BRASSEY'S
CENTRAL AND
EAST EUROPEAN
SECURITY YEARBOOK

BRASSEY'S
CENTRAL AND EAST EUROPEAN
SECURITY YEARBOOK

2002 Edition

Edited by Daniel N. Nelson
and Ustina Markus

BRASSEY'S
Washington, D.C.

ISBN 1-57488-331-3 hardcover
ISBN 1-57488-332-1 paperback

Printed in the United States of America on acid-free paper that meets the American National Standards Institute Z39-48 Standard.

Brassey's, Inc.
22841 Quicksilver Drive
Dulles, Virginia 20166

First Edition

10 9 8 7 6 5 4 3 2 1

Contents

Part III: The Baltic States

Part IV: Southeastern Europe

F.Y.R.O.M. indicates the former Yugoslav Republic of Macedonia. Yugoslavia is comprised of the republics of Serbia and Montenegro.

Acknowledgments

Brassey's Central and East European Security Yearbook, now part of a two-volume endeavor in concert with *Brassey's Eurasian Security Yearbook,* was generated by the collaboration of Don McKeon at Brassey's, my coeditor Dr. Ustina Markus, and the substantial assistance of a superb and patient staff at Brassey's. For this collection, Christina Davidson was both editorially efficient and substantively astute; we appreciate her attention to every detail.

Mr. Eden Cole, on whom far too much of the formatting and manuscript preparation rested, deserves a particular note of appreciation. In the midst of his own graduate work and other endeavors in the U.K., Eden provided enormous energy to this project, and I am indebted for his assistance.

Many of the authors in this volume are, in their own right, very visible scholars and policy analysts. To produce a timely annual volume is no small task, and their cooperative and positive approach to the enterprise was essential.

Daniel N. Nelson

Introduction

Daniel N. Nelson

From the Baltic to the Bosphorus, and the Adriatic to the Black Sea, 2000 and the early months of 2001 were more than auspicious. At the end of the millennium, change was in the air and on the ground.

In the Baltics, vigorous diplomacy lobbied heavily for inclusion—in the EU (European Union) and the North Atlantic Treaty Organization (NATO). Prognoses were less positive than Vilnius, Riga, and Tallinn might have hoped, but the effort was extraordinary. Poland lurched politically, although its security was assured; Hungary and the Czech Republic, very secure externally, fought with their own domestic identities and illiberal tendencies. Romania's election ushered in an entirely new government with a substantial mandate from the left, and Bulgaria prepared for a June 2001 vote that seemed certain to end the 1997–2000 Union of Democratic Forces government.

Meanwhile, in the former geopolitical space of Yugoslavia, Slobodan Milosevic was finally ousted, Franjo Tudjman's death was followed by a social democratic electoral victory, and conflicts in Bosnia-Herzegovina continued while fighting between Albanians and Slavs spread to Macedonia.

It was a busy year.

It was active and seminal in part because the definition of European security became a matter of fundamental debate. For almost a half century, NATO, born in 1949 with the signing of the Washington Treaty, was the West's principal security institution. North Atlantic in scope, anti-Soviet in origin, NATO survived the Cold War to begin a metamorphosis from an alliance of common defense with military means as its core capacity to something akin to an organization for cooperative security (and, perhaps, collective security). Many people, offices, interests, and governments within NATO resisted this metamorphosis.[1]

But in 2000 the debate became louder. As a consequence of American dominance both in the Gulf War of 1991 and the Kosovo conflict in 1999, plus substantial doubt about U.S. efforts to develop a national missile defense (NMD), European Union plans for a "European Security and Defense Policy" with some kind of autonomous rapid deployment crisis response capability were pushed forward. French, German, and other "national" interests played a role, but the larger U.S.-European debate about who did what for whom in terms of security was raised as it had never been in the past decades.

In this volume of the *Brassey's Central and East European Security Yearbook,* we begin with several essays that address this vital issue of 2000 into 2001. And the debate will not soon be resolved. Key players in this debate include such well-known figures as Robert Hunter (former U.S. ambassador to NATO, 1993–98), and other known participants in European security discourse such as Alpo Rusi (Finland), Heinz Gartner (Austria), Peter van Ham (Netherlands), and Maria Clement (France). Via these arguments, both overlapping themes and substantial differences are heard— with Rusi, Gartner, and van Ham stressing new identities and alternative structural arrangements, while Hunter emphasizes continuity and strength of existing transatlantic ties and Clement notes the substantial value of pressing ahead with new EU-focused preparations. These essays, taken together, suggest that Central, Southeast, and East Europe will have a range of alternatives from which to "select"—none of which will be as clear, concise, simple, or satisfying as was an alliance for common defense against a certain foe.

Yet this was also a period during which some of the issues, concepts, and cleavages became clearer. In this volume, unquestionable evidence is seen—in the Czech and Hungarian cases, particularly—that joining NATO is no panacea and that security uncertainties are not resolved simply because accession to the Washington Treaty occurs. We also read how important NATO and EU integration would be for Lithuania, Latvia, and Estonia, and how difficult such integration seems sure to be. For Romania, the largest remaining "Balkan" country, the challenge will be to avoid renationalization of security policy, while Bulgaria's progress and effort on many fronts could be challenged by an uncertain coalition and political vicissitudes after the June 2001 election. Very difficult hurdles for post-Milosevic Serbia, the likelihood of more unrest in a weakened Macedonian state, Albania's fragility, and Croatia's failure to thus far rid the system of authoritarian and corrupt vestiges, leave ample cause for a volatile 2001–2002.

In each of this yearbook's chapters, authors tackle parallel themes. They set the *background* for their analysis of 2000 and the first months of 2001 principally by looking back to the end of the 1980s and the evolution of post-Communist systems in the 1990s. Thereafter, each essay examines the *threats* that are real or perceived for each state, to include a broad definition of such a concept—domestic socioeconomic perils as well as any residual external danger, whether emanating from another state or a transnational origin. *Capacities,* by which the yearbook implies both military and larger socioeconomic and political strengths, are also considered in each chapter. Naturally, these comments provide particular attention to armed forces and defense ministries; but, where appropriate, economic growth, social cohesion, and political consensus are assessed.

Each country-specific chapter, too, offers analyses of *policy innovations* since early 2000 through early 2001—with such innovations, including domestic and international measures taken by a state and government in response to opportunities or threats, or efforts to pursue interests and policy priorities. The thrust of these comments, however, is on new steps in the last year. Contributors also provide a glimpse into and over the near-term horizon with a *future prospects* section, looking not just through 2001–2002, but also a bit further into this decade. A *chronology* concludes each chapter, stressing principal events in 2000 through early 2001.

Our goal in such annual volumes is, in part, to chronicle events, but far more to analyze and assess. We are *primarily* interested in the concept of security—a dynamic balance between threats and capacities[2]—as it plays out in the policy making of the Baltic to Balkans corridor of Europe. Hence, in last year's Brassey's yearbook we devoted attention—both in introductory and concluding chapters and in each contribution—to broader issues of European security as they affect Central, Southeast, and East Europe. This year, we focus attention on the EU-NATO security debate and revisit such long-term concerns in each chapter's "future prospects" section, because the balance between threats and capacities is no longer a matter of military means alone and no longer vested in an alliance designed to deter or defeat.

Heightened complexity is the theme of this year's *Brassey's Central and*

East European Security Yearbook. While NATO and the EU continue their discussions about enlargement, they have also entered a debate regarding future hard and soft security tasks. For each country in the region, this bodes neither ill nor good—just far more assessing and judging. For those countries already in NATO, security seems no longer questionable. Yet, domestic politics and doubt that accession to NATO will provide everything both mean that the EU is increasingly attractive. And, for countries still outside NATO and facing a long process before EU membership is in sight, impatience with both institutions and promises of political moderates has already enhanced the appeal of the right and left.

We thus confront, in 2000–2001, an intriguing security environment. While ample avenues exist by which to pursue security and the institutional framework is rich, countries from the Baltics to Balkans are still knocking at the clubhouse door. Others (Poland, Hungary, Czech Republic) are "in," but not quite as fully as they wish because of their own limited reforms. If this condition persists, the balance between threats and capacities is likely to see persistent worries about threats absent the capacities with which to meet or counter such perils.

NOTES

1. Regarding such resistance, see Daniel N. Nelson, "America and Collective Security in Europe," *Journal of Strategic Studies* 17, No. 4 (December 1994): 10–124.

2. This notion of security has been developed in a number of articles and volumes. For example, see, Daniel N. Nelson, "Security in a Post-Hegemonic World," *Bulletin of Peace Proposals* 22, No. 3 (September 1991): 333–45; and, Daniel N. Nelson, "Great Powers, Global Insecurity," *Contemporary Politics* 3, No. 4 (December 1997): 341–63.

PART I:
THE NATO-EU
SECURITY DEBATE

1 ✦ The Transatlantic Security War?

Robert E. Hunter

Ten years after the end of the Cold War, the transatlantic world has more or less completed the process of returning to normality. It should not have been surprising that it took so long for statesmen, experts, and advisers in the key nations to adjust psychologically to the end of what was, in fact, Europe's longest war in five centuries. The inertia of the Cold War was found not just in the institutions that were spawned in the West by its demands—principally the North Atlantic Treaty Organization (NATO) and the European Community (now Union—EU)—but also in habits of mind that assumed the enduring nature of transatlantic associations, even though the ostensible original purpose for those associations had now disappeared.

In attitudes and relations across the Atlantic that were so much associated with the two great institutions, the 1990s were marked by one important thing that did happen and one that did not. The former was the acceptance of NATO's continued importance and its centrality, leading to its regeneration as an alliance appropriate to the years ahead as it had been so useful for the years just past. The United States confirmed its strategic and political presence on the Continent as a European power, reflecting that presence most directly through the military alliance with which it feels most comfortable—and that it continues to lead. Alliance leaders, parliaments, and attentive publics accepted that NATO should also continue as a factor in predictability for its members—among other things, not "keeping Germany down," as at its founding, but certainly aiding the new Germany in demonstrating to its neighbors that its rising importance would be expressed through grand institutions (NATO, EU), not as a free-floating single state. The Alliance also gained a new vocation, spreading stability—and engagement—eastward to embrace, progressively, all the classic European nations of Central Europe; and it was ratified as a critical instrument for dealing with Russia and demonstrating America's European role to that end—a potentially cooperative Russia to replace the hostile Soviet Union. And NATO also showed that it could be an alliance of action as well as an alliance of passive watchfulness, a sword as well as a shield, by assuming responsibility for imposing peace on at least part of the fractious Balkans, one classic conundrum that had so bedeviled past empires over at least three centuries. Recreated by the late 1990s, NATO thus settled down to a respectable and almost-universally accepted role as a critical political-military mechanism for the future of European security.

All this happened. What did not happen in the 1990s was a great trade war or other form of significant economic conflict across the Atlantic. This had been widely predicted when the scaffolding of the Cold War was dismantled. The logic was that the United States and its European partners had for so many years muted natural disagreements between economies that were more competitive than complementary because of the twin demands of presenting a united front against Soviet and Communist power and menace and of producing the wherewithal for prosecuting a long, drawn out, and quiet "war of attrition by non-warlike means"—at the end of which Moscow and its acolytes collapsed from internal decay.

But despite a congeries of disagreements between the United States and the European Union during the 1990s—bananas, genetically modified organisms (GMOs), extraterritoriality—the relationship did not degenerate into mercantilist competition or a breakdown of international economic institutions: indeed, the two economic giants led a major round of global trade negotiations and fostered the transformation of the General Agreement on Tariffs and Trade (GATT) into the World Trade Organization. This was no accident. For one thing, the collective U.S. and EU economies have proved, at least so far, to be more complementary than had been assumed, in terms of the synergies that advanced postindustrial economies could develop with one another. For another thing, the two great economies found that their collective leadership—and underlying collective comity—was critical for the overall functioning of the global economic system: an elevation of the EU's role to become, if not equal to that of the United States, at least indispensable. Furthermore, it now appears that the renewed U.S. strategic and political role in the Continent has not been without added benefit: once again, a sense on the part of most Europeans that working effectively with the United States on economic matters is essential if they are to rely on continued U.S. geopolitical efforts on their behalf. And lastly, the cumulative effect of political cooperation among this clutch of the world's leading democracies is proving to have benefits across the board—validating, even in a nonmilitary way, Emmanuel Kant's dictum about the impact of democracy on the behavior of states toward one another.

Given these twin developments—the regeneration of NATO and the preservation and extension of a critical political-economic relationship between the United States and the EU—it is remarkable that the two great institutions have had so little direct engagement with one another: it is often said that "NATO and the EU are two institutions living in the same city, but on different planets." That "security" on the Continent and in the broader transatlantic relationship are intertwined, however, has long been evident. From the late 1940s onward, there had been an unspoken division of labor. Roughly speaking, this meant NATO provided "external" security, while "internal security"—protecting societies against major political instability or Communist inroads and, later, to spur reform in Central Europe—was provided by economic efforts, notably the Marshall Plan and later the European Union.

But this division was never rigid: the United States (either bilaterally, through NATO, or through its relations as progenitor of the Marshall Plan and then in its work with the EU) was always engaged in promoting the economic and political well-being of Western Europe; and the Europeans always had an ambition of adding a foreign policy and defense dimension to European integration. For several decades, however, the latter was less a practical project than a distant goal—after all, the ultimate cession of sovereignty for any state is to be found in relying on others, or a collectivity, for defense of the realm. But from 1954 onward, there developed a halfway house: the transformation of the fledgling Western Union of 1948, precursor to NATO, into a body—the Western European Union (WEU)—that gave some expression to defense aspirations of European association. In practice, for many years WEU served as a sort of buffer between NATO and the EU—with the latter represented by officials who came from the world of defense and security issues, and hence somewhat apart from the principal EU preoccupation with economic matters.

In the early 1990s, European integration reached the point that common foreign and defense policies were less distant goals. While EU coordination on such matters was a "work in progress," and had certainly not supplanted the foreign and defense policies of individual states or the Alliance, the United States (and thus NATO) came to accept the value of an EU Common Foreign and Security Policy (CFSP) and, within that, its European Security and Defense Policy (ESDP). Two things were clear, however. First, it was logically and politically certain that European governments would not spend the money to create two sets of military forces and associated infrastructure. Second, it was clear that even a successful ESDP would not be of a size or of a capacity to rival or obviate NATO and its critical engagement of the United States. Both logic and politics argued against such a course.

The bargain struck and ratified at the June 1996 foreign ministerial meeting of the North Atlantic Council was, therefore, to create the new European defense entity *within* NATO. This new entity would be "separable but not separate" from it (to be activated as the WEU)—potentially using, to a considerable degree, what were euphemistically called "NATO assets." This bargain gave expression to aspirations for European integration; it preserved the essential primacy (and the institutional integrity) of NATO; and it recognized that the United States remains indispensable to long-term European security. And if short-term proof of that last proposition were needed, it was provided by the conflicts in Bosnia and Kosovo, as well as by continuing uncertainties about the future of Russia.

At the same time, the development of ESDP in the 1990s had two subtexts, both reflecting competitions about political influence, as played out within the context of security issues and institutions—competitions that were only made possible because neither NATO nor the EU faced a realistic external threat. In both cases, France took the lead. Regarding internal European developments, the augmented WEU provided France with the potential for exercising leadership within Europe in at least one area of activity, following the inevitable rise to political and economic prominence of a newly unified Germany. Regarding external developments, the French saw an opportunity to exploit confidence in peace and stability to gain some ground in its long-standing political and even cultural competition with the United States.

These competitions emerged with significant force with the December

1998 Franco-British summit at Saint-Malo, when the British government, unable to enter the fast-building European Monetary Union, with its soon-to-be-dominant euro, sought an alternative for pursuing influence within the EU and threw in its lot with France on ESDP—at least in rhetoric, while it remained mindful of watchful and skeptical eyes across the Atlantic. The uncertainties about the relative balance of defense institutions for Europe's future—a statement about politics and influence, not about military effectiveness—included whether NATO would remain preeminent or whether it could acquire a competitor in ESDP. While unlikely to rival NATO for the capacity to act, the emergence of such a putative political competitor *could* raise questions in Washington about the willingness of European allies to place capacity for defense above jockeying for political position. Further, Washington has begun to wonder about the question of influence and about its own preeminence in Allied councils. Implicit to these issues is the most fundamental point—whether European security would continue to be seen as principally transatlantic and thus writ large or, as seen by many Europeans, as inward looking, and thus writ small.

At the formal level, this debate was resolved at the December 1991 EU summit at Helsinki, when the Europeans agreed that their proposed Headline Goal Task Force (Rapid Reaction Force) of more than sixty thousand personnel would, on activation in 2003, be used only "when NATO as a whole is not engaged"—that is, in effect, "NATO first," and "only with U.S. concurrence." But at the level of practical application, the struggle for influence represented by the development of ESDP has continued. France periodically has emphasized its desire that the Rapid Reaction Force be able to act autonomously and completely outside the framework of NATO—surely a bluff, if there were ever a serious need for the use of military force, but otherwise a useful device for pursuing influence within the EU and vis-a-vis the United States. And clearly the EU has focused its energies and attention on developing ESDP rather than on enhancing capabilities for NATO requirements, as set forth in the agreed NATO Defense Capabilities Initiative (DCI) of April 1999.

For its part, the United States has been concerned that Allied states like Turkey—a regularly disappointed aspirant to EU membership—be eligible to take part in ESDP efforts, from start to finish. From Washington, too, warnings have been issued that ESDP, as it builds its capacities, should neither waste money that could otherwise bolster NATO nor try to duplicate NATO's military planning and command capacities. The latter step, should it be attempted, would likely produce more confusion than success, particularly if EU states that belong to NATO do not caucus and create common positions before engaging in general debate and decision at the North Atlantic Council.

None of these problems poses a fundamental challenge to transatlantic defense relations. But, to ensure no challenge arises, European Allied states need regularly to remind themselves of the limits of playing politics with defense within Europe, lest they exceed the bounds of U.S. tolerance or erode NATO's competence by accident; and the United States needs to separate out the rhetoric of European ambitions for ESDP (significant) with the likelihood that it could become a serious rival to NATO, even politically (slim, but with potential for misperception).

But these modest and useful prescriptions do not account for two other important factors: one is the great unresolved issue about NATO's future— the compass of its concerns and possible activities. For the United States, European security might still be the preeminent charge on U.S. foreign engagements; but in the absence of local threats, in the predominant view in Washington, Western military interest and capability should be directed to areas of greater concern—both potential regional conflict (for example, the Persian Gulf and beyond) and potential source of challenge to allied territory (for example, terrorism and weapons of mass destruction). For most Europeans, by contrast, solidifying gains in Europe, including completion of the work of dismantling the Cold War system, bringing Central Europe fully into the West, stabilizing the Balkans, and reaching out to Russia, should take precedence. This debate will no doubt continue, with no resolution in sight, but with significant possibilities of friction: two of prominence are, first, whether the United States will recognize that its leadership of the Alliance requires its continued willingness to share risks and burdens with Allies in Balkan peacekeeping; and, second, whether the Alliance will manage without serious crisis to cope with the deeply fraught matters of defense against ballistic missiles.

The other important factor is the long-term reshaping of political influence within the West, of which defense issues are only one aspect. The development of the EU's CFSP and ESDP is, in part, a sign of its slow and still uncertain coming of age, its beginning to develop a true corporate and collective personality and, in the process, its taking first tentative steps toward emerging from U.S. post–World War II and Cold War tutelage and overall direction of the fate of the Western world. The Europeans have, so far, not fully accepted responsibilities either in defense—even as part of the modernization of NATO—or in looking outward, beyond Europe, toward areas of their long-term interests. Developing these responsibilities and these perspectives must be essential requirements of maturity, and they will be some time in coming. And the United States has not yet understood that the growth of a European personality, including in foreign affairs and defense, need not be incompatible with the pursuit of U.S. interests. Indeed, it is remarkable that, in the aftermath of the Cold War, realized common interests across the Atlantic, applicable to most of the world and most functional relationships, far outweigh differences.

The primary transatlantic issue, in fact, is less about interests than about influence: about whether the United States and the European Union can, over time, adjust their respective roles, their perceptions of one another, and the balance of their influence in the broad sweep of their complex relations with one another, while still retaining the fundamental cohesion on which the strength of the Atlantic world—political, economic, and in terms of security—still depends. The ability of the two sides of the Atlantic to sort out effectively the different and valid roles of NATO and ESDP will be a first test of this reshaping of transatlantic relations and the balance of influence. There would be a "transatlantic security war"—and broader misunderstandings, a loosening of the glue of the Atlantic world that is so important in so many spheres—only if there were a collective failure of imagination and political will.

2 ♦ Mind the Gap! Transatlantic Security and NATO's Future

Peter van Ham

I s the transatlantic relationship in crisis? For more than half a century, academics and policy makers have been asked whether the North Atlantic Treaty Organization (NATO) has arrived "at a turning point," or whether we should be "rethinking the transatlantic partnership"?[1] Predictions of the imminent decline of the transatlantic security relationship have been exaggerated, and NATO is evidently still alive and doing rather well after having faced the famous "crossroads" for more than five decades. It is, therefore, with some reserve that I pose this question again. Still, there are some good reasons for doing so.

NATO's strength has been that it has no less than four raisons d'etre: being a collective defense organization ("keeping the Russians out") with an internal pacifying function ("keeping the Germans down") based on shared transatlantic values ("keeping the Americans in") and determined to organize European security and military cooperation. With Russia both economically and militarily on her knees and the German Gulliver tied up in a dense network of rules and regulations spun by the European Union (EU), however, NATO's future now hinges on only two factors. First, NATO may serve as the transatlantic core of an emerging, but still ephemeral "international community," while it also makes practical contributions to manage European and, perhaps, future global security (namely Kosovo and counterproliferation).

We are, therefore, looking at two, rather dissimilar issues: Do (Western) Europe and the United States continue to see themselves as unique partners occupying the same moral space (which is a question of identity)? Does NATO remain the exceptional organizer of European security?

Although the jury is still out on both matters, there are some strong reasons to doubt the strategic relevance of NATO as we know it. The two catchwords are "identity" and "European Union defense."

Identity

Although the strategic pressures of the Cold War have on occasion overshadowed the significance of values and principles (for example, Turkey's membership in NATO), the North Atlantic Alliance's strength and relevance remain premised on a strong sense of shared identity. Governments as well as public opinion must feel themselves part of a community of states that not only face similar external threats and challenges, but also feel bound together by a shared understanding of domestic and international order.

At NATO's Washington summit of April 1999, member states reaffirmed that their alliance was based on "democracy, individual liberty, and the rule of law"—principles that "embod[y] the transatlantic link that binds North America and Europe in a unique defense and security partnership."[2] Are these values, upon which Western societies have been built, and that ostensibly keep NATO together, of continued relevance? There are a number of reasons why an assumption of shared values should now be seriously questioned.

Looking back, it becomes clear that the Soviet-model offered a unique opportunity to juxtapose "the West" as the guardians of stability and democracy versus "the rest," which could be regarded as threatening and not occupying an identical (or even overlapping) moral/virtuous space. The East-West divide also offered Western states a unique opportunity to accentuate and reinforce the political, economic, social, and cultural qualities that they supposedly had in common. It also proved relatively easy to maintain political discipline within the Alliance by emphasizing the clear and present danger of nuclear war and Soviet infiltration or invasion.

But, as Ronald Steel has pointed out with reference to the United States, "[t]he 'melting pot' was to some extent a myth, and it had a lot of lumps."[3] So, with the Cold War's centripetal dynamic now depleted, NATO's lumps are becoming more obvious and sticky. With the demise of the traditional Soviet threat, the foundational presence of "the West" has crumbled, and with its departure the transatlantic relationship has tumbled into a rather traditional crisis of identity.

Obviously, the influence of the United States in Europe is still significant. The United States is highly effective in employing its so-called "soft power," using its ample cultural and ideological resources to "structure a situation so that other nations develop preferences or define their interests in ways consistent" with its own.[4] As the only remaining military superpower, the United States is slowly turning into a global judge and policeman who, ipso facto, feels threatened by those who fail to share its visions of free markets and liberal democracy.

Partly to counter this U.S.-driven process of economic and cultural globalization, EU member states have decided to pool their individual power resources and introduced the euro to counter the dominance of the U.S. dollar. Further, the EU has blocked the trade in genetically modified organisms (GMOs) and rejected the commodification of cultural "products" within the World Trade Organization (WTO). Although this does not testify to an anti-American popular groundswell, it does add up to a broad transatlantic agenda of quarrels and disagreements that places question marks behind the rhetoric of a Western "community of values."

This comes at a time when European states are themselves trying to find out on which principles their European project is based. With the consolidation of a European foreign, security, and defense policy, EU member states are beginning to ask where European integration will ultimately end. Will there be a United States of Europe or a federal Europe with a common currency, constitution, and domestic and foreign policies? These are still delicate issues on which most European countries do not see eye to eye. But, in the search for its own identity, the EU is looking for a suitable "Other," which—apart from Russia and Islam—can certainly be found in America's overall superiority-cum-hegemony.

Sigmund Freud observed (in 1917) that it is "the minor differences in people who are otherwise alike that form the basis of feelings of strangeness and hostility between them."[5] It is this "narcissism of minor differences" (as Freud labeled it), that explains why Europe's emerging identity is striving to differentiate—and perhaps even emancipate—itself from the United States. The complaints in West European media about the "barbarity" of the death penalty in the United States (and the horrific record of its new president, George W. Bush) must be seen in light of such EU puberty. Similar histrionics pervade the European discussion of American perceptions of the right to carry (and ultimately also to use) firearms, and the freedom of expression that allows right-wing extremist groups to spread their hatred across the world by using the Internet. This list could easily be extended.

Since NATO and the transatlantic relationship are now construed as a "community of values," these differences in the American and European notions of domestic order are no longer trivial, strategically irrelevant factors. On the contrary, they add to the perception of significant *differences culturelles* among the allies. The way society is organized and citizens are governed is considered a reflection of that society's views on global order and justice. The notion of "governmentality" (introduced by Michel Foucault) suggests that the way a state is governed and the way individuals manage their own behavior, cannot be separated but are part of the same social construction.[6]

With U.S. and European governmentalities drifting apart (or becoming more conspicuous after the Cold War's numbing hegemony), it is difficult to see how the idea of a transatlantic "community of values" can be sustained. For Europeans, President Bush's choice to designate the arch-conservative Senator John Ashcroft as attorney general (that is, "minister of justice") may well be more telling than his preference of experienced Cold-cum-Gulf-warriors like Colin Powell and Donald Rumsfeld as secretaries of state and defense. Ashcroft's views on social issues mirror those of the extremist religious right. He accepted an honorary degree from Bob Jones University in South Carolina in 1999, a university that does not allow (among others) dating among students from a different race. He also publicly condemned homosexuality as a sin (and in his home state of Missouri, oral sex is still prohibited by law), and called upon the United States to become a "Christian nation."[7]

One might ask whether these are really the sort of issues that will undermine NATO. Is NATO's existence not based on hard-nosed strategic considerations? I would argue that this is no longer the case. One of the most common arguments for divorce in Germany is: *Wir haben uns auseinandergelebt* (we have become estranged from one another). Clearly, with the end of communism, the glue of transatlantic solidarity has dried up ("the kids have gone to college"); and, if we are not careful, these divergent governmentalities will steadily eat away at the moral foundations of the Alliance.

EU Defense

But it is not only social issues that are undercutting NATO's vitality and strategic relevance. The EU's new defense ambitions have also taken Washington by surprise. After a decade of rhetoric, EU member states have finally started to organize their defense on a European basis without recourse to American leadership and military resources. In a surprisingly short time (starting off with the EU's Helsinki summit of December 1999), a rudimentary, largely intergovernmental military crisis management mechanism has been created, which aims to strengthen the EU's foreign and security policies in and around Europe.

During the war over Kosovo in 1999, European states discovered that as long as they do not have substantial military clout, they will not be taken seriously by the United States. Assembling a nascent European army (although this label is still taboo) is also one more step toward a European federation-of-sorts, a United States of Europe that will not only have the organization set in place to speak with one voice, but that will also announce different political messages from those the United States broadcasts. In short, EU puberty has outgrown its American pacifier.

What does this mean for NATO and the future of the transatlantic relationship? Can NATO remain relevant if EU defense becomes operational, more robust, and effective? Political orthodoxy suggests that EU defense and NATO can go hand in hand, even thrive on each other. NATO secretary-general Lord Robertson has claimed that "building a stronger European role in security matters has become necessary to a healthy transatlantic relationship,"[8] thus suggesting that a strong EU defense is keeping NATO politically afloat. Although there is some merit in this argument of inter-Alliance burden sharing, whether this merit will be sustainable if the transatlantic agenda will be top-heavy with a wide variety of quarrels and disputes can be questioned. Apart from the classical three B's—"beef, bananas, and Boeing," epitomizing the enduring commercial EU-U.S. rivalry—there are numerous security issues that cast a shadow over the Alliance's future.

The Bush administration is adamant to intensify its national ballistic missile defense (NMD) program, which is heavily criticized by most Europeans (with the exception of the United Kingdom and Denmark, which would be countries where future upgraded NMD systems would be based). With only a couple of exceptions, European countries suspect that this program will not only undercut existing arms control and disarmament regimes, but is also testimony to Washington's increasing neounilateralism. The impression is that U.S. policymakers pay no heed to Europe's collective words of concern on this issue. In addition, Europeans' sense of Washington's singular pursuit of NMD fits into a broader and highly negative view of U.S. behavior. Such behavior is thought to include undermining international organizations that strive for more global equity (that is, the United Nations and the International Court of Justice), and ignoring international treaties that would oblige industrialized nations to reduce greenhouse gas emissions that cause climate change (such as the Kyoto Protocol). The public indignation in Europe over the use by the U.S. Air Force of depleted uranium during the Kosovo war only adds to this complex picture of transatlantic trouble and suspicion.[9]

Will the uranium affair hurt NATO? Will the NMD program continue to haunt the transatlantic relationship? Will a more vigorous EU defense ultimately make the Alliance redundant? Anyone who claims to know the answer to this series of questions has failed to learn from past predictions of NATO's imminent demise. Indulging in a narcissistic mind-set of exaggerating minor transatlantic moral attitudes and policy approaches should not be excused; both the EU and the United States should find themselves better and more important things to do.

Nevertheless, if the EU becomes the focal point for Europeans to organize their economic, social, political, and military policies, NATO's future looks bleak. If peace and prosperity are two sides of the same coin, and stability and security are based on complex interdependence rather than military cooperation, the principal European organization will be the EU, rather than NATO. In an era of globalization, "security" has become a package deal, a holistic concept that goes beyond the narrow responsibilities of the Alliance.[10] Especially since the EU is bound to remain a civilian power by nature (and will not act as a classical superpower), Europeans will want to use military force only as a last resort and try out their economic and diplomatic instruments of statecraft first. The United States, by contrast, seems keen to return to a more unilateralist, power-oriented foreign policy on the assumption that its overwhelming economic and military prowess (combined with its "soft power") will be sufficient to sway its "allies" and deter "rogue states."

Who Knows?

Only a few Europeans and Americans would want to do away with NATO or play down the importance of good transatlantic ties. Why should they? The point is, however, that the bicycle theory also applies to the Alliance. As soon as NATO's moral basis is undermined (by casting doubt on its shared moral values) and its practical relevance diminished (among others by the EU's military activities), the Alliance is bound to come to a halt and fall over. Of course, a large bureaucracy like NATO will not disappear. But, it may decompose and, especially after continued enlargement, turn into a convenient but certainly not pivotal talking shop a la the Organization for Security and Cooperation in Europe.

In a few cases, small irritants like divergent identities and values may create the proverbial pearl. But, in the case of NATO, this now seems highly unlikely. An autonomous EU defense will encourage ordinary citizens on both sides of the Atlantic to ask what NATO is still about and for what it still exists. Who knows what the answers may be?

NOTES

1. See, for example, Matthias Dembinski and Kinka Gerka, eds., *Cooperation or Conflict? Transatlantic Relations in Transition* (New York: St Martin's Press, 1999); Max Kaase and Andrew Kohut, eds., *Estranged Friends? The Transatlantic Consequences of Societal Change* (New York: Council on Foreign Relations Press, 1996); and Gary L. Geipel and Robert A. Manning, eds., *Rethinking the Transatlantic Partnership: Security and Economics in a New Era* (Washington D.C.: Hudson Institute, 1996).

2. NATO's Washington Summit Communique (23–25 April 1999). Available at <http://www.nato.int/docu/rdr-gde/rdrgde-e.pdf> (accessed 16 January 2001).

3. Ronald Steel, "Who Is Us?" *New Republic,* 14–21 September 1998, p. 13.

4. Joseph S. Nye Jr., *Bound to Lead: The Changing Nature of American Power* (New York: Basic Books, 1990), 191.

5. Quoted in Michael Ignatieff, "Nationalism and Toleration," in *Europe's New Nationalism: States and Minorities in Conflict,* eds. Richard Caplan and John Feffer (New York: Oxford University Press, 1996), 213.

6. Michel Foucault, "Governmentality," in *The Foucault Effect: Studies in Governmentality,* eds. Graham Burchell, Colin Cordon, and Peter Miller (London: Harvester Wheatsheaf, 1990).

7. Barry W. Lynn, "Wrong Man for Justice," Msnbc.com, 15 January 2001. Available at <http://www.msnbc.com/news/516635.asp?cp1=1> (accessed January 17, 2001).

8. Speech by NATO Secretary-General Lord Robertson, "Turkey and a European Security and Defence Identity," in Istanbul (Turkey), 23 November 2000.

9. See, for example, "Gespaltenes Bundnis," *Suddeutsche Zeitung*, 11 January 2001.

10. The notion of holistic security was expanded in the conclusion to the Brassey's, *East European/Eurasian Security Yearbook 2000* (Washington, D.C.: Brassey's, 2000) by Daniel N. Nelson, reprinted in *Problems of Post-Communism* (September–October 2000) as "Post-Communist Insecurity."

3 ✦ EU-NATO Security Debate in an Enlarged Europe

Sophia Clement

The end of the Cold War has led both the European Union (EU) and the North Atlantic Treaty Organization (NATO) to adapt to new realities in their security environment.[1] Europeans, who had devolved the security of the European continent to NATO at the core of collective defense, have drawn major lessons from the Balkans crisis in terms of European political and military crisis management capabilities and burden sharing at a transatlantic level. The European Security and Defence Policy (ESDP) of the EU, initiated at the Saint-Malo summit in 1998, aims at turning the EU into an efficient and credible actor and partner in crisis management operations in Europe and beyond, with NATO or the UN or in coalitions, for the entire spectrum of the Petersberg tasks. The EU is giving itself the means to bridge the inadequacies between the political role it wants to play and the military capabilities it has at its disposal.

NATO, while essentially aiming at collective defense in Europe, adapted to the new environment by identifying new potential threats, extending the nature of its missions (to operations that do not fall under Article 5) and developing crisis management objectives and mechanisms embedded in its New Strategic Concept. Through Washington's strong political and military participation in crisis management in the Balkans, the United States has imposed itself as a power and a key actor in ensuring the stability of the European continent.

These evolutions have redefined the role and the position of the EU in world affairs as well as the transatlantic relationship. At the eve of the next enlargements, it is urgent for both sides of the Atlantic to address concretely the main challenges and dilemmas they are facing: a redefinition of the transatlantic partnership on a new basis as well as each organization's internal reform and external adaptation. In other words, finding the balance between geographic enlargement, internal cohesion, and mutual relations.

Implications for ESDP in an enlarged Europe

ESDP has important implications for EU security and defense obligations toward candidates and countries at the periphery.

First, *stability* has been the initial motivation and justification of the decision of the EU to enlarge. Europe's leaders have not only a moral and historical duty to overcome the continent's divisions. Given the EU's real power to influence events, they also can generate a fundamental process for stability and peace in Europe.[2] As demonstrated in the Balkans, stabilizing the "other Europe" remains essential if there is to be an enlarged space of peace and prosperity in Western Europe.

Second, the ESDP offers an *integrative approach* to security. Candidate countries and non-EU NATO allies have been linked to security and defense issues of the EU through a series of concrete and extended procedures, especially in times of crisis.[3] A whole nexus of association agreements has been developed, notably with the Balkan countries. The willingness of the EU to guarantee applicant countries' closer ties to Brussels, and to take into account their security interests and concerns has gone as far as the autonomous nature of the EU and its institutional and legal limitations will permit. Above all, the EU members' willingness to preserve the cohesive nature of the EU and to avoid diluting its autonomy of decision and action excluded a transfer of so-called *droits acquis* from the Western European Union (WEU). In addition, EU members exclude any institutional recreation of the WEU model (various membership statuses, complexity of procedures), because it lacked decision-making efficiency and political and military credibility.

Third, ESDP allows the EU to *address the diversity* among candidate countries and between those states and current members. Before enlargement, the EU will have to solve the fundamental dilemma between deepening (more legal and institutional integration) and enlargement (more members) in order to welcome new countries while avoiding weakening the political cohesion and the institutional coherence of the Union. Until the last enlargement, this debate could be conducted in parallel. From now on, unless it first deepens ESDP to prepare for a second wave of enlargement of twenty, twenty-seven, to thirty members, the Union runs a real risk of dilution: enlargement will no doubt aggravate current institutional problems and slow the integration project. (The EU is neither only a big economic market nor just an alliance.)

In so doing, however, two main risks should be avoided. First, deepening ought not to be at the expense of enlargement. Enlargement remains a driving force and an asset for the EU in terms of diversity and richness of experience in security and defense policies at a regional level. In addition, as experience has shown, deepening has not hampered the implementation of the ESDP. Second, the EU must address the main risk of concomitant deadlines, namely that the second wave of enlargement will occur simultaneously with the 2003 deadline for the realization of the EU Headline Goal and the revision of the EU Treaty in 2004. In other words, there will be a timing problem, as the consolidation of ESDP will occur simultaneously with enlargement.

As ESDP matures, it will also have substantial implications for the understanding of Europe's borders—in a sense, a geographic objective of the process launched by the EU at the Saint-Malo summit.

ESDP will play *a role in defining the relationship between Europe and the EU.* While current EU borders are clearly drawn in terms of member states, the conceptual borders of Europe have never been certain. ESDP raises questions about the boundaries of Europe, the limits of which depend on geographic, historical, and cultural approaches. Further, ESDP requires attention to the political and cultural dimensions of the new Europe (its culture and values) and what security order will prevail within its borders. Finally, the presence of ESDP raises the issues of stability in neighboring areas and borders (so-called "arc of instability"), which implies a redefinition of EU's security priorities and the development of cooperative frameworks in order to avoid dividing lines.[4]

EU strategic ambitions will also receive more precise definition. Enlargement will modify Europe's geopolitical environment. ESDP first implies a redefinition of geostrategic priorities, because the EU will have to promote stability at its immediate periphery, and, second, ESDP sets the limits of EU capability to enlarge. By raising the issue of some sort of collective defense or assistance, of course, ESDP evokes more questions than answers. Who and what would Europeans like to defend? For what purpose would European public opinion accept the death of its soldiers? What will be the nature of ESDP if a division of labor is installed where the EU essentially covers "soft security" and NATO covers some kind of "hard security"? What level of shared political responsibility and roles can exist in the absence of shared risks?

NATO, as a military Alliance, only *projects* stability. Hence, there is a direct linkage between enlargement and NATO's internal transformation and its ability to deal with new threats (united inside, stronger outside). This is facilitated by the imperatives set by the Alliance that new members should possess interoperable military capabilities they can project over a long range and for an extended period of time. EU, on the contrary, *integrates* (in)stability as a consequence of the nature of its political integrative project. Attaching a "WEU-type Article 5" to the EU Treaty to include mutual guarantees might become an issue to be discussed in an enlarged Europe at some point, provided the nature of neutrality evolves within some states and a real European defense culture emerges.

ESDP's further impact on Europe's borders will be to *define the EU external model*. The definition of EU borders and strategic ambitions are subordinated to the EU's objectives concerning environment, peace, prosperity (grounded in a single market and one currency), and a sociocultural model (distributive welfare and coexistence of diversity alongside a "common core").[5] Diverse objectives that have to be rethought and updated imply political choices. Only then will it be possible to define an institutional architecture for the EU.

Apart from these geographic objectives of ESDP are several *functional objectives* aimed at generating a more efficient Europe.

The ability to accommodate enhanced diversity and work efficiency will be one of the main challenges in an enlarged Europe. Until now, diversity has not affected the implementation of ESDP because such a policy has defined specific objectives and corresponded to real needs. However, certain dilemmas will have to be addressed before enlargement.

EU partners will have to find a balance between current intergovernmentalism that prevails in the security field and an enlarged EU at twenty-seven or thirty. To simultaneously preserve diversity and avoid excessive centralization means finding *increased institutional flexibility*. On the one hand, the decision-making process might be blocked by the rule of consensus to the detriment of EU action in the security and defense field. On the other hand, EU action can hardly depend upon ad hoc variable conglomerates of nations, which remain conjectural, eminently political, and uncertain.

A "renewed legitimizing political project" for the Union could go beyond the existing framework and options (intergovernmental, national interests, peer groups, federation of nation states) without at the same time questioning the functioning of the whole system. The whole issue will be choosing between federal, intergovernmental, and communitarian models in trying to find a balance between the national and the supranational levels, toward more cooperative or intragovernmental models.

To *rationalize decision making* is another functional objective that involves ESDP. The newly established institutions aim at facilitating decision making and consensus.[6] However, issues such as the generalization of qualified majority voting (QMV), constructive abstention, and reinforced cooperation will have to be seriously addressed to allow flexibility for intervention, such as, for instance, the Alba operation in 1994 in Albania.

Further, the EU will be compelled, as ESDP moves ahead, to *clarify commitments*. The status of neutrality might progressively become incompatible with enlargement. To avoid a dilution of ESDP and increased political strains, an evolution of positions concerning European defense as such, a strengthening of common core values, and concrete involvement in all the global issues the EU is dedicated to will have to be addressed.

True implementation of ESDP implies an *EU common military culture*. None of these changes will be entirely effective unless they are accompanied by the parallel emergence of a common defense culture and clearly defined common interests among EU members that will allow intervention under the direction of the Union and not only of nations themselves.

In addition to geographic and functional objectives, ESDP's development will differentiate between EU and NATO enlargements. EU and NATO processes should not be subordinated or confused. They have different logic, negotiation processes, and agendas and their respective gains and challenges differ.[7]

As criteria for accession are different, there can be no parallelism for eligibility. While EU's political vision is based on strict technical, mainly economic and financial, criteria that can essentially be met in the longer term, essentially political and strategic considerations prevail for NATO and the technical criteria remain secondary. Further, providing security to the Euro-Atlantic zone is the Alliance's main driving political dynamic, while the EU criteria aim above all at facilitating global integration in a number of fields to provide political stability and economic prosperity. Security provided by NATO might bring stability. Prosperity for its part is clearly linked to economic and political developments attached to the inherent logic of the EU. However, Central and East Europeans consider both enlargements as security providers in a strict sense of security, of economic prosperity and political stability.

The last NATO enlargement which included three Central European states, has not weakened the Alliance's operational efficiency. Less financial cost than predicted has been incurred, and there has been no slowing of existing programs or its decision-making process despite the increasing number of nations that have to agree by consensus or any dilution of its credibility. In addition, integration in NATO remains very important in purely security terms for those countries at the periphery for which accession to the EU is remote because of economic or political imperatives.

At the functional level, NATO has developed collective security arrangements. It has expanded its level of ambition to adapt to the new environment through non-Article 5 missions "in and around" the Euro-Atlantic area that are embedded in the New Strategic Concept and the Partnership for Peace (PfP). However, it essentially remains a military alliance whose core function is collective defense. It has no civil-military dimension and is poorly equipped to address proper peacekeeping missions, for instance in the Balkans. Its functional enlargement essentially takes place within the PfP framework. On the contrary, the ESDP is part of a global political project aimed at integration in various fields, namely economic, political, legal, and now defense. It has no Article 5–type commitments for nations but has developed appropriate civil-military tools and concepts of use of force (forces and planning capabilities) as well as a whole range of tools to intervene before, during, and after a crisis in a much larger framework than NATO.

Implications for NATO-EU and U.S.-European Relations

The emergence of a European security and defense dimension has modified in depth the terms of the transatlantic partnership. Drawing appropriate "lessons of the Balkans," EU members decided in Helsinki to develop EU capabilities by 2003, especially strategic capabilities. Their aim was to repair EU military deficiencies, such that the EU could address crisis management alone, with NATO or in coalition. NATO, although supportive of an endeavor that will allow EU members to become more credible and efficient allies, seems to fear a shift of influence that would weaken its global role, the political primacy (centrality of the Alliance in defense issues, political control) and the military efficiency (interoperability, Defense Capabilities Initiative—DCI) of NATO, and the future of transatlantic relations.

Answering these concerns, and convinced that a reinforced EU role would benefit the Union as well as NATO, all fifteen EU members (decision making based on consensus) have provided, in a spirit of no competition, for provisions to allow transparency and coherence between EU and NATO. Among these measures are bilateral meetings at all levels, participation of NATO experts in the EU task force on capabilities, permanent consultation arrangements, and a working group on capabilities to ensure coherence between NATO's force goals and national engagements in the EU as well as the coherence between EU's global objective (forces and capabilities) and NATO's DCI.

However, transparency and complementarity go along with the specificity of each organization, their equal status, and the absence of subordination, which clearly *exclude mutual limitations.* Concretely, this implies:

- autonomy of decision: The final objective is to determine the most accurate and rapid response to a crisis in consultation, cooperation, and complete transparency with the Alliance.[8] EU partners act according to EU's institutional and legal limits embedded in the treaty as well as to the integration political project inherent to the Union. Therefore a decision to lead an operation "where the Alliance as a whole is not engaged" implies that the EU does not rely on NATO's initial choice or right of first refusal, the ultimate decision belonging to EU member states. Thus, there is no competition nor right of first refusal. In addition, in practice, as experienced during the Balkan crisis in a spirit of realism and pragmatism (common set of forces, common members, efficiency), there is no commitment to use force on two distinct theaters of operation through two different structures without prior consultation. Decisions are effectively made through permanent consultation, consensus, and transparency at the level of capitals, leaving each organization to examine and decide which means are most appropriate to deal with a given crisis.

- autonomy of action: In military terms, coherence of action implies for the EU and for any other organization the control of the entire chain of command, including predecision planning, operational planning, conduct of forces, long-term deployment, and maintaining the capacity to control violent escalation. In political terms, it means justifying the engagement of troops on the ground while maintaining the political dynamic and coping with the option of a possible nonengagement of the United States (opposition of the Congress, public opinion, engagement of troops in another theater). By implication, this means avoiding systematic recourse to and dependence on the United States in times of crisis. It also takes into account all political constraints on the Allies (public opinion, parliaments), their evaluation of a crisis at a given time (geographic proximity, vested interests), and the limitation of the Alliance's area of intervention (out of area). EU access to NATO common assets and capabilities has been decided and agreed upon by both the Washington communique and the Nice presidency report. Implementation of these agreements by NATO will allow the development of the ESDI and grant the fifteen member states the flexibility to rely on NATO for assets and capabilities according to their needs. Finally, Europeans would like to keep the possibility to intervene in regional conflicts where they would decide to do so, in Europe or beyond, as in East Timor or in support of UN peacekeeping missions.

Most controversial have been discussions regarding ESDP's impact on relations with the United States. From a European point of view, there are clear transatlantic common interests in the European continent and beyond and therefore no alleged growing disconnect in strategic agendas.[9] The two sides of the Atlantic share geopolitical interests and challenges such as sources of instability and new threats on the European continent and beyond. They also have a similar evaluation of crisis management imperatives as far as principles (avoid territorial fragmentation and arms proliferation, respect the rules of law and human rights) and means to be used are concerned (cooperation, diplomacy). In addition, they support complementarity and transparency with the Alliance, which implies no duplication (common set of forces to be used by both organizations, eleven common members willing to ensure coherence and compatibility of national engagements, continued engagement of the United States in Europe). Finally, it is worth noting the evolution of the French position concerning missile defense (ensure bilateral consultations with Allies, while keeping in mind European priorities such as ESDP and nonproliferation).

However, EU members have both common specific interests and their own evaluation of crises. The Balkan crises were of direct interest to them because of their geographic proximity and the potential spillover effects. The EU, having a much larger range of tools than NATO and being more adapted to the nature of conventional conflicts, can take a global approach to crises from conflict prevention to crisis management. Consequently, EU members have a distinct approach to a series of principles. The United Nations remains the legitimizing organization for the use of force. A mandate, by associating all the countries of the UNSC and giving clear political guidance, provides for better political support and strategic control of an operation. A UN mandate also legitimizes EU operations, especially since participation will be more broad based (with the candidates countries) and geographically distributed (if outside Europe or at the periphery). Above all, the association at all stages of a conflict of Russia (rather than its marginalization) and Moscow's role as an important partner in crisis management in EU's immediate periphery remain matters of concern. In addition, the military tool (notably the use of air force) remains a last resort measure and clearly is subordinated to extensive prior diplomatic and political strategy.

The burden-sharing issue, at the core of the relationship, has not yet been properly addressed either. From a European point of view, a burden-sharing approach based on equity implies *no weakening* of NATO. The

Alliance remains at the core of collective defense in Europe and a "key partner" in crisis management operations. The U.S. continued presence in Europe, notably in the Balkans, remains indispensable for both political and military reasons, as Donald Rumsfeld mentioned during an early 2001 NATO defense ministerial meeting. U.S. withdrawal would affect regional stability, while weakening U.S. capacities to exert influence and political control in proportion to its military presence. It would also be perceived by EU partners as a reduction of U.S. commitment in Europe and could diminish their readiness to engage in coalitions with the United States outside Europe. Finally, it would reduce NATO's credibility for Central and South European countries and affect its centrality in crisis management in Europe.

A sound and equal burden sharing implies risk sharing and responsibility sharing and therefore excludes:

- a functional division of labor between NATO and the EU based on a role specialization where the EU would address long-term soft security issues at the lower end of Petersberg missions (preventive tasks, peacekeeping, post-conflict reconstruction), while the United States would deal exclusively with NATO on crisis management and major threats. The EU would be left muddling through in the long run, bearing alone the costs and the difficulties of common transatlantic initial strategic objectives and results of military decisions (for instance the Dayton accord for Bosnia and UN Resolution 1244 for Kosovo).
- a geographic division of labor, which strategically would leave EU members the responsibility to handle security problems in Europe and NATO, or the United States, outside Europe, thus endorsing Washington's global role. At the theater level, it would imply an asymmetric distribution of forces, where Europeans would provide ground troops in the theater while the United States would only deploy "over the horizon," outside the region, providing logistical support and air power in a United Nations Protection Force (UNPROFOR) 1994-type scenario. Such a scenario would not correspond to the role of the EU internationally and would affect domestic support

for either EU-led operations or for EU partners' participation in coalitions in out-of-area contingencies, as emphasized by the new Bush administration.

Finally, a renewed and sound transatlantic partnership must be based on confidence and a clear U.S. support to EU's capability effort, thus getting out of the vicious cycle of "too little, too much." Until now the U.S. approach has been driven by a major paradox: the development by EU of means to address the lower end of the Petersberg tasks might not threaten NATO or U.S. influence but would certainly not allow them to become credible and efficient partners in coalitions in and outside Europe. It then faces a fundamental dilemma: the necessity to choose between confidence and therefore the development of true partnership or lose their disengagement option in Europe and engagement option outside Europe.

Political influence remains at the core of the transatlantic relationship—hence the difficulties and sensitivities of its redefinition. The relationship would benefit greatly if Washington were to: 1) avoid an approach that seeks systematic divergences and, instead, searches for common objectives; 2) stop opposing EU's principle of autonomy, since it is not antithetical to a sound partnership; 3) get away from the vicious cycle of criticism concerning the development of EU capabilities; and, 4) give EU partners some credit to allow them to become credible and efficient allies. For the EU, development of ESDP is inherently linked to a sound basis for the transatlantic relationship. Similarly, for the United States, a failure of the EU would also mean a failure of the Alliance, an immediate security interest.

NOTES

1. The author is an adviser at the Delegation for Strategic Affairs, in the Europe-Atlantic Alliance Directorate, at the Ministry of Defense in Paris. The views expressed in this essay are the author's own views and do not reflect in any sense those of the French government.

2. Javier Solana, *La PESC dans une Union elargie* (The Common Foreign and Security Policy within an Enlarged Union). Speech at Conference at the French Institute of International Relations (IFRI) 1 March 2001, Paris.

3. Implementation of permanent consultation arrangements in peacetime (extended dialogue through meetings at 15+15 and 15+6, at the level of the Political and Security

Committee/PSC), of experts and with the presidency of the EU; intensification in times of crisis; additional military contributions; right to participate to EU-led operations using NATO means and assets; invitation to participate in EU-led autonomous operations. In which case, they have the same rights and duties as the member states as regards the planning and the conduct of the operation concerned once the decisions of all members by consensus has been taken.

4. Javier Solana, *La PESC dans une Union elargie.*

5. Intervention of Madame Catherine Lalumiere, vice president of the European Parliament at the conference on "CFSP in an Enlarged Europe," Mouvement europeen, Paris, 1 March 2001.

6. Political and Security Committee (PSC), Military Committee (EUMC), and the Military Staff (EUMS).

7. For discussion, see the special issue "NATO Enlargement and Peacekeeping; Journeys' to Where?" *East European Studies, Woodrow Wilson Publications*, Woodrow Wilson International Center for Scholars (Spring 2001) and Daniel Nelson, "Post-Communist Insecurity," *Problems of Post-Communism* 47, No. 5 (September–October 2000).

8. Speech of the French minister of defense, Alain Richard, Informal NATO Ministerial Summit, Birmingham, 10 October 2000.

9. Sophia Clement, "Crisis Management and Transatlantic Relations." Publication of the Proceedings of 19 April 2000 conference entitled *NATO and Europe in the 21st Century: New Roles for a Changing Partnership* (Washington, D.C.: Woodrow Wilson Publications, 2000). See from the same author, "European Defence and Transatlantic Relations," in the forthcoming book, *The Emergence of ESDP* (Vienna, Austria: Diplomatic Academy, summer 2001).

4 ◆ PfP + Petersberg?

Heinz Gartner

The security system in Europe is changing dramatically. The new challenges are diverse, and any adequate response must be flexible. Membership in an alliance is only one answer among others. Nonmembership is another.

Military alliances and neutral states alike have to reconsider their Cold War strategies and resist the natural tendency toward inertia. The North Atlantic Treaty Organization (NATO) wants to keep its collective defense commitments which have their roots in the Cold War, and so does the European defense policy. Neutral states are often loath to relinquish their Cold War self-image despite the changing times.

Security has expanded from a military to a comprehensive concept and, as alliances are changing, so must the concept of neutrality. Neither the nature of neutrality nor its attendant expectations can remain what they were during the East-West conflict. Neutral states today must be willing to participate in international peace operations. They cannot remain aloof from every conflict, for neutrality is not eternal nor does it require an identical response to different situations.

NATO + PfP

NATO is redeveloping its basic structure: preparing for a coalition war is no longer the only or even a primary item on its agenda, and its focus now includes crisis management or crisis response operations, peacekeeping, humanitarian action, and peace enforcement. The "new NATO" looks and acts, in part, quite differently from the old NATO.

Simultaneously, the definition of the NATO area Article 6 of the Washington Treaty is losing relevance—the NATO-led operations in Bosnia, Kosovo, and Macedonia are cases in point. NATO will be focusing on new areas in the time to come. It will not, and can no longer, focus on a single mission of collective defense as it did during the Cold War. If NATO remains a traditional alliance of collective defense as enshrined in Article 5 of the Washington Treaty, it is likely to die out or deteriorate. The new NATO's challenges lie beyond its territory, confronting diffuse threats such as international terrorism, the proliferation of weapons of mass destruction, or the disruption of Gulf oil supplies and instability along NATO's southern and eastern flanks. Since these challenges do not represent a direct threat to NATO territory, the real issue for NATO's future is not territorial defense but rather its structural transformation into a crisis management alliance. However, NATO's capabilities are still aimed at mobilizing large numbers of forces to defend against a major attack in Central Europe, rather than developing the capability to quickly move and support limited forces that are trained and equipped to perform specific crisis management or peace-keeping operations.[1]

The Washington Summit Communique of April 1999 and NATO's new Strategic Concept stress that NATO will be larger, more capable, and more flexible.[2] On the one hand, NATO still will be committed to collective defense; on the other hand, it will be able to undertake new missions, including contributing to effective conflict prevention and engaging actively in crisis management and crisis response operations. If NATO is to meet the challenges of future crises—particularly in response to asymmetric threats—it must streamline its own crisis management planning system. NATO must develop the ability to become truly proactive in its planning and crisis management techniques, outlining clearly a set of political scenarios from which military contingencies can be derived at an early stage.

The Partnership for Peace (PfP) program already has been designed according to the new requirements. More than merely a new form of cooperation, NATO's new instruments and tasks will blur the differences between members and nonmembers (that is, partners). PfP and its political companion, the European Atlantic Partnership Council (EAPC), offer almost all the benefits of NATO except the collective security guarantee articulated in Article 5 of the Washington Treaty. As former U.S. Secretary of Defense William Perry foresaw in December 1996 during a meeting of NATO defense ministers in Bergen: "The difference between membership and non-membership in NATO would be paper-thin." Indeed, in some cases non-NATO members may play an even more important role in the new operations than NATO members do, because NATO's focus gradually shifts away from Article 5 missions (territorial defense) to non-Article 5 missions (crisis management).[3] Washington believes that PfP-EAPC will draw partners much closer to NATO in the field of peace operations, humanitarian intervention, and crisis management. Non-NATO states could participate in those missions and cooperate with NATO while retaining their current defense profile.[4]

A priority for partnerships is to continue to make them more operational and geared toward present-day contingencies. Kosovo clearly demonstrated NATO's dependence on its partners when it comes to crisis management and peacekeeping tasks. Under virtually any scenario, future NATO-led crisis response operations will be conducted together with the partners. It also means that partners that are willing to share the risks and costs of an operation have to participate appropriately in the political control and military command of such an operation. In the four years of its existence, the EAPC has demonstrated its value as a forum for consultation and cooperation in many areas critically important to European security—issues such as regional security, arms control, peacekeeping, and civil emergency planning.[5]

EU + Petersberg

The Treaty of Amsterdam of the European Union of June 1997 included the "Petersberg tasks." It states in Article 17 that "the Union can avail itself of the WEU to elaborate and implement decisions of the EU on the tasks referred to." These are "humanitarian and rescue tasks, peace-keeping tasks, and tasks of combat forces in crisis management, including peacemaking." The Treaty did not merge the Western European Union (WEU) and the European Union (EU). It simply states that "the WEU is an integral part of the development of the EU. . . . The EU shall . . . foster closer institutional relations with the WEU with a view to the possibility of the integration of the WEU into the Union. . . ." The precondition is a European Council decision and adaptation of such a decision by the member states only in accord with their respective constitutional requirements. The EU's

Common Foreign and Security Policy (CFSP) is to include all questions relating to the security of the Union, including the progressive framing of a common defense policy. Where this might lead was, in Amsterdam, left for the European Council's ultimate decision in accordance with each member state's constitutional requirements.

Based originally on a Swedish-Finnish proposal, the Treaty allows "all (EU) Member States contributing to the tasks in question to participate fully on an equal footing in planning and decision-taking in the WEU." Membership in the WEU, therefore, is not necessary to participate in the "Petersberg tasks."[6] The European institutions—WEU and EU—will limit their defense ambitions to crisis management and will try to build up separate force structures for this purpose. The EU, after Amsterdam, has focused on the "Petersberg missions," including crisis management, peace keeping, humanitarian action, and peace enforcement, rather than so-called Article 5 operations (collective defense and security guarantees).

The European Council in Helsinki in December 1999 adopted the two presidency progress reports on developing the Union's military and nonmilitary crisis management capability as part of a strengthened common European policy on security and defense. The Finnish presidency of the EU gave highest priority to the mandate from the Cologne European Council to strengthen the common European policy on security and defense by taking the work forward in military and nonmilitary aspects of crisis management.[7] The document stressed that the Atlantic Alliance remains the foundation of the collective defense of its members.

The common European headline goal has been adopted for deployable military capabilities based on a British and French proposal that called for a European Rapid Reaction Force of up to sixty thousand soldiers capable of deployment within sixty days that should tackle military crises without outside help. The European Council underlined its determination to develop an autonomous capacity to make decisions and, where NATO "as a whole is not engaged," to launch and conduct EU-led military operations in response to international crises. (It is not clear whether the EU first has to ask NATO before it conducts an EU-led operation, however, and this lack of clarity has heightened suspicion in Washington and London.) This process will avoid unnecessary duplication and does not imply the creation of a "European army."

NATO Secretary-General Lord Robertson is very clear in this issue:

> There is, and will be, no single European army. There will be no standing European force. National armed forces will remain just that: national forces, under the command of national governments. Any decision to deploy national forces, on any mission, will remain exclusively the decision of the state concerned: for national, UN or NATO operations. What is being created is a fourth option: EU-led operations, where NATO as a whole is not engaged. It will add another tool to our toolbox of crisis management. A win-win situation for Europe, for NATO, and for the transatlantic relationship we all value so highly.[8]

The member states took part in a capabilities commitment conference in Brussels on 20 November 2000, making it possible to draw together the specific national commitments corresponding to the military capability goals set by the Helsinki European Council. The conference also made it possible to identify a number of areas in which efforts will be made to upgrade existing assets, investment, development, and coordination so as gradually to acquire or enhance the capabilities required for autonomous EU action. The member states announced their initial commitments in this respect. It remains essential to the credibility and effectiveness of the European Security and Defense Policy that the European Union's military capabilities for crisis management be reinforced so that the EU is in a position to intervene with or without recourse to NATO assets.[9]

PfP + Petersberg = Austria

In examining the contribution of EU non-NATO states to new crisis management and response tasks, three criteria are important:

1. The states' participation in PfP;
2. The states' participation in EU-Petersberg tasks;
3. The states' previous contributions to peacekeeping and crisis management in other global contexts.

Austria, for example, has been a member of the European Union since 1995. In February of the same year, Vienna joined NATO's "Partnership for Peace" Agreement, and PfP "plus" in November 1996. Austria concentrates on contributing to security tasks that are mainly covered by the formula "Petersberg plus PfP." Neutrality is not incompatible with international solidarity. For a country with a lengthy tradition of avoiding military alliances, this is an important distinction and conceptual difference. Selective participation in international peace operations is possible for neutral states. Peace operations are conducted in a different environment than traditional military operations and involve operations and objectives quite apart from those characterizing traditional armed conflicts. These include conflict prevention, peacekeeping, peace building, peacemaking, peace enforcement, and humanitarian operations.[10]

Austria participated in Implementation Force (IFOR) and Stabilization Force (SFOR) in Bosnia and contributes to KFOR in Kosovo.[11] As of spring 2001, there are more than a thousand Austrian soldiers active in thirteen peacekeeping operations. Since 1960, about forty thousand Austrian soldiers have participated in more than thirty peacekeeping operations. This demonstrates that Austria, while maintaining a form of neutrality, is not a "free rider" in the sense often understood in literature about alliances. Austria does not need security guarantees, because there is no big threat to Austria. No major attack on Austrian territory is likely. Therefore, membership in a collective defense system is unnecessary. Even though the concept of neutrality is changing, it does not entail or accommodate formal membership in NATO or WEU. Austria could participate in crisis management, peacekeeping, humanitarian action, and even peace-enforcement operations in the framework of the Partnership for Peace while retaining a neutral identity. The new Euro-Atlantic Partnership Council provides the opportunity for Austria—not a NATO member—to take part in NATO's consultative and decision-making processes. Many Austrians would find this step troublesome, because it abandons a long-established identity that eschewed links to alliances.

So far, there is no reason to think that neutrality would be absorbed and erased by an integrated European defense system. A Common Foreign and Security Policy will require that decisions be made by consensus. An EU member can oppose a majority's decision regarding foreign or security policy for "important . . . reasons of national policy." The "constructive abstention" gives each member state the option of not participating in the implementation of a unanimously adopted decision. Such an abstention will not prevent the adoption of such decisions, however. Article 23 of the Amsterdam Treaty makes it clear that decisions having military or defense implications are not decided with qualified majority.[12]

Austria has committed about three thousand soldiers to the European Rapid Reaction Force. The Austrian International Peace Support Command—successor to the former Austrian Training Center for Peacekeeping—specializes in training civil and military personnel and units for peace support operations. For the Austrian obligation, such experience will be invaluable.

Emerging regional arrangements could be the building blocks of a new crisis management organization, with regional cooperation based on the terms of the PfP program. As smaller states are unable individually to provide the resources required for conflict prevention and crisis management, they have to cooperate, pool their resources and share their experiences gained from peacekeeping activities both with each other and with larger states. The mission profile of regional contingents, in turn, could encompass operations in the context of chapters 6 and 7 of the UN Charter.

Support or assistance for conflict prevention missions, peacekeeping, peace enforcement, peace building and peacemaking, as well as humanitarian operations must be among chapter 6 and 7 missions. A modular framework *could* establish multinational contingents that might be used for both PfP operations and "Petersberg tasks." Such regional crisis management contingents could then serve as the nucleus around which a larger force is constituted.

Regional crisis management building blocks are already developing in the Baltic (BALTBAT), Nordic (NORDCAPS), and Central European (CENCOOP) region.[13] In 1994 the Nordic states and the United Kingdom supported the establishment of a Baltic peacekeeping battalion (BALTBAT) to increase the capacity of the Baltic states in peace keeping operations. The new NATO members, Hungary and the Czech Republic, joined as have Austria, Slovenia, Switzerland, Romania, and Slovakia.

Only the Washington Treaty's Article 5 security commitments are incompatible with Austria's neutrality law. Yet, Austria does not need security guarantees along the lines of Article 5, because no major attack on Austrian territory is likely. Therefore, membership in a collective defence system does not automatically increase Austria's security. The concept of neutrality is flexible enough to allow Austria's participation in the "Petersberg tasks" or PfP without necessitating formal membership in NATO or the WEU.

The new governmental agreement of February 2000 between the Austrian Peoples Party (OVP) and the Austrian Freedom Party (FPO) proposes and demands inter alia, however "that a guarantee of mutual assistance between the EU countries become part of the EU body of law . . . in the event of an armed attack on one member state the other EU states will afford it all the military and other aid and assistance in their power, in accordance with the provisions of Article 51 of the United Nations Charter."

After what has been said, why should the EU incorporate in its body of law a mutual military assistance guarantee between EU countries that already exists within WEU and NATO? Why should the European Union "securize" itself? In many respects, there is no compelling reason to do so; such efforts will be a waste because the EU shows no inclination to sign a mutual assistance guarantee for collective defense. The Austrian government's initiative has its basis in domestic concerns: it is a way to unobtrusively revoke Austrian neutrality, which is incompatible with collective defense.

According to various opinion polls, 69 percent of Austrians support neutrality and 73 percent oppose Austria's membership in NATO.[14] Even though NATO membership is opposed or receives limited support, a solid majority expresses willingness to have Austrian troops participate in NATO peacekeeping operations.

NATO membership arguably has never been a real option for the Austrian population. Austrians (a majority in public opinion polls) still regard neutrality as an appropriate means of Austria's foreign and security policy. These figures do not tell us that the Austrian population, when confronted with an actual referendum on keeping neutrality or becoming a NATO member, would vote along the lines of opinion polls. Other dynamics could lead to different outcomes. But, it certainly can be inferred that according to given data, a majority of the Austrian electorate is in favor of maintaining neutrality and opposes membership in NATO. This is even true for the majority of the OVP and FPO electorate, the two parties that advocate a fundamental change of Austria's security identity.[15]

It is necessary to understand that neutrality—which served Austria extremely well during the Cold War period—was no more than a mere instrument, a means for Austria to become and remain politically independent. As such, the concept of neutrality should not be overloaded with ideological illusions of yesterday. Neutrality in present-day Europe has a different role than in the past.

Permanent neutrality between East and West was a more-or-less effective means to protect Austria from the military blocs during the Cold War. Yet, the concept of neutrality has to change along with the concept of alliances. This does not necessarily mean the converse, however—that neutral states will now have to join an alliance. It means only that the status of neutrality must take on a new meaning. Austria's neutrality has already de facto adapted several times to changing situations. Membership in the UN was a move away from the Swiss model. Likewise, permission for coalition forces to overfly Austrian airspace during the 1991 Gulf War was compatible only with a broad interpretation of the legal concept of neutrality. Further, membership in the EU with its CFSP and Amsterdam Treaty (that includes peacemaking) has little to do with traditional understandings of neutrality.

Neutrality has become a function that does not extend beyond the negative definition of nonmembership in NATO.[16] This is not to say that little remains of neutrality. Rather, these changes demonstrate the flexibility of the concept even within its existing legal framework. There is no evidence that the only alternative would be neutrality or NATO membership. Some more alternatives are within reach, such as the formula: "PfP + Petersberg."

Implications for Central-Southeastern Europe

It is surprising that the Central and East Central European States (CEECs) insist on formal security guarantees; no countries had more formal guarantees than Czechoslovakia and Poland in 1938, which did not give any real protection. Conversely, Kuwait had neither formal guarantees nor membership in a military alliance but was liberated with the aid of an American-led, UN-approved coalition in 1991 because it was an important energy supplier.

Contrary to the CEECs expectations, membership in NATO is neither a necessary nor a sufficient precondition for security guarantees.[17] On the one hand, Article 5 neither promises nor guarantees that a country's ally will come to its military assistance if it is attacked but leaves the decision to the individual members, who may well opt to stand aloof. The existence of the North Atlantic Alliance may make it less likely that they do so, however. On the other hand, states may certainly receive the requisite assistance even in the absence of alliance commitments, as did Kuwait in the 1990–91 period. One could conclude that NATO enlargement is not, in itself, important for the national security of the new or potential members. Rather, joining NATO (or the EU) gives new members the moral assurance that they are part of the West and that they are European.

The new NATO members could block NATO reform if they focus exclusively on collective defense. NATO's doors will be kept open for new members. Yet, functional metamorphosis is even more important for the security of CEECs than geographic enlargement per se. NATO's structural reformation to improve its capability to carry out NATO's new missions of crisis management and peacekeeping is, unquestionably, the key to wider security assurance.

When states seek or are invited to join an alliance that no longer denotes itself as a response to an unequivocal threat, membership takes on a different character. Cold War membership made different demands and required a different level of cohesion than NATO members may now be willing to both provide for and ask from their members. No longer preparing only or primarily for a coalitional war, NATO is more likely to expect new members to conform to certain domestic behaviors and to participate in multilateral humanitarian and peacekeeping operations.[18]

Can an enlarged NATO continue to reform? NATO wants to be new, but some of the potential new members are still caught in old thinking. The main reason for their NATO eagerness is their belief that NATO—that is, an old NATO based on collective defense—will defend against the big threat, by which they mean Russia. They are not yet used to the idea of an alliance focused on crisis management, peacekeeping, humanitarian action, and disaster relief. Some of these countries do not have the enthusiasm, money, or the military forces to make a meaningful contribution to such operations. NATO, despite its rhetoric about stringent criteria, has been unwilling or unable to ensure that new or potential members (for example, the Czechs and Hungarians) create such capabilities. NATO should be aware that new members with such an attitude can block NATO's reform process. NATO can harm itself if it is unable to convince countries invited to accession negotiations that their ability to contribute to security rather than consume it will be decisive and that their entry into the Alliance is by no means assured.

NATO should demonstrate that it has left the Cold War behind by not extending collective defense commitments to new members. It should make clear to everyone who wants to join that NATO does not look back, but that it is willing to go on with its reform process. The new members increasingly must become involved in the dynamics of the civil-military conflict management, and they must understand that the growing importance of civil-military crisis management must be considered in the current reform of NATO military structures. This will have implications for the planning of types of forces and equipment to respond to an ever wider scope of operations, which the Allies will be called upon to conduct.

NOTES

1. Dieter Mahncke, "The Role of the USA in Europe: Successful Past but Uncertain Future?" *European Foreign Affairs Review* 4, No. 3 (Autumn 1999), 353–70, here 364–65.

2. "An Alliance for the 21st Century," Washington NATO Council Summit Communique, 24 April 1999; The Alliance's Strategic Concept, Washington NATO Council Meeting, 23–24 April 1999.

3. F. Stephen Larrabee, *NATO Enlargement and the Post-Madrid Agenda* (Santa Monica, CA: Cambridge University Press for RAND, 1997).

4. Stephen J. Blank, "NATO Enlargement between Rhetoric and Realism," *International Politics* 36, No. 1 (March 1999): 67–88, here 69.

5. Lord Robertson, "Promoting Peace through Partnership," secretary-general's Cambridge European Trust lecture, London, U.K., 23 March 2001.

6. Austria presently occupies observer status in the WEU.

7. The Finnish presidency, "Presidency Report to the Helsinki European Council Strengthening of the Common European Policy on Security and Defence: Crisis Management," Helsinki, 11–12 December 1999.

8. General Lord Robertson, speech by NATO secretary, at the presentation of the Chesney Gold Medal to Baroness Thatcher, Royal United Services Institute, London, 1 March 2001.

9. European Union, Military Capabilities Commitment Declaration, issued 20 November 2000.

10. See NATO-SACLANT, "Bi-MNC Directive for NATO Doctrine for Peace Support Operations," 11 December 1995. These are tasks that are covered here by the expression crisis management.

11. Austria's participation in SFOR was terminated in spring 2001.

12. The Treaty of Amsterdam, Article 23.

13. Baltic peacekeeping battalion; Nordic Coordinated Arrangement for Peace Support; Considerations in these directions are made in the "Framework Document for the Central European Nations Cooperation in Peace Support" (CENCOOP, 1998), and in the presentation paper, "Central European Nations Cooperation in Peacekeeping" (CENCOOP, 1998).

14. Survey of the Linz Market Institute, 18 October 1998 and Gallup, April 2000.

15. Heinz Gartner and Otmar Holl, "Austria," in *Small States and Alliances,* eds. Heinz Gartner and Erich Reiter (The Hague, Netherlands: Pinter, 2000).

16. Anton Pelinka, "Austria's Future Is in Europe," *Europaeische Rundschau* 17 (Special Edition, Austria and the European Union), (1998): 78.

17. Bjorn Moller, "After NATO Enlargement What?" *NOD & Conversion* 41 (July 1997): 3.

18. Daniel N. Nelson and Thomas Szayna, "NATO's Metamorphosis and Central European Politics: Effects of Alliance Transformation," *Problems of Post Communism* 45, No. 4 (July–August 1998): 32–43, here 42.

5 • Security Qua NATO and the EU—
A Northern View

Alpo Rusi

As the European Union (EU) and North Atlantic Treaty Organization (NATO) intensified their debate about a transatlantic division of labor regarding security tasks, northern Europe watched and listened with apprehension. From Scandinavia to the three Baltic states, the north includes countries in NATO but not the EU, in the EU but not NATO, and aspirants to both. That both of these key institutions remain healthy and that they collaborate with one another are general and strongly held convictions throughout this broad expanse of northern Europe.

In the 1990s northern Europe enjoyed a high degree of stability despite a "revolutionary" transition. Security was no longer primarily based on a specific balance of power between NATO, the Warsaw Pact, and the "neutral states" but, rather, on a complex interaction between new and old actors and a process of globalization. The collapse of the outer and inner Soviet empires have made Russia a European state much more than was the Soviet Union. The post-Soviet space can show very few success stories. The Baltic states—Estonia, Latvia, and Lithuania—are perhaps the only states that emerged from the Soviet Union where democracy and market economies have been consolidated and that are firmly on a path of European integration.[1]

Northern European security has been affected by three fundamental changes that, together, have redefined and repositioned the region's geopolitics. First, the Russian heartland is closest to the outside world in the northwest, that is, toward the Baltic. Today, Russia borders one member state of the European Union: Finland. In the foreseeable future, the EU will gain four new members bordering Russia, namely Poland, Lithuania, Latvia, and Estonia. The Baltic Sea and northeastern Europe, including the

Arctic region that lies at the fringes, are where we can discern the geographical borderline of the European Union.

Second, creation of the Northern Dimension of the European Union (NDEU), launched by Finland and the European Union in 1997, suggests the phenomenon of shared space that is increasingly noted as a global tendency. More specifically, however, NDEU refers to common policies of the European Union toward the political and economic development of northern Europe, as part of its historical efforts to stabilize the wider European space along democratic lines. NDEU is also an instrument to cope with new security risks such as environmental hazards and crime.[2]

Third, northern Europe is embedded within the overall Organization for Security and Cooperation in Europe security order.[3] However, Estonia, Latvia, and Lithuania have applied for membership in NATO, and Poland joined the Alliance during the first round of NATO enlargement in 1999. Further, Russia and the United States held a summit in Helsinki to set up the permanent joint council between Russia and NATO in March 1997. Finland and Sweden have reevaluated their traditional policies of neutrality and are pursuing an increasingly flexible policy of nonalignment within the framework of the European Union and NATO's cooperative structures. As a consequence, the Alliance is more and more present in northern Europe at the beginning of the twenty-first century. However, the question remains whether Russia considers her role as a traditional geopolitical power or increasingly as a "member state" of European integration and Euro-Atlantic security cooperation.

Russia's Challenge

EU enlargement is essential for the future stability of Europe. In December 1999 a major step was taken at the Helsinki EU summit to consolidate the enlargement and the deepening of integration for the early twenty-first century. On the one hand, the EU will become a more "northern power" as the Baltic states and Poland become members by the middle of this decade. On the other hand, the EU is strengthening its security-political role with its plan to establish a rapid deployment capability for crisis management operations by 2003.

For the first time, a genuine interest in the European Union can be seen in Russia. The political elite of post-Soviet Russia gradually has started coming to terms with the EU's enlargement. The EU's own efforts to strengthen its ties to Russia, however, can be credited with much of Moscow's shifting perspective. By far the most important outcome to date of the EU's Common Strategy on Russia was the decision by the Russian government to reciprocate by developing a Russian strategy for cooperation with the EU. This document was presented by Prime Minister Vladimir Putin at the EU-Russia summit in Helsinki in October 1999. One can expect, however, that the real debate about the terms of cooperation is about to begin within the framework of the EU. The EU's foreign policy coordinator, Mr. Javier Solana, has expressed his dissatisfaction with respect to the present EU strategy on Russia. He seems to want a more assertive approach by the EU that incorporates not only carrots but a few sticks as well.[4]

The destiny of Kaliningrad, a Russian enclave sandwiched between Poland and Lithuania on the Baltic Sea coast, is a vital case in point. In many respects, Kaliningrad has the potential to be the flashpoint of this region and, simultaneously, a microcosm of Russian social problems. The increase of crime and the continuing spread of AIDS are endemic to Kaliningrad and affect the entire region. The most likely issue to create tension is the question of transit to and from metropolitan Russia. As an expert of new Russia explains, "if Kaliningrad is a pilot, it is also a test: a Russian enclave to become an EU enclave."[5]

Notwithstanding the differences, the Finno-Russian border remains the only relevant comparison to the future common border of the European Union with Kaliningrad Russia.

New Northerness?

Regional developments are shaped by the politics of power and institutionalism as well as by the politics of identity. Northern Europe has become, in only a few years, a prominent scene of regionalism whether measured by political events, by institutional changes, or by their results for Europe's wider metamorphosis. In the constructivist outlook, the new northerness can transcend or overcome the peripheral status traditionally connected with the north.[6] As one observer has put it: "instead of being used for a typical case of otherness in the discourse at the centre, Northerness could become a constitutive feature of European change."[7]

In the 1990s multilateral cooperation in northern Europe has consisted of two subregional arrangements or dimensions. First, in the Baltic Sea region, the Council of the Baltic Sea States (CBSS) was established in 1992. The CBSS reflected the traditional leadership of Sweden within the region of northern Europe. The collapse of the Soviet Union opened up new opportunities to widen the scope of cooperation in the Arctic region too. As a result, the Barents Euro-Arctic Region (BEAR) and the Arctic Council were established at the same time. These efforts, in fact, expanded the meaning of "North Europe" to the Arctic region and combined a number of non-EU states, Norway, the United States, Canada, and Russia in particular, to the cooperative arrangements initiated basically by the EU.[8]

The cooperative institutionalization in northern Europe, however, offers particularly for Russia an avenue to European engagement with a new concrete agenda and reciprocal gains. This opportunity is highlighted by the EU's northern dimension (EUND) initiative. St. Petersburg is still the largest metropolis in the Baltic Sea area. The city is a gateway to the enlarging EU. But Russia needs to adopt European norms and standards to cope with EUND. This will not be easy. One of the first tests will be the construction of a harbor for the transit of oil in Koivisto (Primorsk) in the Karelian isthmus and close to the Finno-Russian border. The ecology of Karelia is at stake. But, firstly, the new oil harbor will pose a major environmental risk for the Baltic Sea region as a whole in the near future.

In January 2001 the government of Finland established a National Forum of EUND to frame substantive policy for the initiative. The Swedish presidency of the EU further strengthened EUND during the first half of the year 2001.[9] Through the EUND, the identity of European northerness may grow vis-a-vis national identities among the states of northern Europe. The EUND, however, must demonstratively increase economic prosperity, strengthen security, and create new cross-border connections in order to be compared with the Barcelona process. In 2001 these goals remain distant because the EU has been slow to allocate new resources for its northern dimension. The main responsibility for strengthening the EUND is in the hands of Finland and Sweden but is also shared by EU applicants in the region. This group of countries needs to improve mutual cooperation within the EU in the future.

NATO Enlargement as Seen from the North

In response to new security challenges, NATO has undergone a far-reaching process of adaptation and transformation. The Alliance played a decisive role in peacemaking in Bosnia and Kosovo in the 1990s. Its first round of eastern enlargement has strengthened stability and even improved relations between erstwhile adversaries such as Poland and Russia. Most probably the "open door" policy of NATO that was developed during the Clinton administration will not be challenged by the Bush administration because of the danger of severe damage to transatlantic relations and European stability. However, without strong U.S. leadership, NATO would not have enlarged. In the future, American leadership will be no less necessary.

From the perspective of northern Europe, three factors determine when and how NATO's next enlargement will be discussed. First, the strategic rationale for the next round is not clear. The rationale for the first round—to stabilize Central Europe—was widely accepted. Now, however, there is no consensus whether NATO should be enlarged to southeastern Europe only or not at all. Secondly, there are no clearly identifiable qualified candidates. Although Slovenia may fulfill the criteria, its inclusion in NATO alone would do little to enhance the Alliance's military effectiveness. Thirdly, there is no consensus among the United States and its key allies about the timing or modalities of the next round or the role of Russia in the process. For all of the non-NATO countries discussed in this volume's later chapters (and in a companion Brassey's yearbook on Eurasian security), these questions make NATO a less certain future guarantor.

However, northern Europe from Norway to Estonia expects that NATO's expansion *will* continue for a number of reasons. The Baltic states have applied for membership and are implementing the Membership Action Plan (MAP). Were there a limited enlargement of one or two countries, Lithuania may become a dark horse simply for its achievements and geopolitical location in the neighborhood of Poland and Kaliningrad.

Further, the need to deepen cooperation between the EU and NATO to implement EU foreign and security policy is obvious. For financial reasons, there is no need for "two NATOs," as Finnish Prime Minister Paavo Lipponen stated after the Nice summit in December 2000. The message is clear: the EU should not try to replace the existing alliance but, rather, to develop a European Security and Defence Policy (ESDP) within the transatlantic structure. This factor may play a role when the former neutrals, Finland and Sweden, will consider their positions on NATO enlargement. These two Nordic countries certainly meet criteria for accession, but they have been reluctant to apply at the early stage of proceedings. They have insisted, understandably, that they already have been producers not consumers of security in post–Cold War Europe.

However, the next steps of security institutionalization may change the situation. For example, any thoughts that Stockholm and Helsinki have about playing a central EU role may depend on their willingness to enter NATO as well. NATO has also played a crucial role from the point of view of stability in northern Europe. During the Cold War, NATO's deterrence offered a protective umbrella over Scandinavian neutrals, too. Moreover, the U.S. commitment to the maintenance of European stability remains crucial. The continuation of NATO enlargement continues to be necessary in this respect and, therefore, one can predict that the Alliance's enlargement will stay on the agenda when new efforts are taken to strengthen security in northern Europe.[10] In the long run, members of the EU are most likely to be, or become members of NATO—and this equation is understood in northern Europe. With the development of a European Security and Defence Policy, to include a sixty-thousand-soldier Rapid Reaction Force linked to NATO's own reaction force but deployable under separate command, northern Europe may now have a NATO-friendly security alternative.

However, much will depend on the shape and responsibilities of ESDP within the transatlantic security structure. Baltic states have a lot at stake as the relationship between ESDP and NATO becomes defined. Worries about Kaliningrad and the whole of Russia, Belarus, and Ukraine mean that the EU-NATO security debate has lasting implications for Lithuania, Latvia, and Estonia. In any case, the EU's drive to develop a capability for military crisis management is creating a factor with dynamic implications for the European security order. The EU is now taking a series of decisions to which other key actors on the security scene are reacting and adapting. The combined effects of ESDP developments and reactions of the Bush administration will shape the further transformation of the European security order for the next few years.[11] To the degree that American and EU visions and policies for European security converge or diverge, the Transatlantic Alliance will prosper or weaken.

The morass of Balkan wars in the 1990s that spread in early 2001 further to Macedonia pushed Europe toward the ESDP. The declaration of the Cologne European Council (EU summit of 3–4 June 1999) referred to the broader strategic purpose of their effort by resolving that the EU "shall play its full role on the international stage." To that end, member states agreed "to give the EU the necessary means and capabilities to assume its responsibilities regarding common European policy on security and defence."[12] The Helsinki European Council (10–11 December 1999) asserted that "The EU should be able to assume its responsibilities for the full range of conflict prevention and crisis management tasks . . . which comprise humanitarian and rescue tasks, peace-keeping tasks and tasks of combat forces in crisis management, including peacemaking."[13] Although this view could be challenged, one might insist that these tasks (using combat forces in peacemaking) cannot be implemented by "nonaligned" states. By accepting these documents, Finland and Sweden de facto "joined" a military alliance's security structure. The same issue would concern the Baltic states—or any other state from central and southeastern Europe—were they to join the EU later in this decade prior to NATO accession.[14]

For the EU, taking on military tasks is a novel experience. The EU has set up the headline goals for combined forces (sixty thousand to eighty thousand) and the collective capability goals for strategic assets and support systems. These steps will lead to an overall upgrading of defense forces among leading European NATO countries. But the question is also about the growing technological gap across the Atlantic that was demonstrated in the Kosovo air campaign. An integral part of the ESDP endeavor would be closer cooperation between European and American defense industries. However, EU member states exhibit little inclination to increase their defense budgets—a reluctance that may hamper these efforts.[15]

Baltic states, however, want to fulfill criteria for NATO membership as well as EU accession. As a consequence, they have to increase their defense budgets drastically. Further, they must balance their commitments to NATO with EU responsibilities—both current and anticipated—which is a very demanding political task during coming years. Still, all signs point to perseverance among Baltic states to improve their national security structures and political linkages such that their candidacies for both institutions will have a real chance.

Tension between the EU and the United States regarding both the perennial issue of burden sharing and the political repercussions of an EU military role will cast a shadow over transatlantic relations in the early twenty-first century.[16] The Baltic states see their potential role as problem solvers in such an EU–United States debate over security roles; while they cannot influence the debate substantially, they can adapt to it, thereby avoiding any perception of "taking sides."

The strengthening role of the EU as an international player will also depend on its economic development. The early stage of the twenty-first century may see economic recession that could also hamper efforts to build a more assertive political-military EU in world politics. From the perspective of northern European stability, smooth outcomes of eastern enlargement of both NATO and the EU are needed.

Wider Lessons from the Northern Perspective?

That northern Europe's view of the EU-NATO security debate—with enlargements of both likely to add to ambient security for all, but with troublesome uncertainties ahead—is suggestive for Central and southeastern Europe. Whether among the geographically larger and wealthier Scandinavian "neutrals" or smaller and poorer Baltic states, the development of an EU crisis intervention capacity is perceived positively, except insofar as the larger transatlantic condominium is disrupted or severed. For, from the north at least, both key successful institutions must remain robust and collaborative. Otherwise, the future looks far bleaker.

Central and East Europe ought also to take no sides, counsel unity, and accept no substitutes for brand names in the provision of security. Efforts to identify regionally are more hesitant and limited by conflict and poverty; still, as Visegrad demonstrated, group cohesion in a region and peaceful cooperation among them to accelerate integration is highly advantageous. For southeastern Europe, such identity and cohesion seems more distant.

Whether viewed from north or south or east, however, European security remains intimately linked to ties with the United States cemented through NATO. To that end, a northern vision is one firmly grounded in the benefits of a strong NATO and vibrant EU, both of which ought to take further steps toward enlargement.

NOTES

1. Rene Nyberg, "The Baltic as an Interface between the EU and Russia," Lecture in Tampere, Finland, 29 July 2000, Sixth International Council for Central and East European Studies World Congress.

2. Kari Mottola, "The Northern Dimension: How the European Union, the Baltic States, Russia, and the United States Shape Security and Co-operation in Northern Europe," The New Europe at the New Millennium series lecture at the University of Oregon, 15 May 2000.

3. Helsinki Summit Declaration, paragraph 25, *CSCE Helsinki Document 1992*, Helsinki. The concept of Europe "whole and free" was coined after the fall of the Berlin Wall. No distinction was made between Europe and the whole Commission on Security and Cooperation in Europe region in the Charter of Paris for a new Europe (Paris 1990), but thereafter the dissolution of the Soviet Union and the inclusion of Central Asian states as borderline cases made it logical to be more specific.

4. See Alpo Rusi, "EU's Faceless Foreign Policy," in *Lapin Kansa*, 26 January 2001.

5. Nyberg, "Baltic."

6. See, for example, the view of Sergei Medvedev, "[the __ blank __ space]: Glenn Gould, Finland, Russia and the North," *International Politics* 38, No. 1 (March 2001); 91–102.

7. Mottola, "The Northern Dimension."

8. Lassi Heininen, "The European North as a Multiple Use Region for Different Interest Groups," in *BEARing the European North: The Northern Dimension and Alternative Scenarios*, eds. Lassi Heininen and Richard Langlais, AC Reports, No. 23 (Arctic Centre, Rovaniemi, Finland: University of Lapland, 1997).

9. Information presented to Riksdagen (parliament) on 15 April 1999 by Deputy Prime Minister Lena Hjelm-Wallen on Sweden's presidency of the European Council of Ministers 1 January–30 June 2001.

10. William Cohen, "Meeting the Challenges to Transatlantic Security in the 21st Century: A Way Ahead for NATO and the EU." Remarks at the Informal Defense Ministerial Meeting, Birmingham, United Kingdom, 10 October 2000. See, also Alpo Rusi, Speech at the Paasikivi Society, "Finland and Change in Europe," delivered in Helsinki, 24 October 2000.

11. Kari Mottola, "The EU, the US and the Common European Security and Defence Policy (ESDP)—Towards Equal Competence, Capability and Authority in Crisis Manage-

ment?" Paper prepared for the International Studies Association Annual Convention, Chicago, Illinois 20–24 February 2001.

12. Declaration of the Cologne European Council (EU summit), 3–4 June 1999.

13. Declaration of the Helsinki European Council (EU summit), 10–11 December 1999.

14. "Presidency Report to the Helsinki European Council on Strengthening the Common European Policy on Security and Defence," Presidency Conclusions, Helsinki, European Council, 10–11 December 1999, Article 17.2, Title V of the TEU (consolidated).

15. Neither the headline goal or the collective capability goal have been made public, although they were referred to in the Nice ESDP document. Individual member states have published their offers separately on a national basis.

16. On the evolution of the U.S. policy toward ESDP, see Robert Hunter, "An Expanded Alliance Vis-a-vis the European Union: A Stock-taking on the Dawn of a New Century," in *NATO and Europe in the 21st Century: New Roles for a Changing Partnership*, Sabina Crisen, ed. (Washington, D.C.: Woodrow Wilson Center, 2000).

PART II:
CENTRAL EUROPE
Introduction: Central Europe

Daniel N. Nelson

Where "Central" Europe begins and ends is uncertain. Yet, delineating an area below the Baltic, above the Carpathians, and between Russia and Germany locates a region geopolitically that has had an unenviable fate—caught between two of the continent's great powers with no place to go.

For centuries, this spelled trouble—with state existence threatened from outside and inside. To the carnivorous empires around it, Poland was available for consumption in the eighteenth century and was absorbed by Russia, Prussia, and Austro-Hungary. In the aftermath of World War I, as empires were carved up into constituent nations, the Hapsburg demise, German defeat, and Russian revolution gave rebirth to Poland and life to Czechoslovak and Hungarian states.

Entering the twenty-first century, Poles, Czechs, Slovaks, and Hungarians can—for the first time in recent history—sense that external peril is vastly reduced. None of the four chapters that follow suggest that the world is, as seen from Central Europe, uniformly friendly. Indeed, public opinion surveys and governmental policy evoke continued wariness about what lies around the corner—from an unpredictable or, worse yet, predictably malevolent Russia, or from unforeseen regional disturbances. Moreover, prevalent worries about crime, drugs, and other transnational threats have more than supplanted concern about the intentions of neighboring states or governments.

A balance between threats and capacities, from whence our understanding of security arises, is thus being interpreted quite differently today in

Central Europe than it was less than a generation ago. With NATO membership for Warsaw, Prague, and Budapest, and signs that Bratislava is not likely to be far behind, invasion and war have faded as issues. While whether or not Central European elites and publics should see NATO accession as guaranteeing such security can be debated, the perception of threats and appropriate capacities has now shifted.

Pal Dunay, Andrew Michta, Ivo Samson, and Marybeth Ulrich underscore the fundamentally new security debate in their chapters. Dunay stresses that the political nature of Hungarian democracy, not the direction of the country's foreign or military policy, affects concepts of threats and capacities and government's ability to find resources with which to meet public expectations. Michta makes clear that Poland, while "never having had it so good" (so to speak) in terms of external security, has many challenges ahead in order to play the role that Poles see for themselves in the region and Europe. Ulrich, too, is critical of Czech performance as a new ally and recognizes significant internal difficulties, while Samson notes the very long way that Dzurinda's government must go before Slovakia can fully integrate within Western, democratic institutions.

There is no bed of roses portrayed here. In the aftermath of NATO enlargement to three of the four countries of "Central" Europe, and likely EU inclusion of at least one if not more of these states in its first extension east, it might be hard to imagine any security concerns. And, in the old sense of tank regiments battling at the Fulda Gap, there are none. Each of these four contributors, however, tells us unequivocally that getting keys to the Western clubhouse does not mean that defense ministry civilians or legislators suddenly gain expertise, that senior officers learn to respect oversight and accountability, or that publics will understand that institutional membership is accompanied by obligation.

Most important, NATO and the EU do not "fix" domestic political cultures. Membership or potential accession can be credited, perhaps, with encouraging or nudging legislatures to pass certain laws, ministries to prepare standard documents, and electoral processes to conform to international standards. But, years of NATO and EU membership haven't remade the Italian government, resolved Flemish and Walloon tensions, or ended Basque separatism. Slovaks may know that a government led by a Meciar will not be welcome in Brussels, just as any illiberal tendencies in Hungary are incompatible with Western expectations. The message among these chapters, however, is that such domestic politics increasingly have become the "stuff" of security, because it is from such internal sources that the balance between threats and capacities is most affected. The ambient security of Central Europeans is influenced more by *how* their politicians behave and governments make policy than by whether the army is of a particular size, or MIG-29s are replaced or simply discarded.

This may be an important lesson for future thinking about security—where national security becomes defined increasingly in terms of comportment within and among armed forces, ministries, police, and related organs. How well these elements, and the political and military leadership, "fit" behaviorally into democratic political culture may be far more indicative of national security than their capacity to "defend" territory.[1]

NOTE

1. In this regard, see Daniel N. Nelson, "Civil Armies, Civil Societies," *Armed Forces & Society* 25, No. 1 (September 1998).

6 • The Czech Republic: Negotiating Obstacles on the Way to Integration

Marybeth Peterson Ulrich

Expectations were high for Czechoslovakia at the start of its democratic transition. Its historical experience with democracy and economic success in the interwar period along with its demonstrated propensity to shake off the excesses of Communism during the Prague Spring set the Czechs and Slovaks apart from their Eastern bloc counterparts. The amicable breakup of the Czechs and Slovaks in 1993 freed the new states, the Czech Republic and Slovakia, to pursue their own paths of transition. The Czech Republic quickly broke away from its sister state and became a leading candidate for integration into key European institutions such as the North Atlantic Treaty Organization (NATO) and the European Union (EU).

Economic progress was steady and somewhat heady for the first few years as an independent state, but in 1997 incomplete and mismanaged structural reforms contributed to an economic downturn, from which the Czech economy is just beginning to emerge. As is the case across the European post-Communist states, economic prosperity is uneven and democratic political institutions are still developing. Political interests, corruption, incompetence, and public apathy plague the Czech political scene and form the context of the Czech Republic's pursuit of a national security policy.

The year 2000 marked the Czech Republic's first anniversary as a NATO member. Its first year of Alliance membership featured a patchwork of positive trends amid evidence that the Czech national security system still lacks significant capacities essential to the formulation and conduct of national security policy. Public opinion rebounded from last year's tepid support of NATO that was evident in Czech politicians' and the Czech public's negative reaction to the war in Kosovo.[1] By year's end, 65 percent of Czechs polled responded that the Czech Republic's entry into NATO was the best solution for the country's security situation.[2] However, the number of those polled responding that they are dissatisfied with NATO membership has been steadily increasing since April 1999 and stood at 25 percent at the end of the year,[3] and 47 percent of Czechs in a March 2000 poll likened NATO membership to becoming subordinated to another great power.[4] The Army of the Czech Republic (ACR) also earned its best-ever public confidence rating of 55 percent in 2000.[5] Czech trust in their army has consistently grown since November 1999 and increased by three points from February 2000 polling data.[6]

Six hundred Czech soldiers served as part of NATO's Stabilization Force (SFOR) in Bosnia-Herzegovina. This deployment continued Prague's commitment, begun in 1996, to Balkan peacekeeping missions and to implementation of the Dayton Peace Accord. In Kosovo, at the end of 2000, 170 Czech soldiers were serving along the Kosovo-Serbia border protecting the Serb minority and giving humanitarian assistance to the civilian population.[7] The Czech battalion in Bosnia and the reconnaissance company in Kosovo generally fared well in NATO assessments.[8]

However, throughout the year a debate raged within the Czech national security community over whether or not the Czechs would withdraw from Kosovo at the end of 2000 to focus on their operations in Bosnia. In January the General Staff initiated the controversy with a unilateral statement announcing its decision to withdraw the Czech company from Kosovo to cut foreign operations costs.[9] Later, ACR chief of staff Jiri Sedivy admitted that such a decision must be made by political leaders while emphasizing that he supported the withdrawal of resources from the Balkans.[10] The Czech foreign minister, Jan Kavan, and the Czech Senate weighed in with their support for continued Czech participation in Kosovo Force (KFOR) in light of the fact that the supreme allied commander in Europe, General Wesley Clark, was calling upon Alliance members to reinforce their contingents in Kosovo because of heightened tensions there.[11] In addition, NATO Headquarters sent word that a Czech withdrawal would be considered a shirking of Alliance responsibilities and that even a small symbolic presence was important to the achievement of NATO objectives.[12] By the end of the year, the Czech government concluded that both Balkans operations would continue in 2001 at a total cost of 1.5 billion crowns (about $39 million) and began the search for funds within the state budget to pay for them.[13]

The dispute over Balkans policy highlighted two key features of the Czech national security structure—immature national security institutions and a strapped defense budget. The Czech press carried stories throughout the year that painted a picture of managerial ineptitude within the ministry of defense (MOD). Bungled acquisitions processes and their subsequent impact on the readiness of the already resource-starved armed forces resulted in an increasingly public rift between the General Staff and the MOD.

Referring to the General Staff, one prominent Czech defense analyst noted, "These are unhappy people who are more and more disturbed by the inactivity of the ministry to which they are subordinate."[14] To help fill the vacuum that the generals perceive the chaotic administration produces, a sort of council of generals was established midyear to suggest the direction that continuing military reform should take in the future.[15] The MOD has reportedly been paralyzed by strained relationships and an inability to correct flawed patterns and practices that contribute to the Czechs' slowed progress toward defense modernization and transformation necessary to fulfill the expectations of alliance officials in Brussels.[16]

The institutional incapacity of Czech national security structures is evident in a series of acquisition scandals. These incidents reveal both incompetent civilian defense personnel and inadequate parliamentary and governmental oversight. This is born out in the inability of these actors to correct long-running deficiencies within the defense ministry. The repeated purchases of defective spare parts, over-priced contracts, and allegations of defense ministry personnel favoring specific suppliers in a manner akin to bribery—acts that received considerable play in the Czech press—have challenged both the Czech military's efforts to win the trust of the Czech people and set back its goal of building a professional military.

A few examples will illustrate the sort of fare that was regularly offered to the Czech public in its daily newspapers and newscasts in 2000. The MOD's property section purchased defective spare parts for the ACR's Mi-24 ground attack helicopters for the third straight year. The parts contract was worth several hundred million korunas—a severe strain on a limited defense budget. Such mistakes poison the already tense relationship between the armed forces and the MOD. Air Force commander Ladislav Klima summed up the negative impact such actions have, "What do the constant mistakes in the deliveries of spare parts lead to? This is perhaps clear: It holds up training and provokes distrust in the hardware among the pilots."[17] Meanwhile, General Staff documents indicate that the supply on hand of spare parts for air force aircraft is virtually zero.

Repeated evidence of the defense ministry's incapacity to coordinate major investment programs was the impetus for reorganization. A National Armaments Office and a Defense Planning Section within the MOD were established to coordinate major investment programs. These moves were at least partially linked to the arrests of eight MOD employees at the end of 1999 for irregularities in the Main Property Section.[18] In addition, three officers—one from the General Staff and two from the MOD—were arrested in October 2000 for ignoring regulations calling for the competitive bid of Army contracts. Instead, these officials favored particular firms in a series of sole-source contracts and allegedly personally benefited from such arrangements.[19]

In a tight resource environment, commanders increasingly point their fingers at the defense ministry as a key contributor to their plight: "We have to pay for the incompetence of Defense Ministry Chiefs. Why should we be interested in their constant excuses and problems?"[20] Such angst permeates the intragovernmental process of national security policy making. In November, Prime Minister Milos Zeman called the two main ACR modernization projects—the purchase of subsonic L-159 aircraft and the modernization of T-72 tanks—"stupid projects"—that "unnecessarily swallow up means from the army's budget."[21] Zeman's disapproval was reflected in reports that Defense Minister Vladimir Vetchy would be dismissed by year's end.[22] In an effort to save his job in light of charges that he had lost all control over his subordinates and that the defense ministry was in a state of chaos,[23] Vetchy fired his deputy responsible for acquisitions, Jindrich Tomas, on 21 December 2000.[24] At the end of 2000, several perceptions dominated—that the defense ministry was ineffectively and weakly led, that there were strained relationships between the General Staff and the MOD, and that the Czechs' national treasure was squandered by the administration of incompetent and unprofessional officers and defense bureaucrats.

Responsibility for underperforming defense structures lies in each of the sectors of the Czech national security community. Although the defense ministry has been particularly problematic, the ACR must also take responsibility to efficiently spend its allocated resources and become an active participant in fixing the defense sector. Security committees in parliament must also become fully engaged, be interested in and capable of shaping a defense vision, and be able to fulfill their roles to keep the government accountable in order to contribute to high-quality national security outcomes.[25]

Threat Assessments

Czech national security strategy identifies two primary vital interests: 1. Safeguarding the democratic system of government and freedom of its citizens; and, 2. Protecting the sovereignty and territorial integrity of the country. The strategy further recognizes natural disasters, terrorism, international organized crime, migration resulting from regional instability, and various levels of military attacks as threats to these interests.[26] Another transnational threat that affects Central Europe in general and the Czech Republic in particular is the influx of illegal drugs from southwest Asia and Latin America that transit the country en route to Western Europe.[27]

Illegal immigration has been problematic on two fronts. Some illegal immigrants have been passing through Central Europe on their way to Western Europe, while others have been content to stay in the Czech Republic. The Czechs have had a particularly difficult time with Romania, whose citizens have made the largest number of illegal border crossings. Diplomatic efforts with Romania helped to curb this tide in 2000.[28]

The Czech Republic, where prostitution is legal, has also become a favored destination for criminals engaged in trafficking young women from the East. It is estimated that twenty thousand such women are presently working in six hundred brothels throughout the Czech Republic.[29] The European Commission cited the trafficking of women and children as a problem that the Czech political leadership must address to advance Czech prospects for EU membership.[30] This phenomenon is rooted in a more encompassing threat plaguing the former Soviet bloc—the feminization of poverty, which compels East European women to take risks unthinkable to their peers in the West.[31]

Intolerance toward the Roma, or gypsies, has not yet been eradicated, but the Czech Republic, along with its Central European neighbors, has begun to treat these minorities better in order to qualify for EU membership. The Czech Republic's two hundred and fifty thousand Roma live at the margins of society and are subjected to routine job discrimination, some of which is sanctioned at various levels of the government.[32] The inability to root out these behaviors along with a nationalist-based xenophobic propensity threatens the Czechs' accession to the EU and tarnishes its international reputation.

Sustained economic recovery, the elimination of corruption in politics and business, continued progress toward building strong democratic institutions, and continued integration into Western economic, political, and security structures are the key weapons the Czechs must acquire to secure their future among the democratic and prosperous states of Europe. These objectives are also essential to guaranteeing a Czech contribution to Europe's cooperative-based security, political, and economic institutions.

Capacities

The Czech Republic pulled out of its three-year recession in 2000 by posting a gross domestic product (GDP) of 3.1 percent—the first growth in four years.[33] A robust infusion of foreign direct investment (FDI) and improving demand in key EU export markets were key factors driving the recovery.[34] Unemployment peaked at 9.8 percent in 2000, but it fell to 8.9 percent by year's end.[35] Structural reform and privatization of the Czech banking sector helped to correct the economic mismanagement and banking crises that helped propel the Czech Republic into recession. The Czech government took decisive action in June when its central bank put the country's third-largest bank, Investicni Postovni Banka (IPB) into forced administration. This and other efforts to privatize the remaining state-owned banks, which had been dominated by dubious state-owned institutions, have made the banking sector more competitive.[36]

As is the case with most developing countries, the Czech Republic's imports are dominated by the nearest economic giant, the EU, the source of 65 percent of its imports.[37] A strong manufacturing sector and a highly skilled workforce are positive attributes of the Czech economy. These characteristics help to explain the success of Skoda Auto, the motor of the

Czech economy, which employs 4 percent of the workforce and accounts for 14 percent of Czech exports. Skoda is the most successful former Communist company anywhere and has doubled its sales since 1995 even amidst the recession.[38] Investors still complain, however, that business enterprises cannot thrive without further legal reform. For instance, although the Czech Republic instituted a bold new commercial code by midyear, such measures will be ineffective unless its securities commission gets tougher enforcing violations.[39]

EU assessments placed the Czech Republic among the top seven candidates for accession and stated that this group was "well on track to meet the Union's economic criteria for membership."[40] However the European Commission's annual assessment report also ranked the Czech Republic behind Poland, Hungary, and Estonia in its efforts to meet the European Union's economic standards for membership. The report highlighted unfinished structural reforms, an unstable financial sector, a large amount of state debt, and problems associated with restructuring companies as the key Czech economic problems.[41] While the EU Integration Commissioner, Guenter Verheugen, is insistent that some candidates will be taken into the EU by 2003, he has not been forthcoming with a short list of likely first-wave entrants.[42]

The Czech government has honored its pledge made in June 1999 to guarantee defense expenditures at a rate of 2.2 percent of GDP in order to meet the NATO standard for defense spending.[43] Poland and Hungary have both fallen below the 2.2 percent threshold to 1.93 percent and 1.7 percent respectively.[44] The Czech defense budget for 2000 was 43.95 billion korunas (a bit less than $1 billion), which amounted to 7 percent of the state budget.[45] This was a 2.5 billion koruna (more than $60 million) increase from 1999.[46] Projected GDP growth for 2001 could increase next year's budget by a half billion to a billion korunas (at most, another $20 million); however, some Czech analysts and ACR Chief of Staff General Jiri Sedivy were grim about the mismatch between needs and resources. Payment for the acquisition of the L-159 aircraft, in particular, will exact a high toll on the defense budget for the next few years. This issue will be discussed more completely in the military capacities section of the chapter.

The leftist Social Democratic Party (CSSD) and right-wing Civic Democratic Party (ODS) renewed their opposition agreement in early 2000, which helped to stabilize the Czech political scene.[47] This agreement dates to the June 1998 elections, when the CSSD garnered the largest number of votes but failed to form a majority coalition, forcing it into an alliance with the ODS opposition. Although the frail CSSD-ODS pact held at year's end, the CSSD fared poorly in the November regional elections, where the ODS picked up the most votes. Meanwhile, one-third of the Senate seats in play fell mostly in the hands of the opposition four-member center-right coalition.[48] According to polls carried out by the end of November and beginning of December, just over a quarter of Czechs, 27 percent, are satisfied with the political situation in the country while 69 percent are not satisfied. These results are up from the 20 percent level of January 1999, but they indicate a leveling off from the peak reached in September 2000.[49]

The international media focused considerable attention on the standoff between independent journalists and the newly appointed director of the state-run television service that began shortly before Christmas and continued for a short while into the new year. For a few weeks, the dissident reporters produced parallel newscasts over cable and Internet outlets to run opposite the "official" programs. Many observers considered the Czech TV drama to be a metaphor for the Czech political scene, because the struggle pitted the two power centers—the ODS-CSSD alliance and the four-coalition liberal opposition—against each other. Previously, the two-channel public broadcaster had been associated with the four-coalition liberal opposition.[50] Political analysts suspect that Vaclav Klaus, former prime minister and leader of the ODS, won control over the state television director appointment from Prime Minister Milos Zeman in exchange for supporting the CSSD's budget.[51]

Czechs, urged on by the dissident broadcasts and sensing that the politicians were sacrificing the principle of the free press, turned out in numbers unseen since the Velvet Revolution in Wencelsaus Square to protest the government-backed state television appointment. Although not a member of a particular political party, President Vaclav Havel, partially motivated by an interest in undercutting Klaus with whom he has waged battle politically in recent months, threw his support to the rebel journalists.[52] Behind the power politics is a snapshot of an important aspect of the transition to Western liberal democracy being played out across the former Eastern bloc—that is whether free and independent media can take root and thrive or if, instead, major media organs will be controlled by large political parties and business tycoons.[53]

The earliest possible time frame in which frontrunners among post-Communist countries, the Czech Republic, Hungary, and Poland, could be admitted to the European Union is 2003–2004. The European Commission's annual assessment report noted that the strengthening of public administration and reform of the justice system are the top political tasks that the Czech Republic must accomplish to qualify for accession.[54] EU membership will be a badge recognizing the consolidation of the Czechs' democratic and economic transitions. While serious accession issues persist and much work remains to be done—especially to put in place the requisite legislative regime—some key defense implications emerged in 2000. The EU's growing momentum toward building an independent defense capacity outside of NATO is of concern to the Czechs and their fellow Central European NATO allies, who staunchly support a transatlantic link as critical to ensuring their security.[55] The new allies are also concerned that as European states that are in NATO but outside the EU, they will be put at a disadvantage as the EU builds its own defense identity.[56]

The Czech Republic continued to forge security cooperation ties with many states in 2000. The United States sustained its long-term program of security assistance with a pledge to spend $400,000 in 2001 on projects focused on the continued transformation of the ACR.[57] Britain established a training center to facilitate professionalization,[58] while German, Dutch, and Austrian soldiers participated in joint exercises in the Czech Republic.[59] Additionally, the Czech Republic signed military cooperation accords with the Former Yugoslav Republic of Macedonia and Tunisia.[60] Close cooperation was also evident with Slovakia. Talks were held to discuss transformation issues common to both armies and the possibility of cooperating on defense modernization.[61] Czech and Slovak air force commanders discussed the exchange of small squadrons, and Czech and Slovak defense ministers are also considering the formation of a joint Czech-Slovak peacekeeping unit.[62] A joint Czech-Slovak exercise, Blue Line 2000, was the biggest Czech-Slovak military exercise since the split of Czechoslovakia in 1993.[63] Finally, the Czechs have had an especially warm relationship with Latvia, which has received Czech military equipment and sent officers to Czech military schools.[64]

The armed forces of the Czech Republic consist of ground forces, air forces, territorial defense troops, and support elements. These components make up the aggregate ACR. Separate services with parallel administrative infrastructures do not exist. The active armed forces number 57,700, over half of which are army personnel. More than half of individuals serving in the army and air force in 2000 were conscripts.[65]

The ACR is further divided into Immediate Reaction Forces, Rapid Reaction Forces, and Main Defense Forces. Immediate Reaction Forces have a command structure and logistics support that allows them to respond within ten days to Alliance or national taskings. The Fourth Rapid Deployment Brigade is the core component within the Immediate Reaction Forces. Czech rapid deployment units within NATO may be incorporated into the British armed forces' command structure in 2001.[66]

The Air Force is divided into two main structures—tactical air force and air defense. Tactical, transport, and training units compose the Czech air forces. The Air Force is flying an average of sixty hours per year—well below the NATO standard of 160 hours.[67] Soviet legacy systems or modernized versions of them still equip the entire Air Force, although the more costly to maintain Russian aircraft will be retired as new L-159 aircraft come online.

The first anniversary of the Czech Republic's accession to NATO was marked with a spate of progress reports from NATO officials on Alliance performance to date. These assessments, which were largely directed at the Czech public, were carefully worded to laud the positive strides made while softly noting specific shortcomings remaining. NATO secretary-general George Robertson noted that the Czechs learned quickly in the fire of the Kosovo conflict,[68] but that difficult decisions still lay ahead to carry out reforms that would adapt the armed forces into more mobile, easily deployable, and better equipped units. Robertson opined further that new equipment is needed and investment in defense modernization must be done appropriately.[69] General Wesley Clark, while on an official two-day visit to Prague in March, told the Czech press that while the ACR's units serving in the Balkans had a good reputation, these troops represented only a small segment of the Czech Republic's armed forces, which were still in need of transformation overall. He added that the Czech Army must improve its system of financing, develop its commanders' skills, and improve its English language facility.[70] Clark's replacement, General Joseph Ralston, emphasized on a visit to Prague almost nine months later the importance of balancing the cost of modernization with the costs of training and the need to reach an equilibrium between the army's size, quality, training, and equipment.[71]

Other Western officials admit that practical and political problems have overwhelmed the process of absorbing new members as the new allies' armies are underfunded, badly equipped, and often unready for action.[72] This realization has blunted the appetite for more new members who will be unable to comprehensively fulfill NATO's interoperability requirements because of economic constraints and mismanagement. These limitations make it difficult to field robust and efficient defense budgets. It is widely believed that NATO enlargement hinges on the new allies' ability to rise up to NATO's norms and prove that they can be net security contributors to the Alliance as a whole.

The observations documented above included a long list of requirements to be fulfilled in order for the ACR to complete its transformation into a professional, competent, modern force subject to effective democratic political control. The form, degree, and pace of professionalization of the armed forces are fundamental decisions that Czech political leaders have yet to make. In a June interview, General Sedivy posited that politicians must convey to the ACR whether or not they really want to reduce the size of the Army and if they will pay for such reductions. "But that is not enough; they must communicate how large the Army is actually supposed to be at the end of the reductions and what all it must master."[73] Sedivy realizes that an overarching defense vision that connects professionalization with modernization must guide the moves that the Czech national security community makes in the future. For instance, the ACR still relies on anti-quated Russian radar systems that require a substantial number of personnel to run them. Reductions in these units cannot be made until the Czech government commits to the purchase of modern radar equipment.[74]

In June, the Council of Generals proposed a reduction in ACR ranks from the current fifty-seven thousand soldiers to forty-two thousand by 2010 with the goal that this number would be either fully or partly professionalized. ODS deputy chairman and shadow defense minister, Petr Necas, favors a professional army of thirty-eight thousand soldiers supported by eight thousand civilians. Meanwhile, Defense Minister Vetchy has made it known that he regards a rate of 60 percent professionalization as the optimal number.[75] It is clear that the force sizing numbers being bantered about in the Czech national security community are not the result of a carefully deliberated strategic vision that links national interests, defense requirements—both national and those related to cooperative security commitments—and economic realities to the transformation of the armed forces. By year's end, the General Staff estimated that full professionalization was unrealistic before 2015.[76]

In reality, manning the ACR looks problematic under either a continuation of the conscription course or the pursuit of professionalization. In just the last several years the number of conscript-age youths opting for military service has plummeted. Most young men of conscript age either get an exemption from national service on health grounds or choose to perform their national service in civilian posts even though they must serve six months longer. Up to 85 percent of Czech university graduates are finding ways to avoid performing their military service. These best-educated and best-connected Czechs can obtain the famous "blue book" bogus medical certificate for $500 on the black market.[77] Additionally, of the twenty-five thousand young men called to military service in 2000, only fourteen thousand were completely healthy and could serve without limitations. Moreover, a sharply declining birth rate—down 17 percent from 1998 to 2000—will further limit the military service pool.[78] Such trends, warns Deputy Chief of the General Staff Jiri Martinek, will make it difficult to staff the ACR—even as it gradually continues to become smaller.[79]

Professionalization of the ACR has wide support in the Czech Republic, with 48 percent of Czechs in favor of it and 35 percent opposed. For Czechs under the age of forty, support skyrockets to 61 percent. However, this support is more about the desire to do away with mandatory conscription and is not a positive indicator that young people would be inclined to join a professional army. Indeed, the avoidance of conscript service is rooted in the perception that conscripts are bullied, that officers are of low quality, and that conscript service is a waste of time.[80] Fulfilling the professionalization course depends on two main factors: 1. overcoming the negative images of the Czech military that remain in Czech popular culture, and 2. paying competitive salaries. At present, secondary school graduates earn somewhat less in professional positions in the ACR than they could earn in the civilian sector, while university graduates earn significantly less as military professionals.[81] The Czech Republic and its cash-strapped military will be hard-pressed to fulfill its professionalization and modernization goals. This realization has resulted in some observers calling for dividing the ACR into two components—a conscripted home guard and a professional force.[82] In the meantime, the current mismatch of the few professional units and the weak conscripted mass will continue.

Positive developments toward further professionalization include the arrival of a British military advisory and training team at the Vyskov Military Academy in September 2000. The twenty-four-member team is committed to stay in the Czech Republic for three to five years offering three-month courses aimed at teaching new methods of army command at the platoon and company levels. The courses are open to soldiers from the new allies' and aspirants' militaries in Central and East Europe.[83] Adaptation of the Czech Republic's military education system to serve as an effective instrument of professionalization, however, has been negligible. The military education establishment is still sized to serve a two hundred thousand-strong army and has not adapted its curriculum to meet the ACR's dramatically changed requirements. An even more troubling phenomenon is that the military schools do not seem to be under the effective control of the General Staff. When asked about the charge that the military education system was not meeting the needs of a professionalizing force, General Sedivy replied, "Military schools are under the Ministry of Defense and the General Staff has enough of its own problem anyway."[84] He added that the military schools are not being effectively used by the Army and that the schools train military specialists that the Army does not need.

The Czech Air Force struggled through another difficult year in 2000. Aircraft accidents occurred with a familiar frequency. The Czechs lost an

Su-22 fighter, an L-29 Delphin training jet, and two modernized MiG-21 fighters in 2000. These losses, in the wake of eight other combined losses in 1998–99 led to questions being raised about the adequacy of pilots' training, aircraft maintenance, the management of flight operations, and the overall state of the Air Force.[85]

Current flight operations will remain a challenge for the Czech Air Force, but the major Czech defense story of 2000 was the in-progress procurement of subsonic L-159 jets and the projected acquisition of supersonic fighters. These are issues that reach beyond the Air Force and will have an impact on the future course of the ACR. A closer look at the controversy surrounding the purchase of Czech-produced L-159 aircraft reveals, in microcosm, many of the problems that currently plague the Czech national security apparatus.

In the last week of 2000 the Air Force received is first two new subsonic L-159 jets.[86] However, throughout the year, the Czech press was filled with stories criticizing every aspect of the planes' acquisition: the characteristics of the plane itself, the terms of the contract, the great cost, and the politics surrounding the decision to buy them. The L-159, produced by the Czech firm Aero Vodochody, is a modernized version of the Czech-made L-39 and L-59 training jets, fitted with a more efficient engine, advanced aviation equipment, and other modifications.[87] These jets are the first of a fleet of seventy-two to be delivered over the next two years with the goal of forming the backbone of a modernized Czech Air Force.

Critics contend that when the Klaus government approved the contract in 1997, the defense ministry had yet to produce a medium- or long-range defense vision and that the ACR was not an advocate of the acquisition.[88] NATO officials have also criticized the L-159 because it is not capable of in-flight refueling.[89] Without refueling capability, the plane's effective range is quite limited, and it could not be used, for instance, in operations over Yugoslavia.[90]

This defense decision has been attributed to the chaotic state of defense planning evident in recent years. A diplomat from the foreign ministry remarked, "Those who had planned the purchase of the aircraft from Aero were trying to rescue the Czech aircraft industry, without taking any notice of the fact that we did not need so many aircraft for our defense."[91] The decision to buy seventy-two L-159s seems somewhat arbitrary, because it was not made in conjunction with a specific defense vision and was not coordinated with a parallel decision to buy a specific quantity of supersonic aircraft. Defense ministry officials also curiously decided not to invest in flight simulators for the L-159 at the tine of their purchase, which would have been invaluable in facilitating the pilots' transition to the new aircraft and to flying proficiency in general in an air force that flies a dangerously low number of flight hours.[92]

Perhaps the most serious impact of the L-159 purchase will be the constraining effect that it will have on the rest of the Czech defense budget. Failure to think through the consequences of committing to purchase such a large number of planes along with some disadvantageous contract terms have led to results that are currently overwhelming the Czech defense establishment. For instance, the contract price of the aircraft was determined in dollars and the payments were to be made in korunas. Because the defense ministry's contract negotiators did not elect to pay an additional fee of some millions to ensure against an unfavorable change in the exchange rate, the payments will run an additional 7 billion korunas, or one quarter more than originally anticipated. As a result, 80 percent of the defense sector's investment budget over the next few years will be spent on this project.[93]

The operations and training budget will be a major casualty resulting from the need to recover funds from other parts of the defense budget. Operations and training expenditures are slated to decrease by more than one half in 2001.[94] A reduction of the garrison structure is also being considered.[95] Other investments expected by NATO will have to be foregone such as plans to acquire modern communications systems and some efforts toward English-language training for Czech soldiers.[96] General Staff chief Jiri Sedivy admits that the restricting factor of L-159 payments resulted in the ACR meeting only 22 percent of the tasks that it had pledged to NATO to fulfill in 2000.[97] The L-159-induced budget crunch is also responsible for Czech efforts to cut back on their NATO commitments in the Balkans.

Although the L-159 contract has shown that the defense ministry lacks the experience to manage complex, expensive acquisitions, the Czechs are determined to launch the most costly contract in ACR history in 2001—a tender for the purchase of supersonic aircraft. The projected 100 billion koruna ($2.48 billion) expenditure will be spread over ten to fifteen years. While ACR leaders insist that defense of the Czech Republic's airspace is dependent on supersonic fighters,[98] neither the United States nor NATO is insisting on the purchase. Indeed, U.S. ambassador John Shattuck has argued that a purchase that is ruinous to the budget will have an overall negative impact on the transformation of the ACR.[99] Many Czech security experts, including Petr Necas, chairman of the Chamber of Deputies Defense and Security Committee, do not think that the Czech Republic is legislatively, organizationally, or militarily ready to take on the 100 billion koruna contract. Necas further expressed his concern that the government decided on issuing a tender without a clear strategic vision, "The government has no idea how many fighters the Army needs, what their equipment should be, and in which conditions they should be deployed. You must know all that when you decide on a 100-billion contract."[100] At the end of the year Necas' party (ODS) withdrew its support for launching the supersonic tender in 2001.[101]

The Army's modernization hopes are pegged to the upgrade of its Russian-made T-72 tanks. Of the Czechs' 500 Soviet-era T-72s, 140 are slated for modernization. This number is half that originally planned because of the budget squeeze resulting from the L-159 cost overruns. The project has strong domestic support, because the contract will largely benefit the Czech arms industry, which has high expectations to modernize a significant number of the eighteen thousand T-72s that remain in the former Soviet bloc.[102] The Czech modernization program boasts that it can offer custom refittings compatible with NATO standards—a claim that the original Russian manufacturers, who are also in search of buyers, cannot match.[103] The program, however, has been plagued from the start with delays. The main culprit has been an Italian firm with the subcontract to produce the tank's fire guidance system. The firm had been unable to produce a functioning system in the five years since it was awarded the contract.[104] In August, Czech defense industry officials announced that the fire control tests had finally been successful.[105]

Critics contend that effective modernization of the Czech armed forces is problematic in the long term. Of the two major modernization projects facing the Czech military, the L-159 purchase is cripplingly expensive and thought to be below NATO standards, while the T-72 project is of questionable use. Both programs are captives of domestic politics and of a desire to maintain a viable defense industry.[106] In the end, the Czech Republic is locked into the acquisition of Soviet-era legacy systems, the purchase of which will constrain all other efforts to transform the ACR into a NATO-compatible force.

Policy Innovations

Parliament approved an amendment to the constitution that enables the Czech government to make timely decisions regarding sending Czech soldiers abroad.[107] The constitution previously required the consent of both parliamentary houses before Czech troops could be deployed outside the country. The amendment also strengthens the cabinet's ability to allow foreign troops onto Czech territory and permits the government to authorize overflights of Czech airspace. The legislation permits the government to deploy forces for up to sixty days and to accept foreign troops onto Czech soil for less than two months. These actions can be canceled if either house of Parliament votes to do so.[108] The amendment will facilitate the Czechs' ability to fulfill their NATO obligations as well as to participate in UN peacekeeping operations.

The Council for State Security proposed that the Czech Republic should have the ability to receive assistance from its allies to protect Czech airspace if attacked and the authorization to send Czech planes abroad to assist allies in the protection of their airspace. The current constitution does not allow foreign troops to operate above Czech territory.[109] This measure will have to be approved by both chambers of Parliament before it takes effect.

The ACR came under fire in 2000 because only 5 percent of the required number of soldiers had been screened for security clearances.[110] As a result, insufficient numbers of screened soldiers were available to be sent to key NATO staff positions. Under current law, only the National Security Office can do the vetting.[111] The Chairman of the Defense and Security Committee in the Chamber of Deputies, Petr Necas, blamed the ACR for overclassifying its documents and subsequently mandating that an inordinate number of soldiers receive high security clearances. In response, the government is discussing drafting legislation to allow the defense and interior ministries to do their own vetting to break the current log jam.

Prime Minister Zeman has spearheaded a creative innovation aimed at ensuring that cabinet ministers opposed to NATO do not gain the upper hand in State Security Council deliberations. In the 1999 Kosovo crisis, several "pacifist" ministers were able to derail the Czech government's ability to support NATO's actions. These actions concerned Alliance officials, because a veto from a NATO member state could effectively paralyze NATO operations. Zeman's initiative added two additional ministers to the State Security Council in April. This move strengthens the State Security Council's hand vis-a-vis the cabinet so that it would only have to win over one more minister of the seventeen-member cabinet to prevail in decisions such as those encountered in the Kosovo crisis.[112]

Key consensus is still needed on a defense vision that will provide the political guidance needed to determine the appropriate size and degree of professionalization of the ACR. Parliament and the government must work to forge common goals and expectations for the Czech military. Defense Minister Vetchy promises that the MOD will produce such a document in 2001. However, the political leadership across the Czech national security community should be engaged in this task. Meanwhile, in the vacuum of political guidance, national security decisions are made every day. For example, the General Staff has proposed personnel cuts up to one-third of the current level, but doubts run high that the defense ministry could implement them or that the current government will support such cuts that will affect local interests and constituencies.[113]

Future Prospects

A realization has been settling in across the former Soviet bloc that the road of transition has been and will continue to be more obstacle laden than originally anticipated. The good news for the Czech Republic and its Central European neighbors is that the basic elements of a free and democratic multiparty system, freedom of the press, and respect for human rights are now standard political features of their political systems.[114] The Czechs are generally moving in the right direction and the possibility of returning to the economic and political regimes of the Communist era is near zero.

While national security reform has been somewhat problematic, the fundamental frameworks for gradual professionalization and modernization are in place. Scarce economic resources and the challenges of building a credible and competent defense community will continue to constrain more rapid progress. It is also unreasonable to expect advances in the field of defense reform to outstrip progress made in the areas of general democratic and economic reform.[115] Further progress depends on deepening the democratic institutions that affect national security outcomes.

Greater expertise and assertiveness within parliamentary committees charged with defense oversight, an expanded number of defense journalists working within the media, more competent civilian defense professionals in the employ of the defense ministry, and finally, military leaders willing to engage the national security process at every level will lead to more quality national security policy outcomes. Short-term national security decisions of particular import include forging consensus on a defense vision that can guide subsequent actions, such as major acquisitions, force sizing issues, and the appropriate degree of professionalization for Czech national security needs.

The Czech Republic and its Central European neighbors are determined to remain the leaders of the former Eastern bloc's democratic transition. In doing so, they will make a substantial contribution toward regional stability as the pioneers and role models for other aspiring democracies in the region. The course toward further integration into European structures is set. The only question that remains is the pace, form, and particular obstacles that must be negotiated en route.

Chronology

5 January 2000: Government approves draft amendment to constitution permitting the deployment of Czech soldiers abroad and the presence of foreign military troops in the Czech Republic in certain cases for up to sixty days without the approval of parliament.

18 January 2000: First solo flight of L-159 by Czech Air Force pilot.

17 February 2000: Czech Republic and Former Yugoslav Republic of Macedonia sign agreement on defense cooperation.

16–23 February 2000: Czech Republic participates in NATO-WEU CMX/ Crisex 2000 crisis management exercise.

12 March 2000: First anniversary of Czech Republic's accession to NATO.

18 March 2000: Foreign ministers of Czech Republic, Poland, and Hungary meet in Budapest to assess first year of NATO membership.

10 April 2000: First two L-159 subsonic fighter jets delivered to Czech Army in Caslav.

18 April 2000: Members of the Forty-third Parachute Mechanized Battalion begin replacement of members of the First Mechanized Battalion in Bosnia-Herzegovina (SFOR).

April 2000: Czech and German pilots train to NATO standards in preparation for NATO Clean Hunter exercise.

11 May 2000: Six NATO member states without EU membership meet in Portugal seeking clarification of the role of non-EU member states in emerging defense structure.

8–25 May 2000: Dutch brigade and ACR's Fourth Rapid Deployment Brigade participate in Czech-Dutch exercise at the Hradiste military training area in the Czech Republic.

15–17 May 2000: Forty-six Czech soldiers participate in COLA 2000 (Cooperative Lantern 2000) multinational NATO training exercise in Frejus, France. First time Czech officer commands NATO international brigade.

6–16 June 2000: Clean Hunter 2000 exercise aimed at training tactical grades in NATO interoperability. Common Goal 2000, joint exercise of the Czech and German air forces took place simultaneously at Hradiste military training area in north Bohemia.

28 June 2000: Commanders of Czech and Slovak air forces conduct first-ever talks in central Slovakia.

10 July 2000: Yemeni government receives first shipment of T-55 main battle tanks purchased from the Czech Republic.

9 August 2000: Czech Senate passes constitutional amendment allowing the government, in certain conditions, to send Czech soldiers abroad and to approve foreign troops entry into the Czech Republic for up to sixty days.

28–31 August 2000: Seventy-two Czech soldiers from Forty-third Mechanized Battalion participate in SFOR exercise.

11–13 September 2000: Blue Line 2000, largest Czech-Slovak military exercise since split of Czechoslovakia takes place in north Moravia.

13 October 2000: Czech Republic opens first of thirteen NATO-style army recruitment centers.

25 October 2000: Czech Republic and United States sign military cooperation agreement.

31 October 2000: Prince Charles officially opens British Military Advisory Training Team (BMATT) course in Vyskov.

2 November 2000: Czech-Slovak joint coordination commission agrees to limited cooperation within arms industries.

13 November 2000: Czech Republic becomes member of the Western European Armaments Group (WEAG), a forum for cooperation across arms industries.

20 December 2000: Senate approves government's proposal to join NATO's antiaircraft integrated defense system.

21 December 2000: Economic Deputy Defense Minister Jindrich Tomas resigns.

21 December 2000: Defense Minister Vetchy fires the director of the Office for National Armament, Jaroslav Stefec.

29 December 2000: Czech Army receives first two subsonic L-159s; Su-25K planes removed from Czech air force inventory.

NOTES

1. Marybeth Peterson Ulrich, "The New Allies: Approaching NATO Political and Military Standards," *NATO and Europe in the 21st Century* (Washington, D.C.: Woodrow Wilson International Center for Scholars, 2000), 39.

2. "Poll Shows Most Czechs Consider NATO Entry 'Best Security Solution,' " *Prague CTK*, 19 December 2000. The STEM polling agency for Czech television and Czech radio carried out the poll. *FBIS*, EUP20001219000704.

3. "More Than Half of Czechs Satisfied with NATO Membership—Poll," *Prague CTK*, 30 December 1999. *FBIS*, EUP20001214000177.

4. "Hungarian, Polish, Czech Poll on NATO Membership," *Budapest MTI*, 10 March 2000. *FBIS*, EUP20000310000009.

5. "Polls Show Czech Army Enjoying Strongest Support since 1993," *Prague CTK*, 7 November 2000. *FBIS*, EUP20001107000086.

6. Ibid.

7. "Change of Czech Troops Operating in Kosovo Completed," *Prague CTK*, 31 July 2000. *FBIS*, EUP20000731000047.

8. "SFOR Commander Expresses Satisfaction with Czech Unit," *Prague CTK*, 17 February 2000. *FBIS*, EUP20000217000454; "NATO against Withdrawal of Czech Troops from Kosovo," *Prague CTK*, 7 April 2000. *FBIS*, EUP20000407000341.

9. *Prague Mlada Fronta Dnes*, "General Says KFOR Contingent to Complete Mission in July," 11 January 2000. *FBIS*, FTS20000111001175.

10. "Czech KFOR Participation Still Uncertain," *Prague CTK*, 1 February 2000. *FBIS*, FTS20000202001090.

11. "Czech Unit Should Remain in Kosovo Says Senate," *Prague CTK*, 13 April 2000. *FBIS*, EUP20000413000099.

12. "NATO against Withdrawal."

13. One dollar equals 40.22 *korunas* (crowns); "Defense Ministry Facing Major Problems in Finding Funds for Balkans Missions," *Prague Mlada Fronta Dnes*, 11 November 2000. *FBIS*, EUP20001113000311.

14. "Czech Army to Face Collapse Unless Changes Are Made, Says Daily," *Prague Mlada Fronta Dnes*, 26 October 2000. *FBIS*, EUP20001026000101.

15. Ibid.

16. "Situation in Czech Army on Verge of 'Collapse,' " *Prague Mlada Fronta Dnes*, 23 October 2000. *FBIS*, EUP20001027000214.

17. "Defense Ministry again Purchases Defective Spare Parts," *Prague Mlada Fronta Dnes*, 8 February 2000. *FBIS*, EUP20000209000047.

18. "Daily: Defense Sector Reorganization Triggers Conflict," *Prague Hospodarske Noviny*, 3 March 2000. *FBIS*, EUP20000306000027.

19. "High Ranking Army Officers Arrested over Army Procurement Irregularities," *Prague Mlada Fronta Dnes*, 5 October 2000. *FBIS*, EUP20001006000.

20. "Czech Army Short of Money to Pay for Extra Time Work—Daily," *Prague CTK*, 21 September 2000. *FBIS*, EUP200009210000.

21. "Purchase of New Planes, Tank Upgrade 'Stupid Projects'—Czech Premier," *Prague CTK*, 6 November 2000. *FBIS*, EUP20001107000153.

22. "Czech Daily Speculates about Possible Sacking of Defense Minister," *Prague CTK*, 14 December 2000. *FBIS*, EUP20001214000026.

23. "Czech Daily's 'Sources': Minister's Failed Aircraft Tender Means 'No Confidence,' " *Prague Lidove Nivony*, 20 December 2000. *FBIS*, EUP20001122000483.

24. "Czech Republic: Deputy Defense Minister Resigns," *Prague CTK*, 21 December 2000. *FBIS*, EUP20001221000183.

25. "Prague Daily Views Crisis in Armed Forces, Outlines Action Necessary," *Prague Mlada Fronta Dnes*, 6 December 2000. *FBIS*, EUP20001207000217.

26. *The Security Strategy of the Czech Republic* (Prague: Ministry of Foreign Affairs, April 1999), 5.

27. *CIA World Factbook 2000*, Internet, <http://www.cia.gov/cia/publications/factbook/geos/ez.html>.

28. "Czech, Romanian Premiers Hail Decline in Illegal Immigration, NATO," *Prague CTK*, 9 October 2000. *FBIS*, EUP20001009000306.

29. "Trafficking in Women," *Economist*, 26 August 2000.

30. Shada Islam, "Poland, Hungary, Estonia Lead EU Entry Race as Turkey Trails," *Deutsche Presse-Agentur*, 8 November 2000.

31. "Trafficking in Women."

32. Lucian Kim, "The Wall of Hostility on 'Intolerance Street,' " *U.S. News and World Report*, 8 November 1999, p. 62.

33. "Czech Economy Recovers with 3.1 Percent GDP Growth in 2000," CountryWatch. com, 22 March 2000. <http://www.countrywatch.com> (accessed 23 March, 2001).

34. "Country Review Country Wire, Czech Republic—Economy," CountryWatch.com, <http://www.countrywatch.com> (accessed 23 March, 2001).

35. "Czech Cabinet Approves Action Plan to Boost Employment," *Prague CTK*, 19 February 2001. *FBIS*, EUP20010219000240.

36. "The Last Crisis?" *Economist*, 24 June 2000.

37. "Trading Partners," *Economist*, 2 December 2000.

38. "Slav Motown," *Economist*, 6 January 2001.

39. "Rights Issue," *Economist*, 29 July 2000.

40. The other candidates, ranked from first to last, are Poland, Hungary, Estonia, Cyprus, Malta, the Czech Republic, and Slovenia. Islam Shada, "Poland, Hungary, Estonia lead EU entry race as Turkey Trails," *Deutsche Presse-Agentur*, 8 November 2000.

41. "Reaction to EC Report Possibly Linked to Elections—Cibrian," *Prague CTK*, 16 November 2000.

42. "Majority of Citizens in Central Europe's Big Three Favor EU Entry," *Deutsche Presse-Agentur*, 13 October 2000.

43. "Defense Ministry Drafts Prognosis on Future Arms Spending," *Prague Pravo*, 17 March 2000, p. 19. *FBIS*, EUP20000317000256.

44. "Poles' Per Capita Defense Spending Lowest in NATO," *Warsaw PAP*, 5 December 2000. *FBIS*, EUP20001205000211.

45. *Prague Pravo*, 17 March 2000.

46. "Army Main Beneficiary of 2000 State Budget," *Prague Lidove Nivony*, 6 March 2000. *FBIS*, EUP20000307000072.

47. "Czech Republic: PX-50 up 34% in 2000," *Janet Matthews Information Services*, 21 March 2000.

48. "Right-wing Voters More Satisfied with Politics after Elections," *CTK National News Wire*, 26 December 2000.

49. "Only Quarter of Czechs Satisfied with Political Situation—Poll," *CTK News Agency*, 2 January 2001.

50. Lyle Stewart, "Canadians Could Learn from Czech TV Drama," *Montreal Gazette*, 5 January 2001, p. B3.

51. Steven Erlanger, "50,000 Demonstrate for Dissident Journalists in Prague," *International Herald Tribune*, 4 January 2001.

52. "Czech Media Mount High Horse," *Economist*, 6 January 2001.

53. Stewart.

54. "EC Does Not Like State of Czech Public Administration, Justice," *Prague CTK*, 8 November 2000.

55. "So That's All Agreed Then," *Economist*, 16 December 2000.

56. "Grow Europe," *Economist*, 9 December 2000.

57. "Minister, Envoy Sign Plan on US Assistance to Czech Army in 2000," *Prague CTK*, 25 October 2000. *FBIS*, EUP20001025000211.

58. "British Army to Train Central, Eastern European Instructors in Czech Republic," *Prague CTK*, 25 July 2000. *FBIS*, EUP20000725000240.

59. "Czech, Austrian Generals Discuss NATO, Training Exercises," *Prague CTK*, 25 April 2000. *FBIS*, EUP20000425000299; "Dutch, Czech Brigades Train Together in West Bohemia," *Prague CTK*, 9 May 2000, *FBIS*, EUP20000509000432; "Czech, German Air Force Plan Combined Exercise in North Bohemia," *Prague CTK*, 7 June 2000, *FBIS*, EUP20000607000055.

60. "Visiting Czech Defense Minister Signs Cooperation Accord," *Skopje Radio Makedonija*, 17 February 2000, *FBIS*, EUP20000217000378; "Czech, Tunisian Ministers Sign Military Cooperation Accord," *Prague CTK*, 11 May 2000, *FBIS*, EUP20000511000446.

61. "Czech, Slovak Chiefs of Staff Discuss Army Transformation, Cooperation," *Prague CTK*, 30 October 2000. *FBIS*, EUP200001031000091.

62. "Air Force Chief Expects Czech Pilots to Use Slovak Base Next Year," *Prague CTK*, 29 June 2000. *FBIS*, EUP20000629000362.

63. "Ministers Discuss Plan to Set Up Joint Czech-Slovak Peacekeeping Unit," *Prague CTK*, 2 October 2000. *FBIS*, EUP20001002000338.

63. "Biggest Czech-Slovak NATO-Style Military Exercise Begins," *Prague CTK*, 11 September 2000. *FBIS*, EUP20000912000053.

64. "Czech Minister in Latvia Offers Training, 'Experience' With NATO," *Prague CTK*, 22 June 2000. *FBIS*, EUP20000622000129.

65. The International Institute for Strategic Studies, *The Military Balance* (London: Oxford University Press, October 2000), 55–56.

66. "Prague Official Says Czech Rapid Deployment Units to Be Part of British Forces," *Prague CTK*, 19 June 2000. *FBIS*, EUP20000619000301.

67. *The Military Balance*, 56.

68. For a franker assessment, see Marybeth Peterson Ulrich, "Czech Republic: Integrated, Yet Still in Transition," in *Brassey's Eurasian and East European Security Yearbook*, eds. Ustina Markus and Daniel N. Nelson (Washington, D.C.: Brassey's, 2000), 35, and Ulrich, "The New Allies: Approaching NATO Political and Military Standards," 39–40.

69. "Robertson Satisfied after One Year of Czech NATO Membership, *CTK National News Wire*, 7 March 2000.

70. "Clark Praises Czech Mission in Balkans, Says Army Must Change," *Prague CTK*, 21 March 2000. *FBIS*, EUP20000321000334.

71. "NATO Europe Commander Assesses Czech Army Training," *Prague CTK*, 10 January 2001. *FBIS*, EUP20010110000119.

72. Christopher Lockwood and Tim Butcher, "NATO Plans for Eastward Enlargement Put on Hold," *London Daily Telegraph*, 3 April 2000. *FBIS*, EUP20000403000113.

73. "Generals Decide to Make Radical Cuts, Changes in Czech Army," *Prague Mlada Fronta Dnes*, 9 June 2000. *FBIS*, EUP20000606000072.

74. Ibid.

75. "Czech Civic Democratic Party Advocates Professional Army within 6–8 Years," *Prague CTK*, 11 June 2000. *FBIS*, EUP20000611000092.

76. Pavel Otto, "Professional Army Only in 2015," *Prague Hospodarske Noviny*, 29 December 2000, p. 4. *FBIS*, EUP20010102000008.

77. "Central Europe's Sulky Conscripts," *Economist*, 12 August 2000.

78. "Army Statistics Show Recruits' Deteriorating Health," *Prague Mlada Fronta Dnes*, 17 May 2000, p. 9. *FBIS*, EUP20000517000375.

79. "Growing Proportion of Young Men Avoiding Army Service," *Prague Mlada Fronta Dnes*, 22 February 2000, p. 3. *FBIS*, EUP20000223000202.

80. "Cabinet to Take Measures against Abuse of Civilian Service," *Prague CTK*, 12 April 2000. *FBIS*, EUP20000412000039.

81. The average university graduate could earn 15,400 korunas, while his military pay would be 11,500 korunas. "Growing Proportion of Young Men Avoiding Army Service," p. 3.

82. "Central Europe's Sulky Conscripts."

83. "First British-Organized Military Training Course Ends in Czech Republic," *Prague CTK*, 29 November 2000. *FBIS*, EUP20001129000125.

84. "General Staff Chief Sedivy Outlines Czech Army Reduction Problem," *Prague Mlada Fronta Dnes*, 12 June 2000. *FBIS*, EUP20000613000176.

85. "Su-22 Bomber Crashed in Czech Republic after NATO Exercise," *Prague CTK*, 16 June 2000. *FBIS*, EUP20000616000206; "Czech Air Force Training Flights to Resume after Recent Accident," *Prague CTK*, 8 August 2000. *FBIS*, EUP20000808000140; "Air Force Commander Klima's Fate 'Uncertain' following MiGs' Crash," *Prague Hospodarske Noviny*, 12 October 2000. *FBIS*, EUP20001013000014; "Air Force Commander Klima's Chair 'Shaking,'" *Prague Pravo*, 30 October 2000. *FBIS*, EUP20001031000057; "Czech Republic: Senior Commander, Pilots Discuss Safety of Air Force Flights," *Prague CTK*, 3 November 2000. *FBIS*, EUP20001103000308.

86. "Czech Army Receives First New Subsonic Aircraft," *Prague CTK*, 29 December 2000. *FBIS*, EUP20001230000025.

87. Pavel Otto, "L-159: The Army's Unwanted Child," *Prague Hospodarske Noviny*, 11 April, 2000. *FBIS*, EUP20000411000274.

88. Ibid.

89. "Air Force Takes Delivery of First Two L-159 Subsonic Jets," *Prague CTK*, 10 April 2000. *FBIS*, EUP20000410000151.

90. "Czech L-159 May Be Adapted for Refueling," *Prague Mlada Fronta Dnes*, 19 January 2000. *FBIS*, FTS20000120001510.

91. Jan Gazdik, "L-159 Is More Than Officials Can Chew," *Prague Mlada Fronta Dnes*, 26 April 2000. *FBIS*, EUP20000428000018.

92. "New L-159 Aircraft Nearly Crashes, news Blackout Denied," *Prague Mlada Fronta Dnes*, 23 February 2000, p. 3. *FBIS*, EUP20000223000491.

93. Tomas Horejsi, "A Poorly Drafted Agreement Is Depriving the Army of Billions," *Prague Lidove Noviny*, 16 June 2000, pp. 1–2. *FBIS*, EUP20000619000263.

94. "Budget Constraints May Mean Army Unable to Operate New L-159 Aircraft Next Year," *Prague Mlada Fronta Dnes*, 5 September 2000. *FBIS*, EUP20000907000051.

95. "Chief of General Staff Views Troubled L-159 Aircraft Project, Air Accidents," *Prague Pravo*, 22 August 2000. *FBIS*, EUP20000822000124.

96. Gazdik, "L-159 Is More Than Officials Can Chew."

97. Pavel Otto, "The Army Does Not Even Have the Funds for NATO Tasks," *Prague Hospodarske Noviny*, 18 January 2001, p. 4. *FBIS*, EUP20010119000049.

98. Pavel Otto, "The Army Wants Not Only Fighters, But Also Missiles," *Prague Hospodarske Noviny*, 22 November 2000. *FBIS*, EUP20001123000197.

99. "Daily Quotes US Envoy As Saying That Czechs Do Not Need New Fighter Aircraft," *Prague CTK*, 7 December 2000. *FBIS*, EUP20001207000052.

100. Jan Gazdik, "Base for Fighters Is Lacking," *Prague Mlada Fronta Dnes*, 18 October 2000. *FBIS*, EUP20001019000059.

101. "Czech Opposition Party against International Fighter Aircraft Tender," *Prague CTK*, 11 December 2000. *FBIS*, EUP20001211000388.

102. "Modernized T-72CZ Tank May Provide Lifeline for Country's Industry," *Prague Mlada Fronta Dnes*, 23 August 2000. *FBIS*, EUP20000824000048.

103. Pavel Otto, "Russia Wants To Modernize T-72 Tank with the United States," *Prague Hospodarske*, 28 December 1999, pp. 1,4. *FBIS*, AU2912134599.

104. Tomas Horejsi, "The Prime Minister Has Criticized Vetchy because of the Tanks," *Prague Lidove Noviny*, 20 July 2000, pp. 1, 2. *FBIS*, EUP20000720000226.

105. "Modernized T-72CZ Tank May Provide Lifeline for Country's Industry," *Prague Mlada Fronta Dnes*, 12 August 2000.

106. "Prague: Defense Modernization Checked," *STRATFOR.com Global Intelligence Update*, 10 August 2000. Internet, <http://www.stratfor.com/SERVICES/giu2000/081000.asp>.

107. "Czech Senate Consents to Government Deciding on Military Missions," *Prague CTK*, 9 August 2000. *FBIS*, EUP20000809000076.

108. "Czech Government Receives Authority on Sending Troops Abroad," *Prague CTK*, 25 May 2000. *FBIS*, EUP20000525000161.

109. "Vetchy: Armed Forces to Protect Airspace along with NATO," *Prague CTK*, 17 February 2000. *FBIS*, EUP20000217000422.

110. "Low Number of Screened Personnel May Complicate Army Situation in 2001," *Prague Pravo*, 8 September 2000, p. 3. *FBIS*, EUP20000911000033.

111. "Czech Government to Discuss Security Vetting," *Prague CTK*, 30 April 2000. *FBIS*, EUP20000430000037.

112. Tomas Horejsi, " 'Pro-NATO Wing' in State Security Council to Be Reinforced," *Prague Mlada Fronta Dnes*, 23 March 2000, p. 2. *FBIS*, EUP20000323000235.

113. Michal Sverdik and Jan Gazdik, "The Army Command: We Have to Make One-Third of the Troops Redundant," *Prague Mlada Fronta Dnes*, 3 June 2000, pp. 1, 2. *FBIS*, EUP20000606000072.

114. Patrice Muller, "Life after Communism Leaves Citizens Waiting for the Good Times," *Canadian Business and Current Affairs* (August 2000).

115. Sebestyen L. v. Gorka, "NATO after Enlargement: Is the Alliance Better Off," *NATO Review* Vol. 47 (Autumn 1999).

7 ◆ Hungary: Peace and Quiet of an Increasingly Illiberal Democracy

Pal Dunay

A decade after forming the first democratically elected government in half a century, the transformation process of this medium-size East-Central European country is widely regarded as a success story. Hungary is in the forefront of Western integration, it has stable institutions, and private ownership dominates the country's economy. It seems to have liberated itself from the "ghosts of Trianon," the revanchist feelings toward countries that once belonged, partly or fully, to the Austrian empire or the Austro-Hungarian monarchy and that host significant ethnic Hungarian minorities.

Since the beginning of 2000 through early 2001, Hungary enjoyed a quiet and comparatively easily manageable period in its security policy. In spite of this, there are several signs that indicate Hungary's international situation may deteriorate in the next year or so for reasons that have escaped the attention of those who confine their analysis to traditional problems of international security.

The transformation process of Hungary has been more gradual than that of most other countries of the former Warsaw Treaty, comparable only to Poland. Private economic initiative was tolerated earlier than in other countries, while the dominance of public property was retained until the end of the so-called socialist system. The system change was a "negotiated revolution" between the former establishment and the emerging forces of political pluralism.[1] As a consequence, the former regime was not entirely delegitimized, and the democratic forces were not obliged to fight only other political orientations but also the ghosts of the Kadar era as well.

Since the system change of 1989–90 and the first democratic elections in the spring of 1990, three governments have been in power.[2] They had some common characteristics. Each was elected with the active participation of the electorate through free and fair elections and had unquestionable democratic legitimacy. Each functioned as a coalition government. Each served its full four-year term. Extremist forces have never gained governmental responsibility, although they appeared in the Parliament for the first time in 1998. Each government coalition lost the next elections.[3] This highlights either their inability to cope with the tasks of governance or the impossibility to cope with the complex tasks after the system change.

It was an important common feature of the three governments that they have shared the same foreign policy objectives. As articulated by the government programs, the foreign policy of Hungary had the same "priorities":

- Integration into Western institutions
- Good-neighborly relations
- Support to the Hungarian ethnic minority beyond the border

A closer look at the foreign policy of the three governments would lead to the conclusion that very different practices evolved from identical goals.

The first post-Communist government headed by Jozsef Antall (and, after his death in December 1993, by Peter Boross) had the most difficult task. It had to establish an adequately functioning democratic political system and a market economy, while completing the reorientation of the country's international relations.[4] Antall, with his deep historical beliefs about nineteenth-century liberal public order, had a clear vision about the political system to build. He had very little idea about the economy, but he was helped in some areas by professional expertise. Namely, the Hungarian economy increasingly was open during the two decades preceding the system change as seen by the proportion of gross domestic product (GDP) in international markets. On the one hand, this made the Hungarian economy vulnerable while, on the other hand, it helped develop a certain idea about the functioning of a liberalized market economy early on. The choice to follow the "Treuhand-model" in the privatization of the economy on a company-by-company basis, despite all the problems, has become an important long-term success of transformation.[5] It led to a rapid creation of real ownership in a large part of the Hungarian economy.

In foreign policy terms, the Antall government was taken by subjective impressions and often by prejudices. This was exacerbated by several unfortunate selections of foreign policy leaders. The aim to integrate with Western institutions, the North Atlantic Treaty Organization (NATO), the European Union (EU), and the Council of Europe was one of the priorities. Council of Europe membership was achieved after democratic elections. The country joined the North Atlantic Cooperation Council (NACC) and the Partnership for Peace (PfP) from the onset of those institutions. Hungary, together with Poland and Czechoslovakia, had signed an association agreement with the EC in December 1991 and applied for EU membership in spring 1994 before the Antall-Boross government came to an end.

During that period, Hungary subordinated neighborly relations to the treatment of the Hungarian minority. This resulted in a conflictual relationship with Romania and Slovakia, countries that hosted the largest ethnic Hungarian communities. It was not so much the actions as the rhetoric that was found destabilizing by the country's Western partners. It seemed self-evident that Hungary carried the potential to import conflicts into any organization it joined. The Hungarian refusal to renounce the right of peaceful border revision in case the other side does not respect the collective rights of the Hungarian minority was a particularly dangerous bluff. It not only demonstrated that Hungary was not fully committed to stability, but also gave the impression that the country contemplated being in the position to blackmail its partners.

Governments were replaced in the region almost at every election in the 1990s. The same applied to Hungary. There is no agreement among politicians and analysts why the first conservative government lost so badly at the elections of 1995, and therefore why the three parties that had formed the Antall-Boross coalition held only 20 percent of the seats in the parliament afterward. Prime Minister Antall used to be of the view that he headed a "kamikaze" government. Such a coalition government could not win elections, because it had to adopt and carry out many difficult austerity measures to put the Hungarian economy and society on a new track. There is an element of truth in this. Opposition and independent analysts would probably present a different account, however. They would point to an arrogant communication style, attempts to control an alienated media, nepotism, and some corruption.

The ideological overtone of foreign policy, particularly as far as the treatment of the Hungarian minority was concerned, certainly contributed to the negative assessment received by the government. The overwhelming majority of the Hungarian people have not felt strongly about their own kin beyond the border. They sympathized with ethnic Hungarians, but during economic hardship and rising unemployment, they were understandably reluctant to make any sacrifice for that cause. For more than forty years of socialism, Hungarians in neighboring countries (overwhelmingly in other socialist countries) were powerless and could not be used to mobilize or motivate.

The conservatives were followed by a socialist-liberal coalition. The Socialist Party, formed by former Communists in 1989 (officially the erstwhile Hungarian Socialist Workers' Party), gained an absolute majority in the 1994 elections. To gain international legitimacy and also to obtain a qualified majority in Parliament, it formed a coalition with the liberal Alliance of Free Democrats, the party in which the core anti-Communist opposition gathered.[6] The country was in trouble. The inflation rate was high and external debt had ballooned during the last year of the conservative government. The International Monetary Fund was reluctant to sign a new standby arrangement with Hungary that had a negative impact on private creditors. Moreover, because of the controversial "neighborhood" policy of the former conservative government, the country's international prestige was not at its peak.

The new government had clear ideas about how to improve the international standing of the country. It promised to reestablish the balance among different priorities of foreign policy. This meant that the issue of the treatment of Hungarian minorities in neighboring countries would be reintegrated in neighborly relations and thus resubordinated to it. It also meant that the objective of Western integration regained its absolute priority, and neighborly relations could no longer interfere with it. There was every reason to press ahead with the new agenda. There is anecdotal evidence more telling than long descriptions. When the new Foreign Minister, Laszlo Kovacs, met a high-ranking State Department official during the UN General Assembly session in early autumn 1994, for example, he faced the question concerning the territorial claims of Hungary. Kovacs felt genuinely embarrassed about the question and saw the urgent need to propagate a new Hungarian foreign policy that has renounced every sort of border revision, peaceful and nonpeaceful alike.

The new coalition promised a breakthrough in relations with neighboring countries and the early signing of so-called basic treaties. The basic treaties were to regulate the fundamental issues of each bilateral relationship upon which further detailed agreements could be based. Less important, the conclusion of new "basic" treaties made it possible to say good-bye elegantly to Cold War bilateral treaties between Hungary and other socialist countries denoted by the catchwords "friendship, cooperation, and mutual assistance." The new treaties no longer refer to mutual assistance. The idea to regulate some of the most troubled relationships of Hungary, notably with Romania and Slovakia, represented a strategic change. The promise to achieve new agreements soon was a diplomatic mistake, however. It gave the upper hand to other parties that could use such a promise to blackmail Hungary, forcing Hungary to make compromises and take positions that it would not have done otherwise. Hungary did sign the basic treaty with Slovakia in March 1995 and with Romania in September 1996. The conservative opposition, of course, blamed the government for abandoning Hungary's national interest in both cases. In the latter case, criticism was voiced that the socialist government's treaty with Romania during the last months of President Ion Iliescu's first term in office was concluded in order to help him, unsuccessfully, to election victory.

The declared account of the agreements was to regulate basic issues of bilateral relations and to improve the situation for ethnic Hungarians in the respective countries. Further, it aimed to dissipate residual threat perceptions. Given that the treatment of the Hungarian minority did *not* improve at all during either Premier Vladimir Meciar's or President Iliescu's terms in office it is tempting to ask whether the Hungarian leadership pursued an illusion or whether Prime Minister Gyula Horn and Foreign Minister Kovacs were both naive. I believe otherwise. They were well aware of the purpose of the two basic treaties—primarily to demonstrate to the West that these countries would be able to cooperate. Moreover, basic treaties were to carry the message that, in case of their accession to Western institutions, there is no threat that they would "import" their conflicts. They wanted to meet a formal Western expectation that they regarded an essential precondition of accession.

The new, responsible foreign policy was well received in the West. Hungary was invited to join NATO in 1997 and, by the time the socialist-liberal coalition government lost the elections in summer 1998, the ratification of the accession protocol was well under way. Hungary was also part of the first group that started accession talks with the European Union in spring 1998. To achieve such EU acceptance had required a fundamental change in the economic course of the country several years earlier, via the Bokross plan (the finance minister at that time). This plan led to a severe decline in the standard of living for the rest of the Horn government's term. It is not clear why the Socialist-Liberal coalition was voted out of power (with a much narrower margin than the previous conservative coalition). Perhaps the population made it liable for economic hardships. It is also conceivable that the evidence of corrupt practices contributed to the Horn government's demise. Last, but not least, the poor election campaign of the Socialist Party was an important and proximate cause of defeat.

When the second conservative coalition government was formed in summer 1998, Hungary was on the right track both domestically and internationally. The young and energetic Prime Minister, Viktor Orban, and his highly qualified Foreign Minister, Janos Martonyi, could be expected to continue the process and consolidate the achievements. Yet, a year before the next elections, it is difficult to present the final tally of government performance and achievements. For the first time in the post-Communist period, a Hungarian government has a chance to stay in power after the coming elections. But, despite the excellent starting position of the Orban government, the record is mixed.

Major achievements have coexisted with mistakes that carry long-term risks. Beyond political declarations, problems during the Orban government have been most evident in the transformations of the defense sector, necessary for NATO integration, and that of the health-care system, expected by the EU. In addition, the treatment of the Roma population and attempts to limit press freedom have been troublesome to international and Hungarian observers.

Most severe among policy errors are those that try to interfere with the functioning of the market economy and attempt to constrain democracy. The more the government feels that the society is just as divided as it was when the Orban government came to power, the more it tends to use methods widely regarded as unacceptable in a democracy. There is a race with time. Will the integration process of Hungary be concluded, that is, by gaining EU membership *before* the world concludes that one of the most advanced transition countries of East-Central Europe has been moving in a direction alien from the practice of Western democracies?

In international relations, the Orban government took advantage of its predecessor's achievements and from the results of integration. By the time the government was formed, the country was "on the map." It did not have to fight the "familiarity deficit" with which the first conservative Hungarian government had to struggle. It was far less likely in 1998 than in 1990 that an intolerant nationalistic statement would be regarded as a reason to be concerned about regional stability.

Further, both in the sense of the advanced phase of Western integration and the state of relations with their neighbors, Orban came into office with unprecedented advantages in comparison with previous governments. The country has been integrated in every Western institution where any country of the region could join (Council of Europe, the Organization for Economic Cooperation and Development, NATO) and has been among the lead candidates for EU membership. Good relations were achieved with every neighbor in the region, except with Slobodan Milosevic's Serbia. In Romania, the organization of the Hungarian minority, the Democratic Alliance of the Hungarians in Romania (VDMR in Romanian or DAHR in English) has been part of the government since late 1996. In Slovakia, the fall of the Vladimir Meciar regime was imminent and the Mikulas Dzurinda government formed in autumn 1998 found it necessary to pursue the best possible cooperation with Hungary. The coalition of Hungarian parties joined the new Slovak government. Full attention could have focused on accelerating the approximation process with the EU and deepening regional cooperation with like-minded neighbors. It is against these advantageous conditions that the achievements of the Orban government's international relations must be contemplated.

The Orban government, similarly to its predecessors, shared a broad, elusive concept of security that embraced both its military and nonmilitary aspects. For this reason, it is necessary to analyze a broader range of issues when evaluating the security situation of the country.

Threat Perceptions

Hungary perceived an unstable international environment throughout the 1990s. New neighbors emerged and old ones dissolved. This has affected Hungary severely, because it was the only country that neighbored *all* of the three former multinational federations—Czechoslovakia, the Soviet Union, and Yugoslavia—that dissolved in the early 1990s. Hungarian governments have emphasized regularly that the main security problem in the region is instability accompanying transformation. In some cases this vague formulation was accompanied by more specific mention of intolerant nationalism as a source of insecurity. Jan Zielonka's observation a decade ago also characterized Hungary between the system change and NATO membership: "It is easy to get the impression that different threats are presented to different audiences, depending on the circumstances. One day the audience is confronted with a vision of domestic anarchy and foreign aggression. Another day the same politicians describe their country as exceptionally stable and surrounded by peaceful neighbors. . . . The latter vision is usually presented to Western bankers and investors, the former to security experts."[7]

It should be noted that there was a learning curve in Hungary as elsewhere in the region. Politicians and civil servants increasingly have become careful when speaking about their country's threat perceptions. They have noticed it may deter Western investment and may undermine integration efforts. Furthermore, they have noticed that it may be a self-fulfilling prophecy to name any country as a potential threat. As a consequence, it requires an extremely thorough analysis of documents and official pronouncements to understand what a country like Hungary is *really* concerned about.

The concept of belonging to the zone of instability and being exposed to different threats has eroded steadily since the early 1990s. First, the major shocks from the birth of new states came to an end at least as far as the Soviet Union and Czechoslovakia were concerned. The decline of the standard of living that accompanied the system change did not result in large-scale political destabilization in the neighborhood. Beyond changing conditions, improved communications were also of some importance.

The Socialist-Liberal coalition government, moreover, revised the practice of foreign policy. The priority given to a broader *regional* policy, rather than confining policy proprieties to the treatment of Hungarian minorities, led to a less threatening international environment. Consequently, the Hungarian threat assessment changed favorably before more tolerable nationalists came to power in problematic neighboring countries.

When a moderate conservative government took power in summer 1998, certain questions were posed regarding the continuity of Budapest's international orientation. Nobody had any doubt that the pro-Western orientation would continue. But how could such an "orientation" encompass the representation of interests of the Hungarian minority beyond the border? The question remained short lived, however, since the government program modified emphasis but initiated no major change. It declared that "the objectives of the foreign and foreign economic policies of Hungary have been characterized by continuity for eight years that have passed since the system change."[8] In some cases, the Orban government's change of emphasis was expressed in a nonconfrontational manner. At other times, the new defense policymakers seemed to try to compensate for the inactivity of the previous government.

The latter behavior was exemplified by the government's statement that "the Hungarian state and nation do not coincide."[9] The world should understand that this implies that the Republic of Hungary carries a special responsibility for Hungarians beyond the state's border that gives a unique dimension to the country's foreign policy. Such statement of fact ought not be regarded as provocative by anybody. Yet, the government's reintroduction of the concept of national interest, a term never used by the Socialist-Liberal coalition, suggests the basic principles underlying Orban's foreign policy.

The threat perception of Hungary was significantly affected by NATO membership. The government program emphasized the symbolic importance, rather than the security relevance, of NATO: "by NATO membership Hungary has ultimately gained place in the community of Western democracies."[10] A few months later, the Parliament passed a resolution replacing the two resolutions passed in 1993 on the principles of security policy and national defense. The new resolution came into force the day Hungary joined the Atlantic Alliance and took the responsibilities stemming from membership into account. It emphasized, among the objectives of security and defense policy inter alia, that Hungary would "Contribute to the implementation of what has been laid down in the North Atlantic Treaty and to the security of its Allies, to facilitate the preservation of international peace and enhancement of security and stability of the Euro-Atlantic region, Europe, and its neighborhood."[11] Since then, the prime minister has emphasized regularly the contribution of the Atlantic Alliance to the security of the country. References have most often been made to the Kosovo conflict: "Due to our fast NATO accession we have arrived at the outbreak of the warlike conflict not defenseless, lonely but as equal member of the strongest military alliance."[12] Precisely a year later the prime minister expressed his view that "Hungary has a mission; we were taken to NATO to have a stabilizing effect in the region of Central-Europe and in particular in the region of South-eastern Europe through our foreign policy."[13]

In sum, the political mainstream of Hungary regards the Atlantic Alliance as a significant influence on threat perception. As a consequence of NATO membership, traditional forms of threat have been reduced to a nearly unmeasurable level. In security terms, the transition era for Hungary came to an end. Hungary entered the zone of security. The country, according to the Hungarian view, is primarily a security provider and no longer a consumer of security. That alliances may simultaneously contribute to members' security while "distributing" each member's threat perceptions to all others is a possibility thus far unrecognized by the Hungarian elite. The only case when indirect reference was made to the "dangers" involved in NATO membership happened during the Kosovo conflict when certain opposition MPs of the Socialist Party raised the issue of whether Hungary, the only NATO neighbor of Serbia, could face mission creep.[14] The argument did not influence the politics of Hungary in the Kosovo conflict. It had only a side effect; it gave the government an opportunity to present the Socialist Party as internationally irresponsible.

The threat perceptions of Hungary were not put to test in 2000. No major change in Budapest's relations with contiguous countries has taken place since the fall of the Meciar government in the second half of 1998. Given such advantageous international conditions, Hungary's relations with neighboring countries was fairly easy. One has to add, however that the Orban government pursued a pragmatic policy toward Romania, Slovakia, and other states next door. It did not overplay Hungarian minorities in neighboring countries, and its mistakes remained sporadic.

Among Hungarian conservatives, such pragmatism suggests how important a change of generation can be. To Orban and his entourage, all born in the 1960s, territories that once belonged to Hungary do not represent a sensitive issue. They demonstrate interest in Hungarian minorities to the extent that cannot be regarded suspicious by the countries that host ethnic Hungarians. Further, for some neighboring countries, primarily Romania and Slovakia, which would like to join institutions in which Hungary is a member or has a fair chance to soon gain membership, it would be foolish to confront Budapest, whose support they will need to join NATO and the EU.

There are, of course, residual threats and concerns. The prime minister gave his insight into the thinking of the government when addressing the military leadership. He has demonstrated that there are residual, somewhat vaguely defined threats that Hungary has to address. According to Orban:

> After Hungary has occupied her place in NATO and determined its development path characteristic of western societies, Hungary will take its place in the European Union and irrevocably become part of the West. . . . Hungary has occupied its place in the western world while its geographical position did not change. Hungary does not regard the countries further to the east as enemies, and we seek to co-operate with them. . . . I would like to make two matters clear— that Hungary is a committed supporter and part of the western security system and that we seek to good economic relations with Russia do not contradict to each other. . . . We seek good relations, want to strengthen our economic relations, and we are gladly taking part in co-operations of cultural character. But, there is a clear dividing line between us in the sense of security and defence policy. I could say the more intensively we co-operate economically, the

clearer and sharper dividing line has to be drawn between us, the eastern-most member-state of NATO and the territories further to the east, in the field of security and defence.[15]

It is clear from Orban's statement that his most important security-related preoccupation is the instability of the region further to the east of Hungary.

When Orban took a closer look at the region itself he observed that: "We can see in this moment the region is stable in military-security sense, I can say more stable than a year ago. . . . Its reason is that matters south from us on the territory of Yugoslavia are in better shape than they were a year ago. With this I do not say that every danger has come to an end as the democratic transformation has not been completed, yet. In spite of all this, I feel that the region is stable today, and one of the pledges of this stability is Hungary."[16] Orban thus has clearly expressed that he shares, knowingly or not, the democratic peace theory. Countries that are internally stable have completed their democratic transition and have embarked on the way to prosperity are *peaceful*—and thus contribute to the stability of other states in the region or more broadly. He is hopeful that the same will characterize the area of the former Yugoslavia. Interestingly, he has not expressed any similar hope concerning the area east of Hungary, primarily that of the former Soviet Union. Arguably, therefore, the official threat assessment of Hungary is close to the position of mainstream Western scholars of international relations.

Some members of the foreign policy leadership, however, feel more strongly about the Hungarian ethnic minority than others in the political establishment. The political state secretary of the foreign ministry, Zsolt Nemeth, for example, finds threats in developments about which others do not comment. Nemeth continues to see the evolution of neighboring countries through one prism—the treatment of ethnic Hungarians. Right after the first round of the presidential elections in Romania, he declared that "democratic forces suffered a land-slide defeat in Romania and this gives reason for being concerned. At our eastern neighbor an extremist, anti-semitic and anti-Hungarian political force has strengthened. Our country will form its relationship with the new Romanian government on the basis of its concrete steps, nevertheless."[17] It is interesting to note that

Foreign Minister Martonyi rightly emphasized only the pragmatism of the Hungarian government toward Romania, virtually repeating the last sentence of the state secretary's statement.[18] Not long after the new Romanian government was formed in late 2000, state secretary Nemeth paid a visit to Bucharest. Following the end of the official visit, he spent three days in the partly Hungarian inhabited part of Romania (Transylvania), where he had extensive meetings with ethnic Hungarian politicians and cultural representatives. Since this happened without providing any information to Romanian authorities, they did not miss the opportunity to express their reservations concerning this unusual diplomatic step.[19] These examples illustrate that it may well be that people who shape Hungarian foreign policy are incapable of tackling situations that are not entirely harmonious.

In a couple of other cases, Budapest took somewhat unique stances that differed from the mainstream Western position. One of them was the intensive cooperation with Franjo Tudjman's Croatia; the other was the stance of Hungary concerning the new Austrian coalition government that included the Austrian Freedom Party (FPO), and its most well-known figure, Jorg Haider, and the sanctions introduced by fourteen EU member states. Generally, however, the conservative Hungarian government had little chance to introduce a new foreign policy direction because its predecessor had been too successful and recognized, leaving little room for maneuver or innovation. The few areas where attempts were made to be "innovative" were confined to marginal matters.

The foreign political opening of Hungary toward Croatia aimed to establish a strategic relationship between the two countries. It has remained impossible to determine to what extent this meant more than just normal neighborly relations. Gradually, the constituent elements of this policy have become understandable. Several practical steps were initiated, like the free movement of persons using only domestic identification, the privatization of the Croat oil company INA by the Hungarian company MOL, and a free trade agreement. Some of these steps, like the INA-MOL deal, have remained unimplemented.

The Western partners of Hungary followed events closely. Most evident to Western observers were the fundamental differences between Croatian and Hungarian domestic and international situations. Croatia had been, since independence, an illiberal democracy kept distant from the EU and viewed as a country warranting serious international concern about press freedom, minority rights, and corruption. The special ties to Budapest were accompanied by high-level symbolism. The last element of this was Prime Minister Orban's appearance at Franjo Tudjman's funeral. He was the only prime minister present from outside the former Yugoslavia. The EU observed that "Budapest has recently been pursuing aggressively a policy to strengthen its trade and economic ties with neighboring Croatia, which is not a candidate for European Union membership."[20] In the end, well after Tudjman's death and the fall of his regime, the free trade agreement was signed between the two countries under the condition that it comes to an end the day one of the parties, probably Hungary, joins the EU. Free trade will be carried out first on the basis of the bilateral agreement, and later on the basis of the agreement between Croatia and the EU to which Hungary will become a party. The evolution of the two countries' relationship might have thus become largely irrelevant as a result of the belated system change in Croatia and the subsequent warming of EU-Croat relations.

The case has demonstrated, however, two important facts. First, Hungary is ready to take a separate path and give priority to its perceived national interest irrespective of EU expectations. It has also illustrated the admiration of the Hungarian prime minister for a regime that could be characterized as an illiberal democracy, where democratic rights were curtailed and where the public authorities, including President Tudjman and his entourage, used their position to take significant private benefits. The Hungarian prime minister, obsessed by his own power, quickly learned the importance of strong statehood and, early in his government, referred to such a need.[21]

The other point that such a foreign policy initiative demonstrated was Hungary's attitude toward the new Austrian government and EU sanctions. Hungary understandably intended to maintain good relations with Austria and did not join in implementing sanctions. A delicate balance was created regarding Hungary's reaction to the situation in Austria. The foreign minister expressed his views as follows: "We have fears and concerns not constrained to the issue of enlargement because of the coming to power of the Freedom Party."[22] The prime minister drew a somewhat different conclusion and pronounced that Hungary was not endangered by the extreme-right.[23]

In the time since, the relationship has become warmer and warmer between the two countries, including several symbolic gestures. Chancellor Wolfgang Schussel visited Budapest, and the Vienna Philharmonic Orchestra gave a concert in Budapest when their concert was canceled in Israel. Whenever the question was raised whether Orban was planning the "Austrian solution" for Hungary were there a stalemate in the parliamentary elections of 2002, he replied that it would not be necessary. Further, the apparently tense relationship between Orban and West European social-democratic leaders (particularly, although not exclusively, with Germany) complicated the situation.[24] Such tension gave the impression that the moderate conservative coalition government regarded sanctions as heavily influenced by social-democratic governments of Western Europe.

After the report of the "wise men" (the EU's three person top-level delegation, sent by the EU Commission in 2000 to assess the organization's largely political sanctions against Austria and Vienna's response to EU concerns), the Hungarian position—which favored an end to sanctions—was vindicated. Yet, doubts remained over whether or not Prime Minister Orban regarded Austria as a good example to follow. Were the prime minister to treat Austria as some kind of model, however, it would legitimize Hungary's own extreme right and thereby severely damage Budapest's prestige.

Hungary is thus surrounded by an overwhelmingly benign and stable environment. Yet, even if no danger surrounds Hungary, this does not imply that Budapest's third democratically elected cabinet marked the completion of the country's sociopolitical transformation. From Orban's perspective, of course, his election demonstrated that the EU's political accession criteria had been met once and for all.[25]

When the European Commission assessed Hungary's progress toward accession more than a year later it did *not* reconfirm the self-assessment of the government and opined that there were some areas where improvements were needed in the sociopolitical transformation process. It put gentle emphasis on improving human rights, the situation of the Roma population, and the need to strengthen anticorruption measures. Further, it raised concerns about attempts of the government to interfere with the freedom of the press through buying opposition dailies. The report also called attention to the danger inherent in not respecting the independence of the National Bank.[26] Even though the political reservations of the commission were in no way overwhelming, it reflected several areas of EU concern.

After a successful year for the Hungarian economy in 1999 and an extremely promising one for 2000, the government announced in advance its expectation that Hungary would be praised in the report issued in November 2000.[27] Unfortunately, such lofty expectations were met only in part. Most concerns remained largely unchanged. Ill treatment of the Roma population and foreigners by the police were reported. On the fight against corruption, several new measures were adopted by Hungary, although it was concluded that corruption "remains a problem."

Freedom of the press was positively assessed, while the composition of the boards of trustees supervising public service TV and radio was criticized. Critical comments concerning freedom of the press became much harsher in the report of the International Federation of Journalists (IFJ) a few months later. According to the IFJ, independent public media in Hungary is "on the verge of collapse."[28] No further progress could be reported "in ensuring the full independence" of the national media.[29]

The overall very good economic performance was undermined by inflation where the downward trend was reversed. The commission also noted a couple of new worrisome phenomena. Governmental interference in determining the price of pharmaceutical products and natural gas and the decision of the government not to organize a tender for a major highway construction were among the negative examples.[30] When the high expectations of the government were met only partly, the prime minister published a list of opposition politicians who, according to him, tried to undermine the position of the country at the European Commission and in Western public opinion.[31] In March 2001 ten Hungarian Roma from the village of Zamoly got refugee status in France. This meant that Hungary was declared to be a country, according to French authorities, where people may suffer persecution.

The government's interference in economic processes included a 60 percent increase of the minimum wage, populist decisions concerning prices, and nontransparent public procurement and state investment decisions. That inflation began to climb was an early signal of the change of a number of macroeconomic indicators. It was followed by doubts about a lack of progress in reducing the government's fiscal deficit. Hungary, which for many years had attracted the highest per capita foreign direct investment in the region, started to face the withdrawal of foreign capital and bond investors in 2000. The withdrawal reached 327 million euros in the first eight months of 2000 versus 969 million euros influx in the same part of 1999. The ministry of finance attributed "the outflow to the appearance in other post-Communist countries of the quality privatization and other investment opportunities."[32] For 2001 the budget deficit compared to GDP may reach 5 percent, contrary to the 3.4 percent estimated in the budget. Predictions for 2002 already warn that the estimate of the government (3.2 percent deficit) will be exceeded.

Foreign direct investment (FDI) slowed down, whereas foreign profit repatriation has increased. This will pose major problems in coming years. Hungary attracted significant FDI and benefited from this in a number of ways. First, incoming capital made it possible to service foreign debt. Second, productivity increase during the second half of the 1990s concentrated in major foreign enterprises and in Hungarian companies linked to them in one way or the other. Consequently, in case foreign capital investment compared to the GDP declines, debt servicing becomes impossible from that source. Other sources must be found either in the state budget or from loans as a temporary solution to finance the debt. If the government decides to finance debt service through the budget, inflation will quickly rise. Were the Hungarian government to opt for credit, it must consider that the conditions have already started to worsen and that credit is only a postponement strategy in facing the problem. According to the bankers' magazine, *Institutional Investor*, the credit rating of Hungary recently worsened to the greatest extent in the region.[33] The eventual slowdown of the productivity increase may yield a Hungarian currency that no longer appreciates against major currencies. This may further increase the inflationary pressure, although Hungarian exports may become more competitive in the international markets.

No doubt, this is a worst-case scenario. It may happen that the country "escapes" from the trap with a limited and temporary decline. Given that the interference of the government with the economic processes has increased steadily since the Orban government has come to power, however, it may not be entirely realistic to assume that the government will avoid the continuing loss of comparative advantage in the region.[34] Interference has reached the level where major multinational companies no longer participate in public procurement tenders, knowing they will be awarded to companies "close to government circles." It is a combination of economic and sociopolitical factors that will result in fragile economic balances at least for a year or two (2001–2002). Corruption is on the rise and will soon also be noticed by potential investors.

A look at the incomplete integration process of Hungary and its prospects reveals reason to assume that this might have major domestic and regional political repercussions. Hungary has been among the unchallenged, leading candidates of EU integration together with Estonia, Slovenia, and Malta. The Czech Republic has lagged behind somewhat because of problems with the adaptation of its legal system. Poland represents a problem because of its sheer size and its agricultural sector. Cyprus could be an attractive candidate if the fundamental political problem of its division could be solved. It is now known that Poland will be in the first round of eastern enlargement. At the same time, Warsaw was warned that its slow progress could jeopardize early accession of the entire region. Because Poland, with its nearly 40 million inhabitants, represents a burden, member states may not urge the completion of enlargement, notwithstanding verbal commitments. Were Hungary to present a doubtful record in the coming years—economically as well as politically—the incentive for early EU enlargement may vanish. The other unobjectionable lead candidates, Estonia, Slovenia, and Malta, together have fewer than 5 million people and do not represent the critical mass necessary to enlarge the Union in the coming three to five years.

If EU enlargement loses its momentum or purpose, the current Hungarian government may conclude that it can pursue a more independent policy, ignoring the regular warnings of the world at large, including the ones in the annual reports of the EU Commission. Without external influence, the illiberal tendencies present in today's Hungarian political system may gain further ground. Early engagement of Hungary would, of course, be the best way to ensure that pragmatic but corrupt illiberal policies do not prevail in Hungary.[35] The European Union has to understand, however, that unconditional engagement must not be the reward for only partial adherence to fundamental principles of democracy and a functioning market economy. The most important danger, therefore, stems from losing track and thus depriving further Hungarian generations of prosperity and the chance to enjoy democracy after four decades of socialism.

Capacities

Hungary is a typical East-Central European transition country as far as its defense reforms are concerned. This means that the armed forces of the country during the Warsaw Treaty era would have had the not particularly glorious task of carrying out forward defense (the declared rule)—in fact, forward *offense* (as put into practice). Since this would have been in support of the Soviet armed forces, Hungarian units would have been integrated in larger Soviet formations. Hungary's forces thus lacked experience with independent strategic planning and had little professional competence in defense matters.

Hungary inherited, moreover, an antiquated defense structure from the Warsaw Treaty era. Since the country belonged to the southern tier of the organization, its armaments and equipment were less modern than those of the northern tier, primarily of the "frontline" states—the GDR and Czechoslovakia. The threat perception declared by the country was not credible to most of the population except for short, highly ideological periods of time—for example, the core Cold War years in the first half of the 1950s. Hungarian Communist leaders, from the 1970s until the very end of the Warsaw Treaty, were not particularly enthusiastic about Soviet requests concerning the upgrading of defense efforts.[36] This mix resulted in a situation where the defense sector did not develop for decades and the prestige of the military profession was fairly low.

The situation did not improve after the system changed. Four reasons for such stasis are evident. First, that Hungarians have not perceived any major threat has not created a particularly favorable environment for increasing defense efforts. And it is inherently difficult to make the public understand the move from threat-based to capabilities-based armed forces and thus generate the necessary support. Second, no defense reform has the chance to succeed unless it has the support of all major political forces.

It seems, that this backing now exists. Third, between 1987 and 1997, the defense budget was the "softest"—that is, it could be reduced in case of unexpected difficulties in other portfolios. Whether the international commitment of the country to increase the defense budget and then maintain it at a certain level of GDP will be sufficient to fight this tendency in the future is open to question. Fourth, subjective factors must be addressed as well. Since the change of the political system in 1990, the leadership of the ministry of defense (MOD) has not been composed of the smartest "political heavyweights" of the government coalition. This has contributed to the weak bargaining power of those in charge of national defense in any matter beyond a narrow definition of such a term. If this situation persisted, the success of the current and future defense reforms could be jeopardized in the long run.

The current military reform was launched in summer 1999 when the above-mentioned factors combined to leave no doubt that the armed forces required urgent attention. Adding to the conditions were Hungary's NATO accession, the Kosovo crisis, and the impossibility of continuing to finance defense from the limited funds allocated in the state budget. The strategic review was initiated by the governmental resolution, which had set forth two major constraints. These were that the review must not exceed budgetary limitations established earlier and that the implementation of the review must not result in an increase of personnel strength.[37]

The review was urgent for two reasons. For domestic politics, a strategic review had to clarify why Hungary could no longer maintain a defense structure that has absorbed major resources without contributing to the country's defense capability. But, it was also vital internationally—to report some achievements to NATO. When presented, however, the review was offered as an excuse for not meeting certain NATO interoperability requirements in time—an admission that was not welcome by the Atlantic Alliance and some of its member states.[38]

A few months after launching the review, the prime minister addressed the defense establishment in the MOD and outlined nine principal points. Among these, he naturally stressed everyone's individual responsibility to implement reforms and the need to use increased appropriations in a transparent and judicious manner, carefully justifying expenditures. Prime

Minister Orban also emphasized that the structural changes and personnel reductions have to be carried out rapidly so that the most "painful phase" of the reform could be completed by early 2001. The (re)integration of the General Staff in the MOD was also to be rapid; it was to be completed by the end of the year 2000. The prime minister went on to address needs for outplacement of military professionals who leave the service, interoperability with NATO, and improving the image and prestige of the armed forces.[39]

Recognizing pressure from different directions, the leadership of the ministry of defense and the Defense Staff took energetic steps to announce their accomplishments early and loudly. It was interesting to notice, however, that more energy was spent on certain bureaucratic rivalries at the expense of some major issues of the defense reform. It was quickly apparent that the integration of the Defense Staff in the MOD was far more divisive than many strategic issues of the defense reform. Particularly delicate was the decision to subordinate the chief of staff and thus the General Staff. The administrative state secretary of the MOD insisted that the General Staff would be subordinated to him. When this issue was resolved such that the chief of staff was directly subordinated to the minister of defense, the administrative state secretary resigned.[40] In the end, the integration of the Defense Staff took place in fall 2000, although parallels between the Defense Staff and defense ministry departments remained.

The reform process was not free of other fault lines, either. The expenses of defense reform were not planned in the 2000 defense budget. Such costs were estimated at 35 billion Hungarian forint (approximately $120 million at current prices), equaling one-sixth of annual defense appropriations. Consequently, the scheduled unit closures and reductions of personnel had to be postponed to 2001, contrary to the prime minister's plan.[41] It has become apparent early that the labor market cannot simply absorb the professional military personnel who are laid off, and no adequate attention was paid to their problems. This was no surprise to many analysts who knew that the reduction of personnel would most severely affect lieutenant colonels and colonels in their late forties and fifties, whose integration in the economy would not be an easy task, if not impossible. The inadequate attention to this problem led to a spontaneous meltdown in the armed forces. Because of often unfounded fears, people with good career prospects elsewhere were the first to leave the armed forces.[42]

The Alliance has remained critical about the performance of the Hungarian armed forces regardless of the ongoing strategic review process. From Brussels, it may have seemed that the announcement of defense reform could be a delaying tactic vis-a-vis living up to certain NATO commitments. The Alliance used different channels to make its opinion known. In November 1999, then-administrative state secretary of the MOD, Tamas Wachsler, returned from his talks in Brussels with the message that "Hungary has been unable to live up to the minimum requirements of NATO defense planning."[43] A few months later, General Wesley Clark, outgoing Supreme Allied Commander Europe (SACEUR), used his farewell visit to Hungary to remind Budapest of the critical assessment of the country's performance. He emphasized the importance of providing the necessary resources to the further development of the armed forces and the importance of improving the English-language proficiency of armed forces personnel.[44]

Again a few months later during a visit of the foreign affairs committee of the parliament to NATO, the language used became less diplomatic. Officials of the Alliance stated clearly that Hungary did not live up to its commitments. Among the main complaints was that Hungary spends too little on defense despite extremely favorable economic indicators.[45] Hungarian commitments are not backed by an allocation of resources. The main shortcomings are in civilian control, officer-NCO ratios, and acquisition of armaments and equipment. Postponing modernization of dated military technology beyond 2005 was not seen positively. Such criticism included mention that Hungary's problems with fulfilling commitments has a negative effect on an eventual further wave of enlargement.[46] Not much later, during his Prague visit, NATO Secretary-General Lord Robertson again drew attention of the three new member countries to the need to improve their military performance.[47]

Although NATO's critical observations seem to be well founded, it has to be taken into account that the whole first wave of eastern enlargement was a politically driven process where military considerations played a marginal role. Military matters appeared at a late stage of the process and were, to a great extent, confined to budgetary considerations, namely to the commitment to increase defense appropriations. Now, with the Membership Action Plan (MAP), the Alliance has become aware that it may have erred when it belittled the importance of military interoperability during the first wave of enlargement. It is clear that the first three former Warsaw Treaty countries now within NATO, with their current military performance, do a disservice to those who are waiting for accession.

Policy Innovations

Less than a year after the strategic review process was launched, the Hungarian parliament passed two resolutions in June 2000. One concerned the long-term transformation of the Hungarian Defense Forces, while the other addressed the modification of Resolution 124/1997 regarding the specific personnel strength of the armed forces.[48] The former emphasized the comprehensive character of the Defense Forces' transformation and the underlying need ranging from the "real security policy conditions . . . the economical performance of the country . . . the consequences of NATO membership . . . the international commitments . . . and . . . the require-ments of the era." After the completion of the reform process, a smaller force will have to be able to fulfill a number of missions. Such multiple missions include assuring the defense of the country, pursuing collective defense tasks, participating in peace support and humanitarian operations within the framework of international obligations, supporting maneuvers and transportation of Allied forces, supporting law enforcement agencies in a domestic emergency declared on the basis of the constitution, and providing assistance in case of national disaster and catastrophe.

The parliamentary resolution set forth a multiphased, long-term transfor-mation that reduces personnel strength and the number of peace and wartime units, while increasing the number of existing peacetime military organizations manned and trained at a level ensuring that they will be capable of rapid deployment for defense or participation in international crisis management operations. The combat capability of the units must improve with new, modern equipment entering into service. The imple-mentation of this transformation process includes four elements:

- The (re)integration of the Defense Staff into the MOD.

- The reduction of the peacetime personnel strength of the units subordinated to the ministry of defense to a maximum of forty-five thousand people, and the authorized peacetime personnel strength must be much closer to its wartime strength than it was earlier. According to MOD estimates, wartime personnel strength will be approximately 50 to 60 percent higher than the authorized peacetime personnel strength of the Hungarian Defense Forces (HDF).[49] This meant that conscription has been maintained for the foreseeable future.[50]
- The service and branch mixture should not change. The proportion of immediately ready forces must be higher. The peacetime and wartime force structure and the command and control system must be nearly the same.
- Those organizations that deal with tasks not related closely to the basic mission of the force as prescribed by law and the resolution on long-term transformation must be removed from the structure and budget of the area of responsibility of the MOD.

Beyond integrating the Defense Staff, the command structure was changed to reduce the number of headquarters units and to transfer personnel to units. By closing down the Land Forces Service Staff and the Air Forces Service Staff, two corps headquarters-level service command organizations have been established while division headquarters simultaneously were abolished. The Army Corps command is located in Szekesfehervar, whereas the Air Force command is in Veszprem. The HDF recruitment, mobilization and training command will be established as a new element of the command and control structure in order to improve the quality of individual training and enhance the efficiency of recruitment efforts. Through such reorganization, the Defense Staff personnel will be reduced by 20 percent and the personnel of the Army and Air Force staffs by 18 percent. Abolishing division commands and establishing of new leadership bodies will result in a 26 percent personnel reduction of senior leadership organizations of the HDF.[51]

The parliamentary resolution divided the Defense Forces transformation between 2000 and 2010 into three phases. During the first phase, through the end of 2003, the emphasis is on the transition to the new structure, relocating troops, establishing adequate and proportionate personnel strength, reducing operational and maintenance costs, improving living and working conditions, and establishing minimum interoperability with NATO. In the second phase, by the end of 2006, programs to improve the quality of life, combat capability, and training will be pursued. Until the end of this phase, Hungarian forces must basically operate using equipment at hand with certain upgrades. Procurement of new equipment must then begin. The main task of the third phase, until 2010, will be equipment modernization in accordance with capability requirements. The main directions of equipment modernization are defined by the required level of NATO compatibility and interoperability. Priority is to be given to command, control, and information, integrated air defense, logistical systems, technical conditions of mobility, host nation support, and the survivability of troops and infrastructure.

There is no doubt that the National Assembly approved a fairly comprehensive strategic review in 2000. It gives hope that Hungary would have an acceptably modern, NATO-interoperable defense force in a decade or so. The prime minister, when he met the parliamentary leaders a few months after the resolution on transformation was approved, placed the emphasis on successfully implementing the project. The defense budget increased to 1.81 percent of GDP from 1.61 percent earlier, the resubordination of the Defense Staff to the MOD was decided, and new leaders were appointed to different commands. These decisions were passed quickly by Parliament, because there was determination to push ahead.

It is difficult to contemplate the real effect of the strategic review in this early phase of the project, however. Will the determination last beyond its first months or years, particularly if and when another government will be obliged to implement it? Some doubt has already emerged among observers. First, intellectual compatibility with NATO has remained fairly weak. The current political leadership of the MOD has demonstrated its incompetence since 1998 several times. This resulted in a situation in which certain decisions, which form part of the exclusive competence of the minister of defense, were made by other persons and bodies like the prime minister or the National Security Cabinet of the government.[52] Further, one factor of civilian control has weakened during the office term of the Orban government. Nearly the entire leadership of the MOD consists of professional military persons. From among the five ranking civil servants of the MOD (the administrative state secretary and four deputy state secretaries), only one has no professional military background. The state secretary is a colonel, whereas three deputies are former generals. The same situation was criticized harshly by Hungarian analysts during the term of the former government coalition.[53] In this respect, the transformation toward the civilian control of the military has not been completed, and changes are not irreversible.

The resolution of the Parliament concerning the long-term transformation of the Hungarian defense force puzzled Budapest's allies, and they have formulated their concerns beyond the problems mentioned above. Postponing the investment-heavy phase of the strategic review beyond the term of the current government and its successor may ease the situation of the cabinet now, but it carries the risk of unpredictability. In light of the high growth rate of the recent years, particularly of the year 2000 (5.2 percent GDP growth), experts have not understood scheduling the heavy investment phase of the defense reform for a distant and uncertain period. Moreover, leaving investments for the 2006–10 period is not the best idea for another reason. According to current plans, Hungary will be a new member of the EU at that time, with aspirations to join the Economic and Monetary Union. This would require keeping the budget deficit low—a target that major defense investments may endanger. In light of this, it might be concluded that the government wants to avoid interfering with its immediate economic plans and cares less about later phases.

In the last months of 2000 and the beginning of 2001, one major exception will have to be made from the "postponement" of investment in the acquisition of new armaments and equipment. The current shape of the Hungarian Air Force obviously must be improved soon and significantly in light of the parliamentary resolution. It declared that the "structure of the air force must be modernized in a way that allows the entire air defence system to operate as a part of the NATO integrated air defence system, aviation units must be capable to assist pursuing operations required by collective defence."[54] The complexity of the unfolding debate makes it impossible to present it in detail. In sum, either the aircraft of the most modern air wing of MiG-29s will have to be modernized, or they will have to be replaced by modern Western planes. Hungarian pilots, because of the poor technical standards of the aircraft, were unable to fly 160 to 180 hours a year (a NATO standard) or even to meet the Hungarian standard of 120 hours. In 2000, the first full year of the country's membership in NATO, Hungarian pilots flew sixty to eighty hours a year on average.[55] The idea to modernize the MiG-29 wing (or half of it) has been gradually replaced by the preference for leasing (used) Western planes—be they F-16s, other U.S. aircraft, or Swedish Gripens.[56] It has also been obvious that the whole decision-making process was overpoliticized. Professional considerations have played little role in the process. No firm conclusion can be drawn whether the current strategic review has a better chance for implementation than earlier ones, or if it will serve only to legitimize the nonfulfillment of the NATO commitments of the country.

Future Prospects

The international environment of Hungary is, for the medium term, likely to remain reasonably benign. Potential adversaries of the West, to which Hungary now belongs in security terms, will not be in the position to challenge it. It may well be a more delicate task to maintain the commitment of the leading military power of the world to East-Central Europe, or to Europe more broadly.[57] Hungarians clearly see the transatlantic link as the most important security guarantee and would not join anything that would undermine it. It requires skillful diplomacy to live up to different expectations at the same time. The prime minister expresses his commitment to the transatlantic idea and U.S. presence in Europe by rejecting the duplication of military structures between NATO and the EU.[58] If one excludes the possibility of abandoning Europe by the United States and extrapolates from the current trends, there is no reason to be concerned as far as political-military threats.

If, however, the international environment is addressed more broadly—and in conjunction with domestic developments—the picture is far less rosy and rather disappointing. The current political and economical trends give no reason to be optimistic. Although Hungary still prospers far more than many other countries in the region, this comparative advantage may not persist.

In case the current moderate conservative government stays in power beyond the elections, which are due no later than spring 2002, it is likely that the populist economic policy will continue. Authoritarian political tendencies will gain further strength, and the respect for human rights, independence of the media, and the functioning of democratic institutions will be even less important than today. As a consequence, society will continue to be severely divided. It will then be easy to describe Hungary with a term that carries multiple meanings—an illiberal democracy. "The tendency for a democratic government to believe it has absolute sovereignty (that is, power) can result in the centralization of authority, often by extra-constitutional means and with grim results."[59] There is reason to assume that the European Union has not developed the adequate policy mix for a situation when one of its lead candidates follows a policy that is contrary to the principles and ideals member states, current and future, should follow.

The assumption ought not to be made that the alternative—a victory of the current opposition and its leading force, the Socialist Party—carries more promise. The Socialists lost credibility with their record in power between 1994 and 1998. Since then, the party has not taken energetic steps to present a morally sound and professionally superior alternative to the conservative government. Further, the Socialist Party's leadership continues to include former Communist Party apparatchiks. Its program is too much "something to everyone," while its communication is inferior to the leading party of the current conservative government and there is no reason to assume that the situation will change soon. Were the Socialist Party to win the 2002 elections, it would take the helm unprepared. The party will be unable to resist an atmosphere of "revenge" and will have to introduce austerity measures to consolidate the economic situation and avoid continuing decline. Such measures will further reduce their popularity. Consequently, it is practically unavoidable that they would lose the elections in 2006. Thus, no Hungarian government seems able to stay in power beyond four years.

Difficult choices are either those between two good or two bad options. Hungary has arrived at a juncture at which it will soon face the latter.

Chronology

28–29 February 2000: British-Czech-Hungarian-Polish consultations at the foreign minister level on Common European Security and Defense Policy.

18–20 April 2000: Farewell visit of SACEUR General Wesley Clark: critical comments on the NATO interoperability of the Hungarian Defense Forces.

9 June 2000: At a meeting of the prime ministers of the Czech Republic, Hungary, Poland, and Slovakia the Visegrad International Fund is set up. The participants urge that Slovakia be given NATO and OECD membership.

21 June 2000: The parliament passes two resolutions on the long-term transformation of the Hungarian Defense Forces and on the specific personnel strength of the armed forces.

14 September 2000: Foreign Minister Martonyi participates in the meeting of foreign ministers of the six European non-EU NATO member states with Javier Solana, high representative of the European Union for foreign and security policy.

24 October 2000: Visit of SACEUR General Joseph W. Ralston. Critical comments on the performance and interoperability of the Hungarian Defense Forces.

8 November 2000: The European Commission publishes its regular report, "Hungary's Progress Toward Accession."

30 November 2000: In reaction to the critical comments of the commission, Prime Minister Orban publishes the name of those "traitors" (opposition politicians, experts, and journalists) who influenced the EU to publish a critical opinion of the country.

21 February 2001: NATO Secretary-General George Robertson, speaking in Prague, called the attention of the three new NATO members to do more to modernize their armed forces.

March 2001: During the month, ten Hungarian Roma get refugee status in France.

26 March 2001: The International Federation of Journalists (Brussels) publishes its report on "The Political and Professional Crisis of Public Broadcasting in Hungary."

20 April 2001: The ministry of defense submits its comparative assessment of different multipurpose aircraft (F-16, JAS-39 Gripen) to the National Security Cabinet of the government.

30 April 2001: In his interview in *New York Times*, the Hungarian prime minister expressed his concerns about the turmoil in Ukraine.

21 May 2001: In his speech at the American Enterprise Institute in Washington, Viktor Orban says that for Hungary the transatlantic link and the participation in the European defense identity is not an "either-or" question.

NOTES

1. For the best and most detailed account, see Rudolf L. Tokes, *Hungary's Negotiated Revolution: Economic Reform, Social Change and Political Succession* (Cambridge, U.K.: Cambridge University Press, 1996), 305–98.

2. There is a mythology that surrounds some major events of the last decade. One of them is the time of the systemic change. The head of the current government, Viktor Orban denies that the year 1989 belongs to it and emphasizes that it is confined to the year 1990. The reason behind this argument is to deprive the Communist establishment of its (undeniable) contribution to the system change.

3. The next elections to the Hungarian legislative are due no later than in the spring of 2002.

4. Such a triple transition was discussed in Daniel N. Nelson, "Democracy, Markets and Security in Eastern Europe," *Survival* 35, No. 2 (Summer 1993): 156–71.

5. The sympathy of Prime Minister Antall to Germany and personally to Chancellor Helmut Kohl was demonstrated several times. Antall was the only nonnative German-speaking head of government who delivered his address at the Paris Council on Security and Cooperation summit in German (the only foreign language he spoke), to the surprise of many.

6. Bearing in mind the absolute majority of the Socialist Party in the legislature, it was a unique coalition. The Liberals were under heavy pressure from Western countries to join the coalition and not to leave the Socialist Party on its own. Western diplomats and politicians argued that a government formed by the Socialist Party on its own would damage the prestige of Hungary.

7. Jan Zielonka, "Security in Central Europe," *Adelphi Papers*, No. 272 (London: Brassey's for the International Institute of Strategic Studies, 1992), 33–34.

8. "Az uj evezred kuszoben: Kormanyprogram a polgari Magyarorszagert" (on the eve of the new millennium: government program for civic Hungary) (Budapest, Hungary: n.p. 1998), 64.

9. Ibid. 63.

10. Ibid.

11. Resolution 94/1998 (28 December) "OGY hatarozat" (resolution of the National Assembly), reprinted in Ferenc Gazdag, ed., *Magyar biztonsag-es vedelempolitikai do-*

kumentumok 1989–1998 (Hungarian security and defence policy documents 1989–98), Vol. 1 (Budapest, Hungary: SVKI, 1998), 53–57.

12. "Parlamenti vitanap: a miniszterelnok expozeja (29 April 1999)" (Day of debate: the expose of the prime minister), p. 1, available on the Internet at <http://www.meh.hu/Kormany/Kormanyfo/2000/04/990429.htm> (accessed 14 March 2001).

13. "Orban Viktor a pozsonyi NATO konferencian (29 April 2000)" (Viktor Orban at the NATO conference in Bratislava), p. 1, available on the Internet at <http://www.meh.hu/Kormany/Kormanyfo/1999/04/990429.htm> (accessed 14 March 2001).

14. It is memorable that Hungary gradually offered more and more to NATO, including providing Budapest Ferihegy airport for refueling aircraft. Fortunately, Hungary was not put to the test whether it was ready to provide its territory for a land operation against Serbia. For more details see "Korlatozott legterhasznalat? Az MSZP modositana a parlamenti hatarozatot" (limited use of the airspace? The Hungarian Socialist Party would modify the resolution of the parliament), *Nepszabadsag,* 4 May 1999.

15. "A miniszterelnok a feladatszabo ertekezleten" (the prime minister at the task assigning conference of the Hungarian Defense Forces), 1 March 2001, p. 2, available on the Internet at <http://www.honvedelem.hu/cikk.php?cikk=717> (accessed 19 March 2001).

16. Ibid.

17. "Zoltan Tibori Szabo, Bukarest: Kisebbsegi kormany?" (Bucharest: minority government?), *Nepszabadsag,* 29 November 2000.

18. "Martonyi Janos kulugyminiszter evnyito sajtotajekoztatoja (the annual opening press conference of Foreign Minister Janos Martonyi), 3 January 2001, p. 5, available on the Internet at <http://www.mfa.gov.hu/Szovivoi/2001/MartonyiJ/0103Omjevk.html> (accessed 14 March 2001).

19. Andreas Oplatka, "Mission Zwischen Rumanien und Ungarn: Kritische Anmerkung eines Ministers in Bukarest" ("Mission Between Romania and Hungary: Critical Commentary of a Minister in Bucharest"), *Neue Zurcher Zeitung,* 5 March 2001, p. 5.

20. Robert Wright, "Budapest's Patience Wears Thin," *Financial Times,* 13 October 1999, p. 4.

21. In one of his first speeches, Prime Minister Orban emphasized the importance of law and order, the elimination of corruption, and the importance of a strong state. See Orban Viktor "Miniszterelnok eloadasa" (the address of Prime Minister Viktor Orban at the meeting of Hungarian ambassadors in July 1998) (unpublished manuscript), pp. 6–7. More recently, "A miniszterelnok a Belugyminiszterium vezetoi ertekezleten" (the prime minister at the meeting of the leadership of the ministry of interior), 7 February 2001, available on the Internet at <http://www.meh.hu/Kormany/Kormanyfo/2001/02/010207 2.htm> (accessed 9 March 2001). Orban expressed, among other things, his view that "a weak nation state cannot enforce its interests appropriately in the European Union." This statement is no doubt correct. One should consider, however, that weak statehood, a widely known phenomenon in

the region, has never characterized Hungary, and after three years of Orban government many people are far more concerned about a too powerful and influential state (government) than about a weak one.

22. Csaba Szerdahelyi, "Felmosoly-diplomacia Budapesten" (half-smile diplomacy in Budapest), *Magyar Hirlap*, 26 February 2000.

23. Eugen Pogany-Falkenhausen, "Eine Diplomatie des gequalten Lachelns: Budapest—Wien: Die EU bestimmt des Verhaltnis der beiden Nachbarstaaten" (A Diplomacy of Embittered Laughter: Budapest-Vienna: The EU Fix for Relations of Both Neighboring States), *Die Presse*, 2 March 2000. The author clearly sates that Orban's statement does not reflect the truth.

24. "Polemia Martonyi meghallgatasan: A kulugyminiszter szerint nem fagyos a viszony a Schroder-kabinettel" (polemics at the hearing of Martonyi: according to the foreign minister the relationship with the Schroder government is not chilly), *Nepszabadsag*, 8 February 2001.

25. "Martonyi: teljesitettuk az unios politikai felteteleket" (Martonyi: the political conditions of the union have been met), *Magyar Hirlap*, 29 March 2001.

26. "1999 Regular Report from the Commission on Hungary's Progress towards Accession," 13 October 1999, 35.

27. "Orban: Korszakvaltas a gazdasagban" (Orban: epoch change in the economy), *Nepszabadsag*, 8 November 2000.

28. "Az IFJ szerint a megsemmisules szelen a magyar kozmedia" (according to the IFJ public media in Hungary is on the verge of collapse), *Magyar Hirlap*, 27 March 2001. The Report of the International Federation of Journalists, "Television On the Brink: The Political and Professional Crisis of Public Broadcasting in Hungary: Report of the IFJ Mission on Inquiry," Budapest, 11–13 February 2001, 60. "IFJ Report Accuses Hungary Over 'Improper Political Influence' As Public TV Faces Bankruptcy," both available on the Internet at <http://www.ifj.org> (accessed on 2 April 2001).

29. "2000 Regular Report from the Commission on Hungary's Progress Towards Accession," 8 November 2000, 16, 18, 50.

30. Because of the governmental cap on increasing the price of gas for private customers, the profitability of the Hungarian oil and gas company MOL was reduced significantly, which contributed to a major and lasting loss of the Hungarian stock exchange index, BUX. See "Veszelyben a MOL jovedelmezosege" (the profitability of MOL is in danger), available on the Internet at <http://index.hu/tozsde/thirek/moldb0223> (accessed on 26 February 2001).

31. Imre Bednarik and Laszlo Szucs, "Orban vadak es cafolatok: Erthetetlennek es nevetsegesnek tartjak az erintettek az osszeallitast" (Orban's allegations and denials: those involved hold the compilation not understandable and ridiculous), *Nepszabadsag*, 3 December 2000.

32. Robert Wright, "Booming Hungary Enjoys Fruits of Liberalisation," *Financial Times*, 26 October 2000.

33. "Romlo magyar hitelkepesseg?" (worsening Hungarian credit rating?), *Vilaggazdasag*, 27 March 2001. Hungary moved from a ranking of 31 in September 2000 to 36 in March 2001.

34. See "Investors Shun Hungary over Government Intervention," available on the Internet at <http://www.centraleurope.com/hungarytoday/business/markets.php3?id= 185802> (accessed on 7 August 2000).

35. There are many ways to illustrate the level of corruption. The European Bank for Reconstruction and Development says that approximately one-third of Hungarian firms are corrupt. See Borbala Bilkei-Gorzo, "Az EBRD ugy latja, a hazai vallalatok harmada meg korrupt" (according to the EBRD, one third of the Hungarian companies are still corrupt), *Magyar Hirlap*, 16 January 2001. The opacity index published by PriceWaterhouseCoopers still ranks Hungary as number two in the region as far as the level of corruption, although its information is dated and does not take into account some recent scandals. It is interesting that Hungary stands better in every other factor of opacity than in the level of corruption. PriceWaterhouseCoopers, *The Opacity Index*, January 2001, p. 10. It may also be illustrative that the father of the prime minister, a village teacher a decade ago, is now ranked among the one hundred richest Hungarians. For the latter, see "A 100 leggazdagabb magyar" (the one hundred richest Hungarians), *Playboy* (Hungarian edition) November 2000, 84. Gyozo Orban, the father of the prime minister, is listed there as the owner of mining companies.

36. Regarding relative defense efforts within the Warsaw Pact and Hungary's distinct reluctance to raise that effort, see Daniel N. Nelson, *Alliance Behavior in the Warsaw Pact* (Boulder, Colo.: Westview, 1986).

37. See "A Komany 2183/1999 (VII. 23.) Korm. sz. hatarozata a NATO 1999. evi vedelmi tervezesi kerdoivere adando magyar valaszrol, a 2001–2006 kozotti idoszakra szolo NATO hadero-fejlesztesi javaslatokkal kapcsolatos magyar allaspontrol, valamint a honvedelmet erinto egyes kerdesekrol" (Resolution 2183/1999 [July 23] of the government on the reply to the 1999 defense planning questionnaire of NATO on the Hungarian position concerning NATO defense development plans for the 2001–2006 period and certain issues of national defense), point 3.

38. For details of the early phase of the reform, see Pal Dunay, "Hungary," in *Security Handbook 2001*, eds. Hans-Joachim Giessmann and Gustav Gustenau (Baden-Baden, Germany: Nomos Verlag, 2001), 249–82, esp. 255–62. Also, Jeffrey Simon, "Hungary: Exorcising Trianon Ghosts," in *Brassey's Eurasian and European Security Yearbook 2000*, eds. Ustina Markus and Daniel N. Nelson (Washington, D.C.: Brassey's, 2000), 67–70.

39. "Orban Viktor miniszterelnok: Beszed a Honvedelmi Miniszteriumban a hadero reformjarol" (Prime Minister Viktor Orban address in the ministry of defense about the reform of the defense forces), 27 March 2000, 3, available on the Internet at <http://

www.meh.hu/Kormany/Kormanyfo/2000/03/000327.htm> (accessed on 14 March 2001).

40. See Peter Matyuc, "Nem higult fel a haderoreform tervezete: A Honvedelmi Miniszterium kozigazgatasi allamtitkara biralja a vezerkar retrograd erot" (the draft of the defense reform has not watered down: the administrative state secretary of the ministry of defense criticizes the retrograde forces of the Defense Staff), *Nepszabadsag*, 24 July 2000.

41. Zoltan Haszan, "A hadero-atalakitas koltsege 35 milliard" (the cost of defense transformation is 35 billion forints), *Magyar Hirlap*, 31 May 2000.

42. Zoltan Haszan and Gergely Szabo, "Tobb lesz a palyaelhagyo katona a tervezettnel" (there will be more military people quitting the armed forces than planned), *Magyar Hirlap*, 30 May 2000.

43. See Zoltan Gyevai, "A NATO maskeppen szamol" (NATO calculates differently), *Magyar Hirlap*, 25 November 1999.

44. "Clark: A NATO johiszemuen biralja hazankat" (Clark: NATO criticizes our country benignly), *Nepszabadsag*, 20 April 2000.

45. The point of reference was probably to the 5.2 percent GDP growth in 2000.

46. Zoltan Haszan, "NATO-biralat a vallalasok elhuzodo teljesitese miatt" (NATO criticism for the belated fulfillment of NATO commitments), *Magyar Hirlap*, 16 December 2000.

47. See "NATO Chief Demands Czechs Upgrade Military," *BBC News*, 21 February 2001, available on the Internet at <http://www.bbc.co.uk/hi/english/world/europe/newsid 1183000/1183118.stm> (accessed on 23 February 2001).

48. 61/2000 (VI. 21.) OGY hatarozat a Magyar Honvedseg hosszu tavu atalakitasanak iranyairol (Resolution 61/2000 [21 June] of the parliament on the long-term transformation of the Hungarian defense forces), available on the Internet at <http://www. kersov.hu/kzldat/O00H0062.htm> (accessed 7 August 2000) and 62/2000 (VI. 21.) OGY hatarozat a fegyveres erok reszletes bontasu letszamarol szolo 124/1997 (XII. 18.) hatarozat modositasarol (Resolution 62/2000 [21 June] of the parliament on modification of Resolution 124/1997 [18 December] of the parliament regarding to the detailed personnel strength of the armed forces), available on the Internet at <http:// www.kersov.hu/kzldat/O00H0062.htm> (accessed 7 August 2000). A not entirely precise English translation is available from the Hungarian ministry of defense.

49. *"Transformation of the Hungarian Defence Forces,"* 4, available on the Internet at <http://www.honvedelem.hu/cikk.php?cikk=582> (accessed on 14 February 2001).

50. 62/2000 (VI. 21.) OGY hatarozat a fegyveres erok reszletes bontasu letszamarol szolo 124/1997 (XII. 18.) hatarozat modositasarol (Resolution 62/2000 [21 June] of the parliament on modification of Resolution 124/1997 [18 December] of the parliament regarding to the detailed personnel strength of the armed forces), point 1. The

resolution regarding the detailed personnel strength, adopted the same day by the parliament, set forth the troop levels to be achieved by the end of 2001 in more detail. The total peacetime strength must not by then exceed 42,900, consists of the following categories: Officers, 8,600; warrant and NCO, 10,230; contract soldiers, 6,700; conscripts, 12,160; students of higher educational institutions, 1,200; civilians, 4,010.

51. "Transformation of the Hungarian Defence Forces," 5–6.

52. To avoid any misunderstanding, it is necessary to point out that this might have resulted in better decisions even though in some cases there was an apparent violation of the law. The question is, however, whether it would not be better to have competent persons in charge of the MOD so that their authority will not be violated.

53. See, for example, Reka Szemerkenyi, "Central European Civil-Military Reforms at Risk," *Adelphi Papers*, No. 306, (London: Oxford University Press for the IISS, 1996), and Rudolf Joo, "The Democratic Control of Armed Forces," *Chaillot Papers*, No. 23, (Paris, France: WEU Institute for Security Studies, February 1996).

54. 61/2000 (VI. 21.) OGY hatarozat a Magyar Honvedseg hosszu tavu atalakitasanak iranyairol (Resolution 61/2000 [21 June] of the parliament on the long-term transformation of the Hungarian Defense Forces), point 4b.

55. Zoltan Haszan, "A legiero nem tudja teljesiteni a NATO kovetelmenyeit" (the air force is unable to meet NATO requirements), *Nepszabadsag*, 19 March 2001.

56. Gyorgy Szentesi, "Hasznalt F-16-osok vagy Gripenek a MiG-29-esek helyett?" (used F-16s or Gripens in place of the MiG-29s?), *Magyar Hirlap*, 21 March 2001. Peter Matyuc, "Nincs olcso amerikai vadazgep: A HM politikai vezetese tovabbra is a MiG-ek atalakitasat tamogatja" (there is no cheap U.S. fighter aircraft: The political leadership of the MOD continues to support the modernization of MiGs), *Nepszabadsag*, 2 October 2000.

57. Difficulties of maintaining the U.S. commitment to Europe in the Bush (II) presidency are discussed in Daniel N. Nelson and Alpo Rusi, "Rebuild Euro-Atlantic Ties: Bush Must Resist Nationalistic U.S. Impulses," *Defence News*, 29 January 2001.

58. "A miniszterelnok a feladatszabo ertekezleten" (the prime minister at the task-assigning conference of the Hungarian defense forces), 1 March 2001, 2, available on the Internet at <http://www.honvedelem.hu/cikk.php?cikk=717>, accessed 19 March 2001.

59. Fareed Zakaria, "The Rise of Illiberal Democracy," *Foreign Affairs*, 76, No. 6 (November–December 1997): 30.

8 ◆ Poland: Becoming a NATO Ally

Andrew A. Michta

In 1989 the Poles ushered in the final stage of Communism in Eastern Europe. The post-Communist Third Republic would emerge as a democratic state in a security environment that was arguably the most favorable in Poland's entire history. The principal national objective would be to join the Western political, economic, and security institutions as quickly as possible. In the new consensus on national security policy, membership in the North Atlantic Treaty Organization (NATO) alliance became the number one priority for both the post-Communists and the post-Solidarity political parties.

Poland's opportunity to overcome its historical security dilemma was produced by the unification of Germany and the collapse of the Soviet empire, the combination of which revolutionized Poland's geostrategic position. Equally important, the Federal Republic of Germany remained committed to the transatlantic security institutions from the start, and it showed no interest in restarting the great power game over Central and Eastern Europe. Because Germany remained a member of NATO after unification, Poland found itself on NATO's border. Polish security and stability became a vital national interest of the German state. The decomposition of the Soviet empire, the emergence of Soviet successor states, and the continued political and economic turmoil in the Russian Federation have transformed the historical Russian threat from an immediate factor into a hypothetical future scenario dependent on the outcome of the post-Soviet revolutionary turmoil.

For Poland to join Western Europe, it had to redefine its historically adversarial relation with Germany. Fortunately for Poland's security, Germany also adopted a policy toward its eastern neighbor that has aimed at cooperation. Germany has been the principal proponent of bringing Poland into NATO and the European Union (EU). The key message that Germany would seek a new partnership with Poland was sent when Bonn opted not to go beyond the existing security institutions after unification. On the Polish side, the policy pursued by the first Solidarity governments was followed by the Sojuszu Lewicy Demokratycznej or Democratic Left Alliance (SDL) and Polskie Stronnictwo Ludowe, or Polish Peasants' Party (PSL) post-Communist government after the 1993 parliamentary election, and by its Solidarity successor. None of these politically varied governments strayed from the outline offered by the country's first post-Communist foreign minister, Krzysztof Skubiszewski.

Skubiszewski compared the historic chance for Polich-German reconciliation, brought about by the unification of Germany within the existing Euro-Atlantic institutions, to that of Franco-German reconciliation after World War II.[1] This policy found a receptive audience in Bonn. It led in 1991 to the signing of two founding bilateral treaties between Poland and Germany that confirmed the existing borders and outlined a new framework for good-neighborly relations. The border treaty in particular was critical to Polish security, as it did away with the Polish fears of German irredentism and also sent a strong message to Warsaw that Bonn was committed to work for Poland's integration in NATO and West European economic institutions. Article 2 of the border treaty contained a specific pledge for both sides to respect each other's sovereignty and territorial integrity.[2] The 17 June 1991 "good-neighbor" treaty gave a further impetus to reconciliation between Poland and Germany. It brought the Poles a firm German commitment to work toward their integration in the European Community. In turn, the Germans got Warsaw's official guarantee of German minority rights in Poland.[3]

Threat Assessment

Poland is today in a remarkably secure situation, with no immediate threat to its sovereignty and territorial integrity. Since entering NATO in 1999, Poland no longer is subject to traditional geopolitical competition for control from the West or the East: it has left the "gray zone" of European security.

Still, Warsaw remains concerned about the direction of political developments in the east, especially the course of political change in Russia. Russia's

Vladimir Putin is viewed in Warsaw as an authoritarian leader committed to restoring his country's great-power status. The Polish government regards the progressive reintegration of Belarus with Russia and the continued pressure on Ukraine, as disturbing developments that may eventually lead to the restoration of a larger post-imperial federation around the Slavic core of the former USSR.

In contrast to the revolution in Polish-German relations, Polish-Russian relations have remained strained. They deteriorated further after the election of Putin as Russia's president and the subsequent hardening of Russia's policy toward its "near abroad." Defined by the recent memory of Soviet domination, the Poles have remained suspicious of Russian intentions. This view of Moscow only deepened as years went by, exacerbated first by the argument over the withdrawal of the remaining Russian troops after 1989, then by Russia's staunch opposition to Poland's goal of joining the NATO alliance before the Madrid Summit. The NATO enlargement issue effectively froze the relationship. Moscow vigorously opposed the policy, while Warsaw asserted that membership in NATO was vital to Polish national security and treated it in part as a test of its regained sovereignty.[4]

The Polish-Russian relationship will remain one of the most problematic for years to come. In light of the developments in 2000–2001, it may take longer than had been expected for the two countries to reach a clear sense as to where their national interests intersect. It is unlikely that Russia will begin to consider Poland as an important regional power in Central Europe, and that Poland will put behind it the historical memory of Russian domination any time soon. At the same time, the Poles have yet to find a way to articulate their national interests in the east that would complement the larger NATO interest beyond the principle that NATO should remain committed to shared values and an open enlargement process.

In 2000–2001 Russian organized crime remained a security issue in Poland, as it did across Europe. Poland is one of the principal transit routes for smuggling stolen cars into Ukraine, Belarus, and the Russian Federation. The Poles estimate that there are currently over two hundred organized crime groups in their country, some of which have extensive connections to the Russian mafia. Because of the strategic location of Poland in the region, Warsaw has been watching with growing concern the rising tide of organized crime in the east and the growing cooperation between the Russian and Italian crime organizations on Polish territory. The Polish government reacted with alarm to reports in the German press that Russian organized crime was interconnected with the Russian intelligence community, and that the Russian Federal'naia Sluzhba Bezopasnosti (Federal Security Service, FSB) (successor the KGB) has reached deep into the structures of Russia's organized crime.[5]

Polish organized crime is an important link in the production and smuggling of amphetamines and other drugs, including in 2001 "designer drugs" as well. It is also a major transshipping route for international drug rings. Drug trafficking through Poland is likely to remain a serious security threat in the years to come. According to official government estimates, Poland is a transit route for 35 percent of the drugs smuggled from South America and Asia to Western Europe and Scandinavia. The scale of the problem is best illustrated by the number of intercepted shipments in and out of Poland: while in 1994 there were only 20 such cases, in 1998 they increased to 252, and the number has reached 162 already in the first half of 1999.[6] Although some of the increase in the intercept rate can be accounted for by the greater effectiveness of Polish police, the trend is alarming. Reportedly, drug trafficking through Poland today has brought Polish gangs into agreements with gangs in Turkey, Afghanistan, Pakistan, Morocco, Nigeria, and Russia. The greatest "bust" of a Polish-Russian ring to date involved the shipment of some ten tons of Afghan hashish intercepted by the police at the Polish port of Swinoujscie. In 2000 the police and customs seized a number of shipments and increased its cooperation with Interpol to apprehend major crime figures. In the last several years, as drug trafficking through Poland has increased, so has the violence as the competing gangs fight over turf. However, the greatest threat that the explosion of organized crime poses to Polish security is corruption and the potential for subverting the country's political and economic institutions. In 2000–2001 corruption has increasingly become an important national concern.

Moscow considers Warsaw's advocacy of further NATO enlargement into the Baltic area (Poland has been a strong supporter of bringing Lithuania into NATO) as damaging to Russian interests. The relationship reached a low point when the press reported in January 2001 that the Russians were deploying short-range nuclear missiles in the Kaliningrad District. Though the decision was not a violation of existing agreements, it was received in Warsaw as an act directed at Poland and a message to future candidates for membership in NATO.

There has been little in the recent history of Polish-Russian relations that could encourage the two countries to cooperate. In the waning months of the Soviet Union, the Polish "two-track" policy of working with Moscow while also maintaining ties with the national independence movements in the constituent republics was viewed by the Russians with suspicion. After the collapse of the Soviet Union, Poland repeatedly voiced concern that instability in the Russian Federation could spread into the entire region, endangering its own security as it struggled to build its democratic institutions and to introduce economic reforms. Moscow considered such Polish statements to be indicative of Warsaw's intent to exclude Russia from Europe.

In the years leading up to Poland's inclusion in NATO in 1999, a major area of disagreement in bilateral relations was the Russian demand for a de facto extraterritorial access route from Belarus through Polish territory to the Kaliningrad District. The discussions of this so-called "transit corridor" had already begun in November 1993 when the question was first raised by Moscow. In the same year, Russia's Gazprom proposed building a gas pipeline to Kaliningrad through Polish territory; in 1996 the Russians announced that they also wanted to build an additional power line through Poland. Warsaw has rejected all such proposals, maintaining that the Polish highway infrastructure allowed adequate access to Kaliningrad without the need for a Russian-controlled transit route.

The post-Communist era of bilateral Polish-Russian relations has left a record of suspicion on the Polish side and frustration among the Russian elite. The Polish government fears that Russian foreign policy toward the West aims to bypass Poland. In Warsaw's view, Russia's German policy has deliberately attempted to ignore Poland, as if "there were no country between the Bug and Oder-Neisse rivers."[7] The level of concern in Warsaw rose again when Russian president Putin launched a diplomatic offensive to build a "strategic partnership" between Russia and Germany and a strong personal relationship between him and Chancellor Gerhard Schroeder.

The enlargement of NATO finally ended the argument between Warsaw and Moscow over Polish membership in the alliance. As such, it holds the long-term potential to improve Polish-Russian relations, as only when it has been securely anchored in the West can Poland begin to come to terms with its past relationship with Russia. Clearly, it will take time before Polish-Russian relations can improve.

The Warsaw-Moscow relationship, however, has been complicated by developments in the Russian "near abroad," especially in Belarus and, more recently, in Ukraine. Poland's relations with Belarus, Russia's closest ally among the former Soviet republics, have continued to deteriorate following the election of Aleksandr Lukashenka as Belarus's president. Warsaw has been critical of Lukashenka's authoritarian domestic policies and his stated goal of Belarus's reintegration with the Russian Federation. Deterioration in Polish-Belarussian relations had already become visible back in 1996, after the vice president of the Parliamentary Assembly of the Council of Europe, Tadeusz Iwinski, declared at a press conference in Warsaw following the return of the assembly's eight-strong delegation from a week-long visit to Belarus in November 1996 that the formation of the new bicameral parliament by Lukashenka amounted to a violation of the law.[8] Lukashenka reacted by accusing Poland of conspiring to organize actions against Belarus. The charge brought an immediate strong denial from Poland president Aleksander Kwasniewski, but it also set the tone for the deteriorating Polish-Belarussian relationship for years to come.

Warsaw has also viewed with considerable concern the new closer economic and political relationship between Russia and Ukraine, especially Putin's all-out support for Ukraine president Leonid Kuchma during the challenge to Kuchma's authority in the winter of 2000–2001.

Early expectations that mutually beneficial economic cooperation between Russia and Poland could hold the key to better relations after 1991 have proved largely unfounded. These expectations were misplaced even before the Russian economic meltdown of 1998; after the Russian economic collapse, only the most ardent optimists would expect economics to drive Warsaw and Moscow closer together. In 1999 Poland ranked below Russia's top-ten trading partners, behind Belarus and the Netherlands.[9] Even though the Russian economy recovered somewhat in 2000, there was no dramatic improvement in Russia's bilateral trade with Poland. Most important, in the aftermath of repeated confrontations over Poland's determination to join NATO, few among Russia's political elite would consider Poland as Russia's potential partner in the region. Conversely, the Poles have come to view Russia as a source of threat and instability on account of its internal political and economic decline.

Moscow's grudging acceptance of Poland's entry into NATO, that is the recognition that Warsaw will choose its allies, might be the most important legacy of the relationship so far. The learning process, however, leaves much room for improvement on both sides. Polish-Russian exchanges on the question of Chechnya do not suggest that the two sides are likely to reach consensus on how to build a mutually beneficial relationship. In January 2000 Warsaw decided to expel nine Russian diplomats accused of espionage, to which the Russians responded with a tit-for-tat expulsion of Polish diplomats. The aftermath of an incident in February, when a group of Polish pro-Chechen demonstrators ransacked a Russian consulate in Poznan with no interference from the police, demonstrated how explosive the situation still was. The inaction of the Polish police during the incident was inexcusable; likewise, Russia's unwillingness to accept the subsequent apology in good faith, and the series of anti-Polish demonstrations outside Polish diplomatic posts was equally distressing. In the end, Russia's Foreign Minister Igor Ivanov canceled his planned visit to Warsaw.[10]

It is uncertain how quickly Polish-Russian relations can improve. In 1998 Russian President Boris Yeltsin went on the record as saying that the time had come in Polish-Russian relations to put the NATO issue aside.[11] However, Putin's policy toward Poland has hardened considerably. Moscow's apparent unwillingness to reengage in a dialogue with Poland in 2000–2001 leaves the status quo unchanged. The planned Polish-Russian summit for 2000 never materialized, though the countries maintained annual high-level consultations.[12] The relationship further deteriorated after the press reports, in January 2001, of alleged Russian nuclear deployment in the Kaliningrad District. The Polish government expressed serious concern about these reports. Poland interpreted the reports of the deployment of tactical nuclear missiles in Kaliningrad as an indication of Russia's intention to treat Kaliningrad as a military outpost from which to pressure the Baltic states and Moscow's former Central European satellites. On 4 January 2001 the Polish government issued a formal call for an international inspection of the suspected arms dumps in Kaliningrad.[13] The Russians denied the accusations.

Capacities

In 2001, and for the foreseeable future, Warsaw is developing its capacities to ensure national security in two principal directions—bilaterally with neighbors and via NATO.

The most important of bilateral relations is, certainly, with Berlin. Practical manifestations of the new spirit of cooperation between Germany and Poland developed rapidly in the 1990s and continued to expand in 2000–2001. The new diplomatic framework of Polish-German relations after 1990 led to close military cooperation, with Bonn serving as one of the most vocal advocates of Poland's membership in NATO. Germany also assisted Poland in the areas of equipment, maintenance, and training. The current six-year Polish military modernization program, approved in January 2001, may include the acquisition of German Leopard tanks, in addition to technical cooperation and joint training.

The most immediate sign of the new relationship in the military arena has been the establishment of the Polish, German, and Danish corps. The Northeastern Corps, headquartered in the Baltic port city of Szczecin on the Polish-German border, was formally established in September of 1998. It consists of three national divisions: in addition to a Danish division (eighteen thousand personnel), the Poles have contributed the Twelfth Mechanized Division from Szczecin (twelve thousand personnel) and the Germans their Fourteenth Mechanized Division from Neubrandenburg (eighteen thousand personnel).[14] The 150 officers serving with the corps' staff are permanently based in Szczecin, while the divisions remain in their home countries. The corps's command will rotate every three years, with the first command assignment entrusted to a Danish general.

Perhaps as important as military cooperation, a rapid increase in the volume of trade and German direct investment in Poland has been evident over the 1990s. Poland's exports to Germany went up from $5,143 billion in 1993, to $9,904 billion in 1999; its imports went up from $5,288 billion in 1993, to $11,583 billion in 1999.[15] In addition, Poland and Germany have worked to open up a dialogue about their past relations, especially the years of the German occupation of Poland in World War II. In 1997 these efforts led to an official exchange of archival documentation by Poland's Main Commission for Research into Crimes against the Polish Nation and the Federal Archives of Germany.[16]

In June 1999 the Center for Public Opinion Research (CBOS) published the results of a series of polls run between 1990 and 1999 on Polish attitudes to Germans and Ukrainians. When asked whether Polish-German reconciliation was possible, in 1990 only 47 percent of the Poles answered in the affirmative; by 1999 the number of Poles who believed that German-Polish reconciliation was possible went up to 73 percent—a 26 percent increase over the decade.[17] In addition, in the five years between 1994 and 1999, the perception of the German minority in Poland was also improved: from 28 percent positive in 1994, to 32 percent positive in 1999. Simultaneously, hostility toward the German minority living in Poland dropped from 30 percent to 24 percent.[18] The positive view of Germany was clearly favored by the younger generation of Poles.

Warsaw considers strong working relations with all the Baltic states, especially Lithuania, important to Poland's national security. In contrast to the poor record of relations with the Russian Federation, Poland has made considerable progress in its relations with Lithuania. In September 1997 Poland and Lithuania established an intergovernmental Cooperation Council to coordinate their policies in what both described as a "strategic partnership."[19] Polish-Lithuanian relations have also benefited greatly from an increase in bilateral trade. In 1998 Warsaw and Vilnius signed a free trade agreement, which lowered and eliminated tariffs on a number of industrial products. The Poles have restated their commitment to maintain an open border with Lithuania even after their admission to the European Union.

Frequent Polish-Lithuanian consultations continued in 2000. Most important, as the Membership Action Plan (MAP) 2002 decision approached, Warsaw remained the strongest advocate of Lithuania's membership in NATO. The relationship matured, as suggested by growing Polish support for Lithuania internationally, increasing military and economic ties and cooperation in the areas of law enforcement. During a visit to Vilnius in

April 2001, Polish foreign minister Wladyslaw Bartoszewski asserted that Polish-Lithuanian relations will become "an example for the world to follow." Bartoszewski also spoke of a vision of regional cooperation among the Baltic states and Central Europe that in twenty years will be like that among the Benelux states, where "European unity holds sway."[20] In addition to government-to-government relations, the lawmakers of both countries have contributed to stronger relations between their countries. In a highly symbolic move, the 9 May 2001 meeting of the joint Lithuanian-Polish parliamentary assembly decided to hold its next session at the beginning of June at the royal castle in Warsaw to honor the two countries' common 1791 Constitution.[21]

The Polish-Lithuanian partnership is strong, although it has had its share of problems. The minority rights issue has at times snagged relations. Ethnic Poles in Lithuania have demanded that their names be transcribed in Lithuanian passports using Polish spelling—a request that the Lithuanian Constitutional Court has rejected.[22] At times Warsaw has complained that Lithuania's policy on Polish language education discriminates against ethnic Poles, while the Lithuanian side has remained highly sensitive to any appearance of Poland meddling in its domestic affairs.[23]

Notwithstanding occasional friction, however, the two countries have made steady progress in bilateral relations in the areas of trade and security cooperation. Poland and Lithuania have built a record of close military collaboration, including the establishment of a Polish-Lithuanian peacekeeping battalion. This battalion, created in 1999, draws on two companies from the Lithuanian "Iron Wolf" brigade and two Polish companies from the Fourth Brigade stationed in Orzysz in northeastern Poland. The battalion headquarters are also located in Orzysz. Polish-Lithuanian military cooperation has two further objectives: cooperation in controlling the airspace of the two countries and Polish assistance in the training of the Lithuanian armed forces. In addition, Poland has transferred equipment and ammunition to Lithuania, and the two countries have worked to include Lithuanian personnel in the Polish chemical warfare unit.

Continued Ukraine independence is viewed by Poland as a key national security objective, as it mitigates against a future resurgence of a Russian threat. Poland considers Ukraine to be a key partner in the east. However, the two countries still have a number of past issues to address. The often-torturous history of Polish-Ukrainian relations includes a legacy of discrimination in the interwar period as well as violence in World War II and its immediate aftermath, when Polish policies toward its Ukrainian minority and the national aspirations of the Ukrainians often clashed. Today, while relations between Poland and Ukraine are very good at the government-to-government level, much remains to be done to build genuine reconciliation between the two nations, as witnessed by the difficult negotiations over the status of the Polish cemetery in Lviv.

Poland and Ukraine have tried to put their history behind them. They have engaged in a number of diplomatic contacts, maintained an open border, and encouraged bilateral trade, though as Poland approaches EU membership, border crossing issues have become increasingly difficult. The most forceful affirmation of the Polish and Ukrainian governments' desire for partnership came in 1997 during a meeting between Presidents Aleksander Kwasniewski and Leonid Kuchma. Though the text of the joint declaration from the 20–22 May Polish-Ukrainian summit (negotiated in advance of the meeting) did not include any formal apologies, it expressly "condemned the past evil" in relations between the two nations.[24]

Polish-Ukrainian economic and military cooperation seems easier to achieve than a resolution of past grievances. Trade is one area where the two countries have been working well together. Ukraine has been the principal target of Polish direct investment in the region. In 1999 Ukraine received $30 million of direct Polish investment, ahead of Lithuania ($14 million) and Russia ($11 million).[25] These numbers, though small by Western standards, are a significant indication of long-term trends, especially considering the fact that Poland still has tremendous capital needs at home. Poland has also been a vocal advocate for including Ukraine as a transit country for a new pipeline linking Russia with Western Europe.

Polish-Ukrainian military cooperation goes back several years and includes a number of military training exercises in Poland and Ukraine before 1997. In 1997 the two nations entered into a formal agreement to create a Polish-Ukrainian peacekeeping battalion in 1998. The battalion headquarters are located in Przemysl, in southeastern Poland. The battalion has been tested in a peacekeeping role in the Balkans, and the overall results have been positive. Military cooperation between the two countries holds potential benefits for the Ukrainian defense sector as well, as the Poles have been considering placing orders with Ukrainian military plants for modernizing their T-72 tanks.[26]

Warsaw and Kiev have engaged in a series of successful joint training exercises for peacekeeping missions. By 1999 training for peacekeeping operations using Polish, Ukrainian, and British forces resulted in three joint exercises held in Ukraine, Great Britain, and Poland, respectively. The "Cossack Plain 99" tactical exercise in Nowa Deba in southern Poland (the third in the series) demonstrated that Poland could play a strong leadership role within the Partnership for Peace (PfP) program, as it reaches out to the east.

There are clear limits, however, to what Poland can do to strengthen Ukraine's independence. While Warsaw has insisted that the new gas line from Russia to Europe should not bypass Ukraine, in the final analysis it may have to compromise on the issue.[27] Most important, because of its limited resources, Poland cannot offer Ukraine much in terms of direct economic assistance. In the end, the gist of Polish support for Ukraine will remain in the political arena.

Within NATO, Poland has begun a concerted effort to be a significant contributor to the Alliance. And considering its strategic location, its population, and the size of its military, Poland has genuine potential to fulfill such a positive NATO role and also to act as a provider of regional security. This requires continued economic reform and growth, further integration with the West through membership in the European Union, and a sustained effort to modernize the Polish armed forces. The later remains a cause for concern. While in the past several Polish governments had gone on record with their commitment to spend at least 3 percent of the gross domestic product (GDP) for military modernization, Poland never exceeded the 2.2 percent of the GDP on defense, and in 2001 it dropped its defense spending to 1.95 percent of GDP. Though Poland's record in the area has been considerably better than that of Hungary or the Czech Republic, it has fallen short of the country's overall needs.

Poland's formal entry into NATO in March 1999 has been a landmark in the evolution of the country's security since the collapse of communism.

It marked the recognition by the West of Poland's progress in terms of its political and economic reform, as well as the institutional restructuring of its military establishment. Poland entered NATO as a consolidated democracy, with several orderly electoral cycles to its credit, the progressive strengthening of its party system, free media, an independent judiciary, and a rapidly rising number of nongovernmental organizations.

Poland also has made remarkable economic progress, which has laid a foundation for the current and planned military modernization programs. The country that, in the final years of Communism, had been raked by hyperinflation and was paralyzed by the mounting national debt, by 1999 has become the flagship of emerging post-Communist economies. Poland has privatized its economy and reoriented its trade to the West. In 1999 Brussels included it among the first batch of candidates to join the European Union early in the next century.[28] In 2000 it made further progress in preparing to meet EU's requirements in the areas of legal reform, common standards, agricultural transformation, and property issues. During the 2000 EU summit at Nice, Poland scored an important coup by winning the same number of votes allocated to it as a future EU member as that accorded Spain, the country with which Poland frequently compares itself. Warsaw's official position has remained that Poland would enter the EU in 2003, although privately Polish government officials recognize that a more realistic time frame would be 2005–2006.

A potentially serious obstacle to Polish membership in the EU is the powerful Polish peasant lobby, which has been intent on preserving the current standards and the structure of employment in agriculture, both of which are incompatible with the Common Agricultural Policy (CAP). The restructuring of Polish agriculture is likely to be the most painful aspect of Warsaw's bid for membership in the European Union. Moreover, to qualify for the unified market, Poland will have to restructure not only its agriculture, but also its steel, textile, and coal industries. In addition, Poland will have to recast its entire legal and regulatory system to adapt to EU standards.[29] In 2000–2001 there were signs that the combination of EU structural funds assistance and indigenous Polish efforts may prove sufficient to overcome resistance in the countryside. Still, the Poles recognize that they cannot count on a money flow from the EU comparable to what the European Common Market was, for example, prepared to transfer to Ireland two decades ago.

The cost of integration with the EU has to be considered against the benefits that have already accrued to Poland, particularly in terms of market access and direct foreign investment. EU membership will give Poland some additional valuable benefits. Most of all, Poland will be eligible for structural funds that it badly needs to upgrade its infrastructure. In 2000 Poland reached a preliminary agreement with Brussels on EU funding for expressway construction south of Warsaw.

The country's internal cohesion and political stability remain important security assets. While divided over class, regional, and economic issues (leading to serious labor protests), Poland faces no internal minority popula-tion pressures, nor is it subject to irredentist demands from abroad. In addition, the country's economic transformation, which has made it into the model for transition from communism to capitalism, has fostered among Poles the general acceptance of democracy as historically and culturally legitimate and made Poland a strong candidate for further integration with the West.

Polish military modernization has been uneven, going through several iterations and plans. The comprehensive military reform program known as *The Army 2012* had only been partially implemented, and was super-seded in January 2001 with a new six-year program that is to bring a large portion of the Polish army up to NATO standards.[30] Currently, while parts of the Polish military have been reformed, the bulk of the forces continue to struggle with the Communist-era legacy. The new six-year program, adopted in late January 2001, will reduce the armed forces overall from two hundred thousand to one hundred and fifty thousand in six years. The officer corps will be reduced by between six thousand and seven thousand. The defense ministry plans to eliminate some forty garrisons and bring the number of military schools from eight down to five. The armed forces will also sell off parts of the redundant infrastructure, estimated at roughly 40 percent of the army barracks, storage depots, and training grounds. Finally, the most obsolete aircraft (MiG-21) and tanks (T-55) will be removed from service. The defense ministry estimates that the realized savings will be approximately PLN6 billion (approximately $1.5 billion), which will be reinvested in the modernization program. Poland anticipates that the money will allow one-third of its armed forces to meet NATO standards. Most important, the government committed to spend over the six-year period 1.95 percent of the GDP. This will address the most urgent need of the defense ministry: the ability to make long-term acquisition plans. The plan should almost double the current spending per soldier, from approximately $17,000 to an estimated $30,000.[31]

Currently, the Polish Air Force and the navy are obsolete, with the air force, in particular, unable to provide effective defense of the country's airspace. Of some 160 aircraft in the Polish inventory, only the MiG-29s, of which Poland has 22, and possibly the Su-22s can be considered adequate for current operations. The ministry of defense has repeatedly stated that it would acquire a new multipurpose aircraft no later than the year 2000, but the funding for the program has remained in question.[32] As of early 2001, no contract for the new aircraft was issued. Instead, it is likely that the Poles will eventually lease F-16 aircraft from the United States, with Poland covering the cost of training and maintenance. In the amended 2001 budget, the government allocated an additional PLN60 million (about $15 million) for the aircraft program, plus PLN37.4 million (a bit less than $9.5 million) to provide the military frequency band.[33] Prime Minister Jerzy Buzek stated that Poland would assess the bids for the aircraft contract no later than February 2001, with the contract awarded by midyear 2001. In the interim, the defense ministry directed the air force to upgrade its MiG-29s and Su-22s, with the cost of the upgrade included in the ministry's budget. Poland also plans to purchase a transport aircraft to facilitate its greater participation in out-of-area NATO missions, possibly from the British.

The new six-year plan will finally eliminate the ancient MiG-21 aircraft. It will also begin to address the readiness level issue. The readiness levels of the Polish Air Force are very low. Polish MiG-29 and MiG-21 pilots log on average forty hours per year of flight time; MiG-23 and Su-22 pilots fly about sixty hours per year. Principal Western air force pilots fly at least triple those rates. The Polish Air Force also needs serious infrastructure investment to bring it up to NATO standards. Polish airfields need to be modernized, especially in terms of their radar, communications, and fuel lines. The Polish government is committed to making six of its airfields ready to receive NATO aircraft by the year 2002. As with the aircraft purchase, funding remains the critical issue.

The Polish Navy operates Soviet-era equipment that is well below the NATO standard. The current defense budget allows Poland to modernize only the units that have been detailed to serve with NATO, including a corvette obtained from the United States in 2000, and to modernize one submarine with a support ship, a rescue vessel, three minesweepers, and one tanker. Most of the modernization of the Polish Navy will not take place until after 2002. In addition, all three Polish naval bases (Gdynia, Hel, and Swinoujscie) require extensive modernization. The same applies to the airfields of Polish Naval Aviation in Oksywie, Darlowo, and Siemirowice. The initial base modernization plan has focused on the ports in Gdynia and Swinoujscie.

The land forces, which constitute the core of the Polish Armed Forces, urgently require modernization. The most urgent need is to upgrade their communications, command, and control systems and to improve readiness levels. Poland still faces the task of completing the conversion of its Soviet-era analog systems to NATO-compatible digital technology. By 1999 only two Polish divisions were equipped with modern communication systems. Included in the modernization program is the plan to upgrade 112 T-72 tanks and the purchase of new missile and artillery equipment and a multipurpose helicopter.[34] It is also likely that the modernized Polish T-72 and T-91 "Twardy" tanks will be supplemented with the acquisition of enough German Leopard 2-A4 tanks to equip the Polish Tenth Armored Cavalry Brigade.[35]

Policy Innovations

The government's approval in January 2001 of the six-year military modernization program is the most important policy in the area of military reform, and the necessary first step to making Poland a strong contributor to NATO. If fully implemented, the 2001–2006 program will finally achieve the necessary modernization goals. The most important aspects of the plan are the guarantee that the military can count on the 1.95 percent of GDP and that it can budget for the duration of the program. Another important aspect of the current program is the government's assurance that the resources freed as a result of further reductions in personnel and the restructuring of the armed forces will not be siphoned off for other purposes, but instead will be returned to the defense budget. Likewise, the Polish Army will get a portion of the proceeds from the planned privatization of several defense industry plants.[36]

Another key goal of the 2001–2006 program is to make one-third of the Polish forces interoperable with NATO and to invest more per capita in personnel, with the goal of doubling the 2000 per capita expenditures. As a result of these initiatives, the Polish government expects to almost double its spending per soldier, going up from the current equivalent of $17,000 per year to about $30,000 in 2006.

The most dramatic change will be the planned reduction in the size of the Polish Armed Forces, down to one hundred and fifty thousand by the end of the six-year plan. Moreover, it is possible that this number may be revised downward even further. The most severe impact of the reductions will be felt in the land forces, which constitute the bulk of the Polish military. There the projected size of the force is approximately eighty-nine thousand by 2003, with further reductions anticipated in the second half of the decade. To put the scope of the change in a proper perspective, suffice it to say that the planned reduction will amount to more than a 300 percent cut in the land forces since the collapse of Communism, down from three hundred and ten thousand personnel in 1989.

Another important innovation that will make the Polish Armed Forces more compatible with NATO is the plan eventually to do away with the military district structure as presently constituted and to rely on the commands instead. Likewise, the Poles are working on a possible transition away from the division system, to the brigade and corps structure, while simultaneously reorganizing the units according to NATO standards.

In terms of hardware modernization, 2001 will see the removal from service of the most obsolete legacy systems, especially the T-55 tank and the oldest MiG-21 aircraft. More important, 2001 should be the year when Warsaw will finally make a decision on the selection of the multipurpose fighter aircraft and reach an agreement on a contract for a wheeled personnel carrier. The Navy will also likely receive another American ship in addition to the former U.S. navy frigate *Clark,* acquired in Mach 2000.

The aircraft purchase decision is the key to the hardware modernization program, as it will be the largest military contract awarded by the Poles, and under the Polish law it must be tied to offset agreements. As the aircraft selection awaits the official decision, the Polish defense ministry will continue the limited modernization of the MiG-29 and Su-22 aircraft to extend their service life.

Like all previous modernization plans, the 2001–2006 program is not being implemented in a political vacuum. In the fall of 2001 Poland will hold its scheduled parliamentary election, and the current polls indicate that the Democratic Left Alliance (SLD) will likely win it by a landslide, displacing the ruling post-Solidarity government coalition. Consequently, the tenure of the current defense minister, Bronislaw Komorowski, is not likely to last much longer. Nevertheless, it is encouraging for the future of Poland's military modernization program that the SLD leadership has affirmed its commitment to the 2001–2006 program, and hence the country should continue on the reform path regardless of which political party emerges as the winner in the fall.

Future Prospects

Since becoming a NATO member, Poland has finally broken out of the Cold War pattern, as it has erased the remnants of the Yalta system in Europe. The current security situation of the Third Republic is arguably the best in the country's history. Poland, which only a decade ago was Europe's economic basket case and the frontline state of the Warsaw Pact against NATO, is today a democracy and the most rapidly growing market economy in Central Europe, firmly anchored in the West through its 1999 membership in the NATO alliance. It faces good prospects for being included in the European Union in the next decade, provided it can sustain its economic growth and the political momentum for institutional reforms.

Poland's security relations with its neighbors vary from close collaboration to merely working relations, with Russia and Belarus constituting the most difficult cases. Germany is Poland's closest partner in Central Europe and its doorway to Europe's political and economic institutions. The United States will remain in Polish eyes an "indispensable ally," needed to sustain the nation's sovereignty and security. Polish relations with Lithuania and Ukraine have grown stronger through a series of bilateral treaties aimed at stabilizing the country's eastern periphery, including military cooperation and joint military units. Both Lithuania and Ukraine see Poland as their conduit to the West. Lithuania, in particular, views Poland as a principal lobbyist for its inclusion in NATO in the next round of enlargement.

In the coming years, Poland's importance to NATO and the Western security system in general is likely to grow, provided it can complete successfully the six-year military modernization program. Together with Germany, Poland could eventually constitute the bulk of NATO's conventional military power in Central Europe. The country's strategic location on NATO's eastern flank gives it additional importance as a means for the Alliance to reach out further east, and to foster stability. Polish-German and Polish-German-Danish cooperation (as exemplified by the establishment of the Polish-German-Danish corps headquarters in Szczecin in northwestern Poland) are likely to grow. Likewise, once the modernization of the Polish navy gets under way, the Poles should be able to contribute meaningfully to joint naval operations in the Baltic. The Polish air defense system has already been integrated to some extent with NATO's, and the completion of the project has been given the highest priority. The acquisition of a modern multipurpose jet should dramatically improve Poland's ability to contribute to the Allied air defense system. By late spring 2001, it was reported that Polish defense officials had decided to replace Poland's Soviet-made fighters with American F-16s, initially with a lease or purchase of sixteen aircraft (a deal worth $1.5 billion) by 2003 and subsequent with acquisition of up to sixty planes.[37]

The record of Poland's contribution to KFOR (Kosovo Force) in 2000–2001 is encouraging. The Polish battalion assigned to the American sector has earned high praise from the U.S. commanders. Poland is likely to increase its contribution to peacekeeping operations in years to come. In recognition of the skill the Poles have brought to peacekeeping in the Balkans, the Polish-Nordic Brigade in Bosnia was placed under the command of a Polish general. In addition to its participation in both the Bosnia and Kosovo forces, Poland has extensive experience in international peacekeeping operations within the United Nations structure that goes back several decades. In the coming years, the peacekeeping training center in Kielce in southern Poland will gain added importance as a hub for training both NATO and NATO partner forces for joint peacekeeping operations. Polish experience working with Lithuania and Ukraine within the PfP should prove to be an important asset to the Alliance. Likewise, Poland's contributions to NATO peacekeeping missions like those in Bosnia and Kosovo will increase as Polish military capabilities improve. In addition, Poland will serve as an important intelligence resource on regional developments in the east, especially if the turmoil in the former Soviet Union continues.

In economic terms, Poland is well positioned to pursue the path of growth and modernization. From the security standpoint, the country needs substantial investment in its infrastructure, especially the long-delayed expressway system project, as well as further upgrades of its national telephone and telecommunication systems. It is reasonable to expect that, short of a wider crisis in Europe, Poland will be able to sustain a 4 percent to 5 percent GDP growth rate into the next decade. This should help it to establish the necessary foundation for increased defense spending. However, the needed rise in defense expenditures in Poland must coincide with a further restructuring of the armed forces away from the inherited Communist-era pattern of territorial defenses, and in the direction of NATO's new mission.

In light of its history and its recent experience, Poland will continue to regard Russia as the principal potential threat to its security. If the developments in Russia lead to the reconstitution of a post-Soviet, Moscow-centered Slavic federation, Poland will have ample time to seek a coordinated response within NATO. Since Poland is arguably the most fervent supporter of a continued U.S. presence on the Continent, it will remain wary of any defense initiatives, such as the EU plan for an autonomous European defense capability outside NATO, that might duplicate NATO's structures and weaken the transatlantic security regime. In 2000 Warsaw watched with growing concern the progress of the European Rapid Reaction Force and the warnings from Washington about the dangers of duplicating NATO's capabilities.

Poland's two most important accomplishments in the area of national security in the past decade are interrelated: its new relationship with Germany and its entry into NATO. By working with Germany within the existing framework of transatlantic security institutions, the Third Republic may have finally found an answer to the "Polish question." The final step on the road to integration with the West will be membership in the European Union. If Poland maintains its present course, by middecade it will have in place the economic and security framework that will make its traditional geopolitical dilemmas a matter of history.

Chronology

January 2000: Defense ministry decides to extend the life of existing MiG-29 and Su-22 aircraft through a modernization program.

11 March 2000: NATO Secretary-General George Robertson announces that NATO will invest $650 million by 2008 to improve Poland's defense infrastructure.

15 March 2000: Poland receives the former U.S. Navy FFG-7 frigate USS *Clark* during a ceremony in Norfolk, Virginia. This is the first of two U.S. ships to be transferred to Poland under the Excess Defense Articles program.

26 March 2000: Vladimir Putin wins Russia's presidential election.

21 June 2000: Deputy Defense Minister Bogdan Klich announces that Poland will need to spend PLN116 billion ($3.6 billion) between 2001 and 2006 to meet NATO standards, with a third of the money to be spent on equipment purchases and modernization.

6 September 2000: More detailed reports are released of Warsaw's plan to modernize its ninety-eight Sukhoi Su-22M4/UM3 fighter-bombers over the next six years to keep them operational until 2012–2015.

21 November 2000: Poland and Ukraine sign a military cooperation agreement that will allow Ukrainian military officers to be trained in Poland for the first time.

1 December 2000: The Polish-designed "Loara" mobile antiaircraft platform unveiled.

7 December 2000: EU summit in Nice affirms the members' readiness to bring Poland into the European Union.

18 December 2000: Defense Minister Komorowski issues a formal request to acquire sixty used multipurpose aircraft for the air defense and aviation

force (the F-16 and the JAS-39 Gripen emerge as the two main competitors for the contract).

22 December 2000: Poland seeks to lease ex-German Leopard-2 tanks.

3 January 2001: The Polish MOD announces that it will create a new territorial support inspectorate (IWT) by the end of 2002 to develop Poland's territorial defense brigades.

30 January 2001: The government adopts a six-year military modernization program, committing to 1.95 percent GDP on defense and the reduction of the armed forces to one hundred and fifty thousand.

31 January 2001: The MOD launches a program to modernize forty of its Mil Mi-24 "Hind" attack helicopters by 2006 to ensure interoperability with NATO.

7 February 2001: During a visit to Warsaw NATO's SACEUR, U.S. Air Force General Joseph Ralston publicly urges Poland to increase defense spending to ensure its forces achieve interoperability with NATO.

14 March 2001: MOD selects EADS's C-295M design for up to ten aircraft for delivery from 2003 to 2006; the decision is subsequently blocked because the selection process is deemed not sufficiently competitive.

11 April 2001: Israel offers Poland two ex-Israel Navy Gal-class small submarines to replace two Polish Foxtrot-class submarines that will be decommissioned in 2003.

18 April 2001: Poland assigns a 480-strong mechanized infantry battalion to the multinational Standby Forces High-Readiness Brigade (SHIRBRIG) for UN peacekeeping operations.

NOTES

1. "Wielkie zmiany" (great changes), *Sztandar Mlodych,* 19–21 April 1991.

2. "Polska i RNF podpisaly traktat o potwierdzeniu istniejacej miedzy nimi granicy" (Poland and the FRG signed a treaty confirming their current border), *Polska Zbrojna,* 15 November 1990.

3. Francine S. Kiefer, "Germans Move to Reassure Eastern Europe," *Christian Science Monitor,* 19 June 1991.

4. "Zalozenia polskiej polityki bezpieczenstwa" (the foundations of Polish security pol-

icy) and "Polityka bezpieczenstwa i strategia obronna Rzeczpospolitej Polskiej" (the security policy and defense strategy of the Polish Republic), *Wojsko Polskie: Informator '95* (Warsaw, Poland: Wydawnictwo Bellona, 1995), 12–32.

5. "Niemiecki raport: Z wywiadu do rosyjskiej mafii" (a German report: from the intelligence service to the Russian mafia), *Rzeczpospolita,* 10 July 1997.

6. Ewa Ornacka, "Polski lacznik" (the Polish connection), *Wprost,* 7 November 1999.

7. *Polityka,* 18 September 1999.

8. *PAP News Wire,* 27 November 1996.

9. Ibid.

10. "Poland-Russia Spar over 'Collision of Interests,' " *Washington Post,* 20 April 2000.

11. "Koncerty prezydenta" (the president's concerts), *Wprost,* 2 July 1998.

12. Rafal Kasprow, "Miliony i prestiz" (millions and prestige), *Rzeczpospolita,* 27 November 1999.

13. IPR Strategic Business Information Database, 8 January 2001.

14. "Poland, Denmark and Germany Sign Military Accord," *Polish Press Agency PAP,* 5 September 1998.

15. *IMF Direction of Trade Statistics Yearbook 2000* (Washington, D.C.: International Monetary Fund, 2000).

16. "Polsko-niemiecka wymiana dokumentow" (the Polish-German exchange of documents), *Rzeczpospolita,* 19 June 1997. The Germans handed over to the Poles the original files of the general government (German government of Polish territories in World War II), and the Poles handed over a portion of the files of the General Directorate of Security of the Third Reich (RSHA).

17. *Polacy o mozliwosci pojednania z Niemcami i Ukraina* (Warsaw, CBOS, 1999), Komunikat #2154, 28 June 1999.

18. *Stosunek do mniejszosci narodowych* (Warsaw: CBOS, 1999), Komunikat #2192, 9 September 1999.

19. Moscow, *ITAR-TASS,* 14 September 1997.

20. *Baltic News Service,* 20 April 2001.

21. *Baltic News Service,* 10 May 2001.

22. "Polskie nazwiska po litewsku" (Polish names in Lithuanian), *Rzeczpospolita,* 23 October 1999.

23. "Polska-Litwa: Zagrozone polskie szkoly" (Poland-Lithuania: Polish schools under threat), *Rzeczpospolita,* 27 November 1999.

24. "Polska-Ukraina: Zdecyduja prezydenci" (Poland-Ukraine: the presidents will decide), *Rzeczpospolita,* 14 May 1997.

25. "Przyczolki biznesu" (the beachheads of business), *Wprost,* 27 June 1999.

26. "MON: Ukrainski zolnierz w Przemyslu" (the MOD: the Ukraininan soldier in Przemysl), *Rzeczpospolita,* 27 November 1997.

27. "Oil Pipeline Deal Poses a Dilemma for Poland," *Christian Science Monitor,* 19 December 2000.

28. For a detailed discussion of Poland's transition to democracy, see Andrew A. Michta, "Democratic Consolidation in Poland after 1989," in *The Consolidation of Democracy in East-Central Europe,* eds. Karen Dawisha and Bruce Parrott (Cambridge, U.K.: Cambridge University Press, 1997), 66–108. Also see Richard F. Staar, ed., *Transition to Democracy in Poland* (New York: St. Martin's Press, 1998).

29. Ben Slay and Louisa Vinton, *Poland to 2005: The Challenge of Europe* (Vienna, Austria: The Economist Intelligence Unit, 1997), 89–90.

30. *Armia 2012: Zalozenia programu modernizacji Sil Zbrojnych w latach 1988–2012* (Army 2012: the framework of the armed forces modernization program, 1988–2012) (Warsaw, Poland: Ministry of National Defense, 1998).

31. "Gonimy sojusznikow," *Rzeczpospolita,* 31 January 2001.

32. Zbigniew Lentowicz, "Na skrzydlach do NATO: Samolot wyladuje w roku 2000") (on wings to NATO: the aircraft will land in 2000), *Rzeczpospolita,* 31 December 1998.

33. "Kluczowa poprawka do budzetu przyjeta" (the key amendment to the budget adopted), *Gazeta Wyborcza,* 1 February 2001.

34. Jedrzej Bielecki, "Armia nie na te czasy" (the army behind the times), *Rzeczpospolita,* 19 January 1999.

35. "Nie zadrzy mi reka: General Edward Pietrzyk, dowodca sil laowych," *Rzeczpospolita,* 30 January 2001.

36. "Gonimy sojusznikow: Rzad przyjal 6-letni plan modernizacji i przebudowy armii" (we chase the allies: the government adopts a 6-year plan for modernizing and restructuring the army), *Rzeczpospolita,* 31 January 2001.

37. *Defense News,* 28 May–3 June 2001.

9 • Slovakia: Toward NATO Indecisively

Ivo Samson

S lovakia became an independent state after the peaceful division of Czechoslovakia in 1992–93. Still within the framework of Czechoslovakia, since the beginning of the 1990s, geopolitics had become perhaps the most popular (sub)discipline of security studies in Slovakia.[1] Slovakia's foreign political position immediately after 1990, and particularly after 1993, can be described as *geographical determinism*. The most important methodological principles of Slovak foreign political behavior concerning future integration in the European Union (EU) and the North Atlantic Treaty Organization (NATO) betrayed a firm belief in the importance of Slovakia's own geopolitical position and assumed that Brussels would take such a factor into consideration when deciding about membership.

Theoretically, such Slovak emphasis on geography was derived from false premises that misjudged developments after the end of the bipolar world. The "new world order" introduced to the post-bipolar world by the first Bush administration included many geopolitical components. Although the "new world order" did involve a shift from a global to a regional and local focus, Slovaks interpreted this trend too unilaterally as favoring the neutral status of small international actors like Slovakia. Methodologically, however, the priority of geopolitics in security policy still steered toward a new bipolar and "catastrophic" vision of the world that was common in Russian security and foreign policy discussions between 1992 and 1997.[2]

At the beginning of the 1990s, Slovak geopolitical research was concentrated in two scientific institutions that worked for the government. Both based their research on obsolete classical geopolitical theories. They tried, in fact, to apply the traditional geopolitics of the beginning of the twentieth century to complex post–Cold War geopolitical relations and to power relations that prevail in Central Europe, Europe, and the world at the end of the millennium. Unfortunately, the geopolitical study produced by the

Center for Strategic Studies was taken by the Slovak government as a guideline for foreign and security policy.[3]

Official government statements reiterate that integration into NATO has remained the basic priority of Slovak foreign and security policy.[4] Many contradictions can be found in such pronouncements, however. Many expressions made by top officials and governing parties' representatives ran contrary to this declared goal. As a rule, views opposed to NATO membership were interpreted as merely private statements. Slovakia's crucial foreign policy deficiency became obvious in the practical steps that were undertaken by the three parties that governed from 1994 to 1998 concerning such sensitive issues as collective defense and the consensus among pro-NATO parties. The certainty of both were repeatedly questioned, and suggestions were made of a Western "diktat." From the end of 1994 to 1998, Slovak policy toward integration was handicapped by the government's composition: leftist nationalists, left-wing neo-Communists, and extreme right-wing nationalists. Whereas the strongest party in the coalition, Vladimir Meciar's Movement for Democratic Slovakia (HZDS), exhibited a confused and controversial attitude toward NATO, the other two government parties openly opposed Slovak NATO membership. That they were bound by the still-valid Program Declaration of the Government (pledging allegiance to both NATO and EU) was, to say the least, interpreted in an unsatisfactory way.[5] As a result, Americans and West Europeans heard not a commitment to NATO but, rather, ample doubt and indecision.

According to the "Defense Doctrine of the Slovak Republic,"[6] produced by the Meciar government and suspended when a new government took over, national security is guaranteed when, in the opinion of the national leadership, no threat of a military attack or coercion in any form exists. Hidden security threats are not considered explicitly, although the key structural components of national security mention political, economic, social, geographic, environmental, and demographic aspects besides purely military security.

A basic reform of the theoretical framework of the defense policy has been introduced because of the country's failure to gain entry into NATO in the 1990s. Important and publicly accessible defense policy documents that had symbolized the bold reform plans of the Slovak Army after 1993 were no closer to being implemented in 1999. At the same time, at least eight new defense policy documents were announced.[7] On 13 October 1999 the government accepted the document titled "Concept of the Reform of the MOD until 2002 (with the Outlook up to 2010)" and on 11 October 2000 it approved the draft of the "Security Strategy of the Slovak Republic."[8]

At the Madrid Summit on 8 July 1997, the secretary general of NATO, Javier Solana, announced that representatives and governments of the NATO countries agreed that the Czech Republic, Hungary, and Poland should be invited to join NATO. Slovakia, one of the applicant countries, was not invited to join NATO either in Madrid or at the Washington Summit in April 1999, although hopes were expressed in Slovakia after the parliamentary elections in September 1998 that Slovakia would receive an invitation. Even by 1996–97, given the long-term trends in Slovakia, it was extremely unlikely that Bratislava would be invited to join NATO in 1999.

The refusal to invite Slovakia in Madrid or, after the 1998 elections, to grant it a "special position" in 1999 at Washington, was not very surprising. The behavior of Slovak decision-making institutions before the 1998 elections, their reflection of Slovakia's security position, and the security system in Europe, did not allow any other result. After the Madrid Summit, the Slovak government reacted by announcing that NATO membership should remain the ultimate security goal of the country.[9] Since then, many predominantly political deficiencies have surfaced—deficiencies that were not automatically ended after the 1998 elections removed Vladimir Meciar from the government. The main thesis of analyzing the Slovak "double failure" is that parliamentary elections alone are not enough to persuade NATO about a long-term trustworthiness of any country. Slovakia had its big chance after the division of Czechoslovakia in 1993; at that time, the Slovak Republic was accepted as a successor state by NATO.[10] Nothing can substantiate the theory of a "secret deal" between the United States and Russia to enlarge NATO with the exclusion of Slovakia.[11]

There are several reasons why Slovakia, even into 2001, has experienced problems with fully meeting all basic criteria for NATO membership. Whereas some criteria could be met at least satisfactorily (compatibility of the armed forces, gradual transition to market economy), some others (transformation from an authoritarian society to a democratic one, good relations with neighbors) could not be fulfilled for a number of reasons in the past few years. The deficit that continued to be acute throughout the year 2000 is the lack of trust in Slovakia's political future.[12]

It would be irresponsible of NATO to rely on the formal side of the political process in Slovakia (elections) and to neglect the political support for the Meciar government by the voters during its time in office, that is, the long-term political will of the population. The roots of the possible relapse into the past have to be seen in a society that elected the authoritarian regime voluntarily, freely, and democratically. In 2000–2001 Slovakia was still in the process of transforming basic values—values that require self-reflection and a decision about the country's future orientation. This problem may have been only partly resolved by the parliamentary elections at the end of 1998, in which the nationalist and anti-Western HZDS (Movement for a Democratic Slovakia) and its allies lost power.[13] Accompanying HZDS's political victories in the 1990s had been social developments and public attitudes that led to a special *type* of post-Communist democracy very similar to experiences in southeastern Europe in the same period (Croatia, Serbia, partly Bulgaria, Romania).

Threat Assessment

Since 1993, Slovakia has not been endangered by armed attack. Economic coercion and political pressure, however, have been conceivable, and Slovakia necessarily has balanced national security interests with a secure political and economic coexistence among its neighbors to ensure that Slovak society can pursue its development. Former Slovak Defense Minister Pavol Kanis summarized the opinion of Army security experts in 2000.[14] For Slovak security, Kanis noted six principal strategic principles:

- The development of international relations in Europe can be characterized as a dynamic process of gradual transition from possible confrontation to new models of cooperation. While the Slovak Republic need not face direct military threat to its territorial integrity and sovereignty, new security challenges, risks, and threats are rising.
- The greatest security risks that can have significant destructive impact on the society and the state are international terrorism, proliferation

of weapons of mass destruction, migration, and the mass spread of drugs and organized crime.

- Ethnic conflicts based on nationalism, territorial disputes, or extension of latent armed conflicts are especially dangerous. These and many other conditions affect the quantity, structure, weaponry, and training of the Armed Forces.
- The government of the Slovak Republic takes into account the new geopolitical situation in Central Europe, where more than 86 percent of the length of Slovakia's border is shared with NATO countries.
- Increased efforts to become an Alliance member, and the complicated situation in the country that influences Slovakia's defensive capability require reform of the Armed Forces.
- Army reform together with cuts in weapons, manpower, and the worldwide trend for greater technological sophistication, all encourage Slovak integration into NATO.[15]

Besides "security risks," official Slovak documents also note "security challenges." One of the crucial challenges is the participation of Slovakia at the forming of European security system.[16] Other "challenges" have been formulated in a very standard and general way to include active participation in Central Europe to develop good-neighborly relations, cooperation within the Visegrad Group, strengthening democracy, the rule of law, and human and civil rights; building a market economy cognizant of social and environmental needs; and accelerating Slovakia's transition from an industrial to an information society.

National interests of the Slovak Republic have been formulated in the draft of "Security Strategy of the Slovak Republic (2000)." Slovakia, like other states, distinguishes between "vital" and "important" national interests. There are four "vital interests":

- Guaranteeing the security of the Slovak Republic, its sovereignty, and integrity;
- Safeguarding and developing the democratic foundations of the state, its domestic security, and domestic order;

- Securing the lasting economic, social, environmental, and cultural development of the society and protecting the important infrastructure of the state; and
- Preserving peace and stability in Central Europe and spreading the zone of democracy, security, and prosperity, including the full membership of Slovakia in NATO and EU.

In addition to such vital interests, there are six "important interests" that have a broad character. First is the preservation of global peace and stability and prevention of tension and crises, or their peaceful solution. Good relations with contiguous neighbors and the development of mutually advantageous cooperation is a second important interest. Nationally, domestic stability based on a social consensus about vital and important interests warrants inclusion. A fourth important interest emphasizes Slovakia's environmentally balanced transition to a market economy. The equality of citizens, regardless of political orientation, religion, gender, ethnicity, and social class is placed among important interests insofar as such equality contributes to social peace and stability. And, sixth, obtaining environmental security is regarded as an important national interest.

This enumeration of Slovak national interests did not ensure that the security decisionmakers, policymakers, and politicians would become fairly educated about such problems, or that they would avoid generalizations and cliches. They approved such a formulation and division of national interests, including overlapping goals and tautological definitions.

To attain the objectives of the program declaration of the Slovak Government,[17] the ministry of defense elaborated the strategic document "Concept of the Reform of the MOD until 2002 (with the Outlook up to 2010," which was approved by the government on 13 October 1999.

This document is meant to eliminate contradictions between demands upon the MOD and the state's resources. By increasing efficiency and making better use of Slovakia's resources, such a study is meant to help improve ministry of defense operations and to create conditions for the country's successful integration into NATO. Simultaneously, the "Concept of Reform" document is expected to resolve principal questions and problems of Slovakia's whole defense system. The new concept of military reform followed the failed attempt in 1994 to reform the army in three stages: 1993–1995, 1995–1997, and 1997–2000. The armed forces' reforms should have concluded in 2000. In 1994, however, the assumption was made that by 2000 Slovakia would be a full NATO member. The document proposes neither a security vision for the country nor a comprehensive program of the defense system, but only a reform within the MOD. The draft reform for the whole defense system is still missing in the 2000–2001 period. The "Concept of the Reform of the MOD until 2002 (2010)" therefore stirred up contradictory reactions both in army circles and in the environment of expert public opinion.[18]

The second important document—the "Security Strategy of the Slovak Republic"[19]—was presented to the public for an open discussion during 2000. It represents a more generalized view of the security position of the Slovak Republic after the failed NATO integration of Slovakia in 1999. The document summarizes and defines ten security risks that can be faced by the Slovak Republic circa 2000.

First, the "Security Strategy of the Slovak Republic" notes that the probability of a global war has remained very low since the end of the Cold War. In a long-term perspective, however, the risk of a large-scale armed conflict cannot be excluded. As unstable countries tend to increase their military capacity, including the accumulation of the weapons of mass destruction, hypothetically Slovakia still faces an armed threat.

Another source of security risk for Slovakia is formed by regional conflicts in unstable regions.[20] Because of the extreme nationalist, religious, and ideological fundamentalists, these risks bear a long-lasting character.

Uncontrolled migration represents a distant, albeit increasing, threat, because Slovakia stands outside the main migration channels. Migration could easily develop into an actual threat, however, as a consequence of regional conflicts. International organized crime has also begun to threaten the vital interests of the Slovak Republic. The "Security Strategy" cites examples such as smuggling of arms, trafficking in women and children, and money laundering.

"Criminalization" of social relations are mentioned, too, in the "Security Strategy," that is, crimes that are particularly modern forms of domestic criminality, particularly racketeering and criminality of minors. Further, security threats to society are seen in corruption, embezzlement, clientelism, xenophobia, and racism. A sixth arena of threat may arise, the document asserts, from the activities of foreign intelligence services. While these services are not specified, it states that their activities will increase with the probability of Slovakia's NATO integration. Interfering with the state's electronic communications as a form of "IT terrorism," which could lead to a total failure of the country's information system, is further noted as a potential threat.

Criticized (but not mentioned by name) is the Slovak Republic's excessive dependence on Russian energy sources. The report claims that "the excessive dependence on unstable sources of basic raw materials and energy, as well as of their transport,"[21] can result in a threat to the security of the state. A ninth threat may occur as negative demographic trends continue—for example, the aging of the population and a resulting inability of the state to secure the social system. And, certainly, environmental threats, including industrial and technical accidents and natural catastrophes, complete the "top ten" potential dangers to Slovak security.

In the list of threat assessments, a repetition of the "national interests" of the Slovak Republic is often seen. Striking, however, is the mixture of politico-military and domestic security problems. The document, however, succeeded in catching some crucial "politico-military" threats almost by name—implying strongly that Russia, or Russian-generated dangers to Slovak security, are a primary concern.

Capacities

Slovakia's participation in the Partnership for Peace (PfP) program has remained a distinct element of the activities in the context of the Alliance in 1999–2001. The military-associated security activities of Slovakia (within the PfP program) are traditionally more explicit than security policy activities.[22] In the framework of NATO, Slovakia supported the establishment of the Euro-Atlantic Partnership Council (EAPC), and up to 2000–2001, the military-associated security actions of Slovakia have been on the increase. Hence, Slovakia appropriately took advantage of its participation in the PfP program, including taking part in PfP exercises.[23]

Even if the participation in the PfP does not provide guarantees within the meaning of Article 5 of the Washington Treaty, it nevertheless provides the opportunity of consultations in case of a threat to national safety. Moreover, Slovakia, like many other of the PfP participants, has always understood the participation in the Partnership for Peace as a preaccession activity intended as a support to integration plans.

The Partnership for Peace program is implemented in particular via the Individual Partnership Program (IPP) between the Slovak Republic and NATO, prepared annually since 1994. Cooperation within the Individual Partnership Program between the Slovak Republic and NATO is conducted in twenty-two areas, which are decisive for reaching the minimum level of interoperability of the Slovak armed forces with the militaries of the NATO member states. A quality breakthrough in the approach toward the IPP appeared after the Washington Summit (1999), in particular after the adoption of the National Membership Action Plan (MAP) of the Slovak Republic (N MAP SR), when in 2000 the IPP clearly focused on the support of Slovakia's accession process aims. Compared to 1999, the number of activities intended by the IPP increased from 267 to 528. This increase did not apply only to the quantity. There has been a qualitative change as well, with a stress on decisive areas that support Slovakia's endeavor to comply with the intents of Chapter 2 of N MAP SR.

The objectives of N MAP SR reflected in the preparation of IPP for 2000 were as follows:

- Conduct a reform of the armed forces of the Slovak Republic while exploiting the knowledge and experience of NATO's defense-related planning
- Achieve the required level of interoperability and compatibility of the command and management structures, communication and intelligence systems, logistics, and infrastructure
- Language training
- Defense-related planning and procurement of resources
- Modernization of armaments, technology, and military material

By the end of February 2000, thirteen objectives of interoperability and three objectives of temporary partnership were met; in seventeen cases, their fulfillment was postponed until the end of the year 2000 and two will be met in 2001. The Slovak Army reached, in total, thirty-five objectives in the year 2000, for which expenditures amounting to SKK (crowns) 560 million were foreseen. The decisions to adopt Partnership Objectives 2000 for the period of 2001–2006 were preceded by comparative analyses, which confirmed consistency of the overall military reform objectives and the objectives of Slovakia's preparation for NATO membership.

During the previous working session with the NATO team held on 22–24 February 2000, Slovak defense ministry experts approved sixty-six partnership objectives of a total number of sixty-nine that were proposed. The objectives were prepared in a way to provide for the necessary level of Slovakia's readiness in military and defense such that, when met, Slovak forces can be included in the NATO collective defense system. Reaching goals for 2000 was a basic prerequisite for fulfilling partnership objectives from 2001 and beyond. Based on preliminary calculations, these objectives require an annual investment of no less than SKK 2 billion Slovak (about $40 million) to develop programs for staff training, communications systems, compatibility, and protection of information systems. Only with such investments could the Government Program Declaration be realistically achieved with an annual increase of the defense budget by 0.1 percent GDP.[24]

An important aspect of preparing Slovakia's defense and military capabilities to meet requirements of joining a system of collective defense has been—since 1999—the implementation of the military reform. Eight priorities for such reform, to be achieved by 2000, can be identified.

- Restructure and harmonize the armed forces to be comparable to the armed forces of the NATO member countries, and adapt them to the human, material, and financial resources available
- Develop the armed forces, while stressing improvement of operational skills, capabilities to operate within international groups, application of doctrines and administrative procedures, modernization of command, management and communication systems, and specialized language training of the key staff
- Decrease of the military staff in number, optimize proportion of ranks across the soldier staffing structure, switch gradually to professionals

in the immediate and rapid reaction forces, apply criteria of intellectual compatibility with the staff in NATO armed forces, and improve the living conditions of soldiers as well as their social security and health care

- Gradually modernize the command, management, and communication systems, armament, and technology of the armed forces; develop scientific and technology-related cooperation with NATO; exploit own-defense industry potential; and develop the country's defense infrastructure
- Shape the defense and military capacities capable of contributing to the joint defense of the member countries after accession to NATO and provide training to the required numbers of military staff to extend Slovakia's representation within NATO and to adequately represent Slovakia within NATO military structures and agencies
- Foster the operational partnership and compliance with the standardization requirements
- Improve the asset and fund management and increase the share of expenditures on development programs
- Rationalize the support activities of the defense sector and eliminate positions not related to the ability to project military forces

Apart from NATO, Slovakia intends to develop a range of security-related contacts and activities. Cooperation with the Western European Union (WEU) in 1999–2000, however, indicated the impossibility of any associated country of East and Central Europe to achieve membership.[25] WEU membership has been automatically linked to EU membership, which is, as it has turned out, harder to achieve than NATO membership.

After 1999, Slovakia had a certain advantage because of its position in the stable sphere of the NATO newcomers (Czech Republic, Hungary, and Poland). The risk of outright conflict in the region in 1999–2000 was even much smaller than in 1993, when Slovakia had emerged as an independent state. In spite of the improved Slovak-EU relationship during 2000, a possible membership in the WEU is still unclear and distant. The WEU has been considered to be an organization that could, under given conditions, be able to contribute to a climate of security in countries that have for certain reasons remained outside NATO. Although the security guarantees the WEU can offer are substantially weaker than those available via NATO accession, even the WEU "defense shield" is regarded as more efficient than anything offered by the Organization for Security and Cooperation in Europe (OSCE)—the latter being primarily a tool for crisis prevention.

In spite of a declared effort to build an independent European security and defense identity, the real interest of Western European countries is a harmonization and linkage across EU-WEU-NATO relations.[26] Through early 2001, the position of the EU in the security of the Slovak Republic was limited, because this organization possesses no entity allowing a common security and foreign policy. Despite the positive declarations at the Helsinki Summit (December 1999), by 2001 nothing could convince the fifteen EU states to submit their security and foreign policy to a supranational level of decision making. For Slovaks' reasoning about the security position of their country, that the EU could claim (even by 2001) a particular security role *only* in conflicts arising from internal problems could not be ignored. But even here, its authority overlaps with the OSCE and the Council of Europe. In this respect, as the official security decisionmakers in Slovakia agreed in 1999–2000, the EU (just as the OSCE, the Council of Europe, or the UN, and even the WEU) cannot replace NATO.

The EU has, however, affected Slovak security by its "approximation" initiatives encouraging the development of cross-border cooperation. While closed borders always signal the presence of security tension, a state's willingness to be open is generally perceived as a sign of security stability. Because of EU pressure regarding visa rules, Slovakia tried to strengthen its security stability by introducing visa obligations against Ukraine and the Russian Federation in 1999–2000.[27] The European Commission enlarged the PHARE program in the mid 1990s by Cross-Border Cooperation (CBC) for all the countries of central eastern Europe that border EU member countries. The aim of the program has been to promote a dialogue and to support particular regions, as well as to prevent a gap from growing between these two sides.[28] Because of its common borders with Austria, Slovakia has also been included in this program. For Slovakia, this means cooperation with its only EU member neighbor state regarding border security.

Policy Innovations

NATO integration has formed one of the three crucial foreign and security priorities (besides the EU and OECD membership) of the Slovak government after the 1998 parliamentary elections. The NATO membership of the Slovak Republic once more has been put into the framework of the "national," or, as the case may be, "nation-state" interests.

The main difference in the proclaimed security orientation of the country before 1999 and after 1999 has consisted not in security policy declarations, but in the ability to persuade NATO partners about Bratislava's real NATO integration intentions. This orientation has been based on the foreign policy initiatives after 1998. Prime Minister Mikulas Dzurinda highlighted the argument that Slovakia had been at the same starting point as the Czech Republic, Poland, and Hungary for NATO admission. During the visit of the Slovak prime minister to Brussels on 27 November 1998, Dzurinda was accompanied by representatives of the three NATO newcomers at his own request, and an intensified Slovak–NATO dialogue finally began. After the visit, a new foreign policy goal was set. The final declaration of the Washington Summit would explicitly characterize Slovakia as one of the most serious candidates for membership.[29] During the visit of Slovak foreign minister Eduard Kukan to Washington on 22 January 1999, then U.S. Secretary of State Madeleine Albright said that Slovakia had entered the club of reliable and democratic countries and that it was well on the way to achieving a full-fledged partnership on the European as well as the world scale. She promised American support for the Slovak efforts to achieve that goal. Meanwhile, she asserted that it was impossible to reverse all the mistakes and shortcomings of the previous government in such a short period.[30]

Catching up on four lost years and reversing the gradual Slovak exclusion from the group of leading NATO candidates is going to be much tougher than was previously admitted by the new government coalition representatives. The atmosphere for further enlargement is not as favorable as it was from 1995 to 1997, when crucial decisions about NATO enlargement were made. In 2000 Slovak diplomacy maintained intensive political and military contacts with NATO, as well as with the Alliance's member states. Slovakia still presented itself as a country, which de facto has already become a NATO member and is ready to accept the role of a reliable security partner.

In Slovakia's preparation for NATO accession, three fundamental issues seem to be the most important. First is the issue of political stability. It is clear that agreement exists between the coalition and opposition about the basic country's course and that the issue of joining NATO is not a subject of argument. There are good prerequisites for an agreement of this type, as the most powerful opposition entity, HZDS, has repeatedly declared its support for Slovakia's accession to NATO and the EU. However, there are also radical groups within the HZDS openly questioning Slovakia's NATO membership—views that cast a negative light on the sincerity of Slovak interests in this vital matter.[31] The HZDS will have to come to terms with the damage any equivocation or doubt may create for Slovak goals. A part of the Dzurinda coalition, conversely, feels an urge to "prove" that the opposition is against joining NATO. This political tactic, however, is highly counterproductive. The governing coalition must therefore react in a more encouraging way toward positive signals related to Slovakia's NATO membership and persuade the public that joining NATO is in the national and state interest of the Slovak Republic, as well as in the long-term economic interest of the Slovak population.

Another problem lies in the field of defense-related planning, in particular stabilizing the financial resources allocated for state defense. To allow defense expenditures to become a subject of ambiguities when approving the state budget every year would be highly damaging to Slovakia's case for NATO integration. The official government policy foresees an annual increase of defense expenditures by 0.1 percent of GDP. With this pace of defense budget growth, the government believes it will be able reliably to comply with the preaccession tasks.

Another issue is the problem of establishing links between Slovakia's defense industry and similar industries of NATO member countries. The public is interested, too, if—apart from expenditures on defense related to the NATO accession—NATO membership would also means positive economic consequences. This interest of the public is reasonable, as Slovakia is in a period of economic recovery linked with a temporary drop in the living standard. The cooperation of NATO and its membership applicants does not have to be (and maybe should not be) restricted to military and political cooperation, but can expand in the field of economic cooperation.

Slovakia's degree of compliance with assignments pursuant to Partnership for Peace, Individual Partnership Plan, Planning and Evaluation Process, and National Membership Accession programs of the Slovak Republic was considered with a team of NATO experts on 22–24 February 2000. Within the same session, the draft Partnership Objectives 2000 (for 2001 to 2006) were discussed. Their fulfillment should establish realistic prerequisites for NATO membership.

On 10 March 2000 the entire issue of evaluation of the compliance with the 1999 accession tests were considered by the Political Military Steering Committee (PMSC). On the same occasion, the methods for implementing Partnership Objectives 2000 were discussed. This session was aimed at preparing inputs for the session of the North Atlantic Council Committee with the presence of the Slovak ministry of defense and ministry of foreign affairs at NATO Headquarters.

On 9 June 1999, the Slovak government approved the program for Slovak preparation for NATO membership under the title name PRENAME (Preparation for NATO Membership).[32] This program should promote the effective coordination of NATO accession activities among respective state institutions (ministries). A special institutional basis[33] was formed and the NP PRENAME (National Program of the Preparation for NATO Membership) could start its activities. The NP PRENAME served as the necessary document for the adoption of the National Membership Action Plan of the Slovak Republic that has been monitored both by Slovak national ministries and by the NATO international staff. In the document, Slovakia's progress toward NATO has been presented to NATO as an annual program. The security goals of Slovakia for the year 2000 have been formulated in this program.

The experience of NATO's newcomers after 1999 could be used to formulate the security goals of Slovakia within the PRENAME program. A general consensus exists that the Czech Republic, Hungary, and Poland had an indirect influence on the security orientation of the Slovak Republic in 2000 in several respects: army reform, compatibility and interoperability with NATO standards, technical and language preparation of Slovak officers, and adaptation of a part of Slovak armed forces for NATO needs.[34]

Slovakia's progress, however, is not without ample problems. In 2000 U.S. experts conducted an evaluation of Slovakia's defense situation. The team was headed by General Joseph Garret.[35] Garret, in cooperation with experts of the Slovak ministry of defense and General Staff, came to disturbing findings. The report ("Study on the Defense Reform of the Slovak Republic") was very critical of the state of Slovakia's armed forces. According to Pavol Kanis, the former minister of defense of the Slovak Republic (until January 2001), the Garret report "analyzes the historical state of the Slovak Army that has been reached after many years. Partly, the problems of the Army of the Slovak Republic have roots in the old regime, partly they are due to the lack of dynamic changes that took place in other countries."[36] The findings of the Garrett report have not been made public, but even the few released details can be regarded as alarming:

- Slovakia belatedly has tried to revise its basic security and defense documents that do not correspond to contemporary defense needs of the state.
- There is a deficit in planning and distribution of defense resources.
- If Slovakia wants to integrate into Western defense structures, it needs to build smaller and more professional armed forces fit for action.
- Most military formations do not have the necessary personnel (on the average, they are at only 70 percent of authorized strength) and depend heavily on national mobilization.
- Despite an annual GDP growth expected to be 2 to 3 percent in the next years, there are no reliable standards by which to plan resources for defense.
- The system of defense in the Slovak Republic lacks a unified command: there still exist military and paramilitary parts of the armed forces that are subordinate to three different ministries (ministry of defense, ministry of interior, and ministry of transport and telecommunications).
- In personnel policy, the Slovak Republic Army still acts according to the principles it inherited from the Communist regime.
- The most important deficiencies may be found in the planning and implementation of military exercises that lack coordination between land and air forces.[37]

In its recommendations for the Slovak Ministry of Defense, the Garrett report proposed that defense planning be prepared several years in advance, that all military and paramilitary elements be centralized under one command (with the exception of police forces), that personnel management be changed drastically, and that training (exercise) programs be made far more efficient. Some findings and recommendations of the Garrett report met opposition in army circles. Certain reservations were expressed by the State Secretary of the Ministry of Defense, Jozef Pivarci (namely, concerning the problem of purchase of military aircraft), which were not recommended by the Garrett team.[38]

Future Prospects

The entry of Slovakia into NATO would, undoubtedly, mean increased expenses for defense. At present, member countries have higher defense expenditures than does Slovakia. The annual contribution of each member country to the running of the Alliance must also be considered.

The process of balancing differences in armaments and readiness must also be considered. Slovak army deficits vis-a-vis West European and North America Alliance countries could take ten to fifteen years to redress. In this period, defense expenditure would be higher. Further expenditures can be expected as armaments produced by the Slovak armaments industries are brought up to NATO standards.

If Slovakia remains outside NATO, which is the first and worst option, other scenarios emerge. Frequent mention is made of the potential for Slovakia to be "neutral." A neutral Slovakia, however, has no widespread support in intellectual, political, and academic circles. Globalization and associated integration processes now include all aspects of economic and social life (new high technologies, information age). Were Slovakia to exclude itself from this global trend, it would not be able to take advantage, via the EU, OSCE, or WEU, of economic growth and positive indicators recorded in Slovakia in recent years. Slovakia must clearly and unequivocally declare its wish to be part of Europe. As military-security attributes of classic neutrality, or "positive" neutrality, or "dynamic" neutrality,[39] have lost their meaning in present-day Europe, economic, military, and political groupings assume that strategic partnerships will become deeper and more advantageous across erstwhile Cold War barriers.[40] And, even among historically neutral states, there is lively discussion on the simplest way to get rid of neutrality—a costly and morally and politically obsolete notion.

Security cooperation with Russia could be a catastrophic scenario for Slovakia, and support of this scheme in Slovakia is now low. Still, according to opinion polls, the next parliamentary elections in Slovakia (fall 2002), could bring a coalition to power that might try to revive the tacit security alliance between Slovakia and Russia that existed in the mid-1990s. In the past, however, the nationalist Slovak government repeatedly used security cooperation with Russia more as a means of blackmailing the West than as a real option.

The first of these alternatives, although certainly not easily realized, seems to be the only realistic one despite the negative attitude of the Slovak population. The response of the society to Western security integration will depend on deepening security links among other European nations. The weakening of the position of the European "nonaligned countries" (particularly of Austria) might have a decisive impact on Slovak society. In this respect, Slovak public opinion is very "elastic."

The defense philosophy of the Slovak Republic consists of looking for answers to two crucial questions—what must be done and what can be done to guarantee the country's security in the critical period after bipolarity and after the so-called guarantees of the WTO?[41] Security risks for Central Europe have not been as fundamental as they have been for southeastern Europe, but they will continue until security integration into a vital alliance has been reached.

The Washington Summit left the door open to future NATO enlargement and introduced the MAP, but without any firm obligations.[42] In considering Slovakia's new military strategic defense concept, it has to be noted that Europe's contemporary security system does not need an immediate follow-up of the first round of eastern NATO enlargement. Slovak defense forces undergoing another attempt at reform would obviously not meet all technical criteria of NATO integration at the beginning of 2001 or 2002 in terms of compatibility.

The compatibility of the Slovak armed forces with NATO and West European military forces has several aspects. The most difficult of these are the compatibility of military thinking and the change of defense philosophy. This change can be brought about only by active personal contacts with NATO and WEU and through rebuilding of armed forces personnel by adding people who have not been linked to the previous Warsaw Pact period. The contacts with Western armed forces, especially thanks to the Partnership for Peace contacts, are absolutely necessary.[43] The preparations of Slovak peacekeeping units are in full progress. Besides this, Slovakia keeps a military mission at NATO Headquarters in Brussels and cooperates closely, especially with the United States, which finances the reform program for the Slovak army and has launched education programs for Slovak army officers in the United States. Since 1995, Slovak soldiers have increasingly taken part in peacekeeping training in the Central Europe region and in the West.

Another problem Slovakia has experienced up until 1999 can be found in the matter of a "common speech," that is, in terminological compatibility. The traditional terminologies still used in the Slovak armed forces very often have their origin in Warsaw Pact language. The problem becomes even more marked, because even among NATO members there is no unanimity about many principal security terms such as strategic interests, security, security policy, grand strategy, national security strategy in the United States, military strategy, and military doctrine.[44] Among the American, French, and German terms, we find several differences in meaning, and Slovakia has to look for equivalents that correspond to Slovak conditions. After several considerations, for example, the term "military doctrine" was rejected and given the denotation "defense doctrine," which might be changed in the new documents on which the ministry of defense is working. A slight confusion still exists about the proper meaning of "security." In the case of Slovakia, however, an effective security cannot be guaranteed when the country is attacked. Instead, Slovakia must rely on prevention and deterrence. Official statements declare that Slovakia realizes that certain requirements must be met if Slovakia wants to be integrated. Through U.S. and British assistance and analysis, Slovakia intends to develop its program in the following deficit areas: command and control techniques; the Air Force; defense planning and spending; long-term finance planning; and restructuring of the state reserve system.[45]

Deficiencies concerning the Slovak armed forces have been regarded as minimal in comparison with the political deficits in the course of the Slovak NATO integration process. The engagement of the Army of the

Slovak Republic in peacekeeping operations has been above average, and the Slovak military has often given these activities as an example of a positive security policy development of the country.[46] But Slovak security integration remains troubled by the country's political past and uncertainties about its political future. Not surprisingly, a politically mature democracy may be the harbinger of Slovak security in this decade.

Chronology

1 October 1999: General Joseph Garrett, director of European and NATO department of the Pentagon, visits Slovakia.

10 October 1999: Hillary Clinton, the wife of the U.S. president Bill Clinton visits Skovakia for six hours. Afterward she leaves for Hungary, where she stays three days.

11 October 1999: Jan Figel and Jozef Pivarci, from the MFA and MOD, present the NP PRENAME (National Program—Preparation for NATO Membership) in Brussels.

13 October 1999: The European Commission recommends Slovakia for the opening of admission negotiations with the EU.

9 November 1999: Foreign Minister Eduard Kukan presents the NP PRE-NAME to diplomats accredited in Slovakia.

11 November 1999: A delegation of the National Council of the Slovak Republic takes part in the meeting of the NATO Parliamentary Assembly in Brussels.

17 November 1999: The U.S. Congress adopts a resolution in which the development in Slovakia after the parliamentary elections of 1998 is evaluated very positively.

22 November 1999: U.S. secretary of state Madeleine Albright expresses the support of the United States for the integration ambitions of Slovakia.

3 December 1999: The presidents of the Visegrad Group meet in Slovakia.

12 December 1999: The Slovak Republic Foreign Ministry expresses concerns about the hardships of the civil population in Chechnya, but voices support for the preservation of integrity of the Russian Federation.

1 January 2000: After the resignation of Russian president Boris Yeltsin, the Slovak government confirms its interest in the development of bilateral relations with the Russian Federation.

21 January 2000: The president of the European Commission, Romano Prodi, visits Slovakia and gives a speech in the National Council.

3 March 2000: Robin Cook, U.K. foreign secretary, visits Slovakia. During his talks with Slovak foreign minister Eduard Kukan, he promises U.K. support for Slovak EU and NATO integration ambitions.

22 March 2000: The National Council adopts a new law on civil (substitute) service. The civil service obligation is reduced from 24 to 18 months.

29 March 2000: Jan Figel, the state secretary of the foreign ministry, and Ronald Wegener, the deputy of the WEU secretary-general, hold negotiations about the European security policy in Bratislava.

7 April 2000: Foreign Minister Eduard Kukan and the Defense Minister Pavol Kanis present the updated annual program PRENAME in Brussels.

18 April 2000: Foreign Minister Eduard Kukan visits Kosovo in his new position as authorized representative for the Balkans of the UN secretary-general.

26 April 2000: Foreign Minister Eduard Kukan holds negotiations with U.S. secretary of state Madeleine Albright in Washington and reports that the United States would support the admission of Slovakia into NATO.

25 May 2000: A Slovak delegation headed by the Foreign Minister Eduard Kukan takes part at the meeting of the EAPC in Florence.

6 June 2000: Austrian Foreign minister Benita Ferrero-Waldner expresses appreciation for the friendly stance of Slovakia toward Austria after the fourteen EU members introduce sanctions against Austria.

6 June 2000: The Russian Federation announces the introduction of the visa obligations for Slovak citizens as of 1 January 2001 as a reaction to a similar step taken by the Slovak Republic.

9 August 2000: Frantisek Sebej, the Chairman of the Committee for the European Integration of the National Council, expresses his full support for the initiative of the United States and of the countries of the former Yugoslavia to exclude the Yugoslav Federal Republic from the UN.

28 September 2000: Donald Johnston, Secretary-General of the OECD, and Eduard Kukan, Slovak foreign minister, sign the agreement on the admission of Slovakia into the OECD. Slovakia becomes the thirtieth member of this organization.

5 October 2000: The Slovak government expresses its conviction that the victory of Yugoslav presidential candidate Vojislav Kostunica in the Yugoslav presidential elections is definite and can not be stolen.

11 October 2000: The new Slovak government adopts the security strategy of the Slovak Republic.

31 October 2000: Marinus Wiersma, deputy of the European Parliament and reporter for Slovakia, notified of a positive European Commission evaluation report for Slovakia.

8 November 2000: According to the annual EU evaluation report, the Slovak EU integration process is hindered by dissension within the ruling coalition.

11 November 2000: Fewer than 20 percent of voters take part in the opposition-initiated referendum on early parliamentary elections. As a result, the pro-Western government of Prime Minister Mikulas Dzurinda will probably be able to serve its term until new elections in late 2002.

19 December 2000: The prime minister of the Czech Republic, Poland, and Slovakia meet their Dutch counterpart, Wim Kok, in Bratislava. Talks focus on the EU enlargement process and on the signs of a German negative attitude to this process.

31 January 2001: During his visit to Bratislava, Russian foreign minister Igor Ivanov meets his Slovak counterpart, Eduard Kukan. Ivanov openly advises Slovakia against NATO integration.

NOTES

1. The division of Czechoslovakia was effected at midnight on 31 December 1992. There was no referendum; in opinion polls in 1992, the absolute majority of citizens in both the Czech Lands and Slovakia was against the division. The separation, however, had a constitutional background, because it was accepted by the Federal Assembly (Czechoslovak parliament) at the end of 1992. In the following years, the partition has been described as "legal" but not "legitimate." See Martin Porubjak,

"Anfang einer liberalen Demokratie in der Slowakei?" (beginning of a liberal democracy in Slovakia?), *Europaeische Rundschau,* 27, No. 1 (January 1999): 81–93.

2. Alexander Duleba, "Geopolitika a zahranicnopoliticka debata v sucasnom Rusku" (geopolitics and foreign policy debate in contemporary Russia), in *Listy SFPA* (SFPA Letters) 10 (October 1998): 9–10.

3. In Slovakia, "Central Europe" is labeled only as the Czech Republic, Hungary, Poland, and Slovakia. They compose the so-called "Visegrad Group," a regional alliance that the (former) Czechoslovakia, Hungary, and Poland formed in 1991; The Center for Strategic Studies of the Slovak Defense Ministry produced "The Geopolitical and Geoeconomic Development in the World and the Position of the Slovak Republic" for the Slovak government on 1 February 1994. Regarding this report, see Milos Ziak, *Slovensko od komunizmu kam?* (Slovakia on the way from Communism where?) (Bratislava, Slovakia: n.p., 1996), 178–90.

4. Marian Leska, "Pribeh sebadiskvalifikacie favorita" (self-disqualification story of a champion), in *Slovensko v. sedej zone?* (Slovakia in a gray zone?), eds. Martin Butora and Frantisek Sebej (Bratislava, Slovakia: IVO—Institute for Public Affairs, 1998), 74.

5. "Programove vyhlasenie vlady SR" (the program declaration of the government of the Slovak Republic), *Sme,* 16 January 1995.

6. Intentionally, the denotation "military doctrine" was avoided. The "Defense Doctrine of the Slovak Republic" was approved by the Slovak parliament on 30 June 1994.

7. "Zakladne ciele a zasady narodnej bezpecnosti SR" (basic goals and principles of national security), "Obranna doktrina SR" (defense doctrine), "Koncepcia vystavby armady SR do r. 2000" (concept of building up the Slovak army until 2000), and "Dlhodoby plan rozvoja armady SR do roku 2010" (the long-term plan of the development of the Slovak army until 2010). See *Zamer spracovania zakladnych koncepnych a legislativnych dokumentov* (the scheme of elaborating basic concept and legislative documents) (Bratislava, Slovakia: Ministry of Defense, 1999).

8. See an analysis of these documents below.

9. The statement of the ministry of foreign affairs of the Slovak Republic on 13 July 1997.

10. Jozef Moravcik, the former foreign minister (1993–94) and later prime minister (1994) of Slovakia is of the opinion that the United States, represented by President George W. Bush, gave consent to the division of Czechoslovakia to Czechoslovak President Vaclav Havel during a meeting at the third summit of the Conference on Security and Cooperation in Europe in Helsinki in June 1992. See Miloslav Beblavy and Andrej Salner, *Tvorcovia obrazu, obraz tvorcov* (creators of image, image of creators), (Bratislava, Slovakia: Center for Social and Media Analysis, 1999), 49.

11. During his time as prime minister most recently, Vladimir Meciar supported this "conspiracy" theory.

12. The open conflicts in the largest government party, SDK (Slovak Democratic Coalition), at the beginning of 2000 were less notable than the "nonstandard" composition of the government ranging from Christian-Democrats on the right via national liberals, greens, Social Democrats and two post-Communist parties. Such a coalition hints at a long process of "normalizing" the political scene in Slovakia.

13. Hnutie za demokraticke Slovenko—Movement for a Democratic Slovakia.

14. Kanis resigned after a financial scandal at the beginning of January 2001 and was replaced by another representative of the post-Communist Party of Democratic Left (legal successor to the pre-1989 Communist Party of Slovakia), Jozef Stank.

15. Pavol Kanis, "Speeches," <http://www.mod.gov.sk, 2000> (accessed 15 June 2001).

16. *Bezpecnosta strategia Slovenskej republiky* (security strategy of the Slovak Republic) (Bratislava, Slovakia: Ministry of Defense, December 2000), 6.

17. "Programove vyhlasenie vlady Slovenskej republiky" (program declaration of the government of the Slovak Republic), section 4 of *Domestic Security, Justice, Defense of the State and Foreign Policy* (Bratislava, Slovakia: Office of the Government, November 1998), 33–36.

18. Peter Bartak, "Vyuzivame poznatky a skusenosti z polskej cesty do NATO" (using know-how and experience of the Polish road to NATO), in *Europska bezpecnost a proces rozsirovania NATO* (European security and the process of NATO enlargement), eds. Ivo Samson and Tomas Strazay, Bratislava, Slovakia: The Slovak Foreign Policy Association, 2001), 11–14.

19. *Bezpecnostna strategia Slovenskej republiky* (security strategy of the Slovak Republic) (Bratislava, Slovakia: Ministry of Defense, December 2000), 22.

20. The document has localized this risk in the regions of southeastern Europe and the Caucasus (pp. 7–8).

21. *Bezpecnostna strategia slovenskej republiky,* 9.

22. Juraj Marusiak, Juraj Alner, Pavol Lukac, Rudolf Chmel, Ivo Samson, and Alexander Duleba, "The Foreign Policy and National Security of the Slovak Republic," in *Slovakia 1998–1999,* eds. Grigorij Meseznikov, Michal Ivantsyn, and Tom Nicholson (Bratislava, Slovakia: IVO—Institute for Public Affairs, 1999), pp. 168–71.

23. Vladimir Bilcik, Martin Brunko, and Ivo Samson, "Integracia SR do EU, NATO a OECD" (integration of the SR into EU, NATO, and OECD), in *Slovensko 2000* (Slovakia 2000), eds. Miroslav Kollar and Grigorij Meseznikov (Bratislava, Slovakia: IVO—Institute for Public Affairs), 351–52.

24. See above the "Program Declaration of the Government," of November 1998.

25. As a non-EU and non-NATO member, Slovakia has been in the position of an "associated partner" within the WEU, compared to the more advantageous positions of WEU-observers and WEU-associated members (the first being the EU non-NATO members, the second being the NATO non-EU members).

26. Radek Kohl, "Europska bezpecnostni a obranna politika—odpoved na evropske bezpecnostni ambice?" (European security and defense policy—response to European security ambitions?), *Mezinarodni vztahy* (International Relations Prague) 1, No. 4 (2000): 31.

27. Whereas the visa obligation for Ukraine was introduced in 2000, visas for Russian citizens have been in force since 1 January 2001.

28. Felix Mittermayer, "Cezhranicna spolupraca: ukazka europskej integracie" (transbor-

der cooperation: an example of European integration), *Listy SFPA* (SFPA Letters) 1 (January 1999), 7.

29. Alexander Duleba, "Slovenska zahranicna politika—bilancia siestich rokov a perspektivy zmeny" (Slovak foreign policy—balance sheet of the last six years and prospects for change), *Mezinarodni vztahy* (international relations Prague) 1, No 1 (1999), 44.

30. Juraj Marusiak, Ivo Samson, and others, "The Foreign Policy and National Security of the Slovak Republic," in *Slovakia 1998–1999,* eds. Grigorij Meszniko and Michal Ivantysyn (Bratislava, Slovakia: IVO—Institute for Public Affairs, 1999), 173.

31. As of February 2001, the HZDS still remained the strongest political party in all opinion polls made by independent institutes, with roughly 25 percent of voters prepared to cast their vote for the HZDS.

32. Document no. 480/1999.

33. "Vladny vybor pre pripravu Slovenska na vstup do NATO" (preparation government committee for the NATO integration of Slovakia), as well as respective working groups.

34. Peter Bartak, "Vyuzivame poznatky a skusenosti z polskej cesty do NATO" (using know-how and experience of the Polish road to NATO), in *Europska bezpecnost a proces rozsirovania NATO* (The European Security and the Process of NATO Enlargement), eds. Ivo Samson and Tomas Strazay (Bratislava, Slovakia: Slovak Foreign Policy Association, 2000), 11–18.

35. At the time the report was prepared, Gen. Joseph Garret held the position of an assistant to the U.S. secretary of defense. His team had elaborated similar studies on the defense situation in the Baltic states, Romania, and Bulgaria.

36. Pavol Kanis, *Obrana* (defense) 17 (2000), 3.

37. These findings have been taken from the article by General Milan Stranava, "Studia reformy obrany SR" (study on Slovakia's defense reform), *Obrana* (defense) 17 (2000), 14–16.

38. Jozef Pivarci, *Obrana* (defense) 18 (2000), 11.

39. These notions occurred as parts of East-West relations during the mid-1990s.

40. Russia, NATO, see "The Founding Act on Mutual Relations, Cooperation and Security between NATO and the Russian Federation" (Paris: NATO, 27 May 1997).

41. Warsaw Treaty Organization.

42. Vladimir Jakabcin, "Informacie o Washingtonskom summite NATO" (information about the Washington NATO summit), "Bezpecnostna situacia v Strednej a vychodnej Europe po Washingtonskom summite NATO" (the security situation in Central and East Europe after the Washington NATO summit) (Bratislava, Slovakia: Slovak Institute for International Studies, 1999), 7–11.

43. See *Exchange of Experience in Partnership for Peace Program Implementation* (Bratislava, Slovakia: Center for Strategic Studies, Ministry of Defense, 1998), 8–13, 14–16, 61–68.

44. Ivo Samson, "Narodna bezpecnost" (national security), in *Slovensko 1998—1999 Suhrnna sprava o stave spolocnosti* (Slovakia 1998—1999: global report on the state of the society), eds. Grigorij Meseznikov and Michal Ivantysyn (Bratislava, Slovakia: IVO—Institute for Public Affairs, 1999), 377.

45. See *U.S.-Slovak Security and Foreign Policy Roundtable Report* (Washington, D.C.: State Department, 26 October 1999).

46. Jozef Margus "Aktivity Armady SR v operaciach na podporu mieru OSN a ialsich medzinarodnych organizacii' " (the activities of the army of the Slovak Republic in peacekeeping operations of the UN and other international organizations), in *Rizika a ohrozenia v strednej Europe v 21. storoei. Vplyv na ulohu ozbrojenych sil* (risks and threats in Central Europe in the twenty-first century: impact on the role of defense forces), ed. Ivo Samson (Bratislava, Slovakia: Slovak Foreign Policy Association, 1999), 89.

PART III:
THE BALTIC STATES
Introduction: The Baltic States

Ustina Markus

Lithuania, Latvia, and Estonia were unique among the former Soviet republics in their transition to a market economy and accompanying economic development as well as their transition to democracy. The processes in those countries were more akin to the processes in the non-Soviet Central European countries than any other former Soviet republics. All three were committed to Western integration from the beginning of the decade, and by 2000 that integration appeared to be approaching an imminent reality. Part of their Western-integration goals included membership in NATO. Having decided that NATO was an inclusive organization after much debate, NATO countries made clear that the Baltics were on the list for future membership despite protests from Russia. The quest for inclusion in NATO led the three to seek solutions to any territorial disputes they had with each other or their neighbors, so that such issues would not interfere in prospective membership.

Estonia was the most prosperous economically and was the front-runner of the three for possible European Union (EU) membership. Its small size, small army, and proximity to Russia made it a less certain candidate for immediate NATO membership if the alliance decided to expand to the Baltics piecemeal. Thus, Tallinn sought to integrate itself into EU structures as much as possible so that it would be so much a part of the Western community that it would, by extension, be a part of that community's defense planning. One notable sign of Estonia's increased sense of security and west European integration was its 2000 military concept that did not list Russia as an immediate military threat to the country.

Both Latvia and Lithuania felt some resentment over Estonia's inclination to join the EU and get into the Western defense alliance through the back door alone, rather than working in tandem with them. Yet both were equally guilty of acting unilaterally if their chances for NATO or EU integration were better alone than within the Baltic group. Lithuania stood the best chance of obtaining an invitation for membership in NATO of the three. It already bordered on one NATO member, Poland, and it had the largest armed forces of the three Baltic states. While the country's armed forces were small, they were active in UN peacekeeping missions and regularly participated in Partnership for Peace (PfP) exercises as a way of building a relationship with Western and international security structures.

Latvia followed a similar strategy to its Baltic neighbors' strategy for Western integration. Its armed forces participated in PfP activities and strove to meet the criteria for NATO and EU membership. Like Estonia, it had resolved its outstanding issues over its treatment of its Russian minority during the first years of independence, so that the Council of Europe and other Western organizations did not fault its policies on minority issues and those did not stand in the way of further European integration.

By the end of 2000, the three Baltic states had made significant progress in reforming their political and economic systems toward a west European model. Not only were they considered serious candidates for future membership in Western organizations, including NATO, but they also stood in marked contrast to the other republics of the former Soviet Union, which had embarked on a trend of increased authoritarianism and were making little headway in economic reform and improving the living standards of their citizenry.

10 • Estonia Reassesses Russia's Threat

Mel Huang

When Estonia declared its independence in February 1918, the country's main national defense priority was to preserve that status from its large, powerful, and ambitious neighbors, Germany and Russia. The secret protocols within the Molotov-Ribbentrop Pact overwhelmed that priority, causing more than a half century of foreign occupation. Many blame then-president Konstantin Pats for not resisting the Red Army during the basing crisis of 1939 and the ensuing occupation and loss of independence in 1940—all of which occurred without Estonia firing a single defensive shot. That resentment was reinforced by the fact that Estonia had won the only armed war it fought, the War of Independence, against German and Russian forces. The resentment brewed for over fifty years in Estonia and among the thousands of diaspora throughout Europe, North America, and Australia.

As a result, upon the restoration of its independence in August 1991, Estonia once again reoriented its main national priority to that of defending its independence with a renewed vigor. With Germany tied into the North Atlantic space and recent memory focused on Russia, Estonia saw its main security threat as coming from the east. Armed units of the Soviet army did not withdraw from Estonia until August 1994, and various war games sponsored by the Russian Federation—most notably Zapad-99, which forecast a conflict with NATO involving the Baltic states—did not enhance the level of security felt by Estonian officials.

Estonia's national defense faced an array of problems in the first half of the 1990s, such as creating a Western-style civilian-controlled military. The legacy of the half-century of Soviet occupation was manifest through the amount of ransacked military installations strewn throughout the small country, as retreating Russian forces looted goods, stripped equipment of metals, and disposed of hazardous items in the environment. For instance, jet fuel was buried in the soil, concrete dropped into the sewer system, petroleum into harbors, and so forth.[1] Other legacies of the Soviet military system also remained, such as *dedovshchina*—or bullying of conscripts. Having to create a military from scratch, the shortcomings in infrastructure and equipment shortages prevented the development of any realistic national defense for many years, while such basics as structurally sound barracks and functioning guns had to be acquired or built.

It was a commendable achievement that in less than a ten-year period since the restoration of independence, the Estonian Defense Forces were slowly becoming a small but credible force, even participating in international peacekeeping operations. When Estonia made it official that it wanted to join NATO when it joined the Partnership for Peace (PfP) program at its start in 1994, the idea sounded preposterous at that time; however, just a few years later, Estonia was considered as a good candidate for the enlargement round expected in 2002, or the round immediately following. Though the problems of equipment, infrastructure, personnel, and funding remained serious, the progress made over the decade created the necessary foundation for the country's national defense.

National Defense Overview

Because of the geopolitical situation of Estonia, the country's national defense officials strove to create a credible defense. As there was no doubt that the country could easily be invaded by its powerful neighbor through a mass mobilization of forces, or by overwhelming bombardment, the focus of its defense planning was on territorial defense. The shortage of heavy equipment that could deflect an attack made Estonia's rejection of a Polish donation of T-55 tanks hard to understand, especially since Estonia did not own one single tank, even for training purposes.[2] Arguably, the Estonian Defense Forces of 2000 could have been defeated by the Estonian military of 1930 on the basis of personnel, leadership, and, most surprisingly, equipment.

Though Estonia is not a party to the Conventional Forces in Europe (CFE) Treaty, Russia is. The United States and its NATO allies—especially Poland, Denmark, and Norway—have kept Russia's compliance with the CFE, especially its flank agreements, under careful scrutiny. For Russia to mount a decisive attack on the Baltics, Moscow would most likely have to violate the CFE flank limitations near the Baltics, something NATO intelligence would notice instantly. Though Estonian officials at times criticize the CFE for being a Cold War relic because the three Baltic countries were nonparticipants, it ensures that any surprise buildup on the Russian side would be countered by a heavy diplomatic response from the West.

The development of Estonia's national defense over the past decade has been territorial. The standing military is comparably small, at about 5,180, with 55 percent conscripts.[3] The reliance, in case of a successful attack, would rest on the 7,500-strong (with associated organizations, the total number is about 14,000) Kaitseliit, the national guard.[4] Those numbers are small, even when compared to 1940, when the Kaitseliit had about 100,000 members.[5] The goal by 2005 is to have a wartime defense force numbering between 25,000 and 30,000 soldiers. However, the military has yet to work out a concrete mobilization plan, something the new Defense Forces commander, Rear Admiral Tarmo Kouts, emphasized as a priority during his parliamentary confirmation in September 2000.[6] Russia's problems with guerrillas in Afghanistan and Chechnya were cited as a reason for such a defense, as well as Estonia's own guerrilla efforts in the 1940s and 1950s from the *metsavennad* (Forest Brothers).

Looking beyond a straightforward military invasion, Estonia has moved to place all border protection services under the aegis of national defense. That included the coast guard and the border guards, which were seen as combining to provide an immediate first line of defense in any crisis that could extend into Estonia's borders. Though the inclusion of a segment of the border guards' budget into that of national defense starting in 1999 was controversial, Estonian officials continue to emphasize the frontline nature of the border guards in its importance to national defense. Visiting European Union (EU) officials continue to remind Estonia that its eastern border could one day soon become the EU's border with Russia.

Of all Estonian borders, the land border with the Russian Federation remains the most contentious. Most of Estonia's other borders, such as the maritime borders and the land border with Latvia, are regulated under agreements. However, there was no progress in negotiations on the Estonian-Russian land border treaty, despite there being no serious disagreements on the physical border location. Over the years, Estonia has backed away from earlier demands concerning Russia's recognition of the Tartu Peace Treaty of 1920, often called Estonia's "birth certificate" (ironically, it is also considered the "birth certificate" of Soviet Russia, because it provided the first international recognition of the Soviet state). Estonia has made clear references that it does not covet territories lost to Russia following the Soviet occupation—a strip of land across the Narva River in the northern border area and the land around the town of Pechory (Petseri) in the southern border area. The latter was a significant emotional issue for Estonia. A kindred nation, the Setu, lives in the region, and the post-Soviet border splits the small Finno-Ugric people on both sides of the border. Despite the relinquishing of the demands, Russia continues to tie the border issue to the treatment of its ethnic kin in Estonia. Russia has unilaterally demarcated the border, and that border is the de facto border for both countries in crossings, trade, and border defense.

One significant development in 2000 was the drafting of a national defense concept by the Foreign Ministry. The document noted that security threats to Estonia came from instability and possible uncontrollable developments rather than a direct military threat from any single country.[7] Significantly, it can be read as a policy statement that Russia as a military power is not a near-term direct threat to Estonia's security. The groundbreaking document cited other dangers as more pressing than a direct military threat, such as international crime, environmental risks, and ethnic problems. The document was scheduled to reach parliamentary debate in early 2001.

NATO as a Defense Priority

The government reiterated and reaffirmed in 2000 its main foreign affairs priority—NATO membership for Estonia. With EU membership issues tied mostly to the harmonization of Estonian laws and regulations with the EU's *acquis communautaire,* the country's diplomatic focus shifted solidly over to NATO.

The government drafted and presented its Annual National Program in September 2000. That was its second annual report to NATO's Membership Action Plan (MAP) for the country.[8] The plan focused on five issues: political-economic issues connected with joining NATO, partnership goals, resources for developing national defense, protection of classified information, and legal issues. The government was active in responding to Brussels over the progress of the programs, and was encouraged by statements made by a series of visiting officials from NATO and member states.

To Estonian policymakers there have been two facets to NATO integration. On the one hand, the country's national defense must be credible and contribute to the overall security of the alliance. On the other, the ultimate decision on membership is seen as a political one. In his semi-annual foreign policy review, Foreign Minister Toomas Hendrik Ilves told the Estonian parliament on 12 October 2000 that to contribute, Estonia must have the "ability to provide top quality expertise in some specific areas which make it possible for our defense forces to complement the forces of the Alliance in some specific sector."[9] Understanding the political nature of any invitation, the Foreign Ministry took the lead in lobbying efforts in all nineteen NATO member countries. Estonia currently has embassies in sixteen NATO capitals and is to open an embassy in Turkey in early 2001; only Luxembourg (served by Brussels) and Iceland (served by Copenhagen) are not earmarked for individual Estonian embassies. A similar policy was implemented several years earlier with EU member states in order to bring Estonia into early membership talks. Relations with periphery countries such as Turkey have increased, notably after Turkish foreign minister Ismail Cem said in June 2000 that "European security is not complete as long as the Baltic states are not members of NATO."[10] Estonia has received affirmative supporting statements on its NATO bid from a host of members, including but not limited to Denmark, Hungary, Iceland, Norway, and Poland.

Strong lobbying efforts were coordinated in various NATO capitals, especially Washington, which was seen as the key decisionmaker in the enlargement process; if Washington supported Estonian membership into NATO in 2002, its allies were likely to be positively swayed. Officials called on Americans of Estonian extraction to intensify their lobbying efforts in Washington, including cooperation with other diaspora organizations. President Lennart Meri opened the quadrennial Estonian world festival in Toronto in July 2000 by using the example of the Polish lobby in North America to mobilize lobbying efforts for Estonia's NATO bid.[11] There remains some dissent over that strategy, as some groups are pushing for a Lithuania-only entry because of its perceived advanced readiness for NATO membership.

One way of demonstrating Estonia's readiness to join NATO has been to increase its participation in NATO military exercises under the PfP program. The country's forces participated in a number of military exercises through 2000, including Baltic Link 2000 (August, Sweden), Baltic Triangle 2000 (September, Denmark), Nordic Peace 2000 (September–October, Denmark), Amber Sea 2000 (October, Lithuania), Baltic Eagle 2000 (October, Latvia), and others, averaging about 200 PfP-sponsored events per year. Estonia has also made a significant effort to take part in global peacekeeping operations, including UN operations in Lebanon and Croatia and NATO operations in Bosnia and Kosovo. For the latter NATO operations, about 100 Estonian servicemen served as peacekeepers in 2000, as well as a team of civil police officials. Prime Minister Mart Laar told the United Nations during the Millennium Summit that Estonia would end the use of an 80 percent discount on its peacekeeping dues as a sign of its commitment to international peacekeeping.[12] Estonia's thirty-one soldiers in the joint Baltic battalion, BALTBAT-3, returned from their tour of duty in April 2000, while fifty-two Estonian peacekeepers joined the Danish deployment in Bosnia in March 2000.[13]

Baltic cooperation has also been used as a tool to show the ability of the three Baltic countries to work together in a larger framework. In fact, cooperation in all aspects of defense has been strong among the three countries. The joint Baltic peacekeeping battalion, BALTBAT, has seen several deployments in the Balkans as peacekeepers. The joint naval fleet, BALTRON, has participated in many exercises and minesweeping maneuvers in the Baltic Sea. The joint airspace surveillance system, BALTNET, came online in 2000. The Baltic Defense College in Tartu opened in 1999 and brought officers from all three Baltic countries and NATO allies to teach and study, making it a model institution linked to the alliance. The 2000 BALTDEFCOL graduating class, its first, consisted of thirty-two officers from Estonia, Latvia, Lithuania, Denmark, Germany, Hungary, Sweden, and the United States.[14] The 2001 class consists of thirty-eight officers from the same countries, as well as the Czech Republic.[15]

Aside from NATO, Estonia has also voiced its commitment to the EU's rapid reaction force. Estonia, looking at EU membership as a "soft" security guarantee, has consistently supported efforts to expand the role of the common foreign and security policy (CFSP) and the Western European Union (WEU). Defense Minister Juri Luik reaffirmed Estonia's commitment of a military police unit, a mine-clearing unit, a civilian-military cooperation specialist unit, and a naval unit of mine hunters and a support frigate.[16] Luik also added that Estonia would add an infantry battalion to the rapid reaction force by 2005.

Funding, Equipment, and Infrastructure

As with all NATO aspirant countries, the issue of defense funding has been contentious and emotional, especially in light of shortfalls in other important sectors such as education, health, and social welfare. In its Annual National Program, Estonia has called for a plan to increase defense spending by 0.2 percent each year, reaching the important 2 percent of GDP in the year 2002. Governmental stability since the March 1999 elections has helped maintain control over the divisive talks on annual budgets, and all three ruling coalition parties have agreed to the defense spending schedule. Though the permanent inclusion of a part of the border guard's budget into the national defense budget in 1999 caused some controversy abroad, especially as it was a lean budget year, the spending schedule was not due to change during the parliamentary cycle ending in March 2003. By that time, the 2 percent mark of budgetary spending for defense should have been attained.

The 2000 state budget allocated 1.6 percent of GDP for national defense. During the budget debates in late 1999, opposition groups argued against the raise, citing other pressing sectors, but did not succeed in derailing the spending raise schedule. The debates for the 2001 state budget proved to be as difficult as the previous year in dealing with the opposition, but again, the opposition did not prove strong enough to prevent the scheduled hike in defense spending, and it was raised to 1.8 percent of GDP.

Nonetheless, issues that arose in 2000 highlighted problems that went beyond the budget allocations, notably the proper use of funds. The highly respected chairman of the parliament's National Defense Committee,

opposition deputy Tiit Tammsaar, questioned the increased defense spending not out of principle, but with the accusation that the Defense Ministry
was guilty of being wasteful, squandering assets, and general mismanagement.[17] A media report claiming that conscripts had to purchase their own
boots because of the shoddy quality of the military's stock drew attention
to some of those problems.

One major problem was infrastructure and the condition of bases. The
vast majority of Soviet military installations were rendered dangerous and
even hazardous after the 1994 troop withdrawal. As a result, the construction
and refurbishment of the infrastructure has swallowed a large part of defense spending. Talks continue on the consolidation of bases in the country
to reduce on costs, but local councils have often opposed the closure of
bases in their areas on the grounds that this may adversely affect the local
economy. An outbreak of the rota virus at the mess hall of the air defense
battalion, making eighty men ill,[18] led to an outpouring of anger from the
public, and the media highlighted the unfit conditions in which many of
the country's conscripts live. A photo of a squalid latrine on the front page
of *Postimees* in October,[19] alongside a report that only two of the thirteen
bases with barracks met minimal health and safety requirements, prompted
the parliament to adopt emergency funding for the military infrastructure,
granting about $1.2 million for emergency base renovations in 2001.[20]
Officials also laid the cornerstone for a new base, the first completely new
post-Soviet base, in the northern town of Tapa in November.

With most defense spending allocated for infrastructure and personnel,
equipment acquisition came mostly from donations. The navy fleet, which
had no fighting ships, was mostly donated. Germany gave several *Lindau-*
class minesweepers in 2000, and the Danish-donated *Hvidbjornen*-class
logistics frigate, renamed the *Admiral Pitka* after the Estonian navy's
founder, was christened the fleet's flagship in November.[21] Sweden's self-
endeavored "year of the Baltics" in 2000 also featured a military facet.
Sweden donated or sold for a symbolic price a large number of surplus
and decommissioned military goods to Estonia, including antiaircraft and
antiarmor weaponry. The United States was also an important donor to
Estonia's military, offering a variety of goods from clothing to light arms.
Estonia received a shipment of over 40,000 old M-14 rifles from the United
States in February.[22] A former U.S. military attache, Peter Hendrikson, chided

Estonia for not taking full advantage of U.S. military assistance, indicating the country could have received more aid.[23]

Though officials have hinted that another large shipment of military equipment was expected, possibly Stinger missiles, the acquisition of equipment appears to rely on donations for the immediate future. The Defense Ministry has come under some criticism for being selective in its acceptance of equipment donations, notably its rejection of Polish T-55 tanks in lieu of a yet-unfulfilled donation of modern Leopold tanks from some unknown country. Estonia had made one large arms acquisition, from Israel, which ultimately played a role in the collapse of the Mart Laar government in 1994. The state had taken on large financial liabilities to purchase a consignment of arms from Israel, but some of the desert-designed equipment was reportedly inadequate in the subfreezing temperatures of Estonia in the winter. Since then the government has not made any sizeable military arms acquisitions.

The most important acquisition in 2000 was a modern airspace surveillance system for use as Estonia's part of the joint-Baltic airspace surveillance system BALTNET. The Defense Ministry came under fire once more from the media when losing bidders in an international tender complained of procedural irregularities. The ministry was forced to scrap the agreement with Thomson CSF and reannounce the tender, which has carried into 2001. Nonetheless, Estonia opened its national BALTNET operations center at the Amari Airbase in October 2000, with the entire network's headquarters at Karmelava (near Kaunas), Lithuania, also becoming operational this past year.[24]

Personnel Problems and Structural Deficiencies

On Independence Day, 24 February 1999, then-Defense Forces commander Lieutenant General Johannes Kert warned of a future crisis in the military's leadership. Though General Kert focused on the lack of university-educated youths in the military, the actions of President Lennart Meri created chaos in the country's military leadership within two years. Since that speech, five individuals have served as either commander or acting commander of the Defense Forces in a convoluted game of musical chairs, an excess of presidential whim that the parliament was unable to control.

Estonia took a serious step toward restructuring its military back in May

1993 when the parliament offered the Defense Forces commander's post to Aleksander Einseln, a diaspora Estonian career officer in the U.S. Army.[25] General Einseln told the U.S. news program *60 Minutes* that the task was much more difficult than he had expected.[26] However, Einseln himself became increasingly involved in politics, especially in ongoing disagreements with then-Defense Minister Andrus Oovel. Einseln soon decided his position was untenable, and many politicians saw his sudden move into politics as a major step backward for Estonia's military reform. President Lennart Meri accepted an open-ended resignation letter from Einseln, replacing him with former Kaitseliit commander Johannes Kert in January 1996.[27]

During his term as commander, General Kert continued to restructure the military, taking advantage of help from non-NATO countries Finland and Sweden—something his predecessor had spurred. However, he was dogged by two scandals. In 1997 fourteen men drowned during a training exercise in Kurkse, which was attributed to a lack of oversight at nearly every level of the command. At the time, Kert offered to resign, but President Meri refused. In a still-unexplained incident in June 1999, a member of the now-disbanded elite Special Operations Group (SOG) was shot in the head during an apparent robbery. Kert and the military were accused of creating secretive structures, and politicians insisted they had no knowledge of the SOG's existence, even though the operations group had been seen on television a few weeks before the incident. Again Kert attempted to resign, but Meri refused once more. In an effort to calm the situation, Kert decided to take a one-year high-ranking officers' course at the U.S. Army War College and was given a one-year leave with the promise by Defense Minister Juri Luik that he could return to his post upon completion of the course.

President Meri appointed Colonel Urmas Roosimagi, head of air defense, as acting commander. The appointment was generally seen as a snub to the highest-ranking and most experienced military officer in Estonia, Major General Ants Laaneots, the chief of the General Staff. General Laaneots has been criticized for his extended service with the Russian military and his role as a Soviet military adviser in Ethiopia. Those charges led to allegations of disloyalty. The pass over by President Meri all but signaled that Laaneots, probably the best and certainly the most experienced military strategist in Estonia, would never rise to command the military, and Laaneots quickly retired. Despite his retirement from the armed forces, the general continued to be active, writing columns in newspapers about military issues and teaching at the Baltic Defense College in Tartu.

There was considerable upheaval in the command of the armed forces in 2000 when Meri sacked the outspoken Roosimagi, citing a lack of diplomatic rapport. The head of the NATO integration division at the General Staff, Colonel Mart Tiru, was named as Roosimagi's replacement. Tiru was seen as more adept at dealing with the parliament and with NATO officials. The parliament reacted sharply to having been kept out of the process of selecting a new acting commander for the Defense Forces, because the legislature was the only body that could legally appoint or dismiss the commander of the Defense Forces. Colonel Tiru's term should have ended when General Kert's one-year leave was concluded. However, Kert was sent on holiday leave and President Meri named Lieutenant Colonel Aarne Ermus as acting commander, with the intention of replacing Kert with Tiru permanently. Kert was sacked by Meri at the end of June. In response, Kert and the parliament protested, calling his removal illegal and unconstitutional.[28] In a controversial parliamentary session in August, an apparently erroneous vote caused a one-vote margin that served to relieve Kert of his position and averted a constitutional crisis.[29]

Through the entire controversy, Tiru's stock dropped considerably, because he was perceived as being too close to President Meri. Among the reasons that Kert fell out of favor with Meri was his objection to Meri's promotion of Tiru to brigadier general. In response, Meri accused Kert of disobeying the civilian command of the military. In the end, border guards director Rear Admiral Tarmo Kouts became the compromise candidate and was confirmed in September. After several months of hesitation, General Kert agreed to accept the post of ground forces commander, a newly created position, instead of retiring. That allowed Estonia's most-respected military leader to continue serving in the country's armed forces despite the whimsical string of presidential decrees that had almost led to his removal.

In another setback for military reform, a new draft peacetime national defense law was rejected during parliamentary hearings. The bill was drawn up partly in response to political outrage at President Lennart Meri's heavy-handedness and perceived extraconstitutional meddling into the Defense Forces' command. The parliament's National Defense Committee rejected the draft law from the Defense Ministry in early November 2000,[30] and accused the Defense Ministry of coveting more power at the expense of the Defense Forces and the president. Defense Minister Juri Luik was strongly criticized by Committee chairman Tiit Tammsaar for trying to turn the Defense Forces' commander into a de facto adviser under the defense minister. As Lennart Meri cannot run for reelection in 2001 because of the constitutional two-term limit on the presidency, the issue of presidential meddling in the defense establishment may become moot.

Aside from the leadership, other personnel problems dogged the military restructuring process. An alarming report appeared on the level of education of conscripts, and General Kert warned that a future leadership crisis was imminent in the military if well-educated youths continued to avoid their national service.[31] The report released by the Defense Ministry in January 2000 showed that in the year 1999 only one conscript had a university degree, while half of the conscripts had not even finished secondary school.[32] In response, the Defense Ministry moved to amend the conscription rules to force university students to perform their compulsory national duty within a specific time frame, ending the evasion practice of extended matriculation by many Estonian youths.[33] Students protested the bill, while the involvement of some military officials in promoting the change publicly angered politicians, who alleged that the military was overpoliticized. The changes were adopted, but they were not implemented fully, because the Defense Ministry had not anticipated the popularity of the scheme for those students wanting to get their national service out of the way early. The conscription period was also reduced from twelve to eight months in accordance with legal amendments proposed by the Defense Ministry.[34]

The advisory National Defense Council, chaired by President Meri, approved a plan to restructure the defense map by reducing the number of defense districts from four to two, a northern and southern, and creating also a ground forces command.[35] When the post of ground forces commander initially was offered to General Johannes Kert, he turned down the job. But in December he agreed to accept the post.[36]

Future Outlook

According to the draft national defense concept, some of the key challenges to Estonia's national security will come from indirect sources, such as regional instability and uncontrollable political developments, or even environmental disasters. A bomb explosion at the popular Stockmann shopping center in Tallinn in May underlined the threat of terrorism to Estonians. In engaging the border guards as part of the national defense, the country made issues such as cross-border crime and drug trafficking security priorities. In the past few years, Estonia has earned a negative reputation as a drug transit point because of its open travel routes by ferries on the Baltic Sea. That unsavory reputation was highlighted in comments made by Finnish interior minister Kari Hakamies in January 2000, when he suggested Estonia's path to the EU could be blocked if the drugs transit problem was not controlled.[37] One positive outcome of that criticism has been that law enforcement officials of the two countries have increased their cooperation in combating the drug trade, which has resulted in several high-profile arrests as evidence of successful cooperation.

Side effects of the increasing drug trafficking were the increased use of drugs in Estonia itself and the spread of associated diseases. In 2000 the incidence of HIV infection in Estonia dramatically increased. A record 211 cases of HIV were diagnosed in 2000 by October, mostly among intravenous drugs users in the northeastern city of Narva. In the whole previous decade, only eighty-nine cases had been diagnosed.[38] Many health-care providers feared the numbers were much higher, because drug users avoided HIV tests for fear of a positive diagnosis. The government created a small emergency fund from reserves to pay for more HIV testing in Narva in September.[39] Health-care providers also feared a lack of resources for dealing with any new diagnosed cases of HIV, noting that resources were already lacking to treat current cases.

While new factors were increasingly seen as security threats to the country, Russia remained a central force in any traditional threat assessment. Instability in Russia could quickly change the risk assessment of Estonia, Europe, and the world. Former U.S. deputy secretary of state Strobe Talbott once called Russia's relations with the Baltic states a "litmus test for the fate of this entire continent."[40] As for other new sources of threat, no guarantee from a foreign country or alliance could counter some of those risk factors facing Estonia, especially health and environmental. For instance, whether a NATO member or not, there would be little Estonia could do if a mishap occurred at the Sosnovy Bor nuclear power plant near St. Petersburg, a possibility that would devastate Estonia and much of northeastern Europe. With the hard security guarantee of NATO membership, however, Estonia would be more protected against some of the more overt risks that a further destabilized Russia would cause.

With Russia in mind, Estonia's main security policy goal remains NATO membership, and the country's diplomatic efforts continue to be targeted at gaining an invitation to join the alliance at its 2002 summit. A review of Estonia's development program for 2001 is essential, as the political decisions in NATO capitals—especially Washington—will likely be made before the 2002 reviews. Intense lobbying will be focused on the Bush administration and the U.S. Senate, as the current composition of the nearly evenly divided Senate could influence the final decision in the enlargement process.

Estonia would not be devastated in its goal of joining NATO if an invitation was not forthcoming in 2002, although the country would clearly be disappointed. Even in the event that only one Baltic state—most likely Lithuania—receives a membership invitation, the pursuit of NATO membership is not likely to decelerate. The current three-party coalition government, with all three parties fully committed to NATO membership, remains stable and should survive the parliamentary cycle to March 2003. There is very little anti-NATO political power in the country, although the large center-left Center Party of Edgar Savisaar has advocated a slower raise in defense spending. By the next electoral cycle, the 2 percent GDP mark should have been reached, however, making the issue less critical for the politicians both foreign and Estonian for whom that figure remains a magical number. The opposition center-left agrarian-interest Estonian People's Party is firmly pro-NATO and agrees with the ruling coalition on defense issues to a high degree so that the parliament's National Defense Committee is the only committee chaired by an opposition deputy—Tiit Tammsaar.

Support for NATO membership in the country has been consistently just below half in 2000, with more Estonian citizens for membership than noncitizens.[41] Many noncitizens, mostly Russian speakers, turned further away from NATO during the Yugoslav bombing campaign, but as those events receded into the past, support for membership grew. A Saar poll found that 19 percent of non-Estonians supported Estonia's NATO membership in 2000, compared to 8 percent in May the previous year.[42] Only a small handful of political parties, on both the right and left periphery and among the Russian-speaking groups, have voiced opposition to membership. In the current parliament, they hold fewer than half a dozen seats out of 101.[43] Unless an unexpected and drastic realignment occurs in Estonian politics over the next two years, the next parliament, regardless of who wins the right to form a government, will contain a solid majority of actively pro-NATO members.

Though the draft defense concept states that Russia is not seen officially as a military threat to Estonia, its history as a former occupier continues to haunt Estonian-Russian relations. With Russia remaining unstable politically, economically, and socially, Estonian politicians see little choice other than to continue the pursuit of NATO membership. Under NATO's nuclear umbrella, they see a solid guarantee against the loss of their independence by their neighbors, ending a centuries-old quest of the Estonian people.

NOTES

1. Former Defense Forces commander Aleksander Einseln shows such scenes to American journalist Ed Bradley in "Help Wanted" from *60 Minutes* on CBS television in the United States, 7 November 1993.

2. "News from Estonia," 21 April 2000, *Central Europe Review,* http://www.ce-review.org/00/16/estonianews16.html

3. According to the web site of the Estonian Defense Forces, http://www.mil.ee

4. According to the web site of the Kaitseliit, http://www.kaitseliit.ee

5. Eerik-Niiles Kross, "Estonia Lost Its Independence but Did Not Submit," in *Estonia: Candidate for Membership in the European Union, International Business Handbook* (Tallinn, Estonia: Euroinformer, 2000), 267.

6. *Newsline,* Radio Free Europe/Radio Liberty, 22 September 2000, http://www.rferl.org/newsline/2000/09/220900.html

7. *Estonian Defense Digest,* 6–21 September 2000, published by the Estonian Foreign Ministry, http://www.vm.ee/eng/publications/Defense/def1.htm

8. *Estonian Defense Digest,* 22 September–3 October 2000, published by the Estonian Foreign Ministry, http://www.vm.ee/eng/publications/Defense/EDD7.htm

9. Toomas Hendrik Ilves, 12 October 2000, *Riigikogu,* Tallinn, http://www.vm.ee/eng/ pressreleases/speeches/2000/Riigikogu_okt2000.htm

10. *Newsline,* Radio Free Europe/Radio Liberty, 12 June 2000, http://www.rferl.org/ newsline/2000/06/120600.html

11. Lennart Meri, 8 July 2000, Toronto, Canada, http://www.president.ee/eng/ e_speeches.html?DOCUMENT_ID=4602

12. Mart Laar, United Nations, New York, 7 September 2000, http://www.riik.ee/ peaminister/k/un070900.htm

13. *Estonian Review,* 19 December 1999–3 January 2000, published by the Estonian Foreign Ministry, http://www.vm.ee/eng/review/1999/REW52.htm

14. *Estonian Review,* 19 June–2 July 2000, published by the Estonian Foreign Ministry, http://www.vm.ee/eng/review/2000/review25-26.htm

15. *Estonian Review,* 17–23 July 2000, published by the Estonian Foreign Ministry, http://www.vm.ee/eng/review/2000/review29.htm

16. *Estonian Defense Digest,* 16–28 November 2000, published by the Estonian Foreign Ministry, http://www.vm.ee/eng/publications/Defense/EDD11.htm

17. "News from Estonia," *Central Europe Review,* 13 November 2000, http://www. ce-review.org/00/39/estonianews39.html

18. *Postimees,* 16 October 2000, http://www.postimees.ee/index.html?number=116&op= lugu&id=1374

19. Ibid.

20. *Baltic States Report,* Radio Free Europe/Radio Liberty, 29 November 2000, http:// www.rferl.org/balticreport/2000/11/36-291100.html

21. *Estonian Review,* 20–26 November 2000, published by the Estonian Foreign Ministry, http://www.vm.ee/eng/review/2000/review47.htm

22. *Estonian Review,* 13–19 February 2000, published by the Estonian Foreign Ministry, http://www.vm.ee/eng/review/2000/review7.htm

23. *Baltic States Report,* Radio Free Europe/Radio Liberty, 31 January 2000, http:// www.rferl.org/balticreport/2000/01/02-310100.html

24. *Estonian Defense Digest,* 4–19 October 2000, published by the Estonian Foreign Ministry, http://www.vm.ee/eng/publications/Defense/EDD8.htm

25. *Estonian Review,* 3–9 May 1993, published by the Estonian Foreign Ministry, http:// www.vm.ee/eng/review/1993/93050309.html

26. "Help Wanted" from *60 Minutes* on CBS television in the United States, 7 November 1993.

27. *Estonian Review,* 21–27 January 1996, published by the Estonian Foreign Ministry, http://www.vm.ee/eng/review/1996/9612127.html

28. "News from Estonia," *Central Europe Review,* 18 September 2000, http://www. ce-review.org/00/31/estonianews31.html

29. "News from Estonia," *Central Europe Review,* 4 September 2000, http://www. ce-review.org/00/29/estonianews29.html

30. "News from Estonia," *Central Europe Review,* 13 November 2000, http://www. ce-review.org/00/39/estonianews39.html

31. *Postimees,* 25 February 1999, http://arhiiv.postimees.ee/leht/99/02/25/uudised.shtm

32. The report also indicated that 10 percent of conscripts failed to even complete a basic nine-year education; *Newsline,* Radio Free Europe/Radio Liberty, 17 January 2000, http://www.rferl.org/newsline/2000/01/170100.html

33. *Newsline,* Radio Free Europe/Radio Liberty, 15 March 2000, http://www.rferl.org/ newsline/2000/03/150300.html

34. *Newsline,* Radio Free Europe/Radio Liberty, 26 July 2000, http://www.rferl.org/ newsline/2000/07/260700.html

35. *Estonian Defense Digest,* 18–31 October 2000, published by the Estonian Foreign Ministry, http://www.vm.ee/eng/publications/Defense/EDD9.htm

36. *Estonian Review,* 18–24 December 2000, published by the Estonian Foreign Ministry, http://www.vm.ee/eng/review/2000/review51.htm

37. *Newsline,* Radio Free Europe/Radio Liberty, 31 January 2000, http://www.rferl.org/ newsline/2000/01/310100.html

38. "News from Estonia," *Central Europe Review,* 6 November 2000, http://www. ce-review.org/00/38/estonianews38.html

39. *Newsline,* Radio Free Europe/Radio Liberty, 27 September 2000, http://www.rferl. org/newsline/2000/09/270900.html

40. Strobe Talbott, Tallinn, 24 January 2000, http://www.vm.ee/eng/pressreleases/ speeches/2000/Talbott_as%20delivered.html

41. Press Release, No. 38-I, 6 December 2000, Estonian Foreign Ministry, http:// www.vm.ee/eng/pressreleases/press/2000/1206NATO-public.op.htm

42. "News from Estonia," *Central Europe Review,* 12 June 2000, http://www. ce-review.org/00/23/estonianews23.html

43. Only five deputies in the faction led by the United People's Party, which includes the Estonian Democratic Labor Party, have explicit programs opposing NATO membership.

11 ◆ Latvia's Year in Defense: 2000

Graeme P. Herd and Mel Huang

Introduction

Latvia, like Estonia and Lithuania, reemerged as an independent nation in 1991.[1] Over the last ten years, Latvian foreign ministers have constantly defended the foreign policy goals chosen by the Baltic states and their wish to acquire security through strategic reorientation and integration westward, arguing that the security of a region or of an individual country cannot be separated from security of the continent, while Europe's security cannot be separated from transatlantic security.[2] Latvian foreign minister Indulis Berzins noted: "This principle is clearly reflected in the Baltic states foreign policy goals to become European Union and NATO members."[3] Most recently, on 25 April 2001, Latvian president Vaira Vike-Freiberga, speaking at a meeting with foreign policy experts in Washington, stated that the Baltic countries were ready to participate in the decision-making process of a free and united Europe. She noted that in 2000 Latvia boasted the most-rapidly growing transition economy in Europe, and that it was determined to devote sufficient resources to the modernization of defense. She also said that of those who apply for citizenship, 95 percent successfully pass naturalization tests, attesting to the country's commitment to integrate and not discriminate against its nonethnic Latvian population.[4]

Russian president Vladimir Putin has said he is prepared to work toward the resolution of all problems in his country's relations with Latvia: "We are prepared to resolve all problems, no matter how acute they would appear. We are open to talks. . . . We only ask that the same rules be applied [in relation to Latvia's Russian-speaking population] as are applied to ethnic minorities in Europe. That would be well [good] enough for both us and our compatriots in the Baltic states, including Latvia."[5] Aleksandr Udaltsov, Russia's ambassador to Latvia, said in a meeting with Latvian

Saeima (parliament) speaker Janis Straume that Russia viewed with understanding the efforts of the Baltic states to integrate into the European Union (EU) but was concerned about efforts to integrate into NATO. He noted that, because nearly 40 percent of Russian exports go to the EU, the Baltic states in the future could become a bridge between Russia and the EU.[6]

Relations between Latvia and her nearest neighbors to the east, particularly the Russian Federation, appear to be strengthening as the legacy of Sovietization is gradually addressed and the psychology of the past replaced by the prospect of Euro-Atlantic integration. Indeed, President Vike-Freiberga marked Latvia as one of the possible intersections on "the new Silk Road," where trade routes from the West, East, north Europe, and south would meet. She has argued that Latvia perceives its future development in three areas: information technologies, banking, and transit—especially via ports. As 60 percent of the Latvian population was already employed in the service sector, in the future Latvia could become one of the European and, possibly, global financial centers, functioning as a motor of integration in the East, similar to that of the Irish "Tiger-economy" in the West.[7]

Those goals raise the question of to what extent the aspirations for the future affect the foreign and security potential of Latvia at the start of the new century. Will closer Euro-Atlantic integration and, in particular, membership in NATO be achieved, in view of the relative weakness of the Latvian military, Russian objections, and NATO's reticence? Other issues facing the state include: obstacles to continued internal stability, the prospect for a breakdown in Baltic cooperation, and the possibility of delayed EU integration.

Foreign Policy: "Three Good Things?"

On the eve of the new century, Latvian foreign minister Indulis Berzins noted: "From as long ago as the time of fairy-tale telling, the Latvians usually like to talk about three good things." The "three good things" that had dominated Latvia's foreign policy agenda in 2000 and 2001 were the beginning of EU accession talks, the start of the Council of Europe presidency, and the Vilnius meeting of the Central and East Europe (CEE) states to discuss NATO membership.[8] Are those "fairy tales" or accurate reflections of a contemporary foreign policy reality?

Latvia has continued to push toward integration with the European Union.[9] At the 1999 Helsinki European Council meeting, it was agreed to widen enlargement negotiations from six to twelve mainly east European states, including both Latvia and Lithuania in February 2000. At the December 2000 EU Nice Summit it was agreed that each country should receive one commissioner, and, more important, that the process of enlargement should continue, despite the doubts expressed before the summit.

The prospect of Baltic-EU integration placed a renewed stress on "third pillar issues" upon the domestic Baltic political agenda. Former prime minister Andris Skele of Latvia hailed the EU invitation to participate in talks, stressing: "The most important emphasis at the moment, of course, will be on co-ordinating legislation. What is important is the emphasis placed on third pillar issues, the issues relating to the internal affairs and justice systems, combating corruption in the country, the further democratisation of society."[10] By December 2000 Latvia had closed nine of the sixteen chapters that were open, but despite progress, three potential stumbling blocks to Baltic-EU integration remain crucial to this outcome: progress made in combating corruption, harmonizing legislation and increasing administrative capacity, and institutionalizing border control regimes. Membership in the EU is seen as a soft security guarantee and a major boost for the country's economic links (and is especially seen as a further separation from Russia). During talks, Latvia, alongside its Baltic neighbors, spoke strongly in favor of the common foreign and security policy pillar of the Union—including the Western European Union (WEU) and the proposed European rapid reaction force.

The latter part of 2000 also saw Latvia take up the rotating presidency of the Council of Europe, the continent's main human rights organization. Though the rotating presidency of the council is not seen as something very significant by most nations, this opportunity became Latvia's first chance at chairing a Europe-wide organization, thus a huge boost to its standing on the continent. Though rhetoric with Russia at times grew difficult, with both Russia's attacks on Latvia's minority and citizenship policies and with concerns by Latvia and others over Russia's Chechnya policy, Latvia used its status to reinvigorate talks with Russia on bilateral relations.

Latvia's foreign policy goal since the restoration of independence has been to reintegrate with the "Western" world and to participate as a full partner in those "Western" organizations, most notably NATO. The reintegration is seen both as a return to Latvia's rightful place among the family of Western democratic nations and as a guarantee for its security against an unstable Russia. Despite Russian assertions that the further eastern enlargement of NATO would destabilize the balance of power on the continent, Latvia and the other Baltic states see NATO membership as the surest and strongest guarantee for its security. The drive for security and NATO membership has in turn bound the three diverging Baltic countries closer to each other in cooperation to reach their mutual goal of membership.

Latvia continued to work toward membership by increasing its lobbying efforts and by taking part in international (and NATO) peacekeeping operations. Though failing to receive an invitation to join NATO alongside the Czech Republic, Hungary, and Poland in 1999, Latvia and the other Baltic states have set their membership goal and hope on the scheduled summit in 2002. In the meantime, Latvia has endeavored to implement as much as possible reform in the military for each of the two Membership Action Plan (MAP) reviews so far issued. The government adopted the 2001 MAP in September 2000, which emphasized the interoperability of Latvian forces with NATO, as well as peacekeeping.[11] MAP became the guiding document within the Latvian military reform process.

In May 2000 Lithuania hosted a summit of foreign ministers of all NATO-aspiring countries, known as the "Vilnius nine." Latvia was among the states that issued a united statement reaffirming their cooperation in reaching their mutual goals and in urging a "big bang" approach to NATO enlargement in the nearest future.[12] Latvia also strongly valued the US-Baltic Charter, signed in January 1998 by four presidents, Bill Clinton (United States), Guntis Ulmanis (Latvia), Lennart Meri (Estonia), and Algirdas Brazauskas (Lithuania), that pledged U.S. assistance and support for the Baltics' efforts to integrate into the North-Atlantic space. Clinton asserted at the signing ceremony that the charter would help allow the three Baltic countries to "walk through NATO's open door."[13]

However, many analysts have commented on the phenomena in CEE of states turning their backs on each other as they seek integration with the West.[14] Pan-Baltic cooperation is widely perceived to have weakened, as reorientation westward has strengthened. President Vike-Freiberga has spoken of the "homework" Lithuania and Latvia still had to do to improve bilateral relations. The key task that fragments the consolidation of Baltic cooperative efforts is the ratification of the Lithuanian-Latvian maritime border in the Latvian parliament, which "was postponed because of concern over the use of traditional fishing grounds." She also noted that the last oil spill incident at the Butinge terminal on the Lithuanian coast underlined the need for the Baltic states to continue to "strive to co-ordinate action in cases of environmental pollution" and characterized safety at Butinge as "a serious problem which needs to be solved, and I'm sure that Lithuania and Latvia have the necessary resolve and political will to solve this and other pressing issues."[15]

Armed Forces

Latvia's armed forces have experienced rapid modernization since independence, although obstacles and challenges remain.[16] In April 2001 President Vaira Vike-Freiberga stated that the defense sphere firmly remains a "very high priority." Although "there is a whole range of problems," the fact that a program for the elimination of those problems has been developed, she argued, was more important than the problems themselves. She noted that the most topical tasks of the army were developing army infrastructure, educating staff, and promoting the compatibility of the Latvian army with NATO in the future. Latvia's top officials have on several occasions reaffirmed Latvia's commitment to meet NATO criteria by its summit meeting in 2002 in Prague so it can receive an invitation to join the alliance.[17]

The National Defense Concept (of June 1999) clearly followed a system of total defense, calling the defense of the state a "national objective." Central to that concept was mass mobilization, if the need arose, that was not limited to the military but that also included the economic realm. One keystone of the total defense program was conscription, and a one-year national service period was made mandatory for all young men. The country was divided into five defense regions parallel to the national administrative divisions. Those were the city of Riga and the regions of Kurzeme, Vidzeme, Latgale, and Zemgale.

The military developed three levels of planning that were tied to its development: short term (annual), medium term (quadrennial), and long term (twelve-year period). In its twelve-year long-term development plan, the military foresaw by 2012 a force numbering about 50,000, with 20 percent in active service (including active members of the national guards, Zemessardze) during any given peacetime. Over 40,000 of the individuals would come under the ground forces, alongside a modest-sized navy (1,200), air force (1,000), and other support, special, and logistics forces. As of 2000, the total number stood at just under half of the target number.[18]

The national guards, Zemessardze (home guards), are to play a significant role in the event of a mass mobilization for defense. During peacetime, a small active portion of the Zemessardze participates in activities common to other national guards around the continent, dealing with disaster relief and rescue activities. However, during times of national emergency, the reserves are activated into two distinct groups—the mobile reserves, composed of those age twenty to thirty-four, and the territorial reserves, age thirty-five to fifty-five. The territorial reserves are designed to operate in local areas unlike their mobile counterpart. The same twelve-year long-term plan foresees a mobile reserve force of 27,000 and a territorial reserve force of 17,000.

The commander of the Zemessardze, Janis Kononovs, was removed from office during early summer 2000 over a dispute with the rest of the national defense leadership, notably military commander Colonel Raimonds Graube and Defense Minister Girts Valdis Kristovskis. In a heated public war of words, Kononovs accused the military leadership of "unacceptable management methods,"[19] which prompted Colonel Graube to respond that Kononovs had a mental breakdown.[20] Juris Kiukucans was appointed to replace Kononovs in August.[21]

Training both active and reserve forces is seen as paramount in the long-term plan to foster a 50,000-strong force by the year 2012. The National Defense Academy in Riga was the primary military academy in Latvia, while the Baltic Defense College (BALTDEFCOL) in Tartu, Estonia, was an advanced school for Baltic and regional officers. The first graduating class of BALTDEFCOL completed its one-year studies in the summer of 2000, with thirty-two graduating officers from Latvia, as well as Estonia, Lithuania, Denmark, Germany, Hungary, Sweden, and the United States.[22] The 2001 class features thirty-eight officers from the same countries, as well as the Czech Republic, focusing on advanced military themes and NATO-related issues.[23]

The Latvian military participated in several large-scale cooperative projects with its Baltic neighbors and other allies. The most prominent was the joint Baltic peacekeeping battalion BALTBAT, which has served in the Balkans for several years. The Adazi training center serves as the primary training facility for BALTBAT. The three countries also participated in the joint naval fleet BALTRON, while the joint airspace surveillance system BALTNET began operations in June 2000 in Karmelava, Lithuania.[24] Throughout the year, Latvian forces participated in many military exercises under the "Partnership for Peace" aegis and hosted several large-scale exercises on its territory (including Baltic Eagle 2000, held in October).

The issue of military spending has been a difficult one in Latvia for both domestic and international consumption. Although the public saw national defense as paramount, the high increase in defense spending in lieu of similar increases for other vital sectors (such as education, which was most obvious in a teachers' strike that carried into 2000) faced resentment.

The medium-term budget plan for the military reaffirmed the promises made by Latvia in its MAP for NATO, to increase defense spending to 2 percent of GDP by 2003. That represented a formal step and a signal to the alliance about the firmness of Latvia's foreign policy course. Using estimates given by the Finance Ministry on 21 March 2000, the 2003 defense budget would reach about Latvian lats (LVL) 99.95 million (about U.S. $169.4 million, using exchange rates of that week), or 2 percent of expected GDP that year. The budget allocated LVL 42.88 million for defense spending in 2000, which is expected to amount only to about 1.05 percent of GDP. According to preliminary data, the 2001 budget will allocate LVL 54.66 million, or an expected 1.34 percent of GDP. The medium-term budget plan foresees a large jump in spending for 2002, with an increase of nearly 47 percent from 2001 to an expected 1.75 percent of GDP. The medium-term budget plan also includes a growing emphasis on infrastructure and procurements, though spending for personnel and maintenance continues to increase at a slower level. A much-needed increase in wages for personnel, an average of 80 percent across the board, was implemented already in the summer of 1999.[25]

Yet, much of Latvia's military hardware was still equipment donated by NATO member states and friendly Nordic countries. For example, in 2000 Latvia received T-55 tanks from the Czech Republic, as well as armaments from Sweden (including Bofors antiaircraft artillery), and others at no cost or for a token sum.[26] A disputed arms deal with Slovak arms manufacturer Katrim Stella moved closer to resolution after five years, as the Slovak side agreed to take back the faulty equipment it provided Latvia. However, the promise by the Slovak dealer remained unfulfilled in 2000.[27]

Latvia's small military, based on the concept of total defense, struggled to overcome obstacles and challenges to democratic security building through the 1990s. In 2000–2001 the state showed a greater willingness to raise military funding and placed a greater priority on the pace of military reform and modernization in an effort to meet NATO criteria. Yet the question remains whether the Latvian military would be capable of responding to the real threats and risks that threaten security and stability within the state.

Threat Assessment

Of the three Baltic countries, Latvia was clearly in the most fragile and precarious position with regards to its relationship with its nearest and largest neighbor—Russia.[28] Latvia's economic health was the closest tied to that of Russia, mainly by way of the profitable but highly influential oil transport business. The ethnic balance in Latvia was the most dramatic of the three countries, with Latvians accounting for only 57.6 percent of the country's population from preliminary data of the 2000 national census; in fact, no major cities had a Latvian population of more than 52 percent. More important, only about 40,000 individuals have been naturalized as Latvian citizens since the restoration of independence a decade earlier, leaving hundreds of thousands in the country as either Russian citizens or "stateless" individuals with no citizenship at all.[29]

Russia has used those statistics to its advantage in exerting influence on both the country's economic and societal security developments. A strong warning was issued in a summary to the Year 2000 White Paper on National Defense: "NATO must also be realistic about the Russian Federation's attempts to keep the Baltic States, especially Latvia, in a 'gray zone' whereby it can manipulate the Baltic States' economic and security environments for its own political and economic gains."[30] In regards to security, out of the three Baltic states, Latvia feels the most threatened by Russia. In contrast, Lithuania enjoys relatively good relations with Russia, while Estonia issued a policy statement in 2000 that stated that Russia posed no direct military threat in the near term.[31] However, the Latvian National Defense Concept that was adopted by the government in June 1999 clearly stated that "the internal situation in Russia is unstable" and "its domestic and foreign policy is difficult to predict."[32]

Russia's leverage over Latvia was largely economic, based primarily on the oil transport business. The oil pipeline from Russia to the port city of Ventspils, which according to city data, accounted for 15 percent of Russia's crude oil exports in 2000, provided a significant amount of revenue for Latvia's economy (exceeding U.S. $100 million annually), and was a source of substantial income even during the Russian (and later regional) economic crisis of 1998–99. That economic lever for Russian influence in Latvia was further complicated by the development of a Russian-EU partnership based on the export of hydrocarbon energy. Not only was the EU interested in using existing energy and other transit routes between Russia and the West, including those that crossed Latvia, but also, according to Latvian transport minister Anatolijs Gorbunovs, it was also prepared to invest in that infrastructure.[33]

Though Russia was not in a position to use its oil exports as a bargaining chip against Latvia because of its own precarious economic state and its need for oil revenues, the power of "king oil" grew into a powerful political lobby. Several political parties, most notably the large centrist Latvia's Way, were perceived to have a very cozy relationship with the oil shipment business, and the influence of Ventspils was seen as dominant within the country. Ventspils's mayor, Aivars Lembergs, was seen by many as the most powerful politician in Latvia. Often Ventspils's interests would pressure the rest of Latvia to concede to Russian demands for the sake of improving business—or oil transhipment—ties.

The most worrisome development as far as threats to Latvia's national security over 2000 was terrorism. The first instance occurred in September, with an explosion at the old town Centrs department store in Riga that caused scores of injuries and one death.[34] A second terrorist act happened on the eve of independence day, when members of the ultraradical Russian group National Bolsheviks threatened to detonate a grenade on the spire of the historic St. Peter's Church in the heart of Riga's old town in protest against the prosecution of Soviet officials for genocide and against Latvia's bid for NATO membership.[35] Russian officials had warned their Latvian counterparts of possible disruptive actions committed by extremists in Latvia.[36] At the same time, the right-wing Latvian nationalist Perkonkrusts were also exacerbating tensions by launching a small-scale bombing campaign against Soviet-era monuments, and several of the organization's members were convicted of terrorism in mid-2000.[37]

An offshoot of that threat was a series of attacks on Latvian diplomatic properties in Russia, especially the Latvian consulate in St. Petersburg. The consulate experienced several fire bombings in 2000, and calls by Latvia for Russian officials to provide additional security were not acted upon. The National Bolsheviks were active in organizing protests outside of Latvian diplomatic compounds throughout the Commonwealth of Independent States, and many officials feared there was a direct link between the protests and the fire bombings. Another radical group, Workers of Russia, threatened the Latvian ambassador in March with kidnapping in retaliation for Latvia's prosecution of former Soviet officials for genocide.[38]

Finally, an indirect but serious threat to Latvia's security was the rapid growth of HIV infection. In 2000 just under 500 individuals were diagnosed with HIV, bringing the total infection rate in the country of 2.4 million close to the 1,000 mark.[39]

The extent to which the EU influenced the treatment of minority and refugee and asylum issues in Latvia, by implicitly lending external support and legitimization to particular sections of the elite that opposed moves to further tighten citizenship and related legislation, has been noted.[40] The fact that the EU produced such a powerful critique revealed not so much the breadth of the minority problem itself, but the extent to which EU integration had come to shape the political and policy-making landscapes within the Baltic states. As Latvian foreign minister Indulis Berzins noted in August 1999: "As this country integrates into transatlantic structures, so will Russian speakers integrate into Latvia."[41] By May 2000 Swedish foreign minister Anna Lindh announced that Sweden was in favor of the Organization for Security and Cooperation in Europe (OSCE) winding up its missions in Estonia and Latvia. She pointed out that Latvia and Estonia have observed practically all of the recommendations made by OSCE high commissioner to national minorities Max van der Stoel. That was the first statement by a respected Western politician unequivocally favoring the closure of the OSCE missions in Estonia and Latvia.[42]

Future Prospects

Latvia's political elite argued that it was on the fast track to first-wave EU integration, a process that was progressing well. One recent trend, however, threatened to undermine that progress—the growing role of Latvian public opinion in shaping state policies toward integration. While the issue of EU integration had not caused a political cleavage among parties by the late 1990s, the possibility of elite political consensus fracturing under the frustration of delayed integration was present by the end of the decade. By 2001 Latvian foreign minister Indulis Berzins argued that the setback suffered by "pro-European" governing parties (the People's Party, For Fatherland and Freedom, and Latvia's Way) in municipal elections in Riga (11 March 2001) was in no way indicative of growing Euro-skepticism.[43] However, looking to the 2002 Saeima (parliament) elections, it appeared that the number of Euro-skeptics and Euro-skeptic parties (Social Democrats, the leftist movement "For Human Rights in a United Latvia") were increasing in strength, thus endangering a possible referendum on EU accession. Growing Euro-skepticism was a trend notable among other states within the region, particularly Poland, Romania, and Bulgaria.

Although Russia opposed NATO enlargement, specifically the possible admission of the three Baltic countries that were on the waiting list along with nine other contenders, NATO consistently argued that the central and east European states would be judged on eligibility for NATO membership on the basis of their own ability to demonstrate successful democratic security building policies, rather than on Russian interests or objections. U.S. secretary of state Colin Powell directly told the Latvian president:

"Russia would never be given a veto over who is or who is not part of NATO and we will examine each country in accordance with the conditions and standards put forth."[44] In February 2001, on a trip to Moscow, NATO secretary-general George Robertson played down Russian fears that the European security balance would be destabilized by the eastward expansion of the alliance. "I know that Russia has reservations to what it sees as the eastern expansion of NATO. But I do not believe that any expansion or any enlargement of NATO threatens to upset any existing balance." He added that, "the fact that a few new countries may join the NATO alliance would in no way upset existing balances or threaten any good relationship that exists between NATO and Russia." Although there had been Russian worries over first-wave enlargement (Poland, Hungary, and the Czech Republic), "membership has now produced a zone of real stability in Central Europe, which I believe has been to the advantage of Russia. Indeed the political geography of Europe remains very similar and would remain very similar after any potential enlargement."[45]

Latvia and the other two Baltic states have consistently promoted stability and security as foreign policy goals, and they have promoted democratic security building within the armed forces as a means to that end. Baltic foreign and security policies were prompted by the historical experience of Soviet occupation and a desire to "return to Europe" and share the benefits that stability within an enlarging "zone of democratic peace" brings. Although the Economist Intelligence Unit published a report in February 2001 expressing skepticism about Latvia's ability to attain its key foreign policy aims by the declared minimal deadlines—joining NATO already in 2002 and the EU in early 2004[46]—there was no doubt that all three Baltic states would achieve EU and NATO integration criteria over the next five years.

Still, some ask whether the attainment of NATO integration criteria will bring NATO membership. Latvia, Estonia, and Lithuania posed an existential question for NATO, as painful as that asked by Kosovo in April 1999. The ethnic cleansing within Kosovo forced NATO to adapt its strategic concept, to move from collective defense to collective security, or risk being fatally undermined by its lack of a raison d'etre in the contemporary world. At the other end of the spectrum of state-building projects, the consolidated democratic Baltic states that had demonstrably met the required criteria by 2005 should be integrated by NATO, not so much for the sake of enhancing their stability, but more to protect the integrity and credibility of NATO. If NATO fails to integrate states that fulfill objective criteria but cannot attain "strategic acceptability," that raises the question of what is the purpose of NATO in the twenty-first century.

Failure to enlarge undermines the theoretical and ideological underpinning of NATO, delegitimizing it and also destabilizing Europe's security environment. Latvian foreign and security policy is therefore likely to continue to provide us with a contemporary litmus test of the direction and pace of the development of the European security order.[47] The ultimate result of Latvia's quest for NATO membership will demonstrate whether the West opts for integration and enhanced Baltic security or the extension of "gray zones" and the institutionalization of a dependent eastern periphery. That quest has become the defining leitmotif for European security eleven years after the end of the Cold War.

NOTES

1. We gratefully acknowledge helpful comments and references from Dr. Armands Gutmanis, undersecretary of state, Ministry of Foreign Affairs, Latvia; Valerie J. Collins, University of Aberdeen; and the Latvian embassy, Washington, D.C. All errors of fact and interpretation remain our own.

2. R. Karklins, *Ethnopolitics and Transition to Democracy. The Collapse of the USSR and Latvia* (Washington, D.C.: Woodrow Wilson Center Press, 1994); C. Archer & G. Herd, "The Baltic and Beyond: Does Europe End at the Urals?" in *The Unification of Europe? An Analysis of Enlargement.* Jenkins, C., ed. (London: Centre for Reform, 2000), 47–56.

3. BNS news agency, Tallinn, 4 December 2000.

4. The president participated in a round-table discussion called Baltic Dimension of New Europe, held at the Center for Strategic and International Studies, where leading European affairs experts in Washington took part. This deliberately echoed former U.S. president George Bush Sr.'s speech made in Germany in 1989, in which he called for establishing a free and united Europe. LETA news agency, Riga, 25 April 2001.

5. Interfax news agency, Moscow, 11 February 2001.

6. BNS news agency, Tallinn, 16 February 2001.

7. BNS news agency, Tallinn, 26 January 2001.

8. Latvian Radio, Riga, 19 December 2000.

9. S. Arnswald, *EU Enlargement and the Baltic States. The Incremental Making of New Members*. Program on the Northern Dimension of the CFSP. (Helsinki, Finland: Finnish Institute of International Affairs, 2000).

10. Latvian Radio, Riga, 10 December 1999.

11. News from Latvia, *Central Europe Review*, 25 September 2000, http://www. ce-review.org/00/32/latvianews32.html

12. *Baltic States Report*, Radio Free Europe/Radio Liberty, 22 May 2000.

13. *Newsline*, Radio Free Europe/Radio Liberty, 19 January 1998. See also: "The Baltic States": "The special nature of our relationship with Estonia, Latvia and Lithuania is recognized in the 1998 Charter of Partnership, which clarifies the principles upon which U.S. relations with the Baltic states are based and provides a framework for strengthening ties and pursuing common goals. These goals include integration of Latvia, Lithuania and Estonia into the transatlantic community and development of close, co-operative relationships among all the states in Northeastern Europe. Through the Northern European Initiative we seek to strengthen regional coopera- tion, enhance regional security and stability, and promote the growth of Western in- stitutions, trade and investment by bringing together the governments and private sector interests in the Baltic and Nordic countries, Poland, Germany and Russia." *A National Security Strategy for a New Century, The White House December 1999.* For PDF full text, see: http://www.dtic.mil/doctrine/jel/other_pubs/nssr99.pdf

14. Z. Ozolina, "Latvia, the EU and Baltic Sea Co-operation," in *The European Union and The Baltic States. Visions, Interests and Strategies for the Baltic Sea Region,* S. Arnswald and M. Jopp, eds. Program on the Northern Dimension of the CFSP. (Helsinki, Finland: The Finnish Institute of International Affairs, 1998).

15. BNS news agency, Tallinn, 15 March 2001.

16. I. Viskne, "Latvia and Europe's Security Structures," in *The Baltic States Security and Defense after Independence,* Peter Van Ham, ed. Chaillot paper No. 19. 1995, www.weu.int/institute/chaillot

17. BNS news agency, Tallinn, 19 April 2001.

18. "White Paper" 2000 report by the Latvian defense minister. See http://www.mod.lv/ english/

19. *Newsline*, Radio Free Europe/Radio Liberty, 7 July 2000.

20. News from Latvia, *Central Europe Review*, 10 July 2000, http://www.ce-review.org/ 00/27/latvianews27.html

21. *Baltic States Report*, Radio Free Europe/Radio Liberty, 1 September 2000.

22. *Estonian Review*, 19 June–2 July 2000, published by the Estonian Foreign Ministry, http://www.vm.ee/eng/review/2000/review25-26.htm

23. *Estonian Review*, 17–23 July 2000, published by the Estonian Foreign Ministry, http://www.vm.ee/eng/review/2000/review29.htm

24. *Newsline*, Radio Free Europe/Radio Liberty, 7 June 2000.

25. Budget data from the Latvian MOD web site: http://www.mod.lv/english/

26. News from Latvia, *Central Europe Review*, 2 October 2000, http://www.ce-review. org/00/33/latvianews33.html

27. *Baltic States Report*, Radio Free Europe/Radio Liberty, 20 November 2000.

28. For further discussion, see: A. Stranga, "Baltic-Russian Relations: 1995—Beginning of 1997" in *Small States in a Turbulent Environment: The Baltic Perspective*, A. Lejins and Z. Ozolina, eds. (Riga, Latvia: The Latvian Institute of International Affairs, 1997), 184–237; A. Moshes, *Overcoming Unfriendly Stability. Russian-Latvian Relations at the End of the 1990s*. Program of the Northern Dimension of the CFSP (Helsinki, Finland: Finnish Institute of International Affairs, 1999); S. Medvedev, *Russia's Futures. Implications for the EU, the North and the Baltic Region*. Program on the Northern Dimension of the CFSP (Helsinki, Finland: Finnish Institute of International Affairs, 2000).

29. News from Latvia, *Central Europe Review*, 12 March 2001, http://www.ce-review. org/01/10/latvianews10.html. See also: M. Cichock, "Interdependence and Manipulation in the Russian-Baltic Relationship: 1993–1997," *Journal of Baltic Studies* 30, no. 2 (1999): 89–117.

30. "Report of the Minister of Defense to the Parliament (Saeima) on State Defense Policy and Armed Forces Development for the Year 2000" (White Paper, English-language, summer), chapter 2, http://www.mod.lv/english/09inform/2dala.php

31. *Estonian Defense Digest*, 6–21 September 2000, published by the Estonian Foreign Ministry, http://www.vm.ee/eng/publications/Defense/def1.htm

32. National Defense Concept of the Republic of Latvia, adopted by the government on 6 June 1999, http://www.mod.lv/english/08akti/02defense.php

33. ITAR-TASS news agency, Moscow, 9 March 2001. See also: D. Gowan, *How the EU Can Help Russia* (London: Centre for European Reform, 2000).

34. *Newsline*, Radio Free Europe/Radio Liberty, 18 August 2000. Previously explosions occurred either in peripheral locations (gas or old munitions) or specific targets (often linked to rival organized crime groups), but this was the first real incident of terrorism directed at the general public. Though the bombing remains unsolved and investigators hint at a possible economic motive to the attack, it nevertheless opened the eyes of officials to the danger terrorism presented.

35. News from Latvia, *Central Europe Review*, 20 November 2000, http://www. ce-review.org/00/40/latvianews40.html. Though the grenade turned out to be a toy and the perpetrators eventually were apprehended, it nevertheless brought fears of terrorism by radical organizations to the public. Several members of the group from Russia were also apprehended the same week for illegal entry into Latvia, while some others were believed to have absconded after sneaking into the country.

36. *Baltic States Report*, Radio Free Europe/Radio Liberty, 29 November 2000.

37. News Review for Latvia, *Central Europe Review*, 5 June 2000, http://www.ce-review. org/00/22/latvianews22.html

38. News Review for Latvia, *Central Europe Review*, 27 March 2000, http://www. ce-review.org/00/12/latvianews12.html

39. News from Latvia, *Central Europe Review,* 12 March 2001, http://www.ce-review .org/01/10/latvianews10.html. Unlike Estonia, Latvia has yet to address the issue of new threats to its security within its national security concept.

40. M. Jubulis, "The External Dimension of Democratization in Latvia: The Impact of European Institutions," *International Relations* 13, no. 3 (1996), 59–73.

41. RIA news agency, Moscow, 23 August 1999.

42. BNS news agency, Tallinn, 29 May 2000.

43. Latvian Radio, Riga, 13 March 2001.

44. BNS news agency, Tallinn, 15 March 2001.

45. ITAR-TASS news agency, Moscow, 19 February 2001.

46. BNS news agency, 2 February 2001. The Economist Intelligence Unit (EIU) working on a regular report about Latvia's political and economic development prospects came to this skeptical conclusion. It argued that EU enlargement is stalling over the uncertain fate of internal institutional reforms and that NATO enlargement is also likely to be delayed over differences between European and American factions, especially as the alliance seeks to improve relations with Russia.

47. This idea echoes that of C. Bildt, "The Baltic Litmus Test," *Foreign Affairs* 72, no. 5 (1994), 73–85, who in the early 1990s argued that Russia's policies toward the Baltic states were a litmus test for its respect more generally for democratic values, sovereignty, independence, and international law.

12 • Lithuania Continues Pursuing NATO

Graeme P. Herd

Ten years after the collapse of the Soviet Union, the three Baltic States collectively commemorated the "January 10–13 Events" of 1991.[1] In Vilnius and Riga, conservative Communist factions had attempted a coup to enforce the territorial integrity of the Soviet Union. Paradoxically, those events had the opposite effect: they consolidated Lithuanian opinion against Moscow and heightened the perception that Soviet president Mikhail Gorbachev had lost control over domestic events and the USSR's foreign policy agenda. The "January Events" and bloodshed in Vilnius and Riga finally brought into international focus the likelihood that the Soviet Union would collapse and consolidated the international communities' policy responses to ensure a "soft-landing" transition. It provided a crucial bridge to final Western recognition of sovereignty and territorial integrity (which occurred following the abortive August coup of 1991), by promoting Russian president Boris Yeltsin's power base and the status of the Russian Soviet Federated Socialist Republic (RSFSR) in relation to the USSR and legitimizing the emergence of the Russian Federation. As Latvian president Vaira Vike-Freiberga commented: "Ten years ago on January 13, 1991 the Soviet elite units, attacking the Vilnius television tower, killed over 10 unarmed civilians. A week later a similar attack in Riga caused new bloodshed and losses of lives again. The cruelty of these attacks shocked the international community and triggered its support for non-violent independence movements in Latvia, Lithuania and Estonia."[2]

While the quality of democratic transition was mainly determined by the length and character of Communist dictatorship (for example, seventy years in Ukraine, forty years in Lithuania), it was also influenced by the nature of the political system before the Communist takeover and the pace of development since then. The "barricades period" has proved to be a critical stepping-stone for post-Soviet Lithuanian state building, setting the tone for interethnic relations, national self-definition, and state-building projects. It also helped shape post-Soviet Russian attitudes and relations with the former republics, particularly the Baltic states. Undoubtedly, the legacy of Sovietization was the key determinant in shaping the foreign and security policies of the three Baltic states. Issues relating to the lack of agreement on border delineation, the withdrawal of Soviet military units, energy dependency on Russia, and the exercise of full control over an inherited nuclear power complex dominated the early post-Soviet period (1991–94). Although linked by history and geography, in two important respects Lithuania did not share common security concerns with Latvia and Estonia: the "diaspora question" was absent from internal security discourse, while the "Kaliningrad question" was predominant.

During the first republic period of independence (1918–40), various minorities (mainly Russians, Poles, and Jews) whose local culture had been shaped over generations lived on Baltic territory. Here the "native" population, by this time defined more by language than by any standards of ethnic purity, was in the majority: in Estonia 92 percent; in Latvia 77 percent; and in Lithuania 83 percent. However, wartime occupation by German and Soviet forces and subsequent reoccupation by Soviet forces (1944) resulted in drastic changes in the ethnic compositions of Estonian and Latvian societies, but only a gradual diminution of Lithuania's titular majority. While in the 1960s, 1970s, and 1980s mainly Russian-speaking workers came from other parts of the USSR to work in all-Union factories in Estonia and Latvia, this was much less a characteristic of Lithuanian migratory settlement. In this respect, Lithuania reflected other European states, where less than 10 percent of the population is foreign born, while according to the 1989 census, in Estonia and Latvia, around 26 percent of the population was foreign born.[3] The overall changes in the ethnic composition of Lithuania are placed within a Baltic comparative context in table 1 below.

As is clear from the data, both Estonia and Latvia experienced a severe decline in the relative proportion of the native population by 1989, while in Lithuania the indigenous population remained dominant. This is attributed to an overall larger population and higher rate of population growth; a slower pace of industrialization, which did not justify such a large migrant

TABLE 2. Percentage of Titular/Native Population in the Baltic States

	1939[4]	1959	1989	1991	1999[5]	2000[6]
Estonia	92.4	74.6	61.5	62.0	65.2	67.0
Latvia	77.0	62.0	52.0	54.0	56.0	57.0
Lithuania	83.9	79.3	80.0	81.0	82.0	83.0

labor force; and the availability of labor from rural areas for urban industries. Note also that the majority of nonnative residents are Russians in Estonia and Latvia, whereas in Lithuania they are divided mainly between Russian speakers and Poles. The slight increase in the native population since independence is attributed in part to emigration, which reached its peak soon after independence (for example, the departure of military forces and defense industry employees) and has now dropped to more expected levels.

Perceived socioeconomic inequalities and naturalization and resident permit frustrations in Estonia and Latvia have allowed Moscow to argue that the treatment of Russian minorities and retired Soviet military pensioners constituted a serious point of contention in their bilateral relations. However, since at independence Lithuania declared that all Soviet citizens living on Lithuanian territory at the time of independence would automatically gain Lithuanian citizenship (the "zero option") and given the homogeneity of Lithuania's population, the question of the treatment of the diaspora did not cloud Lithuanian-Russian relations.

Threat Assessment

Given that Lithuania's foreign and security policy core objectives remain full NATO and EU membership, all obstacles and challenges to integration can be considered threats to Lithuanian stability and should be assessed. Although the geostrategic, economic, and political shift of Europe's center of gravity eastward—exemplified by the movement of Germany's capital from Bonn to Berlin and first-echelon NATO integration—has strengthened Lithuania's claim to lie at the crossroads of Europe, second-echelon integration is still deeply contentious. While the Russian Federation welcomes Baltic integration into the European Union (EU)—subject to certain considerations—it vehemently opposes NATO expansion in the region. Russia has been accused of accepting that the Yalta line has been breached but attempting to hold the so-called Ribbentrop line.

On 18–19 May 2000 the foreign ministers of nine applicants for second-echelon NATO membership met in Vilnius. There they devised a common strategy to NATO integration and issued the Vilnius Statement/Declaration: "While each country should be considered on its own merits, we believe that the integration of each democracy will be a success for us all and the integration of all our countries will be a success to Europe."[7] Lithuania's central role in coordinating a united central and east Europe (CEE) "big bang" approach to integration reflects both its status as a second-echelon front runner and its exasperation at the loss of enlargement momentum. Such an attitude is underlined by a reassessment of Lithuanian diplomatic efforts to gain NATO membership. In 2001 the appointment of a fourth deputy foreign minister within Lithuania's Ministry of Foreign Affairs most clearly delineated its foreign policy priorities. Antanas Valionis, Lithuania's foreign minister, has appointed Evaldas Ignatavicius, formerly Lithuania's consul general to Kaliningrad, to head the bilateral relations department, with particular emphasis to be placed on Lithuanian-Russian relations.[8] The other three deputy foreign ministers cover NATO integration (Giedrius Cekuolis), integration with the EU and economic relations (Dalia Grybauskaite), and international law, consular affairs, and UN relations (Oskaras Jusys).[9] Lithuanian diplomatic representation and activity has also been increased abroad, with a greater focus placed on influencing U.S. political opinion ahead of the 2002 NATO Summit, with 2001 designated "the year of NATO."

However, over the year 2000, a number of powerful factors that had driven first-wave enlargement began to lose their potency, implicitly downgrading further enlargement as an agenda priority. At a meeting with Lithuanian parliament chairman Vytautas Landsbergis, British officials outlined reservations on Lithuanian membership in NATO that reflected views expressed by some allied governments and officials. Some of the counterarguments to Baltic membership were generic—too many member states would make NATO's decision making unwieldy, and further enlargement could only take place once the successful and productive integration of Poland, Hungary, and the Czech Republic had been ascertained. Others were specific to the Baltic states—they were too small to be useful to the alliance, and Russia, while not having a veto, had a voice and it had to be recognized that Europe's largest country vehemently opposed Baltic inclusion. It was argued that the Baltic states were qualitatively different from CEE states in that they had been part of the Soviet Union, and Russia's continual and persistently repeated opposition to NATO integration of the former Soviet republics would precipitate a collapse of Russian cooperation with the European security order. Those influential objections could cause NATO's 2002 summit to postpone a decision inviting the Baltic states to join the alliance.

Moreover, the integration of the former Yugoslavia into the international community became a more pressing priority for NATO, with the initiation of the Kosovo campaign and the withdrawal of Serb forces through 1999, which eventually led to the collapse of the Slobodan Milosevic regime after the October Events of 2000. By early 2001 the specter of a U.S.-driven National Missile Defense (NMD) being implemented raised the prospect that finance and energy would also be directed toward that mainstay of President George Bush's foreign and security policy. Furthermore, within Europe, Germany ceased to be the motor of enlargement as Poland's integration into NATO lessened the strategic necessity for further inclusion.

Lithuanian officials argue that they have consistently supported NATO's policy on Kosovo and that Lithuania's inclusion would strengthen the alliance's cohesion and reinforce predictability in decision making. Therefore, they argued that making Lithuania's integration into NATO contingent upon the ability of the Czech Republic to fully support NATO policy, for example, would undermine the principle of being judged on one's own merits and capabilities. In response to another frequently voiced argument against its inclusion, bluntly formulated as "small is useless," it was pointed out that while Iceland and Luxembourg were smaller than Lithuania, they had proven useful to the alliance. Despite its size, Lithuanian officials stressed that the country's strategic location provided a unique and stabilizing asset to the alliance. Failure to enlarge, they argued, would decrease not increase stability, and would serve as recognition of the Soviet incorporation of Lithuania in the past and the acceptance of a de facto Russian veto over Baltic inclusion in the present, penalizing Lithuania for the actions of others and weakening NATO's own credibility and legitimacy.

Armed Forces

Lithuania's armed forces were formally reestablished by the Seimas on 19 November 1992 and consist of the regular armed forces (ground, air, and naval forces), the National Defense Volunteer Forces (NDVF) and the active reserve forces. The ground forces constitute the largest element within Lithuania's military establishment, with 7,500 soldiers (7,200 of which compose the six battalions of the motorized infantry brigade Iron Wolf and Zemaitija), and approximately 4,500 civil servants.[10] The Lithuanian air force has 700 personnel, two active airfields, training and transport aircraft, and transport and general-purpose light aircraft. As of 2000 the air force did not have combat units or combat aircraft. The Lithuanian naval force consists of 600 personnel. Its flotilla of six vessels operates out of the port of Klaipeda with the aim of guarding Lithuania's territorial waters and economic zone. The NDVF is an important part of Lithuania's military forces, composed of approximately 12,000 personnel, is trained for conventional and nonconventional warfare, and will in the future be integrated into the land forces.[11] Lithuania has adopted a North European defense model based on the principles of conscription (twelve months of primary service), mass mobilization, and a "total defense" and territorial defense concept. It has divided the country into three military regions (Western, Central, and Eastern) and served to integrate the different component parts of Lithuania's military establishment within this structure.[12]

Spending on defense within Lithuania has gradually risen from 1.7 percent of GDP in 2000 to 1.95 percent of GDP in 2001.[13] Foreign military assistance has complemented Lithuania's defense expenditure and promoted trilateral military cooperation. The Baltic Defense College (BALTDEFCOL), for example, aims to train the Baltic militaries in higher and senior military education and is located in Tartu, Estonia. It began joint staff officers' education and training in August 1999–June 2000, the first intake consisting of thirty-two students from eight countries, rising to thirty-seven students from ten countries in the 2000–2001 intake. In the spring of 2001, a civil servant course was taught to improve the skills of the students as policy advisers and to deepen their understanding of "the development of security policy and the interaction and interdependence between political decision makers, civil servants, and military structures."[14] Political and economic capital has been spent creating this military interoperable capability in order to underscore a Baltic commitment to "producing" security within NATO rather than simply "consuming" it.

The Lithuanian Individual Partnership Program (IPP) and participation in the Planning and Review Process (PARP) have served to strengthen Lithuania's preparation for NATO membership. Both projects concentrate on improving language training, C3 systems, air defense, and military education. A NATO-compatible Baltic Airspace Surveillance Network (BALTNET) provided a comprehensive regional defensive network and was developed within the framework of the U.S.-sponsored Regional Airspace Initiative in 1994. It had a Regional Air Surveillance Coordination Center (RASCC) based in Lithuania at Karmelava (near Kaunas), which began operating in June 2000. This is linked to three national radar subcenters. BALTNET aims to ensure increased aviation safety and in crisis situations will assist military activity; it does not compete with national systems; rather it helps them integrate their joint capability. BALTNET is compatible with similar systems operating in Sweden, and U.S. Air Force E-3A AWACs based in Keflavik air base (Iceland) could be incorporated into a Baltic regional air coordination system. At Palanga on 19 December 2000, Baltic defense ministers agreed to set up an aerial surveillance training center at Karmelava and discussed the possibility of creating a joint air force transport squadron (BALTWING).

Although practical naval cooperation began with a common exercise called Amber Sea 95, the Baltic Naval Squadron (BALTRON), based at Tallinn, was not launched until 1998. On 16 April 1998 the Baltic defense ministers signed a formal agreement initiating the project that was formally inaugurated on 28 August 1998. BALTRON had a combined mine countermeasures capability (Open Spirit 98, MCOPEST 98, U.S. BALTOPS-99 exercises), as well as search and rescue tasks and maritime law-and-order operations, and contributed to the reduction of environmental damage in territorial waters. Lithuania, like Estonia and Latvia, has made available one or two vessels each year to BALTRON. These consist of German-donated minesweepers (Frauenlob and Kondor class) or minehunters (Lindau class).

Germany has assumed a leading role in setting up BALTRON by coordinating assistance received from other states—particularly the United States and the Nordic sponsors. Involvement in BALTRON has helped develop Lithuania's national naval forces and more generally raised the self-defense capability of the Baltic states. Through the adoption of NATO Partnership for Peace (PfP) naval and staff procedures, Lithuania's participation has also promoted interoperability with NATO PfP navies. This was reinforced by BALTRON's participation in the BALTRON and Mine Countermeasures Force Northwestern Europe (MCMFN) in exercise PASSEX-99.[15]

The Baltic Peacekeeping Battalion (BALTBAT) was developed as a concept in 1993–94, and its headquarters started operating in Adazi (near Riga) in 1996. It has a permanent command structure; its activities are funded equally by the budgets of the three member states and designed for peacekeeping, rescue, and humanitarian operations. Lithuania has contributed through the deployment and rotation of BALTBAT platoons and companies (BALTCONS) within the Danish Peacekeeping Battalion (part of the Nordic-Polish Brigade) in Implementation Force and Stabilization Force operations in Bosnia and with the Polish Kosovo Force contingent in Kosovo. Although the Baltic defense ministers ratified the use of BALTBAT on international missions in support of UN Chapter 5 operations from 1998 onward, it has yet to be deployed as a battalion. Hitherto BALTBAT has been promoted as the most extensive example of trilateral military cooperation, but in 2000 it was acknowledged that this force lacks financial and logistical support from the Baltic states themselves. As one former BALTBAT training team instructor noted, "Both the Baltic States and also some of the supporting countries have clearly shown a lack of interest and will to support the project."[16]

As a result, Lithuania has indicated that trilateral military cooperation may be downgraded in favor of bilateral support and cooperation such as increasing interoperability with NATO and implementing NATO partnership goals. Particularly important in this respect has been the creation in early 1999 of the Lithuania-Polish Peacekeeping Battalion (LITPOLBAT). Polish weapons donations and advocacy of Lithuania's early NATO membership have increased the importance of Lithuania's strategic partnership with Poland.[17]

Foreign Policy in Relation to Security

Lithuania's foreign policy priorities have remained stable over the last ten years, and according to Evaldas Ignatavicius, deputy foreign minister in charge of bilateral relations, "The priority of co-operating with neighbouring states has remained in place, and we see the need for further strengthening and expanding those ties."[18] However, the status of Russia's only exclave has proved a constant thread running through Lithuanian foreign and security policy over the last ten years. It shapes the tone of Russian-Lithuanian relations, influences Lithuania's prospects to integrate into the dual enlargement project, and has a growing impact on Lithuania's strategic partnership with Poland and relations with Belarus. Lithuania continues to develop a pragmatic relationship with Belarus and will attempt to solve the most pressing problems in interstate relations, namely, Belarusian debt for electricity exported from Lithuania and demarcation of the shared border. However, the continued status of Belarus as an increasingly introspective bastion of anti–dual enlargement rhetoric and the growing authoritarianism of its president present Lithuania with a growing security threat on its eastern border.

Beyond that, Russia's Kaliningrad region represents the highest profile of the security issues that dominate Lithuania's foreign policy agenda. Since Russian president Vladimir Putin has argued that Kaliningrad is to be the "pilot project," or litmus test, of Russian-EU cooperative capacity, Kaliningrad presents Lithuania with a seemingly intractable security paradox. Failure by Russia and the EU to accommodate Kaliningrad within an enlarged EU will lead to both Kaliningrad's proliferation of soft security threats within the region and its increasing economic and political dependency upon Moscow. However, a successful integration of Kaliningrad into the EU is contingent on a reduction in Moscow's sovereignty over this region, and so a possible growth of autonomy and even separatism within what will become an EU enclave.[19]

The elaboration and implementation of EU policies toward Kaliningrad is largely dependent on Russian, Polish, and Lithuanian cooperation and collaboration. Lithuania is linked to Kaliningrad through joint participation in the envisaged Baltic Euroregion, and the Neman Euroregion (linking Lithuania with Kaliningrad and Belarus) and Saule Euroregions (linking key Kaliningrad towns with Lithuanian, Latvian, and Swedish participants). More concretely, on 10 February 2000 Russia and Lithuania submitted a list of joint project proposals to the EU Commission (the Nida Declaration) for consideration by the Northern Dimension Action Plan. These proposals (e.g., transport modernization, environmental protection, cross-border cooperation) were approved by the EU Feira summit in June 2000 and represent the emergence of regional and subregional interdependency.[20]

The EU pushes before it a massive wall of regulation, which some analysts have referred to as a de facto "silver" or "paper curtain" that must be swallowed whole on membership. However, since Lithuania and Poland will join the Schengen agreement as part of their preaccession procedures, the impact of the EU will first be felt through the formation of an EU border policy. This border policy will be shaped by EU perceptions of Kaliningrad. Does it represent a "Baltic Hong Kong" in the making or a "West Berlin of the twenty-first century," or a "collapsed" Russian province, a forgotten backwater with the potential to destabilize the entire Baltic region? Kaliningrad has suffered from a growing reputation as an unstable and poorly administered center for the proliferation of soft security threats. The role of organized crime gangs, drugs, small arms, and illegal migrant networks within the black economy is complemented by accusations that elite politicians (such as the outgoing governor, Leonid Gorbenko) have managed insider privatization projects in the shipyard industries, suggesting that crime in Kaliningrad is endemic and systemic.

As this negative perception increases, it is highly questionable whether the visa-free regime with Kaliningrad can be maintained. The strict enforcement of a visa regime would undermine Kaliningrad's status as a Special Economic Zone and prove detrimental to local business, particularly the role of tourism and shuttle traders (the main source of income to 10 percent of the region), who buy goods in one republic to resell in the flea markets of another. It would increase the region's dependency on subsidies from Moscow (80 percent of food stuffs are imported from Lithuania, Poland, and Germany), and it would undermine Kaliningrad's participation in the development of European-Baltic energy and regional transport infrastructure projects, such as the Trans-European Networks and the Pan-European Transport Corridors.

In January 2001 Russia denied accusations made in *The Washington Times* (3 January 2001) that Russia had transferred to and deployed tactical nuclear weapons in the Kaliningrad region in June 2000 as a response to NATO enlargement. This followed Russia's organization of a major war game scenario (West 99) in the Baltic region, which simulated an attack by the alliance against Kaliningrad from Poland, which had joined NATO that year. Other analysts attributed the move to President Putin's new military doctrine on first use of nuclear weapons. Lithuanian president Valdas Adamkus noted that, although it was necessary to clarify the matter, there was no reason to panic, because "it is against Russia's interests to introduce nuclear weapons in an isolated zone, cut off from the rest of its territory. This is not logical from a military point of view."[21]

Future Prospects for Lithuania

Ten years after the "January Events" of 1991 Lithuanian prime minister Rolandas Paksas indicated that Baltic strategic cooperation was no longer the priority that it had been in the early 1990s. The romantic interpretation of Baltic cooperation, he argued, as "a paradigm of the past" ought to be rejected with the realization that the Baltic states were now normal competitors.[22] At the same time, Lithuania planned to raise the controversial issue of Russian compensation for damages Lithuania suffered under Soviet occupation: "We are obliged to do so by a referendum held in Lithuania and by legislation adopted, and Russia has certain obligations in these matters as well."[23] While the "paradigm of the past" still has some resonance in contemporary Lithuanian security politics discourse, what are the future prospects for Lithuanian security?

Lithuania signed its Europe Agreement in 1995 and has placed EU integration as a foreign policy priority. Lithuania's political and psychological strategic reorientation westward has been most obviously reflected in the growing role of the EU as an economic partner at the expense of Commonwealth of Independent States (CIS) trade and its ability to overcome outstanding barriers to integration. In 1994, 48.61 percent of trade was with the CIS, 26.10 percent with the EU. By 1999, 45.40 percent was with the EU and 21.53 percent with the CIS, with 63.14 percent of all direct foreign investment coming from the EU states. Following the 10 December

1999 Helsinki EU summit, Lithuania began the accession negotiations with the EU on 15 February 2000, and by February 2001 had closed ten of the thirty-one chapters.

According to the EU's Agenda 2000, Lithuania has no territorial disputes with any EU member or candidate states—a necessary precondition for integration. The presidents of Russia and Lithuania signed an agreement on marine and terrestrial borders on 24 October 1997, and that agreement was ratified by the Lithuanian Seimas in 2000. However, the Russian State Duma has still not ratified the accord. Latvia and Lithuania had signed an agreement on their sea border in July 1999. The EU is to provide 1.33 million euros for the demarcation of 110 kilometers of Belarus's 520 kilometer Lithuanian border under a memorandum that the Belarusian State Border Troops Committee signed with the European Commission on 23 January 2001.

Apart from the assistance the EU has promised to provide for border demarcation, it has also promised aid toward closing Lithuania's Soviet-era nuclear power stations. On 29 December 2000 the EU signed a financial memorandum on the closing of the first RBMK-type nuclear reactor at the Ignalina Soviet-built nuclear power plant, following an agreement between EU member states in June 2000 to provide 265 million euros for closing the first reactor. Lithuania's national energy strategy pledges to close the first reactor by 2005 and to decide the fate of the second reactor in 2004.[24]

The December 2000 Nice EU summit broke candidate states into first and second echelon, improving the prospects for advanced candidate countries to join the EU in early 2003, with Lithuania joining Ireland and Denmark with seven votes in the Council of Ministers while Estonia and Latvia continued to have four.

Although there is progress on the thorny issue of the Ignalina nuclear power plant, Lithuania still has other difficult chapters to be negotiated, particularly those relating to agriculture and the free movement of labor. Moreover, the EU member states have still to agree on changes in the union's own common agricultural policy and to carry out other fundamental internal reform that will facilitate enlargement. In stipulating that all candidates must demonstrate in advance of integration an ability to implement commitments undertaken, the EU appears to have shifted the burden of proof onto the shoulders of the candidate states, thus creating a further and high hurdle toward integration. The Swedish EU presidency (January–June 2001) appears genuinely committed to concentrating on closing as many chapters as possible with EU candidate countries. Sweden's ambassador to the EU has stated that at the end of the Swedish presidency it would be possible to establish which countries would be the first to enter and "perhaps even talk in terms of timetables and roadmaps."[25] That will be the litmus test through which the EU presidency is judged, and failure to make substantial gains in this direction, particularly on the complex and difficult chapters that require sacrifice and have the potential to alienate critical political constituencies, will push Lithuanian integration past 2004. It is doubtful whether another EU presidency in the near future will invest as much political capital in ensuring rapid Baltic integration, because other policy agendas and priorities are likely to become predominant.

Delayed EU enlargement has domestic economic and political costs, as well as foreign policy implications, for Lithuania. The political commitment of the elite to this process and the final goal is not wholehearted; politicians will increasingly have to struggle to ensure that this commitment and enthusiasm are sustained among their own electorate. The longer Lithuania delays taking the appropriate measures to ensure its eventual membership in the EU, the longer it will take to actually join the EU. In the meantime, as prospects for EU membership become more distant, enthusiasm for it is likely to diminish. The implementation of measures for EU membership will prove to be the central axiom in Lithuanian enlargement politics.[26] In Vilnius, some citizens may enjoy lifestyles approximate to those in western Europe, but this is accompanied by growing inequalities between rich and poor, skilled and unskilled, young and old, urban and rural, which could become seriously destabilizing in the context of delayed enlargement. Lithuania's competitive advantage of having a low-cost, skilled, and versatile workforce will be eroded. Moreover, delayed enlargement will also place stress on Lithuania's relationship with its strategic partners—Denmark, Poland, and Sweden, undermining the expectation of extensive synergies between Lithuania and its western neighbors.[27] As it is argued that "it is easier talking to the Russians from within the EU than from outside it," delayed integration will also cause tensions in Lithuanian-Russian relations.[28]

NOTES

1. I am grateful for the helpful comments, particularly on the military capabilities section, made by Vaidotas Urbelis, acting head, Security Policy Division, Policy and Planning Department, and Migle Budryte, acting head of the International Organizations Division, International Relations Division, Lithuanian Ministry of National Defense. All errors of judgment and fact remain mine alone.

2. BNS news agency, Tallinn, 12 January 2001. All media reports are translated by the BBC Monitoring *Summary of World Broadcasts,* Part 1, Former USSR.

3. Andra Sipaviciene, *International Migration and the Baltic States: New Patterns and Policy.* Helsinki, Finland. Report prepared for Baltic Assembly/Nordic Council Seminar on Migration Issues Relevant to the Baltic Sea Area (1996), 17.

4. Includes data from 1923, 1935, 1939.

5. Estonia, Latvia, and Lithuania in figures 2000. *Statistical Office of Estonia* (Tallinn, 2000), 4.

6. *Eesti Statistika Aastaraamat 2000/Estonian Statistical Yearbook 2000* (Tallinn, July 2000).

7. The conference proceedings were published: *NATO's Role in the Changing Security Environment in Europe,* Lithuania-Slovenia, 18–19 May 2000, Vilnius, 1–103.

8. Lithuania has also established the post of defense attache in Moscow to ensure a more comprehensive and accurate acquisition of information on Russia's armed forces, as well as one to the United Kingdom and an additional one to the United States. AVN Military News Agency web site, Moscow, 10 January 2001.

9. BNS news agency, Tallinn, 5 January 2001.

10. The creation of a possible third brigade will be decided in February 2001.

11. It is supplied with transport aircraft but has no combat capability. Lithuania's National Military Strategy can be read at: http://www.kam.lt/english/Military_Defense.html

12. "White Paper '99," Ministry of National Defense, Lithuania, 1999, 1–53. This is available at the Lithuanian MOD web page located at: http://www.kam.lt. A new Defense White Paper is expected in spring 2001.

13. BNS news agency, Tallinn, 20 December 2000. Lithuania does not envisage acquiring or deploying major weapon and equipment systems in 2001.

14. In addition, the Civil Servant Course will cover policy planning, management and administration, logistics, political studies and strategy, staff duties, total defense, and military technology. The BALTDEFCO web site is located at http://www.bdcol.ee/bdc-b.htm#Top

15. Juozas Alsauskas, "The Baltic Naval Squadron—BALTRON," *Baltic Defense Review* 3 (2000): 33–37.

16. Major T. D. Moller, "BALTBAT—Lessons Learned and the Way Ahead," *Baltic Defense Review* 3 (2000): 38–42. Major Moller was second in command of the Baltic Training Team, 1 August 1999–31 January 2000.

17. Migle Budryte, "Lithuanian Foreign Policy and Dual Enlargement," in *Democratic Security Building: Cases from the Baltic and Black Sea Regions,* Unto Vesa, ed. Occasional Paper, Tampere (Finland) Peace Research Institute (2000), 125–49.

18. BNS news agency, Tallinn, 18 January 2001.

19. Igor Leshukov, "The Regional-Centre Divide: The Compatibility Conundrum," in James Blaxendale, Stephen Dewar, and David Gowan, eds., *The EU and Kaliningrad: Kaliningrad and the Impact of EU Enlargement* (London: Federal Trust for Education and Research, 2000), 127–42.

20. David Gowan, *How the EU Can Help Russia* (London: Center for European Reform, December 2000), 34.

21. *Le Monde* web site, Paris, 10 January 2001.

22. *Postimees* web site, Tallinn, 13 January 2001.

23. BNS news agency, Tallinn, 18 January 2001.

24. On 3 January 2001 the Lithuanian government endorsed a program for the decommissioning of No. 1 reactor of the Ignalina nuclear power plant; it is highly likely that reactor No. 2 will be turned off by the end of the decade. BNS news agency, Tallinn, 31 January 2001.

25. Ahto Lobjakas, "Outlook for EU Expansion Improves," *Newsline,* Radio Free Europe/Radio Liberty, 4, No. 243, part II, 18 December 2000.

26. For an analysis of party attitudes toward EU integration, see: Lauras Bielinis, "Lietuvos politiniu partiju nuostatos Europos Sajungos integracijos klausimu," *Integracijos zinios* 1, no. 10 (January 2000), cited in Migle Budryte, "Lithuanian Foreign Policy and Dual Enlargement," 141.

27. Klaudijus Maniokas, "Methodology of the EU Enlargement: A Critical Appraisal," *Lithuanian Foreign Policy Review* 1, no. 5 (2000): 35–60.

28. Vijai Maheshwari, "Elites Favour EU but Voters Worry," *Financial Times,* 24 October 2000, quoting Raimundas Lopata, director, Institute of International Relations and Political Science, Vilnius University.

PART IV:
SOUTHEASTERN EUROPE
Introduction: Southeastern Europe

Daniel N. Nelson

A chille's heel, powder keg—we all know that these adjectives are imprinted indelibly on the map of southeastern Europe. Known more generically as "the Balkans," an indiscriminate label is erroneously applied to the entire region stretching from the plains of Pest to the Bosporous, and from the Adriatic to the Black Sea—a vast and diverse zone of Europe.

That "the Balkans" geographically refers to a mountain chain through central Bulgaria to the Black Sea, not a subcontinental region, seems to matter little. To the extent that "Balkan" is equated in the global press with Europe's southeastern peninsula, no state, nation, community, or government from this vast region can escape the derogative attributions of instability, corruption, and conflict.

No one who studies or lives in this corner of Europe can accept such generalizations with equanimity. Too much diversity and too many variables mean that descriptions and analyses of Slovenia would err ridiculously if guided by expectations based on Romania, Bulgaria, or Macedonia.

Yet, we are compelled to group these states and nations. Geographic contiguity, some similar socioeconomic challenges, and overlapping political histories—sharing the experience of either Ottoman or Hapsburg rule, and sharing the experience of having been part of the large Yugoslav federation created after World War I and maintained by Tito—lead us to join states of southeastern Europe.

In 2000 and early 2001, experiences among these eight cases could not differ more from each other. Failed states, pseudo states, nonstates, and weak states cohabit the region with a couple of countries that, right now at least, have greater resources. Albania's implosion in 1997 (caused, immediately, by a failed pyramid investment scheme), Bosnia-Herzegovina's dubious claim to unified statehood even six years after Dayton, Kosovo's nonstate international protectorate status, and Macedonia's ruptured peace, *all* rest uncomfortably in the Balkans.

As contributors each assess one country, intriguing comparisons emerge. For chapters about southeastern Europe, several authors refer to sense of "Western" movement in policy and socioeconomic conditions. This is particularly true of Margarita Assenova on Bulgaria, Jed Snyder on Croatia, and Ivan Hostnik's essay about Slovenia. For these authors and the security environments about which they write, the desire to move "West" is a matter of these nations' identity and keen hope for heightened safety and prosperity. Beyond identity and hope, however, are pragmatic policies— efforts by political and military leaders to become more attractive to Western investors and the North Atlantic Treaty Organization (NATO) and the European Union (EU), while altering domestic perspectives on politics, economics, *and* security.

For a number of the countries in Part IV, the turn of millennium brought little good fortune. Fabian Schmidt conveys the clear sense that Albania's condition remains far from stable, while Jay Wise summarizes the dismal state of the fractured Bosnia-Herzegovina, where 2000/early 2001 saw yet more nationalist unwillingness to collaborate across ethnic divides. Justifiably expressing the greatest doubt about future security is Biljana Vankovska's essay on Macedonia; certainly, as her country faced the onset of a potential calamity in early 2001, security seemed to have evaporated. Stan Markotich, too, raises questions about the direction that Serbia and Montenegro will take, not just because of the continuing tension between Belgrade and Podgorica, but also because Kostunica's own nationalism may yield further crises with the country's minorities, neighbors, and the European or international community. Romania, too, has trouble coming to grips with its own continued exclusion from the core of European security, and Daniel Nelson notes trends in that country's security discussion that evince such uncertainty.

From cases that seem decisive about their direction, if not their speed, to others where even rudimentary foundations of security continue to be absent, southeastern Europe represents a diverse and challenging milieu for analysis. But, to be sure, the region cannot be subsumed under a single, pejorative description; these eight chapters provide a full account of substantial diversity and insecurity.

13 • Albania: Precarious Stability

Fabian Schmidt

A lbania, a country now with 3.37 million inhabitants has experienced repeated outbreaks of violence since the end of Communism.[1] Both internal instability and other neighboring regions in crisis, especially the former Yugoslavia and Kosovo, hurt Albania by pushing away foreign investors. Nonetheless, Albania gained relative economic stability caused by a rapid privatization policy and fast liberalization of the market.

With the end of Communism in 1991, Albania faced famine and extreme poverty. In several waves, over three hundred thousand people left the country, most of whom emigrated to Italy and Greece. The collapse of pyramid investment schemes in 1997 led to widespread social unrest, during the course of which state institutions collapsed almost completely. After a period of relative stabilization, the Kosovo war in 1998 and 1999 brought over six hundred thousand refugees to Albania at the height of the crisis, which amounted to more than one-fifth of Albania's total population.

Since the end of the Kosovo war, with the return of refugees and the launching of the EU's Stability Pact for Southeastern Europe, Albania's government has engaged in promoting regional cooperation and good relations with all its neighbors. After overcoming latent disputes with Greece in the mid-1990s, Albania also improved ties to Macedonia and Montenegro. Relations with Serbia remain strained, however, because of Belgrade's slow release of Kosovar prisoners from Serbian jails and its limited cooperation with the International Criminal Tribunal for the former Yugoslavia (ICTY).

Home affairs since 1991 have been characterized by a bitter animosity between the anti-Communist Democratic Party (PD) and the Socialist Party (PS), the successors to the Communist-era Party of Labor of Albania (PPSH). In the course of the 1990s, however, the PS made a transformation to a social-liberal party with a Western-style social democratic program.

In the first multiparty elections of 1991, the PPSH had gained the majority of votes, supported by the conservative rural majority. The party was incapable, however, of dealing with imminent problems facing Albania, and the leadership had little vision of how to start the reform process. Protests and the first refugee exodus of about seventy thousand people forced the government to resign. A subsequent coalition government collapsed few months later, and, finally, parliament appointed an expert government to organize new elections. The PD, which had grown out of the anti-Communist student movement that overthrew communism, won these elections in a landslide in May 1992.

The first PD government started a reform program that was liberal in character but that neglected essential institutional reforms. Albania experienced a substantial growth that was not self-sustaining. While the gross domestic product (GDP) fell by 28 percent in 1991—and dropped a further 7.2 percent the following year—the new government managed to turn around that trend. In 1993, Albania reached a growth rate of 9.6 percent, which remained high and only slowly declined to 8.2 percent in 1996. Inflation also declined drastically after the government changes. In 1991 inflation was around 104.1 percent and reached a peak of 236.6 percent at the time the government took office in 1992. The new government managed to reduce it in steps, however, to 30.9 percent in 1993, 15.8 percent in 1994, and 6 percent in 1995. Unemployment declined from 27 to 12.3 percent between 1992 and 1996.

When inflation grew again to 17.4 percent in 1996, it signaled the beginning of the coming crisis and reflected the exaggerated shadow capital market and increased spending by pyramid scheme investors. Despite the apparently strong economic development, state institutions proved unable to control the dramatic social transformation institutionally. The weakness and inexperience of the justice system and the lack of banking controls both contributed to the emerging crisis.

Before the 1996 elections, the internal political conflicts between the PS and PD sharpened. The arrest of PS leader Fatos Nano for alleged misappropriation of aid funds additionally aggravated the confrontation. The opposition charged the PD with abusing the justice system for persecuting political enemies and the independent and opposition media.

Nonetheless, the PD won in the elections against the opposition, which charged the government with election fraud. The Organization of Security and Cooperation in Europe (OSCE) then confirmed the charges of electoral irregularities. The PD repeated its victory, however, in local elections in October 1996, and subsequently gained most of the mayoralities in the country.

Since 1994, several entrepreneurs had started to create investment companies that paid unusually high interest rates of up to 100 percent per month. The owners of the schemes pretended to invest the money in different businesses, but they mostly paid the interest from the input of new investors. At the end of 1996, seven such companies collapsed and were unable to pay back the credits. This triggered massive unrest.

Despite early warnings of the International Monetary Fund and the World Bank, the government failed to stop the schemes from operating. According to estimates, several hundreds of thousands of investors had put their money into the fraudulent companies, amounting to between 20 and 60 percent of the GDP in 1996.

With the unrest, Albania slipped into a state of general anarchy. Starting in southern Albania, but also in several northern places, citizens looted arms depots of the army, and state order almost completely ceased to exist by late 1996. According to estimates of the authorities, about six hundred thousand light arms, most of which were machine guns, got into civilian hands. As a result, armed criminal gangs began to control entire areas of the country.

A mission of the OSCE mediated a compromise in early March 1997 between the opposition and the government. It provided for the creation of a transitional government charged with organizing new parliamentary elections. That government invited an Italian-led international military presence named Mission Alba into the country, which created the framework conditions for reestablishing public security and protected international aid deliveries.

In the course of the crisis, the GDP growth declined to minus 7 percent and the unemployment rate grew to 14.9 percent. The PD lost the electoral majority to the PS. Most voters held the PD responsible for the crisis and charged the government under President Sali Berisha with failure to control the fraudulent schemes. Others charged PD officials with gaining from the schemes, but the charges were never substantiated.

In June 1997 most voters gave their support to the PS-led center-left coalition again, and in local elections in October 2000, the Socialists managed to win the mayoralities in most towns and communities throughout Albania.

The government faced its worst crisis after 14 September 1998, when riots erupted following the murder of famous opposition leader and PD legislator Azem Hajdari. Opposition supporters, who charged the government with having masterminded the murder, attacked the prime minister's offices and stormed the building of public TV. Since then, the PD has repeatedly boycotted the work of the parliament. Meanwhile, in March 2001, the prosecutor general's office identified Hajdari's killers, an achievement that will quiet the opposition, which had accused the government of a cover-up and which had used the murder as a pretext for a parliamentary boycott.

Reasons for the success of the Socialists, despite these incidents and frequent charges of corruption in the media, are found in continuing implementation of reforms toward a free market and especially in efforts to strengthen and reform institutions. They also claim credit for reestablishing the rule of law and basic security after 1997. The government managed to reestablish freedom of movement throughout Albania by summer 1999.

The opposition, however, has not managed to present itself as a strong and credible alternative, largely by discrediting itself through repeated boycotts of parliament. This has led to a further fragmentation of the opposition after a reform faction (headed by Gene Pollo) split off from the PD and formed a new party with the cooperation of some smaller rightist parties in January 2001.

Threat Assessment

Under communism, Albania perceived threats to its security primarily as external in origin. The Hoxhe-era Communist military doctrine aimed at enabling the population to fight back an invasion of both the Warsaw Pact and NATO at the same time. Paradoxically, it was precisely the heritage of widely spread access to arms and a culture of violence and isolation, cultivated by the Communists, that turned out to become the most real danger to internal peace and stability in the post-Communist era.

The main external threat perceived by the Albanian government after the end of Communism was linked to the crisis in Kosovo. Although Albania never recognized the sovereignty of the self-declared Kosovo Republic (declared in 1991), tensions between Belgrade and Tirana were traditional and often severe. While politicians in Belgrade charged Tirana with supporting Kosovo's independence movement, Albanian officials criticized Belgrade's human rights record in the region but reaffirmed the OSCE principles, ruling out any violent change of borders in the region.

Albania, faced with Slobodan Milosevic's Serbia as an unpredictable and highly armed neighbor, was mainly concerned with security threats coming from Belgrade. The government expressed particular concern over incursions by agent provocateurs of the Yugoslav secret services or about border violations and violent incidents, all of which were regular occurrences during the 1998–99 Kosovo crisis. Yugoslav artillery repeatedly shelled villages on Albanian territory, while the Kosovo Liberation Army (UCK) used Albanian soil as a staging ground for attacks in Kosovo, coming from the lawless northern region of Bajram-Curri. A large-scale Serbian attack against Albania was nonetheless unlikely, because invading Albania was not a serious option for President Milosevic. Nonetheless, the Albanian military certainly had to take that remote possibility into account. With the end of the Kosovo war in June 1999, and the ouster of Slobodan Milosevic from power in October 2000, the picture changed dramatically. With the new Belgrade government committing itself to a policy of nonaggression, Albania has no neighbors left in the region that pose an open military threat.

Reconciliation with Greece in 1995 led to the development of substantial economic and cultural ties, even though tensions occasionally arise over discriminatory treatment of Albanian migrants in Greece.

The relationship to Macedonia is marked by pragmatism in defining common interest, especially in developing economic ties and promoting trade. The March 2001 crisis, in which ethnic Albanian irredentists launched a rebellion in the Sar Planina mountains near Tetovo, highlighted the high level of restraint on the Albanian side, where politicians called for a peaceful solution to all minority questions that remain open and condemned the rebellion. Further, no important Macedonian government officials publicly put the blame for the developments in its own country on Tirana even though it is likely that some of the guerrillas used Albanian territory as a base. But, certainly, Macedonia has no intention or capability to destabilize, or much less attack, Albania.

The same can be said about Montenegro. Its relationship to Albania has further improved since the end of the Milosevic regime. It has become common for politicians, journalists, and officials from Albania to visit the neighboring republic, although concrete cross-border cooperation is only slowly starting in the framework of the Stability Pact for Southeastern Europe. Possible independence of Montenegro, in case of a future referendum, would be supported indirectly by Albania. Tirana would certainly welcome such a move, hoping for improving bilateral arrangements and seeing Belgrade's regional influence weakened. Albania's government will probably also support a referendum for the independence of Kosovo, which will come on the international agenda in case Montenegro leaves the federation. UN Resolution 1244 defines Kosovo as a part of Yugoslavia. If Yugoslavia ceases to exist, Belgrade will find it difficult to demand a reintegration of Kosovo into Serbia on either historical or constitutional grounds, since the Yugoslav constitution of 1974 defined Kosovo's position as a unit of the federation.

Albania's external threats today come from organized crime involved mostly in smuggling activities across the region. Albania remains a transit point for heroin from Turkey and Western Europe. Reports have also documented prostitution rings that kidnap girls and young women and send them into prostitution in Western Europe. Corruption in the customs service has been a particularly acute problem, which the Albanian government repeatedly tried to tackle by sacking high-ranking officers. The Italian customs agency (*Guardia di Financa*) has increased its presence in the Adriatic sea and cooperates closely with Albania's police to stem the flow of illegal immigrants across the Straits of Otranto. Internationally coordinated police operations throughout the region have led to the breakup of several prostitution rings in early 2001.

Organized crime in Albania developed because, in part, the state lacked functioning institutions and suffered abrupt social changes and inexperience in democratic culture after the end of Communism. Besides high expectations and—for a European country unusual—backwardness, a lack of democratic traditions in Albania's history provided a fertile ground on which violence grew quickly in settling everyday conflicts. This was aggravated by the abrupt transition from a Stalinist system to party pluralism with a market economy.

In Albania's historic development, the relationship between citizen, society, and state was strained. Especially in traditional rural areas, which predominate in the country, a segregative social structure prevailed. The family provided individual security and freedoms within the family context, while the public space was considered insecure. In contrast to an open society, in which citizens perceive the public and social control exercised by the state as a protector of individual freedom, the segregative society perceives the public realm as a potential threat. The open society, however, observes the self-imposed isolation of families in such societies with mistrust.

The segregative social organization goes back to the Ottoman millet system, when village communities organized along religion were allowed to run their own affairs—as long as they were paying taxes. Especially in northern Albania, common law (known as the *Kanun of Lek Dukagjini*) regulated social relations on a principle of honor. The code regulated the restoration of honor through vendettas. A close identification of individual, state, and society did not exist.

Neither the Albanian kingdom, created in 1913, nor the Communist dictatorship that ruled between 1945 and 1990 broke that tradition. The experience of collectivization in the Communist era, moreover, aggravated the mistrust of individuals toward state institutions, especially among those whose land was nationalized.

Indeed, the specific Albanian variety of Communism strengthened the withdrawal of villagers into the family rather than breaking the trend. The use of draconian penalties for blood feuds and the repressive system, built on fear and subordination, was able, however, to reduce considerably the number of blood feuds. But since the end of Communism, the society has lacked a clear framework of values. The disappearance of Communist repression made space for the reemergence of a crude version of common law, especially considering the weakness and minimal trustworthiness of the post-Communist justice system.

Given the background, the weakness of democratic institutions and functioning checks and balances became the most serious threat for Albania's security. Absent an efficient justice system, people turned to self-justice, arguing with common law. The creation of a post-Communist justice system has been marred by difficulties that were partly the result of corruption and a blatant disregard of high-ranking justice officials, including judges of the constitutional court, for the laws. The inability of the public institutions to address challenges became obvious in the 1997 crisis, when it became clear that there were insufficient banking controls, and no protection for the inexperienced citizens from large-scale fraud. Moreover, courts refused to accept cases form investors who had lost their money.

While internal political conflicts—surfacing mainly in oral accusations and counteraccusations between politicians from both political camps—are declining, there is still no overall consensus on the constitutional order of the country. Berisha and the Democratic Party have repeatedly boycotted parliamentary sessions and put into doubt the legitimacy of the country's constitution, adopted by the Socialists in November 1998. But the possibility of the Democrats breaking the general underlying constitutional consensus is very unlikely. Thus far they have used the boycott mostly to bully the government into making concessions in drafting laws and regulations. They did, however, participate in the local elections of October 2000, which the Socialists won in most regions.

Although there were some violent incidents between opposition supporters and the police in 2000, none of them got out of hand as they had done in September 1998, when opposition supporters captured a tank and stormed the prime minister's office and the public radio and television building.

Capacities

Albania has shown severe weaknesses in addressing both internal and external threats. The army is almost incapable of fulfilling basic tasks, which makes Albania dependent on the support of NATO countries in case of conflict. The weakness of its own institutions became evident in 1997. At that time the country had to ask for an international military intervention to get its own institution-building process back on track.

It was clear, since the collapse of the Albanian Army in 1997, that the country would have been unable to counter a potential Serbian military offensive on its own. Therefore, Albania continued to rely on NATO's military capabilities, which would pose a sufficient deterrence against any possible aggression. The country has less than a handful of antiquated MiG fighter jets from the 1960s, and its ground forces consist of little more than regular infantry with few tanks and artillery pieces. Foreign assistance addressed, foremost, the needs of clothing, transport capabilities, reconstructing of two of the navy's decrepit ships, training, and the introduction of modern communications equipment.

Through diplomatic efforts, and more recently through the Stability Pact for Southeastern Europe, Albania has gained significant support from the Western community. The country's loyal position to NATO and its involvement in the Partnership for Peace program, along with a moderate and restrained foreign policy have helped the country gather international support during the Kosovo crisis. During the war, foreign countries built up the transport capabilities of the airport in Tirana, and the United Arab Emirates built an airstrip in the northern town of Kukes that can accommodate Hercules transport aircraft. At the height of the Kosovo refugee crisis, when Albania had to accommodate around six hundred thousand refugees, up to one hundred humanitarian support aircraft landed in Tirana each day, at an airport that usually handles fewer than ten passenger planes per day.

Albania sees itself integrated into the Euro-Atlantic security area and, recovering from its army's collapse, is focusing its efforts on restructuring of its armed forces to bring them in line with NATO standards. Nonetheless, the likeliness of a speedy integration is low because of the lack of funding, proper equipment, and training.

Policy Innovations

Based on the new constitution of 1998 and assisted by the Council of Europe, Albania's parliament adopted a law on the civil service in November 1999. The significance of the new law was that it introduced, for the first time in Albanian history, the concept of a depoliticized civil service that would not be prone to corruption, with permanent employment, strong job security in law, and special benefits. The law provides controls, checks, and balances to protect civil servants against arbitrary political decisions, but it also clearly defines the duties of the civil servants. The law will help—legislators hope—to improve the integrity of the public sector and to prepare the administration for European standards.

The main policy innovations in the security field came with the launching of the Stability Pact for Southeastern Europe in 1999. All of the projects in the pact's quick start package had been launched by March 2001.

The main instrument of the Stability Pact is its regional table, which is the main coordinating body, and includes the governments participating in the table as well as international financial and other institutions. Under the level of the regional tables, three "subtables" are working on the issues of democratization and human rights (Working Table I), economic reconstruction, development, and cooperation (Working Table II), and security issues (Working Table III). Issues that are touching on the competencies of more than one working table are presented to the regional table, dealing with cross-table issues.

Albania benefits from the Stability Pact's security-related activities mostly in the field of home affairs. Institution building and training for public officials top the priority lists of donors. Here, a strong focus is on capacity building, particularly through the programs of international organizations such as the OSCE and the Council of Europe. Also, the projects in the field of infrastructure, which provide the most visible effects in the short term, are important to Albania's internal security by alleviating social disparities of remote regions. Water supply, electricity, roads, health, and school projects benefit directly those who want to stay but who are considering migrating for lack of opportunities.

Among the cross-table issues, Albania is involved in an anticorruption initiative under the guidance of the Council of Europe, designed to tackle origins of corruption and close legal and administrative loopholes. Furthermore, the Gesellschaft fur Technische Zusammenarbeit (GTZ) GmbH (German Technical Cooperation) is preparing a project involving local organizations for a trauma and reconciliation project targeting children and adolescents.

On Working Table III in the field of arms control and nonproliferation, Albania, together with Hungary and Bulgaria, proposed the establishment of a network of destruction facilities for arms, mines, and ammunition.

This project is closely linked to mine-clearing projects for northern Albania and Kosovo, where tens of thousands of mines were used during the war. The Kilkis Multinational Peacekeeping Center, near Thessaloniki, will host a series of seminars, exercises, and training sessions using experience from peacekeeping and similar operations, including the Western European Union (WEU's) police training mission in Albania. The Deutsche Stiftung fur internationale Rechtliche Zusammenarbeit e.V., in cooperation with the German justice ministry, is also assisting legislative and judicial reform in Albania. The Council of Europe has supported reform of criminal legislation in several southeast European countries. In Albania, the criminal code and code of criminal procedure were adopted in 1995 following expert advice from the council. Council of Europe experts are cooperating with Albanian commissions to ensure conformity of these codes with the new constitution. OSCE's Office of Democratic Institutions and Human Rights intends to assist in prison service reform. It has been assisting the prison services of Albania, Croatia, and FYROM since 1997. The programs are aimed at upgrading prison administration. The assistance takes the form of ongoing expert advice, training, and study visits. The program is carried out in cooperation with the British and the Polish prison services. A similar project on the organization and operation of the prison system comes from the Council of Europe, which currently is developing an action plan for prison reforms in Albania.

Projects of the Stability Pact's Working Table I have had less immediate impact on Albania's security.[2] But at the same time they promote essential understanding for democracy and human rights, which are equally relevant for sustainable security. Albania is involved in at least two projects in this framework. The first is an awareness-raising campaign by the Council of Europe aimed at improving ethnic relations in multiethnic societies of the region. The project aims to promote tolerance and nondiscrimination among the public. The second project comes from the Center of Studies and Programs for Development. It is titled: "Citizens: Pillar for good governance in SEE." This project aims to build up a "communication environment between the local public authorities and the NGOs [nongovernmental organizations] interested in promoting citizen participation to the elaboration and adoption process of the public decision."

The Task Force on Good Governance focuses mainly on the development of local government, the creation of effective ombudsman institutions, and public administration and administrative law. Albania, however, already has an ombudsman, specified by the new constitution. Also, over the past years, the Council of Europe and the OSCE have given very active support in public administration through expert advice. It remains unclear, however, whether the Stability Pact will add a new quality of cooperation to existing efforts. On 28 June 2000 the Council of Europe issued a declaration that praised Albania for the progress it had made specifically in the field of institution building since its crisis of 1997.

The Gender Task Force has given its highest priorities to national programs to empower women politically and increase the representation of women in political life. External donors have earmarked, through this Stability Pact task force, a total of 169,000 euros for Albania for four projects focusing at women's political empowerment. Here as well, the Council of Europe and OSCE's ODIHR have taken the lead in the implementation, although they will work with local governments and NGOs in designing specific projects.

In the media field, the BBC prepares Albanian-language educational programs and a children's radio service. Besides Albania, the project targets Kosovo and Macedonia. There are other cross-border media projects involving Albania by European Center for Common Ground in Skopje, the Council of Europe, the Southeast News Service Europe (SENSE), and other media institutions.

The Royaumont Process has developed a priority list for promoting parliamentary cooperation with training and exchange programs for newly elected parliamentarians and staff members as its highest priority. The projects intend to educate parliamentarians and parliamentary staff members, improve cooperation between legislators and NGOs, and widen parliamentary cooperation.

The main priorities of Albania's government are in hard infrastructure development. The projects of Working Table II reasonably can be expected to be implemented in the next couple of years. Most of these projects include road and railway construction and rehabilitation, power grids and pipelines, wastewater clearing systems, and bridges.

All road projects in the Quickstart and near-term packages focus on the rehabilitation of the existing roads. But roads throughout the country are in a terrible shape. The only stretch of autobahn, or superhighway (four lanes), runs from Tirana to Vlora, and it is less than twenty kilometers long. That highway was built between 1993 and 1995, but pedestrians and cattle also use the road.

The Stability Pact intends to repair some single-track railway stretches in Albania and to complete a new three-kilometer stretch to Macedonia. The problem with that connection is in Macedonia, however. The closest railway connection is in Kicevo. The Stability Pact has identified the construction of a new thirty-five-kilometer track as a project, but a feasibility study is required first. Kicevo itself is about sixty kilometers from the Albanian border. The two ports that received support through Stability Pact projects are Durres and Vlora. In Durres the project included the rehabilitation of quays and storage facilities, while in Vlora the intention is to upgrade the port to minimal standards. The European Investment Bank (EIB) and the European Bank for Reconstruction and Development (EBRD) support the rehabilitation and extension of the passenger terminal and air traffic control operations at Rinas airport. The airport has received substantial upgrades in lighting and radar equipment in 1996 and 1997 and of its cargo capacities during the refugee crisis in 1999. Further, donors agreed to upgrade the powerlines between Albania and its neighbors and to link the country up to international power providers. Lines to be built include Elbasan to Podgorica (Montenegro), Zemlak to Bitola (Macedonia), and Fierze to Prizren (Kosovo).

Other infrastructure projects include gas and oil pipeline interconnection and water supply and wastewater rehabilitation in numerous cities. In total, the infrastructure projects will cost about 112 million euros for the Quickstart package and 320 million for the near-term projects. Construction of a separate, privately financed Trans-Balkan oil pipeline was expected to start by summer 2001 by an Albanian-Macedonian-Romanian consortium. In environmental protection, the Stability Pact has launched a post-conflict environmental assessment in Albania. And the United Nations Environmental Program (UNEP) Balkans Task Force is working to create transboundary nature protection areas and proposed creation of the Prokletije National Park, situated on the border between Kosovo-Montenegro and Albania.

Albania has also accelerated the privatization process and started, in 2000, with the privatization of some key industries, including mobile tele-communications.

Future Prospects

Albania's general perspective toward security has changed significantly with the end of the Kosovo war and the launching of the Stability Pact for Southeastern Europe. The government has been working to establish cooperation with its neighbors, specifically Macedonia, Montenegro, and Greece, as part of a long-term strategy of European integration.

Expectations about the speed and quality of integration are often unrealistic, however. Many citizens regard the Stability Pact as a massive drive to boost economic development and infrastructure rehabilitation and expect that European integration will come sooner rather than later. They do not see the complexity of the efforts within the Stability Pact in helping the enhancement of human rights, democracy, and regional cooperation, however, which is reflected through the lack of ownership of political initiatives.

With this background in mind, the international community has taken a target-driven approach, rather than a demand-driven approach, hoping to involve local players eventually through those initiatives it starts and by triggering development, while not waiting for the local communities to formulate their needs first. Albania's government has welcomed that approach, understanding that the Stability Pact can give an essential impulse for domestic initiatives to boost substainable development.

In the third Albanian democratic local elections on 1–2 October 2000, the PS took most of the seats from the PD throughout Albania. Now the Socialists hold most of the city mayoralties in Albania. The local elections were a test case for the parliamentary elections in June 2001, the results of which favored the Socialists.

Thus, the PS-led government sees its reform course confirmed. The outcome also reflected the limited capabilities of a divided opposition. The PS gained over 42 percent countrywide while less than 38 percent of the voters supported the PD. The small Social Democratic Party (PSD) gained 7.11 percent of the votes, thus entering the Parliament—and the mainly ethnic Greek Human Rights Union Party (PBDNJ) won 4.34 percent of the votes. The Democratic Alliance, which is inside the coalition (together with the PSD and the PBDNJ) received 3.43 percent of the votes. Outside the PD, the two main opposition parties gained only 2.38 percent (United Albanian Right) and 2.28 percent (Republican Party).

The PS candidates gained mayoralties in 49 cities and 238 communities, the PD in 15 cities and 58 communities, the PBDNJ in 5 communities and the tiny monarchist Legality Party in 1.[3] In Tirana, former Culture Minister and independent Edi Rama won a seat for the PS.

A reason for the Socialists' victory also lies in their successful economic policies, including continuing privatization. In 2000 Albania had a growth rate of 8 percent, the same as both 1998 and 1999. Inflation was 2 percent in 1999 and reached zero inflation in 2000. Unemployment grew to 18.4 percent in 1999, largely caused by the privatization of state industries.

Besides the new constitution, which strengthens local government and a thorough reform of the civil service, and which therefore depoliticized the administration, the government took steps to legalize private broadcasters and to reform the state radio and television systems into a public broadcasting company following Western models. Also, Albania has taken numerous steps, adopting Western expertise, toward adjusting its laws to European standards and installing checks and balances. As a result of that process, by the end of 2000, Albania opened negotiations with the EU about a stabilization and association agreement.

Albania's main problems for a sustainable development, however, are numerous investment risks, such as a corrupt judiciary and a high crime rate. According to estimates, there are still about five hundred thousand firearms in private hands. There are about three hundred Italian medium-sized enterprises working in Albania, and a smaller number of Greek or other foreign companies, many of which merely open offices to be present in the market.

The government, which went through a series of reshuffles since 1997, has always reaffirmed its commitment to Euro-Atlantic integration. Therefore, Albania develops its foreign policy toward its neighbors, such as Macedonia and Montenegro, in close cooperation with Western partners. Albania's Kosovo policy is, in many aspects, more moderate than observers would expect. Albania did not object to the admission of the Federal Republic of Yugoslavia into the OSCE, although the very legal and de facto existence of that federation is currently in question.

The Albanians look forward to the EU association and stabilization negotiations. Long-term development perspectives on the way toward European integration include the construction of an East-West corridor, which will link the ports of Durres and Vlora with Macedonia, Bulgaria, and, finally, Istanbul. The corridor is expected to give a boost to regional trade of goods and services and to the integration of the region.

The opposition, however, stands before its most difficult situation in recent years.[4] It will have to face up to a new reality in which it must work more creatively on developing credible political alternatives to the current government. If the PD wants to gain more votes, Berisha eventually will have to give up his often-aggressive and irreconcilable rhetoric. Over the last four years, it has been a key strategy of the PD to embarrass the government with charges of corruption and involvement in smuggling, which they often could not prove. The PD repeatedly demanded early elections. Conversely, the PD neglected the very intensive reform process that the government led and ignored the need to present qualified and credible policy alternatives.

Most voters have clearly noticed improvements in their economic situation and in the level of public security. They also fear a return to anarchy, as in 1997, too much to vote for change. Thus, an election victory of the Socialists is less an indicator of ideological support for that party than a sign that the voters trust the PS enough to let it continue its path of reforms in administration and economy.

A return to situations like what existed in 1997 seems unlikely given such conditions; as long as the institution-building process continues, the living standard in Albania will improve steadily. Recent clashes between police and opposition protesters have been less violent than in the past, indicating that there is political constraint among party supporters. External threats, moreover with the exception of organized crime, have diminished significantly. Meanwhile, further steps toward strengthening law enforcement and the justice system are also showing results, even though the fight against organized crime will take many more decades, considering the high profit margins from smuggling compared to regular salaries, which are currently around $100 per month for qualified labor.

Chronology

11 January 2000: Prime Minister Ilir Meta fires Minister of Public Economy and Privatization Zef Preci, who was an independent member of the cabinet, and Minister of State Prec Zogaj from the Democratic Alliance (AD), a smaller coalition partner. Meta accuses them of abusing their power and favoring certain business interests to the detriment of others.

14 January 2000: The government approves a memorandum on good understanding, designed to strengthen relations with Montenegro.

3 February 2000: Italy launches investigations into allegations that corrupt officials in its Tirana embassy have been selling visas to Albanians for three years.

24 February 2000: Albania and Montenegro reopen their border. It had been closed since the Kosovo war period in 1998.

15 March 2000: Foreign Minister Paskal Milo warns ethnic Albanian guerrillas in Kosovo and southern Serbia not to "sabotage the already difficult peace process in Kosovo." He adds that "the Albanian government does not agree with those extremist nationalistic circles that might be acting in Presevo, Medvedja and Bujanovac."

9 May 2000: Parliament approves the Electoral Code.

14 May 2000: Former president Sali Berisha acknowledges mistakes in handling the fraudulent pyramid investment schemes that triggered the 1997 riots. The remarks are made during a rally in Vlora, his first visit since the city was swept by anarchy.

23 May 2000: The prime ministers of Albania and Montenegro meet in Shkodra to inaugurate a telephone link.

24 May 2000: President Rexhep Meidani visits Kosovo and holds a speech at the university, rejecting the idea of a "Greater Albania" and calling for a Europe of the regions.

1 June 2000: President Rexhep Meidani inaugurates the Prespa National Park, which links Albania, Greece, and Macedonia.

6 June 2000: EU praises Albania for progress in improving law and order and privatization.

20 June 2000: Prosecutors in Albania and Italy agree to foster closer cooperation in combating crime.

5 July 2000: Meta sacks three ministers. Ilir Gjoni, Meta's chief of cabinet, replaces Socialist Luan Hajdaraga as defense minister and Arben Imami of the AD replaces Ilir Panda—an independent member of cabinet—as justice minister. Ilir Zela of the Socialists, who was minister of state, replaces Arben Demeti of the Democratic Alliance Party as public affairs minister. Ndre Legisi, another Socialist, becomes minister of state.

10 July 2000: The Albanian, Macedonian, and Montenegrin prime ministers meet in Durres to discuss regional cooperation and stability.

12 July 2000: The interior ministers of France, Germany, and Italy propose installing an international center for the control of illegal emigration and prostitution trafficking in Vlora.

24 July 2000: A Yugoslav Army roadblock bars Albanians from entering Montenegro.

2 August 2000: Shkodra police chief Arben Zylyftari is killed in an arrest operation.

15 August 2000: Hundreds of armed people attack the police station in Kukes to protest against the taxation of the trade with Kosovo. The riots start after special police forces crack down on a car smuggling ring involving high officials at the city's local police department.

16 August 2000: Villagers blow up the Kukes water supply line in a dispute with the local waterworks over distribution of water.

18 September 2000: Parliament passes a tough law against smuggling of humans, in a belated response to Italian pressure.

26 September 2000: Prime Minister Meta is forced to cancel a rally in Tropoja after opposition supporters storm the square. Meanwhile, unidentified attackers apparently shoot at opposition leader Sali Berisha.

1 October 2000: The Socialist Party wins overwhelmingly in local elections. The leadership of the opposition Democratic Party (PD) refuses to recognize

the results. Many elected PD mayors and city council members take up their positions, however.

15 October 2000: Democrats and Socialists join forces to prevent an ethnic minority party from wining the runoff elections in the southern city of Himara.

18 October 2000: Greece threatens to halt its aid to Albania to retaliate against alleged vote manipulations in Himara. The government denies manipulations.

26 October 2000: Thousands of DP supporters gather in Tirana's main square to protest against alleged vote rigging. Protests continue until 23 December.

8 November 2000: Meta sacks three ministers. Outgoing Defense Minister Ilir Gjoni replaces Interior Minister Spartak Poci. Poci accepts the ministry of public works, replacing Ilir Zela. Meta's previous chief of cabinet, Ismail Lleshi, becomes defense minister.

14 November 2000: OSCE spokesman Giovanni Porta leaves the country after death threats.

15 November 2000: The National Council of Radio-Television awards national coverage licenses to the private TV stations Klan and Arberia.

20 November 2000: Berisha supporters pelt the parliament building with stones and set a car ablaze.

20 November 2000: Two men are killed in clashes between police and pro-opposition demonstrators in Bajram Curri.

6 December 2000: Meta visits Kosovo, marking the first official visit by an Albanian head of government.

7 December 2000: OSCE ambassador Geert-Hinrich Ahrens publicly accuses the Central Elections Commission of bias.

11 December 2000: Dynamite explodes on the Tirana-Fushe Kruja road, minutes before a convoy of Meta is scheduled to pass. Police arrest six men.

14 December 2000: Socialist Party officials urge CEC members to resign, but they unanimously refuse to step down.

22 December 2000: Amnesty International expresses concern over reports that PD supporters have been ill treated.

NOTES

1. "Shqiperia ne Shifra" *(Albania in Figures)*, *Instat* (Tirana: The Albanian Institute of Statistics, Instat, September 2000), p. 4.

2. Special Coordinator of the Stability Pact for Southeastern Europe: "Report of the Special Coordinator for the Regional Funding Conference for South East Europe, Brussels, 29 and 30 March 2000" (Brussels, Belgium: EU, 27 May 2000), 10.

3. *Albanian Daily News*, 10 October 2000.

4. *Koha Jone*, 4 October 2000.

14 ◆ Bosnia-Herzegovina: Security and Other Dilemmas

John R. Wise

Since the signing of the Dayton Accord, Bosnia's progress toward functional statehood has been halting at best. Using mechanisms of power and influence carried over from the war and from Bosnia's authoritarian past—and aided by an electoral system that required Bosnians to construct civic identity on the basis of ethnic identity—the three large, ethnically based parties remained in control at nearly all levels of government. They found common cause less in alleviating the wartime results of rampant corruption and ethnic enmity than in exacerbating and perpetuating them for political gain and retrenchment. A substantial *nomenklatura* of each ethnic group controlled most state institutions and economic concerns, leading both to endemic corruption and to a fundamental lack of economic reform.

The international community was either unable or unwilling to halt this development. The delineation of responsibilities to the Implementation Force (IFOR) and local police under Dayton had been the result of negotiation in Washington nearly as intense as that in Dayton; U.S. commanders were anxious not to be involved in what was perceived as the quicksand of ethnic conflict,[1] and they demanded that the International Police Task Force (IPTF) not be given the authority to arrest or significantly intervene in civil disturbances, lest IFOR be forced to assume responsibility for rescuing the IPTF. At the same time, the High Representative arrived in Bosnia with no staff or funding and little guidance as to how to carry out the already-vague tasks of implementing the civilian aspects of the agreement.

As a result, while the military aspects of Dayton were implemented relatively easily, a vacuum existed in the sphere of law and order. This resulted in little progress on two key components of Dayton—the return of refugees to prewar housing and the arrest of war criminals. Several war criminals indicted by The Hague, and many who had been secretly indicted or who were the targets of investigation for their roles in the war, still lived in Bosnia. Many retained significant roles in the political or economic life of the country, particularly in the Republika Srpska (RS, which is the Bosnian-Serb enclave in Bosnia-Herzegovina), and remain significant factors in the effort to block political progress in Bosnia.

Similarly, the return of refugees was blocked by the intimidation of local gangs—often acting in complicity with local police or government. Added to this was the intransigence of local government officials, whose political support depended on the preservation of the prevailing ethnic mix, and whose patronage networks often depended on the ability to dole out premium apartment space that had once belonged to refugees or displaced persons.

Republika Srpska's political leadership has wavered between outright hostility toward Dayton and grudging or partial acceptance of Dayton's terms. In 1996 the Serbian Democratic Party (SDS) won an overwhelming victory in Bosnia's first election. Despite widespread reports that the party was still linked to indicted war criminal Radovan Karadzic (Organization for Security and Cooperation in Europe—OSCE—rules forbade the connection of any party to indicted war criminals) the international community allowed the election results to stand.[2]

In 1997 the Republika Srpska leadership began to fracture between hard-line, SDS officials based in the RS wartime capital of Pale and more moderate accommodationist officials in the present RS capital, Banja Luka. RS president Biljana Plavsic, who had been an enthusiastic supporter of the war effort, broke publicly with other SDS officials, espousing a nominally more pro-Western, pro-Dayton line and establishing a breakaway party. The ascension in late 1997 of Milorad Dodik to the post of RS prime minister in a coalition that excluded the SDS seemed to vindicate Plavsic's approach. Despite this break, however, the RS moved very little, if at all, toward integration with state-level institutions. Dodik was unable to form a smoothly working majority in the RS parliament or to overcome public perceptions of weakness in the face of Western pressure and of widespread corruption. Hard-liners continued to wield significant political power in the RS, and the SDS has enjoyed a recent political resurgence.

While power within the RS vacillated between Pale and Banja Luka, real power within the federation remained concentrated at the cantonal levels (for largely monoethnic cantons) or lower (where multiethnic cantonal governments frequently came to loggerheads or had their work obstructed by politicians from either party). Each canton has its own constitution, assembly, and interior ministry, complete with control over cantonal police forces.

Bosnian Croats established an illicit parallel state, complete with "national" telecommunications and logging industries and a military force.[3] This parastate received strong support from Croatia's Tudjman regime, in return for its strong political support: Bosnian Croats voted in Croatian elections and even received parliamentary representation in the Croatian parliament, the Sabor. The Bosnian Croats became a key part of the Croatian Democratic Union (HDZ) political apparatus within Croatia. No political party emerged between 1996 and 1999 that was perceived by Bosnian Croats as an alternative to the HDZ. The Bosniak-led Party for Democratic Action (SDA), however, continued to press for steps to make Bosnia a more unitary state. But it also maintained separate institutions—including its own intelligence organization—that were underwritten by a network of illegal economic arrangements.[4]

The international community, led by the United States, helped to ratify this result by inaction. The West's ginger treatment of ethnic parties as the established postwar powers following the Dayton agreement and scheduling elections less than a year after the war's conclusion, gave Bosnia's ethnic divisions a chance to harden. Further, by doing little to break the *nomenklatura* networks throughout its occupation of Bosnia, while avoiding the arrest of several war criminals and exhibiting reluctance to remove from power individuals violating the Dayton agreement, the West lost critical opportunities to break down such divisions.

The United States had also set a year-long deadline for the deployment of IFOR troops in Bosnia, a position that convinced many radicals to "wait out" the international forces. In particular, the decision to leave the tasks of "law and order" to the local authorities—already controlled by the ethnic cliques they were supposed to police—has resulted in superficial stability but little real change throughout Bosnia.

By the beginning of 2000, the international engagement in Bosnia might have seemed a success. The war, after all, had ceased. Statewide, cantonal and local elections were held repeatedly and largely without major incident. Bosnia retained the illusion of working government, with a presidency, a national parliament, and singular representation in international bodies. Despite these superficial indicators, a closer look suggests that by the end of 1999, Bosnia looked not unlike it had at the end of 1996: one restive entity held together mainly by the will of the international community, joined in statehood with another entity, again on the insistence of the international community. The state, such as it was, was bounded by larger powers to the north and east, respectively—powers that actively sought to undermine the putative Bosnian state. Though the year 2000 brought the collapse of regimes that had ruled those neighboring states, it did not solve the problem of Bosnia's instability.

Threat Assessment

Bosnia is not currently threatened by external, overt attempts at destabilization. However, perhaps more than anywhere else in the region, Bosnia is most imminently threatened by its own lack of coherence as a functioning state.

Throughout much of 2000 and into 2001, Bosnia's major state institutions continued to appear fundamentally weak. The major organs of government—the three-member Presidency and the Parliamentary Assembly, each controlled by the three major ethnic parties—proved unwilling to pass major legislation touching on Bosnia's identity as a state; where political debate has broken down, the High Representative (HR) has established laws on several aspects of Bosnian life, including the establishment of a customs union, common passports, license plates, and even a national anthem.

Even if statewide institutions could pass such legislation, however, it is possible that law could go unimplemented by the entity itself, since there is no description within the Dayton agreement of the legal relationship between the entities and the statewide government. When Bosnia's fiscal and economic systems are examined, this point becomes even starker. Areas of responsibility between the federal government and the entities on every aspect of fiscal policy—from tax policy to infrastructure—are only vaguely defined.[5] The result is both horizontal and vertical gridlock.

At the same time, as foreign aid to Bosnia continues to dwindle, it is becoming increasingly less likely—for the reasons given above and below—that foreign investment will take its place.[6] As a result, notes one analysis, "the danger that the Bosnian state and economy will fail is real." Although the World Bank has identified five major areas of reform as prerequisite to sustained economic growth (the establishment of a transparent and predictable business environment; privatization of state-owned businesses; reform of the banking sector; and reform of labor markets), these developments are virtually precluded by the lack of a central treasury system, along with endemic corruption and the weakness of its lawmaking and executive institutions.

Official corruption is helping to strangle the Bosnian economy and leading to the weakness of central state institutions. About half of Bosnia's gross domestic product (GDP) is generated by underground economic activity, and considerable problems with tax collection and evasion remain,[7] limiting the ability of the government to generate revenue. Moreover, organized corruption has rendered the economic environment so unpredictable as to drive away most potential foreign investors.[8] At the same time, each ethnic group has its own set of monopolistic utility companies, each of which is controlled by that group's political party. These companies serve as fronts for illegal activity and play a role in preserving ethnic separatism; they also drain funds from Bosnia's central government.

Two cases during 2000 involving SDA members—banker Alija Delimustafic and then prime minister Edhem Bicakcic, respectively—and the embezzlement of tens of millions of U.S. dollars in aid and investment illustrated the degree to which corruption had permeated the SDA.[9] The political leadership of the Republika Srpska and of the Bosnian Croats is similarly tainted. Massive budget shortfalls in both entities this past year were likely caused by "excessive government expenditure, tax evasion, and smuggling."[10] Despite the cutoff in funds from Croatia, the HDZ has been able to stay in control of Bosnia through its patronage network, which, in turn, has been supported by extremely profitable smuggling activities between Croatia and Bosnia.[11] One major beneficiary of this network has been the Bosnian branch of HVIDRA, the Croat veterans association, which has threatened the safety of Bosnian Croat officials or politicians deemed accommodationist. World Bank officials in September even accused the Bosnian government of siphoning money from the international program to remove land mines.[12] In November, Office of High Representative (OHR) Chief Wolfgang Petritsch forced three demining commissioners to step down.

By many accounts, the armies of each "ethnicity" are good examples of this dynamic. The UN special representative to Bosnia has stated: "wartime underground networks have turned into political criminal networks involved in massive smuggling."[13] Serving as sources of patronage and political muscle, the armies also help prop up ruling parties in the RS and among the Bosnian Croats.[14]

Corruption—by draining public resources from state coffers and propping up illegal parallel institutions that further weaken the state and alienate the electorate—threatens both the viability and the legitimacy of the state, weaknesses that further reinforce each other. As long as the central state is undermined, Bosnians, especially Bosnian Croats and Serbs, have little reason to look beyond their own ethnic parties. In short, Bosnia's weak institutions and ethnic tensions appear locked in debilitating symbiosis.

One manifestation of this dynamic is the slow pace of refugee return. According to the UN High Commissioner for Refugees (UNHCR), the number of refugee returns continues to increase, albeit slowly. Although nearly seven hundred and fifty thousand refugees are listed by UNHCR as having resettled in Bosnia, only a fraction of them qualify as minority returns: the return of Bosnians to homes they left during the war (the rest have resettled in areas of ethnic political or military control). As of 10 May 2000, the number of minority returns had climbed to 210,759, out of a total of 2.2 million originally displaced by the war, or slightly less than 10 percent. One encouraging sign is the rapid pace of return and property repossession by Bosniaks to Croat-controlled areas of central Bosnia, possibly symbolizing the decline of HDZ rule there.

However, nearly all refugees face discrimination and obstruction by local authorities; recent events in the Republika Srpska (discussed below) illustrated that refugees still have to fear extremist groups acting with what might be described as passive acceptance at best and tacit encouragement at worst. Nearly all Bosnian Serb political parties and the HDZ regard potential minority return as a threat to the very purpose of their current political arrangements and to the material and political sources of their support.

Capacities

The weakness of Bosnia's control over its own forces—those charged with preserving law and order and those charged with protecting the state—is a reflection of state capacities.

RS police are some fifty-six hundred strong, according to one recent analysis,[15] and are under central control by the RS ministry of interior. Described as wartime "storm troopers" for the SDS,[16] the RS police force has, at least by standards of multiethnicity, improved measurably. Under a 1998 Framework Agreement on Police Restructuring Reform and Democratization, the RS accepted limits on the number of police it could employ as well as on a minimum percentage—25 percent—of Bosniaks and Croats among new recruits. Nearly all RS officers have completed IPTF training.

Nevertheless, it is clear that RS police are often still unable or unwilling to take action to prevent the intimidation of refugees or international officials. RS police were accused in March 2001 by the Federation Ministry of the Interior of beating a group of refugee returnees.[17] And in an event discussed below, RS police stood by when a violent mob put a halt to the May 2001 rebuilding of mosques in two separate cities.

Within the Federation, police forces—with a total personnel strength of eight thousand—fall under direct command of the interior ministry of each canton. While the IPTF established new police forces in eight of ten cantons, police forces in Croat-controlled cantons "appear to be particularly obstructionist, often openly backing secessionist aims." In Stolac (Canton 7), for instance, in 1999 IPTF monitors discovered police cooperation with the illegal Herceg-Bosna intelligence agency and an illegal cantonal defense ministry; most of the officers were in fact demobilized Croatian Defense Council (HVO) officers.

In January 2000, HR Petritsch imposed a law creating a state-level multiethnic State Border Service (DGS). The DGS then began taking over customs posts in July 2000; as of March 2001 it employed 1,350 people and covered 60 percent of the border crossings in Bosnia. Nevertheless, one report noted in March that "a major source of revenue for the institutions of

Herceg-Bosna comes from smuggling operations that exploit Bosnia and Herzegovina's porous borders with Croatia. The heaviest cross-border trafficking occurs at the numerous border crossings not currently manned by the state border service."[18]

The post-Dayton military story follows the larger historical arc: an uncertain and sometimes ambivalent push for state-level institution building by the international community meeting intransigence from the three ruling ethnic parties, especially those of the Bosnian Serbs and Croats. Formally, Bosnia's military is composed of two armies: the Bosnian Serb Army (the VRS) and the Federation Army (VF), which is theoretically composed of units from the Bosniaks and the Bosnian Croats. In reality, there are four military structures: the VRS; the VF, which remains a largely theoretical concept; the Bosnian Croat HVO; and the Bosniak Army, the Army of Bosnia-Herzegovina (ABiH).

With some one hundred thousand soldiers during the height of the war in Bosnia, the VRS currently numbers about ten thousand. As noted above, the VRS was originally a mix of Yugoslav Peoples' Army (JNA) professionals, local self-defense forces, and paramilitary organizations. The army is composed largely of infantry brigades with some organic armored and artillery support. Small armored units are equipped with Soviet-era T-34s and T-55s, and some M84As. Artillery units use traditional mortars as well as antiair artillery. All units almost certainly suffer from a current lack of training and modern equipment.

The VRS has received significant financial and material support from Serbia, even following the war in Bosnia. Throughout the period in question, and despite continued uncertainty in Federal Republic of Yugoslavia (FRY)-RS relations, the VRS was supported to some degree by the FRY. Officers were paid from FRY coffers, and officers from the general staff rotated through the Yugoslav Army (VJ), and vice versa. Moreover, the RS intelligence office remained close to the Serbian intelligence service. In 1999 the relationships between the VJ and the VRS were evident, but the dismal economic condition of the FRY diminished any kinds of support for the VRS. VJ and VRS trucks were reported in 1999 moving between the RS and Serbia without being stopped by Stabilization Force (SFOR) officials.[19]

The VRS has been affected by war crimes prosecutions. In 1999 Plavsic ally General Momir Talic was arrested in a sealed indictment from The Hague while visiting Austria for a U.S.-sponsored trip. The episode displayed the difficulty of trying to engage with an RS military leadership still firmly rooted in the Bosnian war. RS leaders have reportedly prepared a list of some sixty-one persons who may be listed on secret indictments at The Hague.[20] The secret indictments, particularly in the wake of the Talic arrest, have contributed to an atmosphere of persecution and paranoia within the VRS ranks. The VRS currently suffers from a lack of equipment and low morale. Thousands of soldiers are reported to be in need of housing, and the VRS's equipment is old and in some cases failing. In May rumors circulated in Banja Luka that RS helicopter pilots were considering going on strike to protest low salaries and the poor shape of their equipment.[21]

Since the development of the Plavsic-Krajisnik split in late 1997, the VRS officer corps has been split among several directions: modernizers wishing to work with the West regardless of political beliefs; those loyal to the Slobodan Milosevic regime; and those primarily loyal to hard-liners within the RS. In the past, the international community has tried to use the isolation and equipment deficit of the VRS to pressure it into increased international cooperation. To the extent that the Kostunica government will be able to support the VRS, this may allow the VRS to avoid pressure by the international community to work closely with the ABiH. VRS leadership has continued to argue against the prospect of working closely with the ABiH even while representatives have helped draft a document that at least discusses the prospect of shared command and control.

Established under the 1994 Washington Agreement, the VF is supposed to combine forces from the HVO and ABiH. The VF is currently composed of 23,000 soldiers,[22] some 16,000 from the ABiH and some 7,000 from the HVO. Under the agreement, three ABiH corps and one HVO corps form a single federation army (the train and equip program envisions a federation army of approximately 45,000 soldiers, or eight Bosniak and four Bosnian Croat brigades). A joint ministry of defense exists in Sarajevo, as does a joint military command; Bosniak and Bosnian Croat generals serve, respectively, as commander and deputy commander of the force. Defense planning calls for a "rapid reaction brigade" (RRB) composed of one Bosnian Croat battalion and two Bosniak battalions, but this capacity is mainly theoretical: the battalions are based in separate areas and remain under ethnic command until the RRB is "activated in time of crisis."[23]

The HVO, however, still reportedly maintains a large number of reserves under arms; these forces serve as "Home Defense Regiments." Neither the Bosnian Croat nor the Bosniak reserve forces fall under the command structure of the VF.[24]

Both elements of the Federation Army have received significant funding from external sources. One important aspect of structural change (or the lack thereof) within the Bosnian army would be the train and equip program. In a resolution passed in December 1995, the U.S. Congress made the deployment of U.S. troops to Bosnia contingent on a program to retrain and reequip the Bosnian federation army, a condition accepted by President Bill Clinton.[25] The program set forth in the resolution would partially fund certain approved defense expenditures by the federation army, within the parameters set by the Dayton Accord (and discussed above).

Explicitly, the United States placed two conditions on implementation of the program: that the ABiH and HVO commands are merged and that the Bosnians cease military cooperation with Iran and any irregular armed Muslim groups. These conditions were judged satisfied on 9 June 1996, with the passage of the Defense Law by the federation parliament. Under the train and equip (T&E) program, a total of $152 million was donated by Saudi Arabia, Kuwait, the United Arab Emirates, Malaysia, and Brunei to provide for the modernization and training of the Federation Army. The United States pledged an additional $100 million. These donations paid for the Federation Army's training contract with Military Professional Resources Incorporated (MPRI), the construction of military facilities and barracks, the purchase of major military equipment from third countries (including refurbished U.S. military equipment), and the production in Bosnia of artillery, ammunition, helmets, and insignia.[26]

According to most accounts, the equipment delivered kept the Federation Army well below the arms control ceilings established in the Florence Agreement, although the equipment was far superior to that of the Bosniaks during, and at the end of, the war. Moreover it is also probably qualitatively superior to that of the Bosnian Serbs.[27] While some of the equipment has consisted of relatively sophisticated defensive antimortar radars and antiaircraft systems, the deliveries (from states such as Qatar) have also included twenty-five AMX-10 main battle tanks, forty AMX-30 main battle tanks, howitzers, and other artillery.

Policy Innovations

Bosnia's political economy has been altered immeasurably by regime changes in Croatia and in the FRY. Croatian president Franjo Tudjman's December 1999 death left the HDZ rudderless and facing elections against a revived democratic opposition. Signaling a sea of change in Croatian politics, the opposition swept to power in the elections; Croats elected President Stipe Mesic, who had actively protested against the war in Bosnia in the early 1990s. Mesic has repeatedly denounced any territorial designs on Bosnia; he has dismissed separatist ambitions in Bosnia as "delusions"[28] and has consistently rejected appeals by Bosnian Croats for diplomatic, political, and economic succor. In this, he has supported, and had been supported by, Ivica Racan, Croatia's new prime minister. In a severe blow to the HDZ, he agreed in November 2000 that aid from Croatia to the Bosnian Croats would go through Bosnian state institutions and be transparent to the international community.

The effect of this cutoff has been ambiguous. While the Bosnian HDZ has been cut off from a significant level of financial and political support, their isolation has changed the traditional dynamic between Croatia and the Bosnian Croats. That Croatia's HDZ no longer rules in Zagreb has freed the Herzegovina Croats from even limited constraint. Demands of the Western community, then, have led not to more acquiescence but, rather, to radicalization. With the SDP-led coalition, including several alternative Croat-Muslim parties, holding a slim majority in both the federation and state parliaments, the HDZ is unable to push to the fore its own candidates for state enterprises and agencies.

In Serbia, after years of disarray, the opposition closed ranks around a single presidential candidate—heretofore obscure Serbian nationalist politician Vojislav Kostunica—in time for a September snap election called by Milosevic. After clearly wining these elections, the opposition called for a series of demonstrations until the victory was recognized; the demonstrations resulted in the overthrow of Milosevic in November, his arrest in March 2001, and extradition to The Hague Tribunal in late spring 2001.

Kostunica and his party are perceived as close to the SDS;[29] Kostunica himself (like much of the Serbian opposition) was an advocate of "Greater Serbia" in the first days of the Bosnian war. In the first days of his administration, an international crisis was barely averted when Kostunica modified plans to make his first state visit to Bosnia by going to the Republika Srpska.[30] He pushed for and signed a special agreement establishing parallel relations with the RS. While these ties are explicitly allowed under the Dayton Accord, it is striking that Serbia should expand them at the same time similar arrangements are being cut back or eliminated by Croatia.

The relationship between Serbia and the Bosnian Serbs, then, is likely to look similar to the relationship between Croatia and the Bosnian Croats before Tudjman's death. To the extent that they embarrass Kostunica's government, obstructionist tendencies may be reigned in, but Bosnian Serbs now have a more internationally credible—and passionate—advocate in Serbia than at any time in the past five years. This may encourage continued obstructionism and defiance of the international community. Nevertheless, public sentiment within Serbia has been reported by some observers to be running against emphasis on "national issues," perhaps limiting the degree to which Kostunica's government would be able to focus on Bosnia.

In short, Croatia's clear-cut transformation (discussed further in Jed Snyder's chapter in this volume) has had an ambiguous impact on Croatia-Bosnia relations. Depending on the long-term future of the HDZ, Croatia's transformation may signal the total unraveling of the HDZ's network of patronage and intimidation. Serbia's transition is murkier but perhaps holds clearer implications for relations between Serbia and Bosnia. The Bosnian Serbs may be less radical but more quietly obstructionist. Overall, neither transformation is likely to radically ameliorate the interlaced threats faced by the Bosnian state and described above: weak institutions, pervasive corruption, and strong ethnic cliques.

If the threat facing Bosnia-Herzegovina is a fundamental and chronic absence of robust state capacities, this threat in turn presents the international community with a difficult question: how to help build enduring state institutions around the dominance of the three major ethnic parties—and around the strong public sentiment that has allowed them to remain in power.

Mindful of Bosnia's lack of enduring progress, Western officials had hoped the year 2000 would bring about decisive changes in Bosnia's political landscape. They believed that statewide elections might prove decisive in uprooting Bosnia's main ethnic parties—the Bosniak-Muslim dominated SDA, the Bosnian Serb SDS, and the Bosnian Croat HDZ—from power.[31] In particular, Western officials pinned their hopes on the successes of rivals to the SDA and the SDS, hoping to encourage the formation of governments without the help of the ethnic parties. The most significant of these rival parties, the Social Democratic Party (SDP), ran on a specific platform of ethnic reconciliation.

Superficially, at least, the November elections were a limited success, resulting in formations of moderate, if tenuous, ruling coalitions in the state and Federation parliaments. The importance of this shift should not be underestimated. Cooperation between the Federation entity and state-level governing structures should increase dramatically. Recent steps (described below) taken against the Bosnian HDZ sources of funding may prove similarly useful in diminishing the hold the HDZ once held over the political economy of Herceg-Bosna.

However, the elections also exposed the degree to which ethnicity remains a defining component of Bosnia's politics, and to which the ethnic parties maintain a stranglehold on Bosnia's political economy. The HDZ and SDS each won overwhelmingly among Bosnian Croats and Bosnian Serbs, respectively. Despite mounting a campaign intended to appeal to all ethnic groups, the moderate SDP was unable to draw support from either Croats or Serbs and only fared well among Bosniaks in and around urban areas. Indeed, the SDA campaign slogan, "All the Others Have Chosen Their Ethnic Groups,"[32] seemed particularly effective both as slogan and description of Bosnia's current polity.

As of early 2001, Bosnia faces an immediate threat to its own security growing directly from the results of these elections: the prospect of the secession of the Bosnian Croats from Bosnia-Herzegovina. While this immediate threat will likely be weathered, it is representative of the long-term challenge to Bosnia's security and stability. That challenge is still best described as the self-reinforcing linkage between corruption, the weakness of state institutions, and ethnic separatism.

The nature of the international community's commitment to Bosnia has been gradually stabilizing and even intensifying. In two seminal 1997 Peace Implementation Conferences (PICs), the Contact Group furnished the High Representative with a list of discrete tasks for civilian implementation. They further authorized him to take actions against political representatives who fail to attend meetings without good cause or who the High Representative sees as having violated legal commitments made under the peace agreement.

As state institutions have continued to stagnate, the High Representative has used these powers to take a stronger, more interventionist role in Bosnian politics. Since the Bonn conference, the High Representative— first Carlos Westendorp and now Wolfgang Petritsch—has unilaterally established over eighty laws and binding decisions, touching on issues from passports and license plates to a state border service. The June 2000 PIC set as a goal the securing of economic reform, including the establishment of several common institutions, including a statewide regulatory regime, a state treasury and a professional civil service. These steps, if eventually implemented by the HR, would follow on the heels of the creation of the state border service (described above). Finally, the High Representative has become increasingly interventionist in the political process, dismissing some eight public officials in the last year.

The international military force has undergone a similar evolution. Although its force level has declined (from sixty thousand under IFOR to twenty thousand today), when IFOR "switched over" to SFOR at the end of IFOR's one-year deadline, the scope of its mission has increased significantly. SFOR now takes a more active role in assisting the civilian side of the mission, including coordinating and preparing for refugee return with the rest of the international community in Bosnia. Perhaps most important, SFOR stepped up the arrest of war criminals in Bosnia as well, although some indicted war criminals—particularly in the RS—remain at large and maintain a significant role in Bosnia's political and economic life. SFOR also continues to shy away from involvement in civil unrest, preparing to leave those situations to local police under the guidance of the IPTF.

Close attention, however, should be paid to the U.S. position on the continued deployment of troops to the SFOR. George Bush promised during the presidential campaign to review U.S. peacekeeping deployments, and a month before the election, an aide suggested strongly that Bush would establish as an objective the withdrawal of U.S. troops from the Balkans.[33] In a presentation at a conference in February, top Pentagon official U.S. General Joseph Dayton, while making it clear he was speaking on his own behalf, suggested that the "principals" in the new administration had agreed to drastically reduce troop presence in the Balkans and hinted a full withdrawal could occur by the end of Bush's first term (though these statements were enthusiastically countered by a U.S. State Department representative). At the least, these episodes give a strong indication of the degree to which many in the U.S. military and in the current U.S. administration believe the time has come for the United States to sharply reduce its presence in the Balkans. At most, they herald pressure for troop reductions in 2001–2002.

At the moment, no institution so clearly exemplifies the halting and uncertain peace effort of the West's in Bosnia as that of Bosnia's military. During 2000, the most important innovation in Bosnia's military involved neither policy nor procurement, but administration. In December of 1999, the Standing Committee on Military Matters (SCMM) formed a working group to discuss the development of a common, state-level defense policy. That working group, composed of two high-level officers from the ABH, VRS, and HVO, met at nearly monthly intervals during 2000. With a final meeting in January 2000, the working group returned a draft to the SCMM, albeit with a multitude of bracketed (contested) passages, and the SCMM is scheduled to agree to a formal version sometime in 2001.

The real question for 2001–2002 concerns the mechanisms of command and control. Despite repeated statements by NATO that no army but a larger Bosnian force will be accepted within PfP, NATO VRS representatives continue to claim that the VRS must join PfP as a distinct force rather than within a larger Bosnian army.[34] VRS representatives also dismiss the idea of a joint Bosnian force.[35]

Nevertheless, all parties seem to be moving toward gradual acceptance of a military structure in which units under a nominal control structure are based in regions of their own ethnicity. A military adviser to HDZ president—and Croat member of the Presidency—Ante Jelavic called for a similar structure, noting that "we would be finding ourselves in a situation where we do not mind the national features, the language, creed, customs, and culture of the others."[36] ABiH General Atif Dudakovic has suggested an army with units and command dispersed "to ensure that the national interest of the predominant peoples in a certain area are met."[37] It is perhaps significant that the HR is placing a clear premium on the slow development of consensus among Bosnia's three parties, rather than the imposition of a solution.

All sides, regardless of short-term developments, will be pursuing long-term cuts and demobilization. As discussed above, the militaries are under severe financial strain. Both parts of the Federation Army were placed on leave for a large part of December.[38] In addition to discussions on command and control, the SCMM process set a series of limits on military force in the region. At an August 2000 meeting in Oberammergau, the three sides in the SMCC process agreed to lower the number of troops in armies in Bosnia to 19,800 at most: 6,600 for the RS and 13,200 in the federation. The parties also agreed to limits on the number of potential reservists that could be placed under arms.[39] In a December interview, senior American emissary Robert Barry called for a final reduction to 15,000 of all armed forces in Bosnia.[40]

Future Prospects

The last few months of 2000 and the first months of 2001 in Bosnia were particularly eventful. In the Federation, the HDZ, reacting to an unfavorable change in election law only three weeks before the November elections, and an unfavorable postelection ruling removing ten HDZ representatives from cantonal governments, stated it would no longer work within the Federation, and declared a "temporary Croat-self government." The HDZ tried to revive the institutions of Herceg-Bosna, calling on Bosnian Croat members of the Federation Army to desert their barracks. The international community reacted by appointing a special auditor to oversee affairs at the Herzegovacka Banka, known to be a central institution in the HDZ network of smuggling and patronage. By late May 2001, the HDZ effort appeared to be crumbling. HVO defense officials had publicly sworn loyalty to the federation defense ministry—the minister of which is a member of the

SDP-led coalition, illustrating the immediate effects of the moderates' take-over of the federation parliament—and soldiers were returning to barracks.

In the Republika Srpska, so-called "mobs," by some accounts clearly organized, used physical intimidation to halt two mosque rebuilding cere-monies, one in Banja Luka and the other in Trebinje. In a particularly humbling moment, several international officials were trapped inside a hotel in Banja Luka as Bosnian Serb police did little to disperse the crowds and SFOR declined to step into the situation.

Both events displayed the problems and possibilities of Bosnian security. HDZ intransigence, like the riots in RS, apparently are the result of calculated decision making, and have strong public support. Nevertheless, it is becom-ing apparent from the recent behavior of the HDZ that the effort to maintain parallel structures, particularly in light of the seizure of Hercegovacka Banka, will be exceedingly difficult.

In short, the uncertainty surrounding Bosnian security is best presented as a series of seeming contradictions. With apologies to Winston Churchill, Bosnian security is neither as robust nor as precarious as it appears to be. The 2000 elections, heralded by international community representatives as a fundamental change in Bosnia's political future, did not actually repre-sent a significant change in the electoral attitudes of most Bosnians. How-ever, the administrative control gained as a result of the election by the moderate SDP and its coalition partners—both at the state-level and at the federation level—does represent a significant shift in the polity and a potential shift in the political economy of the entity.

Conversely, while the stunning changes in Croatia and Serbia have ripped away some of the financial props upon which the political economy of obstruction had rested, the political effects of those changes have yet to be fully gauged, and, particularly in Serbia, may not have an entirely positive effect on Bosnian security. Finally, the increasing involvement of the High Representative at this stage of Bosnian political development acts as both help and hindrance to Bosnian political development.

Chronology

1 January 2000: The position of the federation president and vice president rotates; Ejup Ganic becomes the Bosnia-Herzegovina (BiH) federation pres-ident and Ivo Andric-Luzanski the vice president.

3 January 2000: Croatian parliamentary elections held; the HDZ loses the majority of seats in the Parliament to a coalition of opposition parties.

14 January 2000: The ICTY sentences five Bosnian Croats to six to twenty-five years. The five were charged in connection with their role in the attack on the village of Ahmici in central Bosnia in 1993 and the massacre of 116 Bosnian Muslim inhabitants of the village.

24 January 2000: Croatian presidential elections held; Croat peace activist and politician Stipe Mesic finishes in front of reformer Drazen Budisa. The HDZ finishes a distant third.

25 January 2000: IFOR detains Mitar Vasiljevic, a Bosnian Serb and suspected war criminal, who was a member of White Eagles, a paramilitary group headed by Vojislav Seselj. He was wanted under sealed indictment by the ICTY for war crimes committed from 1992 to 1994 in the area of Visegrad.

15 February 2000: Two-day meeting of the Stability Pact Working Table on Security Issues started in Sarajevo. The BiH Parliament House of Representatives rejects the draft election law.

3 March 2000: General Tihomir Blaskic found guilty on all charges by the ICTY in The Hague and sentenced to forty-five years imprisonment.

5 March 2000: SFOR detains Dragoljub Prcac, a Bosnian Serb, charged with grave breaches of the Geneva conventions, violations of the laws or customs of war, and crimes against humanity at the Omarska camp in 1992.

13 March 2000: The Hague ICTY initiates the trial of Gen. Radislav Krstic, charged with genocide, crimes against humanity, and war crimes in connection with massacre in Srebrenica in July 1995.

20 March 2000: The trial of Dragoljub Kunarac, Radomir Kovac, and Zoran Vukovic begins at the ICTY in The Hague. All were accused of crimes against humanity (rape, torture, enslavement) of Bosniak women in Foca in 1992–93.

23 March 2000: Croatian president Stipe Mesic arrives for a two-day official visit to BiH.

3 April 2000: SFOR detains Momcilo Krajisnik under a sealed indictment by the ICTY for war crimes.

8 April 2000: Municipal elections held in Bosnia and Herzegovina. Non-ethnic parties make some gains, although the HDZ remains in control of Croat cantons.

14 June 2000: The High Representative meets with the newly appointed chairman of the BiH Council of Ministers, Spasoje Tusevljak.

25 June 2000: SFOR detains war crimes suspect Dusko Sikirica. He is charged with crimes against humanity, violations of the laws or customs of war, and grave breaches of the Geneva Conventions of 1949.

29 September 2000: The High Representative imposes amendments to the Law on Travel Documents, introducing a single national passport. Meeting of the BiH Presidency, which nominates Martin Raguz for the new chairman of the BiH Council of Ministers.

5 October 2000: Supporters of Kostunica storm the parliament building in the FRY, eventually winning recognition of Vojislav Kostunica's victory.

14 October 2000: Zivko Radisic takes over duties from Alija Izetbegovic as the president of the BiH Presidency. President Alija Izetbegovic withdraws from the BiH Presidency and is replaced by Halid Genjac.

18 October 2000: The BiH House of Representatives confirms Martin Raguz as the chair of the BiH Council of Ministers. The BiH House of Representatives adopts the Law on Freedom of Information and the Draft Law on Ombudsman.

20 October 2000: The High Representative, Wolfgang Petritsch, meets with the new Yugoslav president Vojislav Kostunica in Belgrade.

10 November 2000: The BiH Presidency meets with Javier Solana, EU High Representative for the Common Foreign and Security Policy.

11 November 2000: General elections held for BiH House of Representatives, RS Presidency and RS National Assembly, Federation House of Representatives, Federation cantonal assemblies, and the municipality of Srebrenica.

15 December 2000: BiH and the FRY establish diplomatic relations.

11 January 2001: High Representative Wolfgang Petritsch issues a decision establishing constitutional commissions in both entities.

12 January 2001: Former RS president Biljana Plavsic pleads not guilty to charges of committing war crimes, after voluntarily surrendering to the ICTY.

13 January 2001: Representatives of ten parties (SDP, SBiH, NHI, BPS [Bosnian Patriotic Party], Republican Party, GDS [Civic Democratic Party], HSS [Croat Peasant Party], and others) create the Democratic Alliance for Change.

15 January 2001: Constitutive session of the Federation Parliament's House of Representatives; SBiH's (Party of BiH) Enver Kreso elected chairman. HDZ deputies leave the session in protest. Senior HDZ official, Ivo Andric Luzanski, says the session marks "the beginning of the end of the BiH Federation." RS prime minister Mladen Ivanic asks ministers in his government to suspend their party memberships and assume the role of independent experts. U.S. government asks Ivanic to dismiss minister and SDS member Goran Popovic.

18 January 2001: Controversial SDS minister in the RS government, Goran Popovic, is withdrawn from his post, as a result of international pressure.

19 January 2001: FRY President Vojislav Kostunica pays his first official visit to BiH.

25 January 2001: Ante Jelavic assures the High Representative that HDZ does not want to create a third entity in BiH. *New York Times* publishes Thomas Friedman op-ed calling for BiH partition.

31 January 2001: The Alliance names Bozidar Matic, a prominent intellectual and successful business manager, for the chair of the Council of Ministers. Standing Committee on Military Matters convenes. Common defense policy close to being completed.

6 February 2001: Deputies in the BiH Parliament's House of Representatives reject Martin Raguz (HDZ) for the post of the chairman of the Council of Ministers.

9 February 2001: High Representative asks the BiH Presidency to appoint without delay a new candidate for the chair of the Council of Ministers. On 10 February, Alliance parties propose Bozidar Matic, a prominent academic and a successful business manager, as the Presidency's candidate.

13 February 2001: The Bosniak and the Serb member of the BiH Presidency endorse the candidacy of Bozidar Matic for the chair of the Council of Ministers; Croat member, Ante Jelavic, walks out of the session.

22 February 2001: BiH gets its first government in a decade without national-ist parties—Bozidar Matic is named the chair of the Council of Ministers.

22 February 2001: The Hague Tribunal sentences three BiH Serbs from Foca (Dragoljub Kunarac, Radomir Kovac, and Zoran Vukovic) to prison for leading a campaign of mass rape during the war in BiH; media mark this a historic verdict, because the ICTY has punished sexual assault as a crime against humanity.

26 February 2001: The Hague Tribunal gives prison sentences to two senior Croat officials, Dario Kordic and Mario Cerkez, for crimes against humanity committed in Central Bosnia. Bosniaks are appalled by the "light sentence"; Croat veteran associations and the HDZ say the "unfair" ruling places collective guilt upon Croats in BiH.

28 February 2001: Federation Vice President, Ante Jelavic, the Croat member of the BiH Presidency and HDZ leader, sends a letter supporting two sentenced Croat war criminals and says that the Federation is solely a Bosniak entity.

3 March 2001: The Croat National Assembly (HNS) declares interim "Croat self-rule." Marko Tokic (HDZ) is elected president of the so-called Self-Rule. The HNS threatens to break away permanently unless the international community and political partners in BiH meet demands within fifteen days.

5 March 2001: The president of the Federal Republic of Yugoslavia, Vojislav Kostunica, and the RS (Republika Srpska) president, Mirko Sarovic, sign an agreement on special relations between FRY and the mainly Serb entity.

5 March 2001: Croatian Prime Minister Ivica Racan and the country's presi-dent, Stipe Mesic, condemn the decisions of the Croat national assembly and stress that all issues should be resolved through legally established insti-tutions.

7 March 2001: The High Representative, Wolfgang Petritsch, removes Ante Jelavic as well as three other senior party colleagues. Petritsch says Jelavic and his colleagues violated the constitutional order in BiH.

9 March 2001: The Presidency of the HDZ rejects the decision of the High Representative to remove its officials from all public functions, but Ante Jelavic says he will "voluntarily resign" from the BiH Presidency.

12 March 2001: Nearly four months after the elections in November, the BiH federation gets its first nonnationalist government led by Alija Behmen (SDP).

16 March 2001: The Croat National Assembly (HNS) postpones the self-proclaimed Croat self-rule in BiH for another two months.

23 March 2001: The Croat National Assembly (HNS) welcomes the decision of a number of Croat officials within the Federation ministry of defense and the joint command of the Federation army to offer their services to the HNS.

26 March 2001: The chief UN prosecutor for the ICTY, Carla del Ponte, arrives in Banja Luka for a three-day visit to BiH; Del Ponte calls for the arrest of indicted war criminals Radovan Karadzic and Ratko Mladic and announces new indictments against other war crimes suspects in BiH.

28 March 2001: After the Croat National Assembly calls for temporarily disbanding the Croat component of the Federation army, a number of Croat officers and soldiers in Vitez, Livno, Mostar, and Kiseljak walk out of their barracks. Federation Defense Minister Mijo Anic dismisses three additional Croat commanders for their disloyalty to the Federation Army.

1 April 2001: Former FRY President Slobodan Milosevic arrested in Belgrade.

6 April 2001: The High Representative, Wolfgang Petritsch, appoints a provisional administrator to Hercegovacka Banka to investigate information that public funds had disappeared possibly to finance Croat "self-rule."

6 April 2001: An attempt ordered by the OHR, SFOR, and the provisional administrator to take control of the offices of the Hercegovacka Banka in Mostar and other towns in Herzegovina is met with well-organized violence, resulting in twenty-two injuries among international officials.

NOTES

1. Richard Holbrooke, *To End a War* (New York: Modern Library, 1998), 221–22; James Kitfield, "Lessons from Kosovo and Bosnia," *The National Journal* 32, 23 December 2000: 52–53.

2. Julian Borger, "Karadzic Spectre Hangs over Poll," *London Observer*, 8 September 1996, p. 20.

3. *Reshaping International Priorities in Bosnia and Herzegovina: Part One* (Sarajevo: European Stability Institute, 1999).

4. *Reshaping International Priorities in Bosnia and Herzegovina: Part One*, op. cit.

5. European Stability Institute, "The End of the Nationalist Regimes and the Future of the Bosnian State," 22 March 2001, 18–19.

6. John Schindler, "Bosnia Prepares for Life after Izetbegovic," *Jane's Intelligence Review* 13, no. 2 (1 February 2001).

7. U.S. General Accounting Office, *Bosnia Peace Operation: Crime and Corruption Threaten Successful Implementation of the Dayton Peace Agreement*, GAO/NSIAD-00-156 (Washington, D.C.: July 2000).

8. Schindler, "Bosnia Prepares for Life after Izetbegovic."

9. Ibid. R. Jeffrey Smith, "West Is Tiring of Struggle to Rebuild Bosnia," *Washington Post*, 25 November 2000, p. A1.

10. Janez Kovac, "Bosnian Smuggling Revival," *IWPR Balkans Crisis Report* 154 (7 July 2000).

11. International Crisis Group, "Turning Strife to Advantage: A Blueprint to Integrate the Croats in Bosnia and Herzegovina," Technical Report No. 106, Brussels and Sarajevo, 15 March 2001.

12. R. Jeffrey Smith, "West Is Tiring of Struggle to Rebuild Bosnia," *Washington Post*, 26 November 2000, p. 1.

13. World Bank, *Bosnia Peace Operation: Crime and Corruption Threaten Successful Implementation of the Dayton Peace Agreement* (Washington, D.C.: World Bank, 2000).

14. Jon W. Western and Daniel Serwer, *Bosnia's Next Five Years: Dayton and Beyond*, (Washington, D.C.: U.S. Institute of Peace, 3 November 2000).

15. "Security and Foreign Forces," in *Jane's Sentinal Security Assessment—the Balkans* (23 August 2000).

16. International Crisis Group, *Is Dayton Failing?* (Brussels: International Crisis Group, 1999), 111.

17. "Federation MUP Says Bosnian Serb Police Beat Up Bosniak Returnees in Kotor Varos," Sarajevo *ONASA*, 7 February 2001.

18. International Crisis Group, *Turning Strife to Advantage: A Blueprint to Integrate the Croats in Bosnia and Herzegovina*, March 2001. Available on the Internet at http://www.crisisweb.org (accessed 12 April 2001).

19. International Crisis Group, *Is Dayton Failing?*, 5.

20. Zeljko Cvijanovic, " 'Secret Hague Indictments' Exposed," Institute for War and Peace Reporting, Banja Luka, Balkan Conflict Report 172 (15 September 2000).

21. Milkica Milojevic, "Corps Commander's Salary KM380: Officers and Their Families Live in Barracks, Where Weaponry Has Not Been Replaced since 1990, Like in Refugee Camps," Banja Luka, *Nezavisna Novine*, 19 May 2000, Printed in FBIS as "Report Reviews RS Army Status on Army Day," (23 May 2000), EUP20000523000167.

22. *OSCE Fact Sheet on Entity Armed Forces (as of April 2001)*. Available on Internet at <http://www.Oscebih.Org/Regstab/Eng/Regstb-Forces.htm> (accessed 3 April 2001).

23. "Security and Foreign Forces."

24. Ibid.

25. A 1997 report by the International Crisis Group notes that this resolution was rooted in two important political-diplomatic touchstones: the pre-Dayton enthusiasm of the U.S. Congress for arming Bosnia during the war and the concept—embodied in the 1994 Washington Agreement—that the arms could be used as an enticement for Bosniak-Bosnian Croat cooperation.

26. *"U.S. State Department Fact Sheet on the Train and Equip Program"* (Washington, D.C.: U.S. Department of State, February 2001).

27. Enis Dzanic and Norman Erik, "Retraining the Federation Forces in Post-Dayton Bosnia," *Jane's Intelligence Review* 10, no. 1 (1 January 1998): 14.

28. Tony Gabric, "Zagreb Spurns Bosnian Croat Separatism," Institute for War and Peace Reporting (Split, Croatia), Balkans Crisis Report 197 (21 November 2000).

29. Schindler, "Bosnia Prepares for Life after Izetbegovic."

30. Gabriel Partos, "Analysis: An Uneasy Relationship," *BBC News* 19 January 2001. Available on the Internet at <http://news.bbc.co.uk/hi/english/world/europe/newsid_1126000/1126346.stm> (accessed 25 January 2001)

31. International Crisis Group, *Bosnia's November Elections: Dayton Stumbles*, no. 104 (Sarajevo, Bosnia-Herzegovina: 18 December 2000).

32. Schindler, "Bosnia Prepares for Life after Izetbegovic."

33. Michael R. Gordon, "Bush Would Stop US Peacekeeping in Balkan Fights," *New York Times*, 21 October 2000, p. A1.

34. Patrick Murphy, "Bosnian Serb Army Rejects Bosnia-Wide Force," *Radio Free Europe/Radio Liberty Newsline*, 29 March 2001.

35. Ibid.; *Bosnian Serb Television* (Banja Luka, 9 August 2000), reprinted 12 August 2000 in BBC Summary of World Broadcasts as "Joint Army 'Not Realistic,' Serb member of Presidency Tells NATO" (EE/D3917/C).

36. "Interview by Djuro Kozar with Brigadier General Miroslav Nikolic," Sarajevo *Jutarnje Novine* 18 December 2000, reprinted in FBIS as "Jelavic's Military Adviser Sees Single B-H Army as 'Our Destiny,' " EUP20001120000141.

37. "Interview of Gen. Atif Dudakovic by Antonio Prlena," Sarajevo *Oslobodenje*, 20 January 2001.

38. Sanjin Becirajic, "Generals of a Hungry Army," Sarajevo *Jutarnje Novine* 12 January 2001, reprinted in FBIS as "Daily Assesses 'Financial Dire Straits' of B-H Federation Army," EUP20010126000184.

39. "Interview by Djuro Kozar with Brigadier General Miroslav Nikolic," Sarajevo *Jutarnje Novine* 18 November 2000, reprinted in FBIS as "Jelavic's Military Adviser Sees Single B-H Army as 'Our Destiny,' " EUP20001120000141.

40. Habul, "Commentary Views OSCE Proposal to Reduce Number of B-H Troops to 15,000."

15 ◆ Bulgaria: Driving to the West

Margarita Assenova

The most frightening is that Bulgaria's population has decreased by one million during the last decade, while in all wars of the 20th century the country lost 150 thousand people. The essence of the nation has emigrated. Bulgaria not only loses its lifeblood, but also experiences a brain drain.

—Stefan Tzanev, Bulgarian poet

The year 2000 was marked by the start of Bulgaria's accession negotiations with the European Union (EU), the government's efforts to fight organized crime and corruption, and the battle against Russia's plan for regaining its influence in the Balkans. However, the fighting in Macedonia at the beginning of 2001 posed the biggest security challenge to Bulgaria since 1989.

The door to Europe finally opened for Bulgaria after the EU Justice and Home Affairs Council decided to lift visa restrictions for Bulgarian citizens on 30 November 2000. President Stoyanov stated that "the Berlin Wall fell for the Bulgarians on that day." Although geographically Bulgaria has always been in Europe, the country was politically isolated for more than half a century. In 2000 Bulgaria symbolically regained its position, and the event lifted the spirit of the tired and impoverished people.

During the first years after the fall of Communism, Bulgaria had fluctuating success in trying to overcome its international isolation and extreme dependence on Russian foreign policy. Although the country established diplomatic relations with the North Atlantic Treaty Organization (NATO) in 1990, the dramatic shift in foreign policy and security priorities was not completed until 1997, when Bulgaria declared its desire for full membership in NATO and launched a more active regional diplomacy.

In 1991–92, the first government of the Union of Democratic Forces (UDF) established the foundations of a Euro-Atlantic policy by opening

Bulgaria to Europe and keeping a reasonable distance from Russia. Bulgaria established closer relations with Turkey after years of alienation following the Communists' forcible assimilation of the sizable Turkish minority.[1] Despite perceptions that Bulgaria harbored territorial claims toward Macedonia, it became the first state to officially recognize the Republic of Macedonia in January 1992 after the disintegration of Yugoslavia. These two new foreign policy directions raised suspicions in Greece over the intensification of Bulgarian-Turkish relations and created tensions over Macedonia's name.

Bulgaria's UDF government fell in November 1992, lacking the time to pursue its initiatives toward European integration and the assumption of a more important regional role. The next four years of Socialist rule largely returned the country to international isolation. The Socialist government of Zhan Videnov preferred to intensify Sofia's relations with Moscow, Athens, and Belgrade, practically closing the country inside this triangle.

Sofia drifted away from the West and NATO at the time the Alliance refined its criteria for future enlargement. In 1996, after three rounds of discussions with NATO concerning prospective desires to join the Alliance, the Socialist leadership decided not to pursue membership. The government's isolationism, combined with a disastrous economic policy, led to large-scale social unrest in the winter of 1996–97.[2] Barely avoiding "grave civil clashes, which would have jeopardized the country's European and Atlantic integration" as President Petar Stoyanov pointed out,[3] Bulgaria finally embarked on economic transition, international integration, and a balanced regional policy after a democratic government took office in 1997.

In February 1997 the government officially declared Bulgaria's objective to become a NATO member. The major political parties supported this goal with the exception of the Socialist Party, which insisted on neutrality and a public referendum on membership.[4] The government approved a national program for Bulgaria's accession to NATO and created several institutions and working groups to help the country meet the criteria for future accession. These steps were the first sign of unity on key foreign policy issues between the executive and legislative branches of government.

Bulgaria's decision to strive for NATO membership put an end to the country's unsolved problem of finding valuable allies in the Balkans and Europe. It also removed the ambiguity in Sofia's relations with Russia.

In the spring of 1999, the Kosovo crisis brought to the fore the sense of threat caused by regional destabilization. For the first time after the fall of Communism, Bulgaria had to seek protection for its national security from NATO after the country declared full support for operation "Allied Force" against Serbia and allowed air corridors for Allied aircraft.[5] The Kosovo crisis became a test for Sofia's determination to pursue collective security and defend the human rights of oppressed minorities. With its actions and diplomacy during the war, the government underscored the degree of political change that had taken place in the country toward a pro-European and pro-Atlantic orientation.

Threat Assessment

The year 2000 provided conditions for intensive reconstruction and regional cooperation in the Balkans after the war in Kosovo. Although tensions between Serbia and its neighbors remained high for most of the year, the fall of the Slobodan Milosevic regime brought about hope for a better future for the region.

The external risks to Bulgaria's security during the year stemmed mainly from three sources: 1. the activities of radical groups on the territory of former Yugoslavia; 2. political and economic instability in the region; and 3. the increasing criminalization of the Balkans.

The radicalization of the south Balkans after the war in Kosovo became the most serious threat to the security of the entire region. Although the actions of militant groups remained limited to the territory of Kosovo, southern Serbia, and Macedonia, there was uncertainty whether the guerrilla war could be stopped and there was a danger of a spillover to neighboring Bulgaria and Greece.

The continuing disintegration of Yugoslavia and the unwillingness of the international community to decide on the status of Kosovo created conditions for rapid radicalization of certain groups among the Albanian community. The actions of extremist groups, the ethnic confrontation between Albanians and Slavs, and the difficulties in building civil structures and dealing with Kosovo's humanitarian problems produced obstacles to the region's stabilization. Political and economic insecurity in the region had a negative impact on Bulgaria and delayed the process of economic transformation. The general uncertainty in the region hampered foreign investors' participation in Bulgaria's privatization and established conditions for the arrival of illicit money.

The crises in the region accelerated the emergence of criminal organizations, which rapidly built bases and channels for illegal activities. The Balkans became an arena for the activities of Albanian, Serbian, and Russian criminal networks. Despite the government's struggle against mafia-type groups operating on Bulgarian territory, the country remained vulnerable to penetration by criminal networks, because of the overall high level of crime in the region and Bulgaria's location on the major road from the Middle East to Europe. Bulgaria has long held a strategic position on the drug-trafficking route, connecting sources of supply in southwest Asia with major markets in western Europe.

The role of Albanian criminal networks in transnational crime, and especially in drug trafficking, increased. In 2000 one-fifth of all discovered attempts of drug smuggling were committed by the Albanians. The profit from these activities is believed to be one of the main sources for financing radical forces among the Albanian community in the Balkan peninsula.

There is a growing danger of Bulgarian citizens being involved in criminal structures in drug trafficking channels as well as building drug depots on the territory of the country. During the year 2000, there was increasing drug trafficking in the southwestern direction along the so-called "Balkan route" across Bulgaria to the western Balkans; the northern trail of the "Balkan route" across Romania to western Europe, Moldova, and Ukraine; and from Turkey and Latin America into Bulgaria.

Drug smuggling along with the illegal immigration, which uses the same routes into Europe, caused serious problems for the government, especially after the EU lifted its visa restrictions for Bulgarian citizens in the fall of 2000. The existing organized criminal groups in Bulgaria continued to be a security risk. Various forms of smuggling, fiscal and financial fraud, illegal gambling, money laundering, and the illegal export of capital have not been eliminated.

The Bulgarian government considers that foreign special services were using the structures of organized crime to attain their own goals in the country.[6] Bulgaria encountered attempts by the Russian secret services to regain political influence by using criminal networks and the instruments of the gray economy.

According to experts and political observers in Sofia, Russia's attempts to heavily influence the political process in Bulgaria have not ceased since Todor Zhivkov was ousted in 1989. However, the means of achieving this goal have changed since Russia was no longer able to directly dictate its political will to the new and not always accommodating Bulgarian administrations. Russia's former security services became involved in developing criminal networks throughout the country, which not only increased overall criminality, but also corrupted the economy and undermined the political system.[7]

Some of the major players of Russia's organized criminal networks were former Soviet intelligence officers such as General Vladimir Gorshenin, who was involved in the arms trade, illegal compact disks manufacture, and diamond smuggling before being expelled by the Bulgarian government in the summer of 2000. Another major player, Michael Chorny, who was also expelled from Bulgaria and banned from entering the country for ten years, ended up on the FBI's list of people suspected of money laundering. According to a *Fortune* magazine article in May 2000, the Trans World Group, run by Michael Chorny and his brother, was involved in the money laundering scandal at the Bank of New York.[8]

In August 2000 the Bulgarian government expelled five Russian and seven Serbian businessmen for posing as threats to Bulgaria's economic and national security. The Serbs tried to smuggle military equipment, including rockets, to their country through Bulgaria.

The tensions between Bulgaria and Russia further escalated after Kostov's government asked three Russian diplomats to leave for Moscow in March 2001. The government had evidence that the Russians were involved in spying on Bulgaria's defense secrets. One of the diplomats tried to promote the establishment of leftist organizations in Bulgaria to help the former Communists defeat the ruling coalition in the coming elections. Russian diplomats were also involved in mobilizing Russians who were naturalized Bulgarian citizens to render support to the former Communist party.

Although there were no significant security-related threats to Bulgaria's internal stability, the domestic political situation kept tensions high and political confrontation escalated in anticipation of the general elections in 2001.

The cabinet of Prime Minister Ivan Kostov, who also led the Union of Democratic Forces (UDF), became the first government to accomplish a full mandate in the post-Communist period, thus contributing to Bulgaria's stability. The reformist majority that had ruled the country since 1997 continued to pursue its policy of economic reforms and integration of Bulgaria into the European Union and NATO. While all major political forces in the country have favored European integration for almost a decade, only in 2000 did the Socialist Party declare its support for Bulgaria's bid to join NATO.

The Socialist decision came as a result of growing public support for NATO accession, which has risen significantly as a result of the firm and successful policy of the government during the war in Kosovo in 1999. The Bulgarian government adopted the behavior of a loyal NATO ally during the bombing of Yugoslavia and played an instrumental role in preventing Russian forces from preemptive deployment to Kosovo. Bulgaria refused to give an air corridor to Russian planes carrying soldiers to Pristina and thus precluded Russia's plan to divide the province. Though these policies created public anxiety and fears at the time of the bombing against Yugoslavia, the Serb withdrawal convinced the larger part of the Bulgarian population that the government had adopted the right course of action.

In May 2000 the national assembly adopted by consensus a declaration on foreign and security policy, which demonstrated broad political support for joining the alliance. Accession negotiations with the European Union started in February 2000 after the Helsinki European Council formally invited Bulgaria into the EU in December 1999.

Bulgaria started 2000 with a major change of government ministers. Ten out of sixteen ministers were replaced following decisions on restructuring of key ministers and the creation of new European integration structure. However, behind the official explanation of these changes was the prime minister's intention to remove from the government several compromised or corrupted political figures. Unfortunately, Kostov did not admit publicly the real reasons for the dismissal of some ministers, and this created conditions for speculations and more corruption accusations. As a result, the government spent a significant amount of time and effort trying to neutralize the struggle for power within the ruling coalition.

One after another, corruption scandals started to unfold and undermined public support for the government. The former minister of interior, Bogomil Bonev, dismissed for alleged connections with Russian criminal network leaders, fought back after his firing and demanded Kostov's resignation, accusing him of corruption. He failed to bring down the government and resorted to forming a new coalition to run against the Union of Democratic Forces in the June 2001 general elections. Counting on support from the Bulgarian monarch in exile Simeon II, the new formation intended to attract votes that traditionally went to the UDF. This plan failed, however, after Simeon II formed a separate movement upon his return to Bulgaria in April 2001.

The corruption scandals continued throughout the year and involved, among others, the former deputy prime minister, Alexander Bozhkov, who was dismissed as Bulgaria's chief EU negotiator. Two deputy ministers and the cabinet's newly appointed press officer also fell victims of corruption accusations. Kostov and his family also paid a high price in the ongoing political war when it became evident that Mrs. Kostova had accepted donations for her charity from the Russian businessman Grigorii Luchanski shortly before Bulgarian authorities accused him of money laundering for the former Soviet security services.

In the summer of 2000, the Bulgarian public was baffled again by a wiretapping scandal after Attorney General Nikola Filchev discovered listening devices in his apartment. The homes of seven hundred government officials were carefully checked for "bugs," but the police could not find proof that the secret services had undertaken an illegal operation of political surveillance. Several months later a similar wiretapping scandal unfolded in Macedonia. The former Macedonian prime minister, Branko Crvenkovski, broke the scandal after his visit to Bulgaria, where he met with Socialist Party functionaries, some of whom were former Communist security services officers. Crvenkovski tried to implicate Bulgaria and its current security services in spying activities in Macedonia.

However, under the surface of political scandals and partisan struggles for power, Bulgaria has been gradually developing its democratic institutions. The country has achieved a strong measure of institutional stability by guaranteeing democracy and the rule of law. The Bulgarian parliament has established a pattern of smooth and constructive work on the enormous amount of new legislation, the adoption of which is necessary to be in compliance with the European Union. The government continued to implement its reform program toward establishing a private economy and a free market. Even in the midst of political turmoil, the government was implementing policies that led to Bulgaria's international recognition for its reform effort.

At the end of its mandate, Kostov's government was able to show substantial progress in economic development. Bulgaria's gross domestic product (GDP) reached 5 percent, which is the highest for the last eleven years. The country's exports rose by 20 percent as a result of the liberalized foreign trade.

The government has accomplished the privatization of over 77.5 percent of the enterprises designated for sale. The contribution of the private sector to the gross added value was 69.9 percent at the end of 2000. The restitution of agricultural lands to their legitimate owners increased from 80 percent in 1998 to 99.8 percent at the end of 2000. Foreign investments for 2000 were $1.1 billion, according to the Foreign Investments Agency, which constitutes a rise of 36.5 percent compared to 1999.

The current macroeconomic picture in Bulgaria seems stable, although the level of economic activity still has to reach the pretransition levels, while the trickle down effect of economic benefits is still not evident for most people.

The establishment of the Currency Board in 1997 helped to reverse the downward trend in the main macroeconomic indicators. However, the standard of living in Bulgaria has worsened in recent years, while the social assistance system has not been in a position to respond effectively to the most needy and vulnerable groups.[9]

Bulgaria's high dependence on external supplies of energy resources continues to present a specific economic risk, which also becomes a security risk, because most of the supplies come from a single country—Russia. This extreme dependence creates conditions for Russia to use energy blackmail for political purposes, as past experience has shown.

The social cost of the transition in Bulgaria is one of the highest in Central and East Europe. Although the transition process resulted in gains for the people in terms of human rights and civil liberties, a large proportion of Bulgaria's people have experienced a decline in their general quality of life, through mounting poverty, decreasing incomes, rising unemployment, and greater inequality and insecurity. The official UN Human Development Index (HDI) ranking for Bulgaria has declined from 33 in 1991 to 60 in 2000. The rate of registered unemployment reached 19 percent in 2000.

The level of wages in Bulgaria is still one of the lowest in Europe. The average wage stands at a little over $100 per month. The majority of Bulgarians remain close to the poverty line, with food expenditures accounting for well over 50 percent of the total household budget. Those particularly affected by the decline in incomes have been public sector wage earners and all social payment recipients. The plight of pensioners, who represent almost one-third of the population (2.5 million), has particularly worsened.[10]

Poverty also has an ethnic dimension, with higher rates of impoverishment found among Roma and Turks. Over 40 percent of Bulgarian Turks and 84 percent of the Roma population are estimated to live in poverty. Poverty and lack of prospects has led to an enormous wave of emigration of well-educated young people to Western Europe and America. The Turkish population has seen a relatively low but steady flow of emigration to Turkey, mostly for economic reasons. Over three hundred thousand Turks left Bulgaria for political reasons in 1989 following the Communist assimilation campaign. Almost half of the Turkish people who had lived in Bulgaria before May 1989 have moved to Turkey.

The dire living conditions and poverty levels have led to a dramatic decrease of the birthrate and increase of the death rate and caused negative natural growth of the nation.[11] Bulgaria became the fastest decreasing nation in the world with the loss of almost 1 million people (11 percent) over the last decade as a result of negative natural growth and emigration.[12]

Capacities

Situated in the middle of a war-torn and crime-riddled region, Bulgaria has made the only realistic choice it could to secure its borders, integrity, and future: the country resolutely took the road to the European Union and NATO. Sofia centered its security agenda on four major objectives: development of dynamic relations with the neighbors to achieve mutual trust with the countries in the region, enhancing Bulgaria's role as generator of security and stability in the Balkans, contributing to the process of integration of southeastern Europe into the European and Euro-Atlantic structures, and implementation of military reform to attain interoperability of Bulgaria's armed forces with NATO.

In 2000 Bulgaria began accession negotiations with the EU. One of the significant results of Bulgaria's consistent pro-European policy was the EU decision to lift visa restrictions for Bulgarian citizens. Public opinion appreciated Sofia's achievements by viewing it as one of the foremost positive developments during the year. Before that, Bulgaria had to accept the European standards and criteria for border control and migration.

In 1994 Bulgaria joined NATO's Partnership for Peace (PfP) program, and in 1997 applied for NATO membership. The policy of seeking integration into NATO and the EU reinforced the government's commitment to reform. Bulgaria's strategy for joining NATO includes active participation in the European Atlantic Partnership Council (EAPC) and the enhanced Partnership for Peace. The government has also developed a clear national strategy to meet the criteria for NATO membership, including reform of the armed forces, strengthening civilian control over the military, and achieving interoperability with NATO forces. The Bulgarian parliament has introduced significant changes to national legislation to facilitate the development of highly mobile, streamlined, more professional and well-equipped armed forces that can meet NATO standards. The steps that have been taken suggest that the country's aspiration to join the Alliance in the short term remains realistic.

The parliamentary decision to allow NATO aircraft to use Bulgarian airspace for bombing raids on Yugoslav targets during the Kosovo crisis in 1999 was followed by an agreement in early 2001 to permit NATO to transit and deploy forces in the country. Bulgaria became the first non-NATO country to sign such an agreement with the Alliance. Prime Minister Ivan Kostov recognized that the agreement would provide additional guarantees for Bulgaria's national security as well as for the security of the region in times of armed conflicts.

After the Kosovo crisis, Bulgarian political leaders promoted the country's central role in advancing regional stability, and Sofia hosted a number of postwar security and reconstruction forums and conferences at various levels. Bulgaria fully embraced the EU-sponsored Stability Pact, which was concluded in June 1999, and the country continues to play host to numerous international meetings, in keeping with the government's aspiration to promote Bulgaria as a factor of stability in a politically unstable Balkans.

The Stability Pact implicitly recognized the need for the EU to promote regional stability after the Kosovo conflict. For Bulgaria, as with other countries in southeast Europe, this raised hopes that EU integration might be hastened to facilitate postcrisis regional reconstruction and rehabilitation. Although Bulgaria was not included in the first wave of planned EU enlargement, the strong commitment to accession by Kostov's government, and the new political situation in the Balkans allowed Bulgaria to begin preaccession negotiations at the start of 2000. Several chapters of the *Aquis Communautaire* (the European Union's body of law and regulations) were closed successfully.

The most recent "Regular Report of the EC on Bulgaria's Progress towards Accession" (November 2000) reiterated its previous judgment that Bulgaria already fulfills the political criteria for EU accession and comments that the government has been able to increase its administrative capacity with regard to staffing, planning, and policy making, although there remains some ground to be covered on this front. The report also identifies the need for significant further efforts and resources to be devoted to the area of judicial reform. It is also noted that the government should further enhance its efforts to create an environment of zero tolerance for corruption and to minimize the potential for corruption when drawing up new legislation.[13]

Bulgaria continued its active relations with all neighboring countries and further developed the policy of avoiding the formation of any axis in the region. During its term in office, the UDF government shifted Sofia's foreign policy from one of seeing preferential allies in Greece, Serbia, and Russia to one of equal attention to all neighbors. The new line is consistent with the role Bulgaria wants to play as a generator of security and stability in the Balkans, but it is also a result of a major shift of the overall foreign policy from a pro-Moscow to a pro-European orientation.

Sofia continued to enjoy the support of Greece for Bulgaria's EU and

NATO membership, including backing for resolving the visa problem. Greece had promised to press for Bulgaria's removal from the EU's Schengen visa blacklist and delivered this promise by actively lobbying on behalf of Bulgaria.

Greece remained one of the leading foreign economic partners and investors in Bulgaria. The two countries realized earlier agreements to propose joint projects for implementation under the Stability Pact. The accelerated implementation of joint infrastructure projects was one of the major priorities for bilateral relations.

Bulgaria's relations with Turkey were based on mutual interest in cooperation on security-related issues. The two countries were also interested in developing active bilateral commercial and economic relations and in combating organized crime. Turkey has supported Bulgaria's effort to become a NATO member. However, the economic crisis in Turkey, followed by a political shake-up, affected some of the prospects for Turkish investments in Bulgaria.

In its relations with Romania, Bulgaria has established an interaction and partnership not only on a bilateral basis but also on the basis of the joint efforts to be integrated into the Euro-Atlantic community. Trade and economic relations have become more dynamic, although the two countries have yet to develop their full potential in this respect. Sofia and Bucharest have established effective cooperation in the field of security and fighting organized crime. The change of government in Bucharest in 2000 did not affect bilateral relations between the two neighbors. Moreover, joint initiatives and regular meetings between the presidents of Bulgaria, Romania, and Turkey continued despite the election of new presidents in both Ankara and Bucharest.

The initiation of the democratic process in Serbia created favorable prospects for establishing bilateral relations between Sofia and Belgrade. Before Milosevic's downfall, Bulgaria helped the Serbian opposition to mobilize its potential and win the September elections. After the victory of the democratic forces in Yugoslavia's parliamentary and presidential elections, Sofia advocated including its western neighbor in Stability Pact projects concerning defense, security, justice, and home affairs.

The ethnic and religious contradictions in certain parts of the western

Balkans represent some of the risks for the national security of the Republic of Bulgaria. This is the reason why the Bulgarian national interests require consistent support for the consolidation and intensification of democratic processes in Bosnia-Herzegovina and in the Federal Republic of Yugoslavia. Bulgaria also attaches great importance to protecting the rights of the Bulgarian ethnic minority on the territory of Yugoslavia.

Sofia's policy toward Macedonia was determined not only by the government's strategy of maintaining good relations with all neighbors, but also by the understanding that the stability of Macedonia remains one of the key factors for the security of southeastern Europe.

The beginning of the guerrilla war in Macedonia raised fears of another Balkan conflict. The sense of threat became visible in Bulgaria as soon as the fighting started around the village of Tanushevci in northern Macedonia in February 2001. When the Macedonian army mobilized its reservists and headed for Tetovo on the tanks donated by the Bulgarian defense ministry a couple of years before, the feeling of danger became real for most Bulgarians. There were three factors that contributed to the perception that a war in Macedonia would affect Bulgaria more deeply than any of the Balkan conflicts in the past ten years: 1) the two countries share a border; 2) they also share history; and 3) a sizable Macedonian minority was present in Bulgaria, which was likely to get involved in a potential civil war in Macedonia.

During the twentieth century, Bulgaria fought four wars over Macedonia with the goal of uniting territories, which at different times belonged to the Bulgarian kingdom. After losing all these wars, Bulgaria learned a bitter lesson and accepted the fact that Macedonia does not want to be attached to its eastern neighbor. With a desire to establish friendly bilateral relations, the initial democratic government in Bulgaria led by Philip Dimitrov became the first European government to recognize Macedonia as an independent state in January 1992.

Although relations were strained for several years as a result of an unresolved language dispute, Bulgaria managed to put an end to this long-standing controversy. It recognized Macedonian as separate from the Bulgarian language in 1999. Consequently, the two governments signed twenty-three agreements for bilateral cooperation, among them economic, trade, and military agreements. As part of the military cooperation, Bulgaria donated surplus Bulgarian military supplies to the Macedonian army, which was stripped by Milosevic of all military equipment in 1991.

A potential civil war in Macedonia may have an even more detrimental impact on Bulgaria than the 1999 war in Kosovo did. Apart from economic losses, such a war could pose serious security risks and cause additional complications:

- Refugee problems could be much more severe, because in this case Bulgaria is a neighboring country.
- Possible attempts to split Macedonia may cause serious complications in Balkan relations, thus destabilizing the whole region for an indefinite period.
- Potential involvement of the Macedonian minority in Bulgaria in military operations in Macedonia and creation of paramilitary units may trouble relations with Albania and Kosovo.
- There is an increased risk of terrorist activities on Bulgaria's territory.
- Criminal activities throughout the entire region are likely to intensify.

At the beginning of the conflict, Bulgarian President Petar Stoyanov offered his Macedonian counterpart Boris Traikovski to dispatch Bulgarian armed forces if Macedonia asked its neighbors or international organizations for assistance. The government, however, quickly realized that such a step could prove unsettling to regional security. Bulgarian Defense Minister Boiko Noev sought to play down the president's remarks, saying there was no need to send troops, and offered to provide the Macedonian army with ammunition instead. The initial offer revived fears in the West of a pan-Balkan conflict centered on Macedonia.[14]

Apart from the first emotional response of the Bulgarian president, the reaction of the Bulgarian government, offering support in the framework of a multilateral initiative, was timely and was aimed at quickly stabilizing the situation. This position of the government was welcomed both by Bulgarian and Macedonian politicians and received a positive response from the international community. The commitment of Bulgaria to provide technical assistance and further diplomatic support is important, because the EU is paying increasing attention to the development of good-neighborly relations in the region.

There were two important steps that the Bulgarian government made early in the crisis in Macedonia, and they remained largely unnoticed: for the first time in a decade the banned Macedonian party OMO-Ilinden in Bulgaria was allowed to have its annual public gathering to celebrate the hero Yane Sandanski without any police disturbance, unlike in the past. Also, the Bulgarian government permitted all citizens whose ethnicity was not included in the official census questionnaire to describe it in writing. For the first time, it gave an opportunity for the Bulgarian Macedonians to self-determine their nationality. The final results of the census will be available in the fall of 2001. Although these two steps do not yet signify Sofia's official recognition of the Macedonian nation, which Skopje expects, they form the ground for a future solution to the only unresolved issue between the two countries.

Policy Innovations

Bulgaria continued to maintain its active preparation for NATO accession. In conformity with the Membership Action Plan (MAP), the ministry of defense drafted and submitted to the headquarters of the Alliance an annual national program for 1999–2000 and later a separate progress report on Bulgaria's participation in the MAP, which was approved and accepted by the North Atlantic Council in April 2000.

During 1999, the United States undertook a defense reform assessment, also known as the Kievenaar study, which became the foundation for Bulgaria's 2004 force plan. The ministry of defense and the general staff envision reducing the armed forces from the present figure of 93,100 to 45,000 by the year 2004. By that date, Bulgaria will only have 590 generals and colonels, 1,250 lieutenant colonels, 1,950 majors, and 4,500 officers of lower rank. A total of 62,120 personnel will be retired or discharged, including 10,620 officers, 12,530 sergeants, 18,630 soldiers, and 20,340 civilian employees.

A total of 989 officers and over 800 sergeants were dismissed from regular military service in 2000. Implementation of these reforms is likely to prove a painful process. The cuts will result in social dislocation among ex-soldiers, will raise unemployment levels, and could increase tensions between civil authorities and the military. Indeed, although the defense ministry managed to establish a good relationship between civil and military leaderships and made the basic preparation for the reforms, most of the cuts were postponed until after the general elections in 2001. The incumbent government feared that a sudden increase of the unemployment among military officers would further reduce the declining popular support for UDF.

Bulgaria faces several challenges in the coming years in preparing for meeting the rigors of NATO membership. In particular, similar to the new Central European members, there is a danger of a two-tiered military structure developing with a small, elite, NATO-ready force alongside a much larger unmodernized, unrestructured, and resource-starved army. Indeed, although restructuring and cuts in the Bulgarian army are still ahead, Sofia already announced that several military units are intensively preparing to become fully interoperable with NATO. Out of the forty target items for interoperability, set in 1997, thirty-two have been achieved so far. This has contributed to the increase of the degree of compatibility of the equipment of the air force and the navy, as well as their ability to conduct joint operations with NATO.

However, these "show-case" units, which consumed a significant portion of the resources for MAP implementation, practically competed with the national 2004 plan for restructuring and modernizing the army. In January 2000, the Bulgarian government realized that many of the NATO partnership goals did not relate to its 2004 defense plan. Sofia had to allocate additional resources for the partnership goals. Bulgaria adopted its national security concept in April 1998, a military doctrine in April 1999, a 2004 defense plan in October 1999, and partnership goals in April 2000. Although the Bulgarians believe these documents are adequate, the defense plan 2004 and MAP are separate and need to be integrated.[15] The NATO 2001 report on Bulgaria's progress on MAP implementation recommended revision of the Defense Plan 2004 to provide for faster achieving of interoperability between the Bulgarian army and NATO.

In 2000 Sofia implemented its plan to cut the number of military educational establishments and to open a new national higher military school.

A process of drastic reduction of the military stocks, including tanks, air defense radars, aviation, and navy equipment, and privatization of much of the country's defense industry has already been launched. However, in its 2001 report, NATO recommended that Sofia cut spending on maintenance of unnecessary military equipment. The military budget for 2000 was 6.45 percent of the GDP.

During the year, the structures of the General Staff and the headquarters of the different armed forces branches were brought in accordance with NATO's standards, which included the creation of special technical support and a strategic communications information system. In accordance with the Law on the Defense and the Armed Forces and the NATO Membership Action Plan, the General Staff of the Bulgarian army drafted the "Military Strategy of the Republic of Bulgaria."

Another important step in 2000 was to improve the financial system following the preparation of a concept for the financial management of the ministry of defense and the Bulgarian army. This concept detailed a program approach for the management of the defense budget.

The successful functioning of the headquarters of the Multinational Peacekeeping Forces in Southeastern Europe (MPFSEE) was confirmed with the signing of a third additional amendment to the agreement concerning these forces.

To master in practice NATO's operational procedures and to prepare army units and individual military servicemen for participation in operations of the Alliance, Bulgarian army units and individual representatives took part in twenty-six exercises included in the PfP Program and "in the spirit" of PfP, as well as in NATO exercises that are open for participation of partner countries. In 2000 eight Bulgarian officers were posted in the headquarters and the different bodies for civilian and military cooperation of Stabilization Force (SFOR) and Kosovo Force (KFOR).[16]

In 2000 and early 2001, Bulgaria continued to participate in various forms of regional cooperation such as the implementation of NATO's Southeastern Europe Initiative (SEEI). Bulgaria also actively participates in the defense ministerial meetings of the countries of southeastern Europe, which comprise NATO member states (Italy, Turkey, Greece, and the United States) and candidate countries for NATO membership (Bulgaria, Romania, Macedonia, Albania, Slovenia, and Croatia). The participation of Bulgaria in BLACKSEAFOR, the operative group for military and marine cooperation between Georgia, Romania, Turkey, the Russian Federation, and Ukraine for conducting humanitarian operations, also has practical orientation. Another initiative in which Bulgaria participates actively is the Stability Pact in Southeastern Europe, which is supposed to be an instrument for the integration of Balkan economies with the united economic space in EU. However, critics say that the Stability Pact increasingly is becoming a bureaucratic institution, which spends more money to fly EU officials to the Balkans than to invest in rational projects.

Bulgaria attaches high priority to some of the projects considered by the Stability Pact: Corridor 4—the construction of the bridge across the Danube between Vidin and Calafat; Corridor 8—the railway connection between Bulgaria and Macedonia and the linking of the electricity transfer system of the two countries with a 400-kV electrical transfer cable; Corridor 10—the construction of the motorway between Sofia and Nis.

In 1999 Bulgarian Prime Minister Ivan Kostov launched an initiative of informal meetings with the prime ministers of countries bordering Yugoslavia. It created one of the most effective forums for neutralizing Belgrade's destabilizing potential. After the fall of Milosevic, a change of priorities of the forum is considered to be in order to make it a helpful tool for Yugoslavia's democratization. Some other forms of regional cooperation such as the Black Sea economic cooperation, the established "troikas" Bulgaria-Romania-Greece, Bulgaria-Romania-Turkey, and Bulgaria-Greece-Turkey, as well as the subregional forms of dialogue in different areas of mutual interest such as Bulgaria-Macedonia-Albania and so forth are also going to be evaluated through the prism of the decisions of the EU summit in Nice in 2000.

After the EU lifted the visa restrictions for Bulgarian citizens, the country will become an important barrier to the new challenges to security, such as terrorism, organized crime, drug smuggling, trafficking and trade of people, illicit arms trade, and so forth. This issue is also connected with the problem of reducing corruption as an important means of opposing the new threats. Organized crime not only benefits from the regional military conflicts, but it also has a multiplying effect on them.

Crime and corruption are among the top five problems Bulgaria faces. Although many people indicate that corruption is morally and socially unacceptable, the most recent corruption indexes published by Coalition 2000 show that corrupt behavior is a widely accepted practice.[17] Over 50 percent of respondents to a survey on corruption claimed low salaries, and the opportunity to make "quick money" lay behind the high incidence of corruption in the country.

Bulgaria ratified the cooperation agreement for prevention and combating transborder crime within the boundaries of southeastern Europe, signed in May 1999. The parliament also ratified the charter for the establishment and functioning of a regional center for combating organized crime.

In connection with the Stability Pact, the Bulgarian ministry of the interior is one of the parties in the initiative for combating corruption, which started in February in Sarajevo at the meeting of Working Table 3 on Security and Cooperation, and its sub-table Justice and Home Affairs in particular. It is also one of the parties to the initiative for fighting organized crime, launched in Sofia in October 2000.

The measures aimed at overcoming crime represent a substantial part of Bulgaria's efforts to limit specific risks and the challenges before the country's security.

At the 2000 UN political conference in Palermo, Italy, the regional cooperation for combating the trafficking of people was given an official start at the political level. Bulgaria signed the declaration of the countries of East Europe for combating trafficking and the UN Convention against International Crime, as well as the accompanying documents for preventing, stopping, and sanctioning the trafficking of people, especially of women and children, and the illegal trafficking of immigrants on land, by boat, or by plane.

In May 2000 the national assembly ratified the Civil Law Convention of the Council of Europe on Corruption, and the convention ratification instrument was delivered on 8 June 2000. The Amending Act to the Criminal Code (adopted in June 2000) criminalized the promise and offer of a bribe to local and foreign officials, as well as the asking for and agreement to take a bribe on part of local officials. The new legislation eliminated the restriction to punish active bribery of foreign officials only in the case of international business transactions. Besides, more severe punishments were envisioned for all offences under the Bribery Chapter of the Criminal Code. A new offence was included in the Criminal Code, holding officials criminally liable for spending of budget resources and subsidies for purposes other than those envisaged in their appropriation. The Transparency of the Property of Senior Officials Act established a public register of annual statements on the property, income, and expenditures of senior government officials and their families. Last year, the perpetrators of 6,788 corruption-related offences were detected. These included 2,393 criminal breaches of trust, 3,217 cases of fraud, 52 cases of bribery, and 938 cases of embezzlement.

Future Prospects

There are three possible scenarios for Bulgaria during the next decade: positive, negative, and grave. The decisive factor will be mostly the degree of regional security followed by progress in domestic reforms. Since the Western military involvement failed to prevent another armed conflict in the Balkans and the fighting in Macedonia was intense at some points in 2001, the possibility for Bulgaria to get involuntarily involved in a war becomes plausible. In such a scenario, terrorist groups may start operating on Bulgaria's territory organizing provocations and Bulgarian militants may join Macedonian paramilitary forces to fight against the rebels. The borders could become difficult to control, and the smuggling of weapons, drugs, and people could spread throughout the country. In an even worse scenario, the fighting may expand to Bulgaria, where the Macedonian minority may become restless and demand more rights in a similar fashion to that of the Albanian rebels in Macedonia. Bulgaria's Turkish and Muslim population may also be engrossed in the Macedonian conflict fighting on the side of the Muslim Albanians. In case of war in Macedonia and a potential spillover to neighboring countries, Greece and Turkey are also likely to be involved, and the scenario will become reminiscent of some terrible periods in Southeast European history.

In the negative scenario, if the conflict is contained within Macedonia's borders, but a low-level insurgency continues to riddle the Balkans, the entire region may become an unstable "gray zone" hole on Europe's periphery. It will be impossible for the country to prove that it is a valuable EU or NATO asset and that the process of integration should continue. In such a negative scenario, it would be very difficult for Bulgaria to attract foreign investment and build a competitive economy. Living standards will further decrease, and pressures for immigration will increase even more significantly. Such a situation also provides the conditions for growing crime and corruption. Cutting the country off from the West may also enhance dependence on Russia for almost 100 percent of Bulgaria's energy supplies and could leave Russia as the primary market for Bulgarian goods. This undoubtedly would force Bulgaria into a tighter political orbit with Russia and will increase the possibilities for economic and political blackmail by Moscow.

In an alternative positive scenario, reliable support and concrete measures by the international community can be expected to stop the violence in Macedonia, provide conditions for the building of an independent Kosovo, and stabilize the weak Balkan countries and their "impoverished democracies."[18] It also requires determination by the government of Prime Minister Simeon Saxe-Coburg to continue the pro-Western policy of its predecessor, to implement the planned economic reforms, to systematically fight corruption and organized crime, and to undertake measures for improving social conditions. If the next government shows the same determination to accomplish Bulgaria's economic transformation and the West rewards it by targeted international assistance, burgeoning private investment, and steps toward European integration, then within the next decade the country can take its place in the Euro-Atlantic family.

Chronology

1 January 2000: Bulgaria introduces visa requirements for the citizens of seventeen of the twenty-four states that are on the EU's list of "high risk" countries effective 1 January 2000.

18 January 2000: Visit of Bulgarian President Petar Stoyanov to Israel, where he meets with Israeli Prime Minister Ehud Barak in Jerusalem. Stoyanov meets in Bethlehem with Palestinian Authority Chairman Yassar Arafat.

22 January 2000: Summit of the leaders of seven states bordering Yugoslavia

in the Bulgarian town of Hissar. High-ranking EU and NATO representatives participate.

24 January 2000: The Turkish Movement for Rights and Freedoms calls for constitutional changes to reflect the existence of minorities in Bulgaria.

28 January 2000: The Bulgarian parliament approves agreements with NATO on Bulgaria's participation in KFOR.

29 January 2000: The Bulgarian premier meets with Kosovo Albanian leader Hashim Thaci, the head of the former Kosovo Liberation Army.

7 February 2000: Romania and Bulgaria agree to settle their long-standing dispute about the construction of a second bridge over the River Danube.

9 February 2000: Libyan authorities charge six Bulgarian medics, detained in February 1999, with spreading the HIV virus and accuses them of conspiracy against Libya's national security.

24 February 2000: Bulgarian president asks Libya's Muammar Ghaddafi to intervene in the trial against the medics.

29 February 2000: The Constitutional Court rules to outlaw OMO-Ilinden-PIRIN, a political party that advocates autonomy for the Pirin region and regards the region's inhabitants as Macedonians.

1 March 2000: As part of the military reform, the Bulgarian General Staff is reduced to six directorates and two deputy chiefs.

2 March 2000: Macedonian President Boris Trajkovski expresses regret at the recent decision of the Bulgarian Constitutional Court to outlaw the ethnic Macedonian political party OMO-Ilinden-PIRIN.

5 March 2000: The foreign ministers of Bulgaria, Greece, and Turkey meet in Plovdiv and call for efforts to be made to ensure "safe living conditions for all ethnic communities" in Kosovo.

9 March 2000: Visit of Bulgarian Foreign Minister Nadezhda Mihailova to Washington, where she meets with Deputy Secretary of State Strobe Talbott and leaders of the Congress.

13 March 2000: The Bulgarian government denies accusations in a UN report that the country has sold weapons to UNITA and trained members of the rebel group in Angola. UN report cites Bulgaria as a chief source

of weapons for UNITA since 1997. The government sets up a special commission to investigate the allegations.

19 March 2000: Prime Minister Ivan Kostov visits Kosovo and meets with ethnic Albanian leaders Ibrahim Rugova and Hashim Thaci, as well as with Serbian leader Momcilo Trajkovic and Orthodox Bishop Artemije.

29 March 2000: Bulgarian Defense Minister Boyko Noev and his Romanian counterpart, Sorin Frunzaverde, agree in Sofia to explore the possibilities for military cooperation with the Dutch contingent in NATO's KFOR mission in Kosovo.

9 May 2000: The government commission investigating allegations in a UN report comes to the conclusion that Bulgaria cannot be charged with violating the UN embargo on arms supply to Angola.

17 May 2000: Mandatory military service is reduced from one year to nine months.

18 May 2000: The Bulgarian government survives a no-confidence vote initiated by the Bulgarian Socialist Party, which accused Kostov of allowing corruption at top levels.

26 May 2000: With a vote of 189 to 3, Bulgaria's parliament endorses a government-sponsored resolution backing the government's drive to join the EU and NATO. The opposition Bulgarian Socialist Party, in a reflection of its recently held convention, votes in favor of the resolution, although it said that it will demand that a referendum be held before joining NATO.

16 June 2000: Defense Minister Boiko Noev tells an international conference in Sofia that Bulgaria "staunchly opposes independence for Kosova . . . and the creation of an Albanian state" in the province.

20 June 2000: Newly appointed NATO Supreme Allied Commander Europe general Joseph Ralston visits Sofia.

27 June 2000: Defense Minister Boiko Noev visits Washington.

20 July 2000: President Petar Stoyanov, Prime Minister Ivan Kostov, and Foreign Minister Nadezhda Mihailova voice dissatisfaction with the Southeast European Stability Pact.

28 July 2000: Listening devices are discovered in the apartment of Prosecu-

tor-General Nikola Filichev. The opposition accuses the government of spying on them.

15 August 2000: CIA director George Tenet visits Sofia in preparation for cooperation with Bulgaria.

18 August 2000: Bulgaria orders five Russian businessmen to leave the country for actions threatening national security and links to international crime organizations. Eight Yugoslav citizens are also expelled for the same reasons.

24 August 2000: The deposed king of Bulgaria, Simeon II, holds talks with President Petar Stoyanov in Sofia.

5 September 2000: UN War Crimes Tribunal chief prosecutor Carla Del Ponte visits Sofia.

7 September 2000: Bulgaria deports two Russian businessmen, accusing them of involvement in international arms smuggling.

23 September 2000: More than 1,100 soldiers from six Balkan countries and Italy launch peacekeeping exercises at Koren, some 300 kilometers southeast of Sofia.

5 October 2000: President Petar Stoyanov, responding to the events in Belgrade on 5 October, orders chiefs of the army, police, and border guards to take special measures to prevent suspected war criminals from fleeing across the border from Yugoslavia.

11 October 2000: Parliament approves a resolution calling on Yugoslavia's new leaders to hand over ousted President Slobodan Milosevic to the international war crimes tribunal.

30 November 2000: Visa restrictions for Bulgarian citizens are lifted by EU. Bulgaria announces that it will introduce visa requirements for citizens of non-EU countries in order to bring its policies into line with those of the union.

4 December 2000: Visiting President Petar Stoyanov and Greek Premier Kostas Simitis say they are determined to overcome delays in the construction of a pipeline project that would transport Russian oil from the Black Sea port of Burgas to Alexandropolis in northern Greece.

4 December 2000: Bulgaria unilaterally abolishes a 1978 free travel agreement with Russia. The move follows the EU decision to lift travel restrictions on Bulgarians.

NOTES

1. In 1984 Bulgaria's Communist regime launched a campaign to assimilate members of the Turkish minority by forcing them to adopt Slavic names, prohibiting them from speaking the Turkish language, and banning Islamic rituals. In the summer of 1989, the Zhivkov regime expelled more than three hundred thousand Turks to neighboring Turkey. The assimilation campaign and the abuse of civil rights in Bulgaria became a strong driving force for the political change in 1989. At the end of 1989, after Zhivkov was ousted from power, Bulgaria restored the civil rights of the Turkish and Muslim population.

2. The consumer price index reached 311 percent in 1996, the annual average exchange rate rose more than nine times, and over one-third of the commercial banks went bankrupt. In 1997 Bulgaria faced a full-scale crisis that was both economic and political. In that year the consumer price index hit 578 percent. Government Information Service, "Information on Economic Reform in Bulgaria," 10 October 1999. http://www.bulgaria.govern.bg (12 December 1999), accessed 15 March 2001.

3. Speech of the Bulgarian president Petar Stoyanov at the National Assembly after the election of the government of Ivan Kostov in May 1997. http://www.president.bg/news_speech.html (22 March 1999), accessed 15 March 2001.

4. The Bulgarian Socialist Party continued opposing an eventual NATO membership of Bulgaria until the spring of 2000, when its leader, Georgi Parvanov, announced a dramatic change in the party's position. Although the moderate leadership formally declared support for Bulgaria's bid to join NATO, the hard-liners still insist that Russia's opinion on the issue should be taken into account. Government Bulletin "22–26 May 2000." http://www.government.bg/eng/gis/bulletin/2000/22_26_May.htm (4 January 2001).

5. According to the letters of NATO secretary-general Javier Solana to Bulgarian president Petar Stoyanov and Prime Minister Ivan Kostov from 20 April 1999, NATO assures that:

   • The security of the NATO member states is connected to the security of all European partner countries, and the security of the Republic of Bulgaria is subject to immediate and substantial concern for NATO.

   • Any threat to the territorial sovereignty, political independence, and security of Bulgaria by the Federal Republic of Yugoslavia would be unacceptable.

   • NATO will react against such threat to the security of the Republic of Bulgaria, which may be addressed because of NATO's use of Bulgarian airspace.

"Letter from NATO Secretary General Xavier Solana to Bulgarian Prime-Minister Ivan Kostov." http://www.government.bg/bg/kosovo/pismo_solana_24_03.html (5 January 2000).

6. "National Security Report, 2000." Council of Ministers, *Annual Report on the State of the National Security of the Republic of Bulgaria in 2000* (Sofia, April 2001) http://www.government.bg/eng/index.html

7. Professor Ognyan Minchev in conversation with author. Ognyan Minchev, *Mediapool. bg.* 23 2000, http://www.mediapool.bg/site/bulgaria/2001/03/23/0001.shtml (24 March, 2001).

8. "George Tenet Arrives, Chorny and Ershov Leave," *Capital Weekly,* no. 33, 19–25 August, 2000. http://www.capital.bg/old/weekly/00-33/2-33.htm (3 September, 2000).

9. "Development Performance and Policies," *National Human Development Report,* UNDP, 2000. http://www.undp.bg/

10. Ibid. "The Sustainable Human Development Perspective," *National Human Development Report,* UNDP, 2000. http://www.undp.bg/

11. Bulgaria's population has decreased by 1 million since 1989. Some three hundred thousand of that shrinkage can be attributed to high mortality rate, while seven hundred thousand resulted from emigration. With a "growth" rate of minus 6.4 per 1,000, Bulgaria has the most rapidly declining population in all of post-Communist Europe. Nearly 9 out of every 1,000 Bulgarians have emigrated since 1989. Similarly, the birthrate in Bulgaria has dropped from 12 per 1,000 in 1989 to 7 per 1,000 in 1999. BTA and Mediapool.bg, 10 April 2001. http://www.mediapool.bg/site/business/2001/04/10/0004.shtml

12. Population Census 2001, preliminary results.

13. "2000 Regular Report from the Commission on Bulgaria's Progress towards EU Accession." Brussels, 8 November 2000, 88–90.

14. *Reuters,* March 2001. Ivan Krastev, "Anxious Bulgaria Looks On," *IWPR Balkan Crisis Report,* 21 April 2001. http://www.iwpr.net/index.pl?archive/bcr/bcr 20010321_6_eng.txt

15. Jeffrey Simon, "NATO's Membership Action Plan and Defense Planning: Credibility at Stake," *Problems of Post-Communism,* vol. 48, no. 3, May 2001.

16. "National Security Report, 2000." Council of Ministers, *Annual Report on the State of the National Security of the Republic of Bulgaria in 2000* (Sofia, April 2001) http://www.government.bg/eng/index.html

17. Coalition 2000 is an initiative of a number of Bulgarian nongovernmental organizations (NGOs) aimed at combating corruption through a process of cooperation among governmental institutions, NGOs, and individuals, drafting an Anti-Corruption

Action Plan for Bulgaria, and implementing an awareness campaign and a monitoring system. Available on the Internet at <http://www.online.bg/coalition2000/>

18. President Stoyanov at the NATO summit in Washington in April 1999. http://www.president.bg/news_speech.html

16 ◆ Croatia: After Tudjman, Finally to the West?

Jed C. Snyder

On 10 December 1999 Franjo Tudjman, architect of Croatian independence, Croatia's first president, and once the youngest of Marshall Josip Broz Tito's generals, died at the age of seventy-seven. Tudjman served as president for eight and a half years. His death, long anticipated after several years with cancer and other ailments, was, nevertheless, received by many Croats and Balkan leaders as a seismic political shock for which neither the Croatian nation nor Zagreb's turbulent neighbors were really prepared.

Led by Tudjman and the political party he created—the Croatian Democratic Union (HDZ)—Croatia declared its independence from the rapidly crumbling Yugoslavia in June 1991. Few who have observed Tudjman over the years would disagree that Croatia's founding president was an imperial and autocratic Croat nationalist. Franjo Tudjman so totally dominated Croatian political life that even his detractors at home seemed at a loss to contemplate life after Franjo. For nearly a decade, he successfully defeated all who dared to challenge his authority either as the head of the powerful HDZ or as head of state. Errant prime ministers also felt his sting. Tudjman's detractors cite similarities in behavior between Tudjman and his one-time mentor, Marshall Tito. Both were fond of imperial trappings; Tudjman often wore a Tito-like white general's tunic and occupied Tito's former presidential palace in Zagreb and his summer retreat on Brioni. Both men were born in the Zagorje district north of Zagreb.

A fierce approach to maintaining nearly absolute power exacted large costs in democratic freedoms, including imposition of the most restrictive press laws and curbs on genuine political pluralism anywhere in Europe, with the ironic exception of Slobodan Milosevic's Serbia. These domestic actions and Tudjman's refusal to cooperate with the International Criminal Tribunal on Yugoslav war crimes (ICTY) in The Hague, his unfaltering support for Bosnian-Croat hard-liners in neighboring Bosnia, and his grudging and minimalist adherence to the tenets of the Dayton agreement (which he signed), combined to isolate Croatia in a way not understood by most Croats until after his death.

Tudjman's near-dictatorial reign delayed Croatia's entry into the Western community of democratic nations and exacted a horrendous economic price as well, as Croatia was unable to conduct normal international commerce for virtually all of Tudjman's tenure as president. Consequently, the genuine sense of mourning at his death throughout Croatia (to include many of his most passionate critics), which testified to his standing at home, was not felt abroad. As an illustration of Tudjman's international isolation, with the exception of the president of Turkey (then Suleyman Demirel, a friend and ironically an ally), Tudjman's funeral was not attended by a single head of state, and the official representation from both Europe and the United States was minimal and relatively low level.[1]

At the end of 2000, the three major regional political figures who had come together for three weeks in November 1995 in Dayton, Ohio, to sign the General Framework Agreement on Peace for Bosnia and Herzegovina, had all left the scene. In October 2000, President Alija Izetbegovic of Bosnia resigned after his party lost the support of much of the Bosnian Muslim population, and that same month Slobodan Milosevic lost the Yugoslav Presidency to Vojislav Kostunica. Five years after Dayton, the three principal actors in the Bosnian tragedy had all been replaced by successors, who, to varying degrees, were even less enamored than were their predecessors of the Dayton construct, which brought about the de facto ethnic partition of Bosnia.

In early January 2000, parliamentary elections were held in Croatia. Three weeks after Franjo Tudjman's death, his HDZ party was soundly defeated in the largest electoral turnout since 1990—over 75 percent of eligible voters went to the polls to expel HDZ leadership from nine of Croatian's ten electoral districts. Despite nearly total control of the country's media by Tudjman loyalists, a left-leaning six-party opposition coalition known as "the Six" defeated the HDZ, winning two-thirds of the seats in the parliament. The Croatian public had reacted to the arguments advanced by the opposition coalition's two leading parties—the Social Democrats (SDP) and the Social Liberals (HSLS), which focused on Croatia's international isolation and its horrendous economic state, illustrated by a 20 percent unemployment rate and a foreign debt that had risen to nearly $10 billion. The six-party coalition's platform promised drastic reductions in public expenditures, privatization of state-run industries, a less imperial Presidency, and an end to the financing of the Croatian "autonomous" conclave in Bosnia-Herzegovina, Herzeg Bosna.

The coalition was led by the SDP and HSLS leaders Ivica Racan (who would become prime minister) and Drazen Budisa, respectively. Budisa was initially favored in most of the polls to become the next president. In fact, Budisa would be defeated in the final round of the presidential election several weeks later. The SDP-HSLS coalition won 40 percent of the vote on its own and thus could have formed a government without the other four coalition members, but chose to build a broader and more representative administration. That would prove to be a fateful decision, as the future Prime Minister Racan would discover soon after assuming office. The six-party coalition would prove to be essentially unmanageable, hobbling virtually every major effort at reform planned by the coalition's leadership. The four smaller parties—the Croatian Peasant's Party (HSS), Croatia's People's Party (HNS), the Liberal Party (LS), and the Istrian Democratic Party (IDS)—together captured only 15 percent of the vote.

The HDZ was devastated by this electoral loss, having won only 24 percent of the vote. Tudjman's successor as leader of the HDZ, his longtime foreign minister, Mate Granic, would run as the HDZ presidential candidate in the first round of the 24 January presidential election. The rivalry that developed during the three weeks between the parliamentary and presidential elections provided an interesting glimpse of the power of history in the Balkan region, and became a window on the Croatian public's deep despair after the autocratic rule of Franjo Tudjman. Granic was regarded by most of the media and electoral observers alike as almost irrelevant to the outcome. Although Granic was on the ballot for the first round of the presidential polling, the race was really always between Budisa and Stjepan (known popularly as Stipe) Mesic, who themselves had been political rivals since 1992 when Croatia became an independent nation.

After the first round, it was clear that most of the Croatian pollsters had been wrong about how easily Budisa would defeat Mesic. Mesic won more than 41 percent of the vote, to Budisa's 28 percent. Budisa had a long history of dissident behavior, having been a very vocal opponent of Tudjman's authoritarian style and a leader of the 1971 "Croatian Spring" movement. He led the HSLS. By contrast, Mesic had chaired the HDZ and led the party's campaign to elect Tudjman in 1992. Mesic, who had become a Communist Party functionary early in his political career, eventually emerged as a dissident leader, calling for increased political freedoms, for which he was imprisoned by the Communist authorities during the Tito years (as was Budisa), in the early 1970s. Nearly two decades later, however, he rose to power first as prime minister in 1990 and then as Yugoslavia's last federal president (before the federation dissolved) in 1991. Mesic abandoned Tudjman (over his prosecution of the Bosnian War), leaving the HDZ in 1994, when he resigned as Speaker of the parliament, to join the HNS. In the end, Mesic appealed to Croats as the "anti-Tudjman" who also made a point during the campaign of condemning the disproportionate influence that the "Herzegovinian lobby" had maintained during the Tudjman era. Budisa was less willing to sever ties between Zagreb and the Bosnian Croat community and during the election campaign declared that he would withdraw funding from the Bosnian Croats *only* if the Muslim community (the Bosniaks) severed their connections with Islamic countries providing aid to their cause. Mesic's harder line on severing funding was probably a contributing factor in his victory.

Between the period of Tudjman's death and the final round of presidential polling in early February, Croatia was governed by the speaker of the parliament, Vlatko Pavletic. Although nearly powerless as an interim figurehead, Pavletic led the country ably during a potentially dangerous period, where the worst of Croatian historical tendencies could have surfaced. During this period, there were meetings among former and current military officers, as well as hard-line Tudjman loyalists that raised public fears of a potential coup by the armed forces in support of an illegitimate (that is, nonelected) HDZ successor regime. Although largely unnoticed by the press, a key figure in keeping the military in the barracks and providing critical assurance to Western governments during this period was Tudjman's last defense minister and a former Chief of the General

Staff, Pavao Miljavac. Miljavac navigated skillfully as the HDZ broke into three rival factions. Two hard-line groups battled against a moderate wing led by Mate Granic, who had the respect of Western powers and the international community, but who was regarded by most Croats as weak and indecisive.

The other two post-Tudjman wings of the party were led by former Tudjman lieutenants. Ivica Pasalic, a ruthless authoritarian and former adviser to Tudjman, as well as the anointed successor to Gojko Susak (former defense minister) as leader of the Herzegovina lobby, urged continued support for the Bosnian Croats. Vladimir Seks, a deputy speaker of the Sabor (the parliament) led a rival grouping. Croatia was fortunate that the acting head of state, Pavletic, and Miljavac both understood the potentially tragic consequences should the dark side of Croatian politics emerge just as the first shoots of democracy were also emerging from a long winter. Much of the speculation regarding a possible coup subsided when Pavletic formally asked Ivica Racan to form a new government on 22 January.

In the second round of polling on 7 February, Stipe Mesic emerged victorious as the second president of the independent republic of Croatia. In the end, Budisa was regarded as an amateur, unable to lead a fractious coalition or to implement the coalition's promises, particularly the pledge to uncover and remove the corrupt officials who by some estimates had established an underground economy that accounted for more than 70 percent of Croatia's gross domestic product (GDP). Mesic, who began the presidential campaign with less than 10 percent of the public's support and who served as Tudjman's first prime minister, appeared serious and, in contrast to his former mentor (and to Budisa as well), very *unimperial.*

There was much rejoicing in parts of Bosnia over the election results in Zagreb. Bosnian Serb and Muslim officials were effusive in their congratulatory proclamations. Former president of the Bosnian-Serb entity within Bosnia-Herzegovina, Republika Srpska, Biljana Plavsic, announced that "the first precondition for the disappearance of extreme forces" had been met. Alija Izetbegovic, the Muslim member of the Bosnian tripartite Presidency (who had delayed sending an official condolence message after Tudjman's death), was among the first to dispatch a congratulatory telegram to the Croatian opposition leaders after the parliamentary election victory.

Predictably, only the HDZ's sister party, the Bosnian HDZ, and its leader Ante Jelavic bemoaned the results.

Threat Assessment

A decade of economic stagnation, rampant corruption, and isolation from most international markets and Western trading blocks had a predictably severe impact on the quality of life of most Croatians. In 1999 the gross domestic product (GDP) per capita was less than $4,400. This was among the lowest of comparable states in the region. The last two years of the Tudjman reign were the most damaging, with real GDP falling almost 5 percent.[2] Final figures for 2000 are not yet available, but the tourist season for the summer of 2000 (the first time since 1992 that Croatian tour operators were able to operate in a nonwartime environment) was expected to boost GDP figures. Depreciation of the national currency, the kuna, (particularly against the U.S. dollar and the German mark) also contributed to a general economic decline. Late in 2000 the new government in Zagreb began to see the same pace of economic rehabilitation that it had witnessed in the defense and security sector. In July Croatia was admitted to full membership in the World Trade Organization (WTO) and earlier in the year, the U.S. government opened an office in Zagreb of the Overseas Private Investment Corporation (OPIC), a clear signal to the American business community that Washington regarded Croatia as a safe climate for investment.

Earlier decisions by the Tudjman regime continued to retard economic progress. Prominent among these was the 1998 introduction of a huge value-added tax (VAT) of 22 percent, which boosted inflation to nearly 6 percent. Trade deficits, a contraction of the manufacturing and industrial sector, and an alarming rate of bank failures further worsened Croatia's competitive position in world markets. Most of these maladies can be traced to the Tudjman government's reliance on *increasing* the state's role in the national economy and the stranglehold of a powerful kleptocracy, fueled by an elite grouping of families close to the president and his family, who were able to siphon off what little investment capital survived the misguided economic and political policies of the Tudjman era.

Societal factors, however, also continued to hamper real growth. Like many other small European countries, Croatia is facing an aging population and a shrinking young workforce. The new government's program called for an annual 2 percent growth rate on GDP in the near term. Stabilizing the currency, reducing inflation and unemployment, promoting market liberalization, accelerated privatization, and institutional reform are the major economic objectives of the Racan government. Reaching a successful negotiated agreement with the International Monetary Fund (IMF) is among the more urgent international economic priorities for Zagreb. Lastly, the defense budget will continue to be a burden for Croatia, although the percentage of GDP devoted to defense has declined substantially over the last five years to about 3.8 percent in 2000.

In mid-March 2000 a NATO delegation arrived in Zagreb to acquaint Croatian defense and foreign ministry officials with the requirements for Partnership for Peace (PfP) membership. During these discussions, Croatian officials briefed their NATO counterparts on the structure and functions of Croatia's national security apparatus. It was during these meetings that NATO was able to get its first glimpse of how opaque Croatia's defense and national security decision-making structure actually was. It became clear to this delegation that several of the key prerequisites for NATO membership were neither in place nor in immediate prospect. The NATO delegation was unable to obtain realistic estimates of Croatian defense spending or of its plans to introduce genuine civilian control of its military.[3] I was involved in assisting the Croatians to prepare for these meetings, where the issue of how the chief of the General Staff and the minister of defense were to interact during peace and war was a focus of discussion.

The new government has resisted NATO calls to insert the civilian Minister of Defense, Jozo Rados, into the peacetime and wartime chain of command. Franjo Tudjman's long-held directive that the president would assert full control of the Croatian military through the chief of the General Staff (the nation's senior military officer and the Croatian equivalent of the Chairman of the U.S. Joint Chiefs of Staff) remained intact. Neither Racan nor Mesic were yet prepared to challenge that concept, which effectively removed the minister of defense from what the United States refers to as the "National Command Authority"—the mechanism through which the commander in chief's orders are transmitted down the chain of command.

In sum, the Croatians were not prepared to agree to the concept of civilian oversight of the armed forces, the sine qua non of Western national security practice. Despite this, the Alliance approved full membership for Croatia in the PfP program at a NATO ministerial meeting in Florence, Italy, in May 2000.

As Minister Rados discovered early, he was *not* to be a key decision-maker in matters of national security. As the first indication of his distance from the president and prime minister on these issues, the selection of a new Chief of the General Staff, General Petar Stipetic, occurred *without* the minister's input. This was to begin a feud (that continued into late spring 2001) between the chief and the minister on virtually all important defense matters. That feud intensified quickly as it became clear that party politics were influencing decision making on national security issues, in-cluding the appointment of senior military officers to command positions. The minister of defense (a senior HSLS party member) was a close political ally of Drazen Budisa, the defeated HSLS candidate for president. The prime minister, the former head of the opposition rival SDP, resented Budisa's continuing contact with his defense minister, which the Croatian press began to highlight. Commentators implied that Budisa and Rados were scheming to undermine Racan's authority. This was a classic example of Balkan intrigue, on which Croatian politicians feed and thrive.

Jozo Rados had been announced as the new defense minister shortly after the January parliamentary election results, when it appeared that Budisa (Rados's political mentor) would be elected president. When Mesic was elected president, he chose not to overturn the Rados appointment as a gesture of solidarity with the other members of the "Group of Six" opposition coalition. Shortly after the presidential election, relations be-tween the armed forces leadership and the new ministry of defense (MOD) leadership deteriorated. Rados looked to the prime minister for critical political support, particularly with the armed forces, whose leaders had not yet become comfortable with the new Racan government. Much of the military resented statements by the former opposition leaders (now in power as the new government) made during the election campaign that attacked the institutions of the Croatian military as key, corrupt, and willing allies of "the dictator Tudjman and the HDZ." Further, the military watched as Rados was forced by the interparty political bargaining (so prevalent when relatively inexperienced, rival parliamentary opposition groups come to national power) to appoint young, unknown political cronies to senior management positions in the MOD.

The relations between Racan and Rados were further strained by the prime minister's inability to initially persuade the president to allow involvement of the prime minister in matters of national security. This was a remnant of Franjo Tudjman era, during which several key cabinet portfolios were designated as "state ministries" accountable to the president, not the prime minister. In addition, Mesic was not yet prepared to disband all of Tudjman's power centers in the government. In some cases, this would have required significant changes to the Croatian Constitution, which Tudjman had carefully crafted to codify and reinforce his absolute governing authority. Further, a commission had just begun to debate the issue of constitutional reform, and Mesic was not yet prepared to preempt their deliberations.

The country's senior policy-making body on matters of national security—the National Security and Defense Council—was one of these Tudjman-created bodies. On paper, it appeared to be a deliberative body similar in concept to the U.S. National Security Council, where all of the senior cabinet-level officials with responsibility for security and foreign policy issues would convene regularly to advise the president. The prime minister was a statutory member of this body. In reality, it functioned essentially as a rubber stamp for Tudjman's decisions, and the prime minister played no significant role in national security decisions during the Tudjman era. Tudjman would simply not allow any interference with his prerogatives as commander in chief, as he defined them. Despite Mesic's promises during the campaign and notwithstanding his private assurances to Western officials, he was not yet prepared to share authority with the prime minister and the parliament on national security decision making.

More surprisingly, President Mesic seemed to be establishing a direct connection with the chief of the General Staff rather than communicating with him through the defense minister, which would be the appropriate chain of command procedure. The man described by the Croatian press as the "anti-Tudjman" was showing the same disregard for the Western civil-military model as his predecessor had. As a result, Racan was initially denied an important set of duties, and that indirectly soured his relations with the defense minister, who was also a representative of a rival political party.

The initial "honeymoon" period between the SDP and HSLS was over. Important questions of presidential power and authority increasingly clashed with the urgent need to open the government's decision-making structures and processes to public and parliamentary scrutiny.

The power struggles became the subject of endless press speculation, further personalizing the substantive disagreements between the chief of the General Staff and the minister of defense to whom he supposedly reported. Regrettably, the prospects that Croatia would actually move to "Westernize" its national security and defense establishment now appeared much less promising.

A new Defense Law, in preparation for months, will presumably address some of the very difficult issues of command and control, jurisdiction, and military authority described here. Unfortunately, the new government in Zagreb has allowed all of these questions to be politicized. Additionally, the Defense Law will not reflect the need for serious reform unless there is direct involvement of President Mesic in the drafting of this important legislation, as well as serious consultation with the leadership of the Sabor (parliament). To date, there is little indication that the president is prepared to assume this responsibility.

Capacities

In 1995, at the conclusion of what Croatians call the "Homeland War," Defense Minister Gojko Susak determined that Croatia must reorganize and rebuild its armed forces, focusing on capabilities for the future and seizing the opportunity to "Westernize" its forces. The strategy was to realign Croatian defense and foreign policy objectives toward the longer-term objective of integrating Croatia into the network of Western multilateral security institutions and alliances. While NATO membership was not envisioned in the short term, it was certainly a goal to look toward.[4] In the meantime, Croatia needed to shift from a wartime structure for the armed forces and ministry toward a reduced, Western-oriented, peacetime defense and military establishment.

Although there was considerable debate within the Tudjman government about Croatia's ultimate orientation, Defense Minister Susak clearly
led a controversial school of thought that argued for a closer relationship
with the West—a view that was in the minority and did *not* initially include
Franjo Tudjman. While Tudjman understood the obvious political (and
possibly financial) benefits of a close relationship with the United States,
he also held great suspicions regarding the West's real agenda for Croatia
and the Balkan region generally. Tudjman's neo-isolationist stance was not
difficult to understand, considering how weakly the Western nations had
initially reacted to the aggression of Milosevic in Bosnia, Croatia, and
Slovenia. The successful campaign of Serb paramilitary forces, which at
one point had occupied a third of Croatian territory, was particularly infuriat-
ing to Tudjman, who was quite bitter about Washington's refusal during
the elder Bush's administration to intervene early in the Bosnian conflict.
This sense of betrayal by the West was compounded by its refusal to come
to Croatia's aid, which Tudjman believed would have avoided the tragedies
of Vukovar and the humiliating shelling of the ancient Adriatic coastal town
of Dubrovnik.

Against this backdrop and these suspicions, Gojko Susak (who died
after a long illness in 1998) began to rebuild the Croatian military. A key
objective of this rebuilding effort was to increase the compatibility of Croatian forces with those of NATO. This was a large task, because much of
the Croatian military structure was Soviet-supplied and was still largely a
remnant of the old Yugoslav National Army (JNA) training system. The
JNA legacy proved to be a very resilient and politically powerful one. Many
of the military officers who fought in the Homeland Wars of 1991–95 lacked
any formal military training, but by necessity they were put in command
of troops trained during the JNA era. Having risen through the ranks himself
and having watched the blatant discrimination against non-Serbs in the
senior officer ranks, Tudjman understood that many of the JNA-trained
commanders were either Serb or Serb-sympathetic and therefore could not
be allowed to lead Croatian forces, which were engaged in a desperate
effort to defeat regular and paramilitary Serb units.

After the Homeland War, a fierce and bitter rivalry developed between
those who had led Croatian forces in that war and those who had risen
through the ranks of the JNA system. In a desperate search for trusted

political allies to lead the ragtag Croatian armed forces, Tudjman had actively promoted many of the Homeland War veterans while ignoring many of the more senior JNA officers. Some of the Homeland War leadership had returned (at Tudjman's personal request) to Croatia from the diaspora (particularly the Croatian community in Canada, including Susak himself). This created an atmosphere of resentment among Croatian officers who were JNA veterans toward these modern-day "carpetbaggers." The remnants of this resentment linger today and continue to hobble the efforts of the younger, reform-minded Croatian officers to modernize training and doctrine for the officer corps.

After Susak's death, the trend began to reverse, with JNA officers receiving a larger share of the promotions, to the point where the political pendulum has now swung toward the other extreme. Today, nearly all of the current Croatian military leadership is drawn from the JNA ranks. As might be expected, the political views of many of the JNA officers are more traditional and in many cases, less supportive of initiatives to introduce Western-style reforms in the structure and character of the Croatian military. To a large extent, JNA officers are more sympathetic to Soviet-era doctrine, training, and operational methods. This has presented a substantial obstacle to introducing Western-oriented concepts and doctrine.

The Susak reforms were introduced with the help of U.S. assistance, both at the official and nonofficial levels. In the mid-1990s, the Croatian MOD signed contracts with a private American firm, MPRI, to begin the multiyear process of advising the MOD on modernizing and Westernizing the Croatian military and defense establishment. Initially, in 1995 one team of retired U.S. military officers was sent by MPRI to live and work in Croatia to assist the minister of defense and the chief of the General Staff in reorganizing and, in some cases, retraining the Croatian military. The MPRI presence in Croatia expanded over several years. At its height in 2000, MPRI fielded three separate teams, totaling more than twenty-five retired military and civilian advisers, including a long-range management program team to focus on introducing U.S. and Western concepts of defense management and strategic planning, to an antiquated MOD.

In 1995 the Croatian defense budget was about $1.8 billion, an unsustainably large percentage of the total national budget, and nearly 12 percent of GDP. It has been reduced progressively since that apogee to about $815 million in 1996 and an estimated $600 million in 2000 (my estimate). The Croatian Armed Forces (CAF), like most Central European militaries, was and remains dominated by a relatively large army and a much smaller air force and navy.

The mission of the CAF is to ensure the territorial integrity of Croatia and to deter aggression by regional neighbors. The deterrent aspect of the mission, however, is discounted, because Croatian military leaders do not today see any imminent, external military threat, nor do they envision one materializing in the foreseeable future. Generic regional threats, including renewed interethnic violence in parts of Bosnia, are included in the Croatian General Staff's list of concerns of events that could require long-term deployment of peacekeeping forces. Croatia *does* seek to increase its level of participation in international humanitarian and peacekeeping missions and has contributed to its first UN peacekeeping mission, in Sierra Leone.

The possibility that Milosevic (or a Serb nationalist successor) could launch operations to recapture portions of the Krajina or eastern Slavonia were regarded as unlikely, second-order threats to Croatian security. With Milosevic's ouster, the only remaining territorial issue that concerns the Croatian military is the question of the Prevlaka peninsula. This is the southern-most tip of the Croatian coast, which is still disputed by Serbia, Montenegro, and Croatia. The area (known as Point Ostro—the Konavle region of Dubrovnik) borders Montenegro on the east; the area's northern border is with Bosnia-Herzegovina. The area's importance is essentially economic. There is considerable potential for development of fisheries and exploratory drilling for oil.

The CAF peacetime strength stands at about 57,000,[5] reduced from more than 85,000 at the end of the Homeland War. Of this number, the army comprises nearly 78 percent of the total manpower, with the Air Force and Navy each contributing about 3.5 percent of the total. The remainder is composed of the Ministry of Defense and the General Staff. Nearly 66 percent are professional soldiers, with the remainder serving as conscripts. All males between the ages of eighteen and twenty-seven are subject to the draft. (Until recently the term of conscription was nine months, soon to be reduced to six months.) In the event of a national crisis, the force can be expanded to more than two hundred and fifty thousand following a general mobilization and a recall of reservists. Nearly 90 percent of the current professional and reserve military personnel served in the Homeland War.

The current force suffers from maladies common to all armed forces caught in the painful transition from executing wartime functions to engaging in peacetime missions. Most of the Croatian military equipment and weapons were either inherited from the JNA units or seized during the Homeland War battles. Much of the current equipment is obsolete and represents a wide range of nonintegratible systems, some of which were acquired illegally during a UN-imposed arms embargo. There is little standardization and even less interoperability among units because of the diverse and largely antiquated state of ordnance and equipment.

The CAF is organized into three services—Army, Air Force and Air Defense Force, and Navy. The land forces are organized into six area commands (at Karlovac, Knin, Pazin, Dakovo, Ston, and Varazdin), as territorially based units of infantry, mechanized armor, artillery, engineers, signal, and reconnaissance. The navy is organized as a fleet, with three naval sectors, operating from one main base at Split. The Air Force operates from four air bases. The nucleus of the Army is a force of seven Guards Brigades (mechanized, tank, and artillery battalions), typically populated by a mix of professionals, reservists, and conscripts. The Air Force has seen the most dramatic transformation of the three services. It was established shortly before Croatian independence and has grown from a few transports to a command with air defense and ground attack fighters, helicopters, and air defense units. Modernization of fighter aircraft is a priority for the Croatians; the backbone of this force today is a small number of largely unserviceable MiG 21s.

The Croatian Armed Forces are now engaged in a five-year reorganization and downsizing effort, initiated by Defense Minister Rados.[6] The effort is designed to reduce the size of the Croatian military, the ministry staff, and the General Staff by at least 20 percent. If fully implemented, this initiative will include new command and control systems, a modernized personnel management system, and a Western-style financial management structure. In addition, the General Staff is to be transformed into a joint staff. Perhaps the most daunting challenge facing the MOD is to trim the disproportionate share of its budget now committed to personnel, which takes more than 70 percent of the budget. More significant, the budget allows for very little money for new procurement and less than .2 percent for research and development. Further, the percentage committed to personnel costs could actually grow as the MOD seeks parliamentary approval for pay raises for its uniformed personnel, even as the overall budget is mandated by the Sabor to shrink. The MOD budget has been substantially reduced even as the personnel levels have remained essentially static.

The current reorganization plan calls for the MOD structure to be streamlined, reducing the minister's senior staff (structured around a deputy minister and assistant ministers) drastically. The initial phase will eliminate three assistant ministers from the current level of eight. Ultimately, only three assistant ministers will remain under the current reorganization blueprint. Similarly, the General Staff will also be reorganized. Unfortunately, the size of the General Staff relative to the ministry staff is likely to increase. This will reduce the prospects for civilian oversight even further. At the end of December 2000, there were barely a dozen civilian officials with management responsibilities at the ministry of defense, out of a total MOD workforce of more than four thousand.

As a recent U.S. Defense Department assessment concluded,[7] the fundamental force issue facing the Croatian military is the aging of the force and the lack of accession of professional soldiers into the force. Put simply, many of those who joined the armed forces and fought in the Homeland War have remained in the service, while conscripts have not been able to enter the professional ranks because of current statutory prohibitions. In addition, the conscription service is poorly administered and starved for funds. Currently, a typical Croatian army conscript will earn less than $20 a month. Further, Croatia has no formal, institutionalized recruitment process for the armed forces. Until antiquated legislative barriers are removed and a functioning military personnel system is put in place, the structural problems facing the military will continue and become progressively worse. A combination of poor quality of life, politicization of the promotion process, and serious pay inequities combine to make professional military service very unattractive for all but a few.

In general, the ministry's leaders oppose or ignore the notion of building multiyear, cyclic resource and acquisition plans to support realistic budgets. The absence, for example, of a functioning planning, programming, and budgeting system (PPBS) compatible with those of NATO nations has created an enormous disadvantage for Croatian MOD officials when dealing with their Western counterparts. Additionally, there is no tradition among Croatian government officials to plan *collaboratively*. Thus, the notion of building an interagency structure to support an integrated, transparent national security decision-making system linking the MOD to the General Staff, the foreign ministry, and the president's office was entirely alien to most. This complicated coordination and preparation for important visits by senior NATO and EU officials, for example, who often arrived in Zagreb to find contradictory declaratory and operating policies between key ministries.

Croatia is in the process of building a national security system to support a capability to link the key defense and foreign policy agencies into an integrated, Western-oriented decision-making structure. Central to this process is the development of key planning documents, including a national security strategy, a national military strategy, a defense planning guidance, and a Croatian Armed Forces plan. Unfortunately, until a fully functioning national security system is in place, these documents (which would be created by this system) are likely to be developed without the appropriate interagency contributions and critical review required. The delay in establishing such a system has already become a serious obstacle in deepening and accelerating Croatia's participation in PfP programs.[8]

Croatia has taken full advantage of available U.S.-sponsored bilateral and multilateral military assistance programs. These have included several years worth of intensive involvement in the U.S. European Command's (EUCOM) Joint Contact Team Program (JCTP), which is designed to acquaint European nations engaged in democracy transition with the structures and functions of U.S. and NATO-related military institutions and processes. Typically, a JCTP Military Liaison Team (MLT) is deployed to the host nation by EUCOM to work with MOD officials and their counterparts in the armed forces.

In addition, Croatia has been the beneficiary for some time of the U.S.

International Military Education and Training (IMET) program, administrated by the U.S. Defense Department. This program provides funds to allow Croatia to be introduced to U.S. concepts of resource planning and defense management. Its programs provide opportunities for Croatian military officers and civilian officials to travel to U.S. military installations, command headquarters, academic centers, and research institutes for intensive interaction with U.S. defense and security planning experts.[9]

Policy Innovations

The day after Stjepan Mesic was elected president and head of state, the new government under Prime Minister Racan released its program to the Sabor and the Croatian public. An impressive document, it outlined an ambitious program of reform in virtually every area of Croatian domestic and international policy and emphasized a strong commitment to creating a civil society and a democratic and market-oriented state within the European Union.

The program frankly stated Croatia's poor economic and financial condition. But, as the new regime soon learned, the severity of the situation was underestimated and the state of decay was not well understood by Racan's team. The combination of officially sanctioned corruption and outright theft of funds had left Croatia essentially bankrupt. Two of the new government ministers told me privately that a conservative estimate would conclude that only a small percentage of the budget was ever visible to any of Tudjman's ministers and that perhaps as much as $30 billion had simply "disappeared" in the last several years of the Tudjman reign. The Racan government's program acknowledged some of the alarming statistics, including a foreign trade imbalance in 1999 of $3.5 billion. There was, however, a deliberate effort to mask the extent of the crisis, since few if any of the new ministers could confidently state that they had found all of the financial land mines left by their predecessors.

The new government's program also acknowledged the lack of general transparency in government budgeting and admitted that, in the past, neither the government nor the Sabor really had knowledge of defense spending. This was an important acknowledgment, since the public had long suspected that much of the officially sanctioned corruption could be traced to the ministries of defense and interior. Finally, referring to the autocratic practices of the Tudjman years, the program stated emphatically that, "Croatia needs a full parliamentary democracy, primarily by reducing the powers of the president of the state and by strengthening the role of parliament and the government."[10]

The use of the word "government" in Croatian English-language documents is confusing, but it also reveals the political adolescence of the Croatian system of governance. Under the Croatian system (codified in the Croatian constitution), the head of state (the president) exercises total authority as the senior public official. The prime minister (the head of government) serves effectively at the president's pleasure and with relatively little authority. Although this is not unique among European parliamentary systems, the president's ability to actually run the most important parts of the government in Croatia was quite unique.

One of Tudjman's earliest declarations was to label the key "power" ministries (defense, foreign affairs, interior, finance) as "state" ministries. This effectively removed the prime minister from any jurisdiction over the daily business of these key cabinet agencies, a fact privately acknowledged to me by Tudjman's last prime minister, Zlatko Matesa. In fact, the president often exercised his authority to appoint both senior- and mid-level ministry of defense officials (much to the chagrin of several successive ministers of defense) and determined the appointments of the nation's senior military leaders. This authority flowed from the president's constitutional designation as "commander in chief." The Croatian description of the "government" generally was acknowledged to mean the executive branch (the prime minister and the various ministries) only. Neither the parliament (nor the judiciary) was regarded as a branch of the "government" despite Croatian pride at describing their system as adhering to a Western "parliamentary" model. It is but one example of the nearly unchallenged, monarchic hold on power that Franjo Tudjman enjoyed for a decade.

The key leaders in the new government are the prime minister and three deputy prime ministers. The first deputy prime minister, Goran Granic (the brother of Tudjman's foreign minister, Mate Granic) functions essentially as the government's chief operating officer. The key cabinet officials include the defense minister, Jozo Rados; the foreign minister, Tonino

Picula; the finance minister, Mato Crkvenac; the interior minister, Sime Lucin; and the economics minister, Goranko Fizulic.

The first several months of the new government's tenure were consumed by efforts to launch its new program and to establish some semblance of fiscal order. In late February 2000, the prime minister was forced to acknowledge that the government was still uncertain as to the extent of its debt, since the notion of transparency was still not accepted by those bureaucrats inherited from the Tudjman era, who continued to manage the government's daily business. This did not deter the Racan administration from announcing its first draft national budget of 45.6 billion kuna ($5.7 billion) in early February. The budget was characterized by the new leadership as draconian. State officials were asked to accept salary cuts of up to 40 percent in some cases.

World leaders began to descend on Zagreb to bless the new regime. Among the first was U.S. secretary of state Madeleine Albright, who arrived even before the final round of the presidential election to announce that Washington would immediately increase its annual financial assistance by $20 million (an increase from $12 million). During this visit, she also declared that the new government's stated intention to cooperate with the Hague Tribunal (something Tudjman had essentially ruled out) would move Croatia closer to a goal enunciated in its new program—membership in NATO's Partnership for Peace. Britain's foreign secretary, Robin Cook, echoed the same sentiments during his visit to Zagreb and also reiterated London's support for an accelerated negotiation with Croatia over the first step toward EU membership—the Stabilization and Association Agreement (SAA) between the EU and the new government in Zagreb.

Croatia's emergence from isolation within Europe was an early goal of the new Zagreb government. Toward this end, Racan's first official trip abroad as prime minister was a swing through key European capitals, first to Portugal, which at the time held the rotating EU presidency. The objective, to persuade the Portuguese to agree to an accelerated timetable for Croatian admission into the EU, was largely met. Even before President Mesic was inaugurated on 18 February 2000 Racan had visited Brussels to confer with EU leaders, including EU Commission president Romano Prodi and to meet for the first time with NATO secretary-general Lord Robertson in the hope of extracting a public pledge to consider early membership for Croatia in the PfP. The Croatians presented Robertson with a formal request to join the PfP. Actually, the Tudjman government had made a similar request some years earlier, but it had been officially ignored.

The Mesic inauguration was a threshold political event for Croatia, which attracted many Western leaders, in stark contrast to the very sparse diplomatic representation at Franjo Tudjman's funeral less than two months earlier. More than seventy official delegations attended, including twelve presidents and heads of state. At a press conference after the inauguration, Secretary Albright stated publicly that both President Mesic and Prime Minister Racan had assured her that Croatian support for the remnants of Herceg-Bosna would cease. She emphasized this point later in private sessions with officials from the U.S. embassy in Zagreb.[11]

Croatia's gradual reentry into European regional affairs began in mid-March, when, during meetings in Budapest involving states neighboring the Federal Republic of Yugoslavia (FRY), Zagreb was asked to join the Italy-Hungary-Slovenia trilateral grouping, which would now be a regional quadrilateral consultative forum on Balkan affairs.

Future Prospects

The new government was very reluctant to openly debate issues that highlighted some of the darker tendencies of Croatia's recent past. These included war crimes charges against Croatian military officers and the general disaffection of the Croatian military with the post-HDZ regime in Zagreb. An early challenge on this issue occurred in March 2000, when The Hague War Crimes Tribunal levied a harsh prison sentence on the former commander of the Bosnian Croat Army (HVO), General Tihomir Blaskic. The International Criminal Tribunal on Yugoslav war crimes (ICTY) charged Blaskic with complicity in the April 1993 massacre at Ahmici. Blaskic was the most senior military officer the Tudjman regime allowed to be extradited to The Hague court. The Blaskic sentencing announcement touched off a large demonstration in Zagreb, centering on a rally outside of the U.S. embassy. The demonstration's leaders insisted that Washington had orchestrated the harsh sentence of Blaskic and that the Racan government's policy of "appeasing the Americans" had fueled anti-Croatian sentiment among the ICTY judges and prosecutors. This theme of linking a desire for a closer relationship to the West with "persecution of Croatian military heroes" had begun to appear in Croatian press editorials, fueling an effort by HDZ hard-liners to call for the government's overthrow.

The month before the Blaskic incident, NATO forces under the Stabilization Force (SFOR) command had seized and silenced a television transmitter controlled by the hard-line Bosnian-Croat HDZ party. The station, Erotel, had been broadcasting messages of ethnic hatred and rabid nationalism, designed to influence impending municipal elections in Bosnia. NATO forces had seized the transmitter of the Bosnian Serb hard-line network, SRT, in 1997. Shortly after that seizure, the office of the EU High Representative in Bosnia had established the Independent Media Commission (IMC) to monitor all radio and television broadcasts in Bosnia in an effort to limit outlets for all extreme nationalist broadcasts.

Following the Blaskic verdict and sentencing, another prominent Croatian officer, General Miro Norac, came under renewed scrutiny for his alleged involvement in the massacre of one hundred Serbian civilians in the Croatian town of Gospic. The Racan government had allowed ICTY investigators access to Gospic, which had been denied to them by the Tudjman government, again fueling criticism of the Racan administration by Croat nationalists. Protestors renewed calls for the overthrow of the Racan government.[12]

The accumulated resentment of the Croatian military leadership toward the Racan government came to a head in late September 2000, when twelve military officers (including seven serving officers) signed an open letter to the Croatian public, expressing outrage over the "criminalization" of the Homeland War (referred to by the signatories as the "Patriotic War") by the new government. The letter condemned statements by the government, which in the view of these military officers, unfairly label patriotic Croatian officers as war criminals. Earlier that month, twelve Croatians suspected of war crimes and listed by the ICTY as suspects were arrested by Croatian authorities. The letter also called for the promotion *only* of Homeland War officers. The letter was extraordinary, since it was signed by several active duty officers, including the (then) current Deputy Chief of the General Staff, Major General Damir Krstecevic (supposedly a representative of the next generation of Western-inclined Croatian military leaders; he had recently returned from a year-long tour at the U.S. Army War College), and the then commander of the Military Training Command, Major General Ivan Kapular (a wartime commander in Vukovar), who was among the most "Westernized" of the Croatian officer corps and a protege of the late Defense Minister Susak. The letter was also signed by two former chiefs of the General Staff and the recently retired Deputy Minister of Defense, Kresimir Cosic, who had been a serving lieutenant general during his tenure as deputy minister.

Many observers assumed that the letter had been encouraged by bitter and disaffected HDZ leaders and cronies of the late President Tudjman. Reflecting this view, President Mesic responded to the letter by saying that it "was organized by individuals who cannot accept the fact that they lost the elections and have to transform themselves from a movement into a party."[13] Shortly after the Mesic statement, his office released a policy statement, emphasizing that serving military officers were prohibited from political activity and that the letter constituted an unacceptable form of communication with the commander in chief. The MOD released a supporting statement in the name of the Deputy Minister, Zlatko Garaljic, saying that the letter was "an unprofessional, inappropriate and irresponsible act that is against the disciplinary code and the decisions of the Minister and the Chief of the General Staff."[14]

The day after the letter was released, President Mesic retired the seven serving officers who had signed the letter, stating that "those who thought a coup d'etat in this country could be achieved with pamphlets have played the wrong card. As of today, they are not members of the Croatian Army (HV)."[15] Prime Minister Racan and Speaker of the Parliament Zlatko Tomcic strongly supported the Mesic decision. Unfortunately, the minister of defense was nearly silent during this period, except to complain privately to MOD colleagues that the president did not consult him. The only early public statement by the MOD suggested that the minister may have disagreed with the decision. A MOD spokesman stated that "the president's decision to retire senior officers of the Croatian Army is drastic and was reached without the knowledge of the Defense Minister."[16] The silence of Minister Rados during this potentially serious crisis of civil-military relations cast a long shadow over the MOD and had a chilling effect on those of us who had thought he represented the new wave of democratically inclined civil leaders, prepared to take Croatia into the Western community of nations.

Prime Minister Racan has learned what many of his fellow European colleagues (particularly those within the European socialist leadership) have known for some time—that governing while attempting to hold together a fractious, multiparty coalition is nearly impossible. He has also learned the very costly lesson of moving too cautiously toward reform, when attempting to break the stranglehold of an autocratically managed kleptocracy, which is how I (and many Croatian democrats) would define the Tudjman years. In the summer of 2000, reports began to surface of widespread corruption, particularly among the military and the former MOD leadership The Racan government hesitated to move vigorously against these individuals, fearing a backlash against the new government from a substantial portion of the Croatian public that still supported many of Tudjman's cronies.

While the response to "The Generals' Letter" was appropriately swift and decisive, it would prove to be an anomaly in the way the Zagreb government would react to serious challenges to the regime's stability. The refusal to publicly condemn and root out corruption (particularly within several of the government's key ministries) has been perhaps the most damaging legacy of the Racan administration. Despite numerous arrests (including a score of former MOD officials and general officers), very few prosecutions have been sought.

Since Tudjman's death at the end of 1999, Croatia has made considerably more progress in rehabilitating its position regionally and internationally than it has domestically. In November a much-heralded EU summit, organized by the nation holding the EU presidency, France, was held in Zagreb. This marked the first time in decades that Croatia had hosted an important international gathering. The summit brought together the fifteen EU member states as well as representatives from the Federal Republic of Yugoslavia, Bosnia-Herzegovina, Macedonia, and Albania. With the overthrow of Milosevic the month before, there was a celebratory atmosphere at the Zagreb gathering. Also, in a victory for the Racan government, the EU leaders agreed that the five states of the western Balkans would be considered for EU membership individually rather than as a group, which had been suggested earlier. Regional reconciliation seemed to be in prospect.

Yet, in a reminder of how some of Zagreb's less attractive political links still survived, the summit was held at the same time that hard-line voices among Bosnian Croats were calling for a third officially recognized entity in Bosnia—that of an autonomous Croatian conclave, similar to the earlier Herzeg Bosna ministate. While the Croatian president publicly condemned such initiatives, Zagreb was simply incapable of controlling the Bosnian Croat leadership. Five years after the Dayton Accord, the Bosnian HDZ leader, Ante Jelavic still condemned an integrated Bosnian state. A year after his death, it seemed that Franjo Tudjman's ghost remained a potent force for this young government in Zagreb.

Chronology

January 2000: Parliamentary Elections; new prime minister appointed by Sabor; first round of presidential elections.

February 2000: U.S. Secretary of State's visit to Zagreb; new government's program released; prime minister and delegation visits Brussels; second round of presidential elections and presidential inauguration.

March 2000: Visit to Zagreb of NATO Delegation; Croatia invited to join Southeast European Trilateral Group; U.S. Sixth Fleet command ship visits Dubrovnik; President Mesic visits Sarejevo.

April 2000: Minister of defense presents plan to president and prime minister to reorganize Armed Forces and MOD; municipal elections are held in Bosnia.

May 2000: Croatia joins Partnership for Peace (PfP) as the twenty-sixth member and the Euro-Atlantic Partnership Council (EAPC) as its forty-sixth member and signs PfP framework document; Croatia joins NATO Parliamentary Assembly as associate member; Croatia participates in the expanded trilateral discussions with Hungary, Slovenia, and Italy.

June 2000: Croatian delegation visits Prague; Croatian government holds initial talks with IMF officials; Croatian President Mesic meets Montenegrin President Djukanovic at Cavtat.

July 2000: Croatia is admitted as a full member into the World Trade Organizations (WTO) as the 137th member; Croatia hosts its first PfP seminar in Zagreb; Croatian delegation led by prime minister visits Bosnia-Herzegovina.

August 2000: President and prime minister make first visit to United States; Croatia attends Southeast Europe Defense Ministerial meeting for the first time; NATO Supreme Allied Commander Europe (SACEUR) visits Zagreb.

September 2000: Croatians arrest twelve Hague Tribunal suspects; Generals' Letter published; Trilaterale is formally renamed as the Quadrilateral Forum, to include Croatia; Croatian first deputy prime minister visits the ICTY in The Hague; Council of Europe ends monitoring of Croatia's democratic reforms and human rights behavior.

November 2000: EU summit held in Zagreb; negotiations begin on an EU stabilization and association agreement (SAA); Bosnian elections.

December 2000: Croatian government sets conditions for cooperation with The Hague; The Tribunal announces its intention to question the Croatian chief of the General Staff in connection with possible war crimes during Operation Storm.

NOTES

1. "Foreign Leaders Skip Tudjman Rites," *International Herald Tribune,* 14 December 1999, p. A6.

2. These figures are drawn from several sources, including *Economist Intelligence Unit, Croatia, 1999–2000* and various issues (1999 and 2000) of *Business Central Europe.*

3. One of the few published discussions by Croatian officials of the civil-military relations issue can be found in Marin Sopta, ed., *European Security Into the 21st Century: Challenges of South East Europe* (Zagreb, Croatia: Croatian Center for Strategic Studies, 1999). See, particularly, Kresimir Cosic and Dragan Lozancic, "Civil and Military Relations in a Democratic Society: Challenges for the Republic of Croatia." Cosic was long-serving deputy minister of defense under Susak, and then also under Andrija Hebrang and Pavao Miljavac, while Lozancic was one of the very few serving civilian officials in the Croatian MOD.

4. At the request of then President Tudjman and Defense Minister Susak, MPRI prepared detailed strategies and plans for Croatia to pursue NATO membership as early as 1997.

5. The figures in this section are drawn from a variety of sources, including Croatian

print media discussions drawn from Croatian MOD planning documents and other open source materials like *The Military Balance, 1999–2000* (Oxford, U.K.: Oxford University Press for the IISS, 1999), 85–86.

6. It was not possible during the Tudjman era to openly pursue such reforms, although Susak's immediate two successors, Andrija Hebrang (whom Tudjman had moved from the health ministry, where he was minister) and the former chief of the General Staff, Pavao Miljavac, began efforts quietly with reform-minded officers.

7. In 2000 the U.S. Defense Department concluded a detailed assessment of the Croatian Armed Forces and the structure and functions of the MOD and all defense agencies. The assessment was part of a series of steps taken by the Pentagon to assist Croatia in moving forward on its modernization programs. I was involved in assisting the Croatian MOD to prepare for this assessment.

8. My discussions with NATO officials.

9. "The Republic of Croatia," *Country Profile Series,* Headquarters, U.S. Army Europe and Seventh Army, October 1998, 5. (Prepared for USAREUR under contract by Science Applications International Corporation.)

10. "Croatian Government Program" in *Croatian Government Bulletin #28,* January 2000.

11. My discussions with U.S. embassy officials in Zagreb.

12. For more detailed reporting on these incidents, see *Institute for War & Peace Reporting,* BCR No. 136 (2 May 2000).

13. See *Media Scan,* Zagreb (29 September 2000), 1. Media Scan is an independent Croatian firm that provides English-language translations and commentary on Croatian media.

14. Ibid.

15. *Media Scan* (2 October 2000), 2.

16. Ibid.

17 ◆ Macedonia: Security Policy without a Compass

Biljana Vankovska

Before its independence, Macedonia was obliged to follow the common security policy of the Yugoslav Federation. Because of the heavy historical legacies of the so-called "Macedonian Question,"[1] the sociopolitical advantages of the federal defense and security system were far more significant to the republic than the military and financial efforts invested in it. The Cold War had frozen all disputes among the Balkan competitors over Macedonian territory and population, while the Yugoslav state provided sufficient security guarantees. At least such was the dominant security perception among Macedonian citizens for decades.

Within a partly decentralized federal system, Skopje had control over the republic's police forces and shared control with the federal army over the militia-type component of the Yugoslav Armed Forces, which was called territorial defense. Because of the implementation of the so-called "national key," Macedonian representatives in federal bodies were taking part in the decision-making process, although their real influence was minor.

As the former Yugoslavia's disintegration progressed, the Macedonian leadership did not take any concrete step toward articulating the republic's own security policy or even a clear political stand toward the ongoing crisis. Many analysts agree that, despite the spread of nationalist fever, Macedonia never had any intention to secede.[2] Consequently, independence was gained without demanding it, that is, today's Republic of Macedonia is not the achievement of an intended state-building policy but a byproduct of Yugoslavia's disintegration.[3]

On 25 January 1991 the Macedonian assembly adopted the Declaration of Sovereignty, albeit with considerable hesitation regarding the final severing of a relationship with the federation. The issue of possible independence was on the agenda of the assembly even on the day war in Slovenia broke out.

Following the independence referendum of 8 September 1991 and the new constitution of 17 November 1991, the first organic law adopted in the assembly was the Defense Law in February 1992. After the Yugoslav Peoples' Army (or JNA) units withdrew from Macedonia by March 1992, the new defense system could be said to have coexisted with the old federal one. The JNA took all movable armament and equipment (and what was not possible to remove was destroyed). From early 1992, JNA officers of Macedonian origin started coming back and were immediately included in the newly formed Army of the Republic of Macedonia (ARM).

Despite prior calls from some political parties, the government began to form the ARM only after the establishment of the political and legal framework. A nationalist party (MAAK) that had called for secession since 1990 proposed a radical solution in September 1991 and issued the so-called "Manifesto for Demilitarization of the Macedonian Republic." Some domestic authors were uncritically euphoric about the document, claiming that the Manifesto implied a specific "Macedonian peace model."[4] It was instead a symbolic cry by a group of intellectuals concerned about Macedonia's future in the hostile Balkans. It was not a product of a mature civil society's demands, and thus it did not echo strongly in Macedonian society. The idea was not inspired by any critical evaluation of deficiencies in the previous security establishment. It was more a product of Macedonia's passivity and self-pity than a concept generated by a proactive and democratic attitude toward national security issues. It is incorrect to conclude that demilitarization and making an "oasis of peace" out of Macedonia were the leading ideas in government policy making in 1991–92.[5] Also, the idea of a neutral Macedonia did not get any public attention and was treated as nothing more than a nice but unrealistic idea.[6]

In early 1992 Macedonia was de facto a demilitarized country, because the JNA did not leave any weapons behind. From the point of view of the new defense system buildup in 1992, the most urgent need was to utilize human and particularly professional potential and material resources. These efforts seemed hopeless in the context of a series of disadvantages, such as the double embargo from the "north" (as UN sanctions against all of the former Yugoslavia were enforced) and from the "south" (by the Greek government because of the name dispute). The UN embargo banned the export of arms and military equipment indiscriminately to all Yugoslav successor states, while the disintegration of the former Yugoslav market pushed down the level of economic development of Macedonia and all successor states.

Paradoxically, in this critical period during which Macedonia was totally disarmed, the country was not directly militarily threatened. The possibility of spillover effects from the war zones in former Yugoslavia was immense, but the traditional rivals over Macedonia did not show serious aggressive intentions toward the young state. The negative effects of the troublesome process of international recognition were decisive; the growing feeling of insecurity regarding the state identity issue inevitably gave impetus to ethnic (Macedonian and Albanian) nationalism. The internal threat of violent inter-ethnic conflict between the two major ethnic groups (Macedonians and Albanians) was becoming more and more salient.[7] It was apparent that the young state possessed a deep conflict potential and lacked democratic culture for a peaceful conflict resolution.[8]

The government's call for an international peace operation in November 1992 manifested a reasonable and critical attitude to Macedonia's own security capabilities. The UN mission's mandate originally was defined as follows: "to monitor the border areas with Albania and the Federal Republic of Yugoslavia; to strengthen, by its presence, the country's security and stability; and to report on any developments that could threaten the country."[9] But an examination of the character and changing mandate of the UN preventive deployment shows that this unique mission was deployed for the wrong reasons.[10] It was established when external aggression from the north was a highly unlikely scenario.[11] By the time the mandate was transformed and focused on internal conflict mitigation, neither the UN officials nor the Macedonian government had admitted officially such a changed mission.[12] The achievements of the United Nations Preventive Deployment Force (UNPREDEP) were most useful in terms of monitoring the porous borders with Albania and Kosovo through which one could document principal routes for drugs and arms smuggling. UNPREDEP did not, however, succeed in alleviating internal conflict potential. The mission helped Macedonian Army border units to perform their tasks to a great extent. In the 1993–99 period, the Macedonian military coexisted with another (international) military force, the mandate of which was not seen as concurrent but helpful.

In the first years of an independent Macedonia, Skopje was preoccupied with political survival and had practically no security policy. For example, in 1993 the UN troops were deployed, and immediately afterward the national assembly declared Macedonia's wish to join NATO. The process in Macedonia was opposite of that of Slovenia, where security matters became "nationalized." All security initiatives were motivated by the need to find a security provider rather than a result of some proactive foreign or security policy. The decision to seek NATO membership was not an outcome of any wide public or expert debate. No other alternatives have ever been considered, because from the very beginning, NATO was imposed as a kind of dogma around which an all-party consensus has been reached. The idea was that helpless Macedonia could survive only with powerful external assistance. Through early 2001, all Macedonian governments have taken for granted a national consensus about NATO. The responsible state actors have successfully avoided the issue of economic costs of entry into the North Atlantic Alliance, while the public has been led to believe that the benefits (in security terms) would be much greater than expenses (in economic terms).

The Status of Forces Agreement (SOFA)—a document that establishes the legal rights and responsibilities of foreign military forces stationed in a country and those of the host state—of June 1996 should have demonstrated the high level of mutual cooperation between Macedonia and NATO and the United States. The government claimed that it was an outstanding achievement of its foreign and security policy and that Macedonia had taken a step forward toward refuge under the Western defensive umbrella. Independent media argued that the government was misusing a rather technical issue to score points with the domestic public.[13]

Given the so-called "Taiwanese adventure" of Macedonian foreign policy in early 1999, when Skopje recognized as a sovereign state the Taipei government and exchanged ambassadors, the termination of the UN mission as a result of China's veto in the UN Security Council was hardly surprising.[14] There are indications that the government had (intentionally) opted for replacing UNPREDEP with NATO or U.S. troops as a better security guarantee. However, NATO's intervention against Belgrade and bombing of targets in Kosovo and Serbia brought the most serious security challenge for Macedonia since 1991. Security challenges of all kinds (military, political, economic, societal, and ecological) increased to dramatic levels, but the Macedonian leadership could not respond in an adequate way. Ultimately, an Albanian insurgency revealed dramatically Macedonia's lack of a security strategy. The lack of an articulate security policy was a severe weakness during and after Kosovo; that the country did not collapse was the result only of some international assistance and coincidence, but the consequences were painfully visible at the outset of 2001.

Threat Assessment

Macedonia, the only Yugoslav successor state that gained independence in a peaceful way, can be seen as the only exception to the rule. Given the peaceful transition, at first glance, it looks like the country historically known as a "powder keg" has become an "oasis of peace." However, an analysis of Macedonia's security plight as well as characteristics of Macedonian security policy readily dispel any optimism.

Assessment of current security threats does not always imply an objective analysis. In a country like Macedonia, subjective perceptions of security threats sometimes weigh more than any objective indicators. The subjective dimension of security deals with more cognitive elements of the process of security policy making. Nations, like individuals, create their own perceptions about reality that may differ dramatically from measurable and tangible indicators of the security threats. Even on a national level, various social segments are likely to have different evaluations of the same "real" content. True or false, accurate or not, the perspectives of a nation or a social group are factors that determine their policy, behavior, and possible responses to the "real reality." Perceptions, in other words, represent reality for the actors that create, bear, and believe in policy alternatives.

The real essence and scope of the security policy at present heavily depends on the actor who defines what security is. In terms of Ole Weaver's concept of securitization, security is a speech act. In other words, "a problem is a security problem when it is defined so by the power holders."[15] The power holders, however, are not the only securitizing agents often being supported by other domestic actors (such as pressure groups, media, economic and military elites, and so forth). Conversely, an illusory alliance is being created between political elites from the West and post-Communist countries. The idyllic picture of unanimously accepted "cooperative security" and the new security agenda might be misleading, indicating a unitary vision of security and a desired level and type of security for everyone at every level when such consensus does not exist.

During a decade of instability, ethnic strife, economic collapse, and individual insecurity in the "gray zone" of southeastern Europe, Macedonia has created its own "virtual world," where many security problems are absorbed into everyday life and have even become a way of survival. Rhetorically, the government is concerned about the so-called new security agenda, while the government itself is part of the country's security problems. It is both fashionable and politically correct to talk in terms of nonmilitary threats. It is the way to catch up and to share the partnership for peace and security with the Western allies.

Until recently, the Macedonian state had adopted none of the NATO-required strategic and doctrinal documents on national security. Without any prior public debate, two documents (the "White Book on Defense of the Republic of Macedonia" and the "Strategy of Defense of the Republic of Macedonia") were issued in August and September 1998. According to official statements, the country does not face any direct military threat and does not consider any country as a potential enemy. Actually, the political and military elites find themselves in frustrating dilemmas. The dominant threat perceptions held by the political establishments are still principally concerned with external sources of insecurity—that is, the Macedonian elites perceive the neighborhood as hostile and dangerous in regard to Macedonian statehood, nationhood, territory, and sovereignty. Yet, this cannot be formulated openly or emphasized in the defense doctrine, since the explicit wish to join EU or NATO structures does not permit hostile perceptions of the neighborhood.

To alleviate this dilemma, Macedonia tries at least to catch up with the developed countries in the rhetoric of a new security agenda. Thus, Skopje's official security policy is focused on transnational terrorism, uncontrolled arms proliferation, ethnic conflict, religious fundamentalism, drugs and arms trafficking, organized crime networks, money laundering, "white slavery," and other social deviations. The vocabulary and rhetoric used in government documents give the impression that all of these negative phenomena happen in an undefined space on earth. This has a touch of absurdity insofar as the Balkan region still represents a focal point for all of these phenomena. In other words, Macedonian policymakers do not consider their own country and society as a fertile ground for all these nonmilitary threats or as a stage for interethnic conflicts. Instead, Macedonia is perceived as an innocent and passive victim of the negative developments from the neighborhood.

The concrete security agenda in Macedonia is tailored in accordance with the self-perception (very often a false one) and political purposes. Even when the security agenda is set up in a way that includes all nontraditional threats, the sources of these threats are most often identified as outside the respective country, most often in the neighboring states. Not surprisingly, Macedonia has not adopted a document on integral national security strategy yet but, rather, sticks to a (military) defense strategy.

A valid threat assessment calls for a prior definition of the level of analysis. The picture might differ depending on whether the analysis is at a regional, state, or individual level. Nevertheless, an analysis along the lines of Barry Buzan's five sectors of security (military, economic, political, societal, or environmental) seems to be the best way to give a full picture of the security threats in Macedonia.

Although southeast Europe is far from being a security community, direct *military threats* to the Macedonian state have not been probable even during the most critical periods of the former Yugoslavia's dissolution. Only in late February 2001, when border incursions by Kosovo Albanians led first to gun battles with Macedonian border units, and then a large artillery and infantry counterattack in March, did a sense of external threat seem relevant. Slobodan Milosevic's nationalist agenda perceived Macedonia as a traditional Serbian territory (that is, Southern Serbia). But, because of the unexpected difficulties on the other fronts in former Yugoslavia (first

Slovenia, and later much more in Croatia and Bosnia, and finally in Kosovo), Macedonia never became a topical and urgent issue in Belgrade's military circles. The constellation of global, regional, and national developments in each of the other three neighbors let Macedonia remain perfectly safe in military terms through 2000.

Instability in Albania and Yugoslavia (Kosovo) affected Macedonian military security only indirectly—at least until February and March 2001. Several armed incidents on the border with Kosovo beginning in early 2000 were serious and pointed toward the danger of a larger confrontation such as was experienced early the next year. The 1997 collapse of the Albanian state imposed serious border problems, but the current situation is different and incomparably worse. First, these armed incidents have shown the military inferiority of the Macedonian defense system relative to illegal terrorist groups from Kosovo. Second, the vulnerability of the Macedonian state has become apparent, since the political-military leadership allowed itself to be blackmailed and even entered into bargaining with illegal Albanian armed groups. Third, the escalation of border incidents into a military security crisis demonstrated that the Kosovo conflict was not stopped by the deployment of international forces in the troubled province and that a widened conflict is very possible. In sum, the capability of the Macedonian state to protect its territory, sovereignty, and citizens constantly has been challenged.

The significance of military security (that is, maintenance of peace in the midst of a turbulent region) has often been used for internal political purposes. The notion of Macedonia as an "oasis of peace" was invented to earn political points and internal legitimacy. Various political elites and groups have claimed peace as their main political capital and historical achievement, although peace in Macedonia has been more a result of a constellation of factors in Balkan affairs and much more a coincidence than a consequence of a proactive policy. The data clearly indicate Macedonia's fundamental military inferiority, despite undeniable improvements since 1991 imposed "demilitarization." Even more indicative is that police forces are much better off (in terms of equipment, training, armament, and salaries) than the army. One may conclude that Macedonia's sources of insecurity are deeply embedded in society and that the so-called internal security doctrine is given de facto priority over external threats.

The sector of *political security* has been burdened with many deficiencies since 1991. A decade later the situation looks no less unstable. The acceptance of Western democratic principles has been limited to two forms of imitation—an intentionally created illusion or even a self-deceit. "Democracy" introduced overnight is usually uncritically praised in the West, thus giving opportunities for new elites to fulfill the lack of internal legitimacy and push back criticism from the opposition and society. Having insisted on the minimal procedures of democratic elections. Western powers tend to support autocracies with such formal legitimacy or highly corrupted elites. The absence of substantive and normative democracy and the dominance of mafia-state regimes, electoral fraud, and media manipulation are all forgiven because of geopolitical interests.

One of Macedonia's main political characteristics is a high level of *ethnification.* In addition to a divided society, the situation is worsened by the intentional ethno-mobilization of the masses by the main political parties (both Macedonian and Albanian). *Ethnification* of political matters is very often seen as the easiest way to get public support and votes during elections. Violent conflict in early 2001 has further solidified this tendency.

Yesterday's ruling party and today's main opposition party, the Social Democratic Alliance (SDSM), uses the rhetoric and the arsenal of the prior opposition and today's ruling party, the Internal Macedonian Revolutionary Organization (VMRO). It seems that behavior and vocabulary used by the political parties depend on the current position they occupy and have nothing to do with the political orientation and programs. The country's political spectrum is split into two heavily antagonized blocks (along the main division between Macedonian and Albanian ethnic groups). Sometimes the divisions within the so-called Macedonian block are much deeper and troublesome than between the states of Macedonia and Albania.

The lack of democratic political culture is evident not only in the parties' structures, which are based of the concept of a "leader" and not on a political program, but also in their readiness to use violence or the "services" of the hard-liners among their ranks. Violence in the political struggle is not limited to instruments of state coercion. Various "party militias" and bodyguards as well can be seen parading in the public and even in the parliament and government building. The most catastrophic indications about the progress of the democratization process became apparent during the presidential (1999) and local (2000) elections. Although the electoral process is a minimal prerequisite for democracy (not democracy itself), Macedonia showed its political immaturity in a dramatic way. While presidential elections were overburdened with irregularities, denial of voting rights, and outright intimidation (especially in Albanian-populated areas) local elections involved at least one death and many armed incidents.[16]

The Macedonian state has no monopoly on coercion or the means of violence, thereby raising doubts about its ability to protect the people, their human rights, and their property. In addition to the emergence of paramilitary groups, "parapolice" forces operate in western Macedonia. To maintain the governmental coalition (that is, marriage of interest with the Albanian partner, the Democratic Party of Albania (DPA) led by Arben Xhaferi, the ruling VMRO (which holds the sector of interior) turned a blind eye in 2000 to clear indications and even official reports from intelligence services of impending difficulties.

After electoral victories, the first move of post-Communist governments (and Macedonia is no exception) usually is to create a symbiotic relationship between political elites and economic monopolies. The new alliances almost immediately identify common interests and transform themselves into criminal structures. Without an independent judiciary and other democratic control mechanisms, such criminal structures penetrate every pore of society. Not surprisingly, governing elites are co-opted by organized crime that, over time, takes over the real political power. The previous SDSM government in Macedonia announced a resolute battle against the so-called octopus-like tentacles of organized crime, while the current government has, from the outset of its mandate, repeatedly spoken about the fight against corruption and organized crime.

The results are nonexistent in Skopje, while the regional situation has become more and more favorable for illegal activities in which state support (or at least, silent approval) is necessary. After the Kosovo war, Macedonia became a transit route for all kinds of illegal trade (stolen cars, narcotics, arms, "white slavery"), and it is believed that some governmental officials and bodies are involved either directly or indirectly in these activities.

International crime experts have been alarmed by the rise of organized crime in former Balkan war zones and the powerlessness of international peace enforcement forces.[17] In 1995, one observer noted:

Socially organized in extended families bound together in clan alliances, Kosovar Albanians dominate the Albanian mafia in the southern Balkans. Other than Kosovo, the Albanian mafia is also active in northern Albania and western Macedonia. In this context, the so-called "Balkan Medellin" is made up of a number of geographically connected border towns. . . . If left unchecked, this growing Albanian narco-terrorism could lead to a Colombian syndrome in the southern Balkans, or the emergence of a situation in which the Albanian mafia becomes powerful enough to control one or more states in the region. In practical terms, this will involve either Albania or Macedonia, or both.[18]

NATO's blunder in Kosovo made one more instance of "collateral damage" for the region. The Italian analyst Francesco Silvestri talks about a drugged future of the Balkans in the following way:

In the meantime, however, the effects of the war between NATO and Serbia are in the center of attention. Above all, there is reason to worry about the effects of the war on the restructuring of the Balkan mafias. The unavoidable reconstruction of the areas destroyed by the NATO bombs will lead to a strengthening of the local mafias that will be able to specialize themselves in the building sector, as the Italian mafias have done in the past, in order then to pour the gains of the reconstruction in the drugs trafficking business. Today, this is only a hypothesis, but whatever will happen in the southern Balkans in the future, will be automatically related to the existence of this underground economy that draws great part of its profits from drugs trafficking.[19]

Today's image of the Kosovo province resembles a Colombia of Europe. There are practically no guarded borders between Kosovo and Albania or between Macedonia and Kosovo. This "advantage" makes it possible for more than 40 percent of the heroin reaching Western Europe to transit through this region.

Not surprisingly, the situation in terms of *economic security* only reflects the catastrophic situation in all society. Official data are either false or cosmetically adjusted either to domestic needs or to demands of international financial institutions. In reality, Macedonia "leads" Europe with a 53 percent unemployment rate. Among the minority who are primarily employed, more than half did not receive salaries for the last several months in 2000 (or even a year, in some cases). Privatization of firms and enterprises has appeared more like a criminal takeover and is perceived as legalized robbery. Particularly in relations with foreign partners, Macedonia has sold its most profitable firms and enterprises for so little that it seems humorous.

Social tensions and conflicts, as a consequence, are increasing, which produces a fertile ground for all other kinds of conflicts in society. In 1999–2000, economic stagnation (or better, regression) was a cumulative result of ineffective economic reforms and the impact of regional turmoil. The so-called "economic medicine" practiced against Milosevic's regime severely hit the Macedonian economy, while the destruction of Yugoslav roads, railways, and infrastructure during the NATO campaign are still among the main obstacles for Macedonian products to find their way to Western Europe. Security analyses usually put emphasis on the military or ethnic problems, but very few identify the tight relationship between socioeconomic factors (underdevelopment, unemployment, poverty, brain drain) and the rise of ethnic hatred and intolerance. Macedonia is a very indicative case in this sense, because the animosity between the majority (ethnic Macedonians) and the most numerous minority (ethnic Albanians) has not had any deep historical roots. Yet, the vicious circle of ethnic intolerance, an unequal distribution of goods and positions in the social structure, and the evident democratic deficit (both in terms of elite and public political culture) are unlikely to be broken soon. On the contrary, these traits provide fuel for an explosion of conflict and a spiral of hostility and violence.

The Macedonian government claims a major achievement because of new financial arrangements with the World Bank and the IMF, which came after a couple years of hard negotiations. However, the best Macedonian economists have a different view on the economic prospects of the country under the conditions prescribed in these agreements. In the words of the leading economist, Dr. Natalija Nikolovska, "the reform package we got from IMF is a part of the Washington consensus, which provides the transitional economies to enter the 'third world' and not the market economy.

The interests of the creators of the IMF programs and the interests of our region are in deep disparity."[20]

Given its multiethnic composition, Macedonian society has been facing tremendous difficulties in terms of *societal security* since 1991. The conflict potential of the country is immense, which gives extraordinary importance to all measures for conflict prevention and mitigation. Unfortunately, the Kosovo war left deep scars on Macedonian society. Such scars are particularly evident in terms of shaken identities and in the rival Albanian and Macedonian security perceptions (but also, of the other ethnic groups in the country). At first glance, it seems that Macedonia is an exception to the rule in terms of the last best hope in the Balkans. Albanian parties have been in all Macedonian governments since 1991, and ongoing efforts are under way to increase the number of Albanians in all state structures. However, the gap between political (macro) and societal (micro) levels is huge. The communication between the ethnic groups is best on a level of political elites. Each political (ethnic) center maintains full control over its behavior and electoral potentials of its own ethnic group, which means that political elites create unprincipled coalitions (either in power or in opposition) and successfully conspire with their own ethnic kin to stay in power.

Ethnic Macedonians and ethnic Albanians live in two parallel worlds with almost no points of contact. The gap of distrust has been present in their relationships especially since 1991. Most often, an ethnic modus vivendi has been practiced—conflict avoidance and isolation in one's own ethnic group. The collapse of the old federal state opened a troublesome period of political and ethnic identification, which in Macedonia appeared to be not only two different but also opposite processes. Strengthening each group's identity (in terms of ethnic symbols, languages, religious affiliation, and culture) has been perceived as an identity threat by the opposite ethnic group. Thus, the so-called ethnic security dilemma is the concept that explains the essence of interethnic relations in the country. The 1999 NATO intervention in Yugoslavia led toward more intensive ethnic homogenization and confrontation between the two groups. The population of Macedonian ethnic origin exhibited overt disagreement with NATO's intervention, while solidarity with the Yugoslav side was based merely on the perception of Albanians as a common enemy.

While the Macedonian government is speaking about "positive energy" and "relaxed interethnic relations," many indications suggest that the feeling of internal cohesion in both the major ethnic groups has increased rapidly. Such internal cohesion has increased not only within the Macedonian-Albanian community in Macedonia, but also between the Albanians in Macedonia and those in Kosovo. The Albanian community in Macedonia has also eschewed identifying with what is seen as a common mighty protector—NATO and the United States. Thus, all eyes are turned toward Kosovo and the hopes and expectations are tightly related to the developments in the neighborhood instead of the future prospects in Macedonia.

The Balkan laboratory represents an excellent setting for analyzing the most serious and interrelated aspects of security. For a decade, southeastern Europe has been repeatedly confirming and denying the differentiation of military versus nonmilitary security threats. The number of so-called nonmilitary security problems is greater than ever, but almost all of them are dependent on military security of countries from the region. It does not necessarily mean that governing elites have defined clear security policy and doctrine in light of reality. Macedonia can be said to be living in a kind of hyperreality or self-perception of being a "normal" country in transition.

Capacities

Efficient security policy calls for a careful evaluation of available capacities and resources, which once put into function, will be able to secure the state and its population from various threats. Absolute security is certainly an unachievable goal, but it is also true that certain threats should be met by adequate security measures and mechanisms. The problem arises when leaders misperceive security threats or their severity and potential.

Macedonia's capabilities to respond to military challenges are still very weak; but, fundamentally, the military threats were not at the top of the agenda until February and March 2001. The official statement that the Macedonian Armed Forces are a "respectable military force" has a meaning only in a "historical" perspective, that is, in comparison to the period of early 1992 when the country was militarily helpless and "demilitarized." The other (political) reason for such a political evaluation is Macedonia's wish to join the Atlantic Alliance. Officially, the government is dedicated to improving the Army's armaments, equipment, and training. The government's emphasis on strengthening the country's military capability seems aimed primarily at pleasing the Western allies and at meeting NATO military standards—not because of imminent military threats endangering state security.

In the Macedonian public, discussions on the difficult professional and social situation in the Army are taboo. Many military professionals feel highly humiliated regarding their professional and social status, particularly by the treatment they receive from the state leadership. Members of special units very often leave the Army because of irregular payments and inappropriate treatment. In addition, the Macedonian defense system faces huge difficulties ensuring the annual conscript contingent is filled. A total of 70 percent of the pool of draft-age youths seek to avoid military service.

For a small and militarily inferior country, diplomacy might have an extremely important role in achieving goals of security policy. However, the young state has a very small number of experienced diplomats, while the state leadership often has no clear idea about the country's foreign policy. Ambassadorial posts are usually bargaining chips in intracoalition political games, so people who represent the Macedonian state abroad rarely meet criteria for diplomats.

With President Boris Trajkovski in office, the relationships between the president's office and the government, and particularly the foreign minister, could be expected to be far more harmonious than in the period of so-called cohabitation between the former president Gligorov and VMRO's government. However, the relationship between the (VMRO) president and the foreign minister, a post allocated to the Democratic Party Alliance (DA) was rather troublesome and not synchronized. One of the first conflictual issues was full diplomatic recognition of Taiwan, which threatened to obscure the pro-European orientation of the country. Even the relationships between the president and Prime Minister Georgievski (both members of the ruling VMRO) have not always been in concordance, which often creates laughable situations before the international community.

The country objectively lacks potential to stimulate economic recovery or to satisfy the basic social demands of society. At the same time, the government has not abandoned the idea to invest more in the military sector in order to meet NATO criteria. Thus, extremely scarce resources were allocated to the military and interior ministry even before fighting began in early 2001. External assistance comes more in the form of "humani-tarian" aid than in the form of real and direct investments, while the "klepto-cratic" habits of a part of the establishment prevent even these insufficient financial injections from reaching those who badly need them.

The political system shows a paradoxical situation: instead of progress in the democratization process, the democratic deficit grows in size and effect. Political institutions that are supposed to be channels and mecha-nisms for peaceful resolution of societal conflicts de facto represent a part of the problem. They produce instability and insecurity among the citizens, who feel left in a lurch while, as ordinary citizens see it, the power-thirsty politicians have only one priority—to stay in power against all odds. The coalition government has not been stable and has not had a consistent policy in any societal sphere since the very beginning of the "marriage of interest." Each of the coalition partners has believed itself to be smarter than the other two, and able to double-cross them.

At the end of 2000, the situation seemed simpler, with the ruling VMRO stronger than ever over the collapsed and confused opposition, which is not necessarily a guarantee that Macedonia is entering more stable political waters. On the contrary, having in mind the VMRO's methods of governing, the situation looks more serious than ever in regard to the democratization prospects. The full control over the military, police, secret services, judiciary, media, and even the university leaves free hands to the ruling elite, while the society lacks efficient mechanisms to limit and control political power.

Serious deficiencies of the political system give no hope for resolving the societal and especially interethnic problems through legal and legitimate channels. Even less capable to do something in this regard is an immature civil society. So far, the interethnic "peace" has been maintained with ad hoc solutions, a half-way "policy" wavering between liberal democracy and nation-state building, unprincipled coalitions, and bargaining over the country's national interest.

Policy Innovations

The developments in the field of security policy making in Macedonia during 2000 could hardly be described as innovative. In the first years after the Kosovo war, the main efforts have been to catch up with developments stopped during the NATO operation when Macedonia served as a logistic base for the operation and was mainly worried about survival.

The year 2000 started with a heavy political mortgage transferred from the 1999 presidential elections. The new president of the republic and commander in chief, Boris Trajkovski entered office with weakened legitimacy and disputed authority and found himself challenged even by the leader of his party and Prime Minister Georgievski. Therefore, for President Trajkovski, it was of utmost importance to demonstrate his capability to exercise the presidency's constitutional rights. One of the first steps of the new president was to appoint a new National Security Council, with a promise that he would make this body workable. However, after the first serious situations (that is, heavy border skirmishes in the spring of 2000), the statements of the council's members were dissonant, additionally confusing the concerned Macedonian public. The orders issued by the commander in chief and the defense minister to the border troops and special units of the Army clearly indicated not only their weakness but also their ignorance of the basic procedures typical for such situations.

The records of the government information office clearly show that the Macedonian establishment has spent many days and hours greeting numerous guests whose final destination was Kosovo, or in meetings with Kosovo Force (KFOR) representatives. Macedonia might be said to have become a transit route to Kosovo and much of the government's energy and time might have been devoted to Kosovo-related issues. Another ambiguous issue is the unclear relationships with KFOR, especially in terms of legal responsibility of the mission's members.

The new president opened the process of reevaluation of Macedonia's official strategy of defense, allegedly to make it compatible with NATO admission requirements. In addition to this reason, however, Trajkovski wished to play the role of a president with his own vision regarding defense matters. The newly appointed working group (formed in the summer 2000) was still, as of early 2001, preparing the draft defense strategy. The work of the group was not made public, but there are indications that it has had some shortcomings such as noncoordination, external supervision, and an open dilemma regarding what comes first—the strategy or the Defense Law.

The new Defense Law is also supposed to be one of the main achievement of the "new" security policy of the current government. In spite of some novelties and the elimination of certain inconsistencies of the old statute, one thing has remained the same. The draft statute was made in a small circle with no public or expert debate, which only proves that transparency is still something unknown for Macedonian security policy making. Moreover, the preparation of the statute basically was made by the members of the private U.S. corporation of retired military officers (MPRI). The same corporation is being authorized to organize the process of reorganization of the defense ministry and the Army General Staff and serves as a kind of supervisor of the defense strategy making. It appears, further, that Macedonia will get another defense statute first, while the strategy will be adopted later. Macedonia, it seems, is building a house beginning with the roof.

The Macedonian president decided to take a regional initiative right after the change in Belgrade, and the so-called Skopje Summit of 25 October 2000 was supposed to be a turning point in reestablishing old bridges among Balkan states. For the first time, Macedonia took a lead in such an (informal) initiative. The apparently successful meeting, however, had just short-term effects. The main innovation was the return of the Federal Republic of Yugoslavia to regional dialogues, while Macedonia tried to compensate for its (in)direct support for the NATO intervention and normalize the relationships with Vojislav Kostunica's regime.

A month later, on 25 November 2000, the EU and Western Balkan countries held another historic summit in Zagreb. Macedonia signed the Agreement for Stabilization and Association with the EU and many bilateral contacts were realized. The whole event, in addition to its real significance, received two interpretations. First, it was falsely presented as (almost) an admission of Macedonia into the EU and as one of the major achievements of the current government. In reality, the so-called "evolutionary clause" was imposed and became a nonnegotiable obstacle for swifter admission of Macedonia into the EU. According to some analysts, it was actually an indication that both economic and political reforms had not been undertaken in a proper manner. Second, it was accompanied with a parallel domestic intragovernmental crisis that left a shameful impression abroad.

The end of 2000 left Macedonia less stable than it had looked at the year's outset, with a crisis brewing that exploded early in 2001. The last month of the year was marked by a deep political crisis. The parliament appeared to be a scene for potential (even physical) conflicts. The inability to achieve at least minimal consensus over the most important issues, such as the Defense Law, indicates that 2001 will have led to few hopeful developments.

Future Prospects

Since 1991 Macedonia has been an object of controversial predictions. One side has seen it as a "powder keg" that had enough conflict potential to ignite a Balkan war. The opposite standpoint argues that Macedonia is the last best hope for the Balkans, that is, the only truly multiethnic democracy.[21] Such competing images of Macedonia are not academic or abstract. At the end of 2000, the question was still open whether peace in Macedonia is a result of a meaningful security policy or a coincidence (and a temporary condition). The security crisis of 2001 has made the question even more urgent.

The set of security (military and nonmilitary) threats to the Macedonian state and population have been numerous and complex. Since they have a potential to feed each other, the best way to cope with them would have been an integrated strategy. The main characteristic of these threats is that they are unrelated to territory and contain dynamic components that cannot be confined within a limited area. The Macedonian government, however, claimed that it had full control over developments. Also, the so-called international community wanted to see a success in the case of Macedonia. Skopje and international actors badly wanted to disregard the catastrophic security situation—at the levels of both the Macedonian state and human security. There was an insistent effort to proclaim Macedonia as an oasis of peace long after such a description obviously had become inaccurate.

Macedonia still looks like a passive observer of its own existence, especially regarding security perspective. In the first months of 2001, new defense legislation and a new defense strategy, both of which are principal tasks of the annual plan for admission into NATO, should have been produced. Unfortunately, a real conflict occurrred—starkly emphasizing that security problems will not be resolved by legal reforms. It is also true that the previously designed reforms of the Macedonian army have little relevance for the security challenges of the Macedonian state.

What really happened in the first half of 2001 can be seen as a sort of "baptism by fire" of the army of the "oasis of peace." Macedonia lost its "military virginity" and was swiftly transformed into the historically well-known "powder keg." The publicly praised "military offensive" against the Albanian insurgents on the Tetovo hillsides in late March 2001 carried the potential to become a Pyrrhic victory of the Macedonian security forces, not in terms of casualties and damages but in terms of deepening distrust between the country's two major ethnic communities.

Some analysts have seen developments of early 2001 differently, and it will take some time before it becomes clear what the crisis was all about. Possible interpretations vary greatly. Was it a "faked war" for which the background might be a previously agreed division of Macedonia? Did the crisis arise from criminal matters in which both Albanian and Macedonian groups were involved? Have Albanians employed concentrated violence to "incite" a dialogue over the political status of Kosovo? Was this an instance of "controlled chaos" used to speed up the process of federalization of Macedonia? Or was the violence generated by problems related to human or minority rights discourses? While these differing views are not mutually exclusive, they do draw attention to highly divergent explanations of Macedonia's security condition and future.

The prospects for the country during 2001–2002 are highly risky. The crisis of Macedonia's political system can be characterized as a total paralysis and collapse of legitimate institutions that are unable to resolve any of society's pending problems. The constitutional crisis resembles the Yugoslav situation of early 1991. The constitutional institutions (particularly the parliament and the government) can hardly function, while there is a quiet promotion of unconstitutional bodies and practices (such as summits of the leaders of the political parties in the office of the president of the republic). More and more international mediation is wanted or unwanted—that is, the Albanian side calls for more internationalization of the conflict, while the Macedonian side is highly suspicious about offers that come from someone who is seen as a person with disputed credentials (such as Javier Solana). Social problems and mistrust have raised the nationalist fever in the country to a point much higher than it was in 1991. For the time being, under an euphoric atmosphere (among the ethnic Macedonians), only vague estimates exist of how much the military "victory" cost in economic terms, let alone possible future investments in the military security.

Throughout 2001 and 2002, it is most likely that Macedonia will continue the old practice of coping with the security problems without any clear long-term policy. Even hypothetical membership in NATO would have been insufficient and inappropriate to resolve the burning problems. In Macedonia's "virtual reality," officials still regard the most urgent security and political act for the coming years to be EU and NATO admission, despite the fact that the population is slowly and silently dying from poverty, a nonexistent economy, growing intolerance, terror, and pollution. One thing is sure—Macedonia is running out of time, and 2001 may bring some outcomes in the security sphere. Were NATO able to address some of these immediate and tangible security issues, Macedonia's population would be well served.

Chronology

15 December 1999: The new president of the republic and supreme commander, Boris Trajkovski, is inaugurated.

13 January 2000: In an action against illegal arms trafficking, three policemen are killed near the Albanian-populated village of Aracinovo, near the capital, Skopje.

30 April 2000: Four soldiers of the Macedonian army are kidnapped on Macedonian territory on the border with Kosovo by a group of Albanian terrorists; after several hours the soldiers are exchanged for an imprisoned Kosovo Liberation Army (KLA) fighter in a Macedonian prison.

5–6 June 2000: Two Macedonian soldiers are wounded in an armed incident on the border with Kosovo and the Federal Republic of Yugoslavia.

24 June 2000: Big opposition rally is held in Skopje as a warning to the government.

4 July 2000: The Macedonian parliament declines the opposition's demand for a vote of no-confidence in the government.

13 July 2000: Prime Minister Georgievski receives the KFOR Commander, General Ortuno, and exchanges views on greater cooperation and border control.

19 July 2000: NATO secretary-general George Robertson pays a short visit to the Republic of Macedonia on his way to Kosovo.

27 July 2000: After the fourth reconstruction of the government of the Republic of Macedonia, Ljuben Paunovski becomes the new defense minister.

15 August 2000: Defense Minister Paunovski receives KFOR logistic base commander, Vice Marshall Tony Stables, and exchanges opinions on cooperation between ARM and KFOR.

10 September 2000: The first round of the local elections is held, accompanied by violence that leaves one dead and scores of wounded people in the western part of the country.

12 September 2000: The draft of the new defense law is approved by the government and put up for parliamentary ratification.

18 September 2000: Foreign Minister Dimitrov takes part in the fifty-fifth annual session of the UN General Assembly.

25 October 2000: Skopje informal summit of the heads of southeast European countries is held.

13 November 2000: Prime Minister Georgievski greets the EU High Commissioner for Common Foreign and Security Policy, Javier Solana.

14 November 2000: Foreign Minister Dimitrov pays official visit to the Federal Republic of Yugoslavia and is greeted by the new Yugoslav president, Vojislav Kostunica.

24 November 2000: Macedonia's president signs the Stabilization and Association Agreement with the EU at the Zagreb Summit.

24 November 2000: Democratic Alternative publicly announces its withdrawal from the governmental coalition and joins the opposition.

30 November 2000: The Macedonian parliament dismisses five Democratic Alternative ministers, and votes for the reconstruction of the government on initiative of Prime Minister Georgievski.

1 December 2000: Deputy NATO Secretary-General Sergio Balancino pays visit to Macedonia and meets President Trajkovski, Prime Minister Georgievski, and the ministers of defense and foreign affairs.

17 January 2001: The leader of the opposition party (SDSM), Branko Crvenkovski, publicly reveals material proof of illegal phone tapping of around one hundred public persons in Macedonia.

22 January 2001: A police station in the Tetovo village of Tearce is attacked by rockets. One policeman is killed and three injured.

25 February 2001: A policeman is shot by two unknown men in an Albanian-populated part of Skopje in the midafternoon.

28 February 2001: Military clashes in Tanusevci between the fighters of so-called National Liberation Army (NLA) and Macedonian security forces begin.

3 March 2001: Macedonian army suffers its first casualties in fighting with the NLA.

14 March 2001: The NLA fighters attack the security forces in the city of Tetovo in the aftermath of street protests organized by three Albanian nongovernmental organizations.

25 March 2001: Macedonian Army and police undertake joint "final" offensive against the extremists in Tetovo.

NOTES

1. The so-called "Macedonian Question" emerged with the decline of the Ottoman empire and the rise of Balkan nationalisms over the territory and the population in Macedonia. Since the late nineteenth century, there has been open dispute over the identity and the distinctiveness of the Macedonian nation and the "ownership" over the territory. It is believed that all wars have been waged, more or less, over Macedonia. See James Pettifer, ed., *The New Macedonian Question* (Oxford, U.K.: Oxford University Press, 1999).

2. Eric J. Hobsbawm, *Nations and Nationalism Since 1870* (Cambridge, U.K.: Cambridge University Press, 1992) 166.

3. See Stefan Troebst, "IMRO + 100 = FYROM?," in Pettifer, *The New Macedonian Question.*

4. Olga Murdzeva-Skarik and Svetomir Skarik, "Peace and UNPREDEP in Macedonia,"

paper presented at the sixteenth IPRA General Conference, "Creating Nonviolent Futures," Brisbane, Australia, 8–12 July 1996, 11.

5. Ibid.

6. Trajan Gocevski, *Neutralna Makedonija: od vizija do stvarnost* (neutral Macedonia: from vision to reality) (Kumanovo, Macedonia: Makedonska riznica, 1995).

7. Since 1991, on the Albanian side there have been several important indications concerning attitudes toward the Macedonian state: Albanians boycotted the referendum on independence in 1991 as well as the census: the Albanian parliamentary group boycotted the vote that adopted the new constitution; in 1992 Albanians held an illegal referendum that demonstrated that 90 percent supported independence; in 1994 they declared an autonomous "Republic Illiryda" in the western part of the Republic. In early November 1993 the police arrested a group of Albanians (including a deputy minister of defense in the government of Macedonia) and accused them of attempting to establish paramilitary forces. Their next steps ostensibly would have been to separate "Illiryda" by force and then to unify it with Albania and eventually independent Kosovo.

8. On several occasions before early 2001 there were armed clashes between the state police forces and Albanian protesters or groups. Each of these clashes have been labeled evocatively, such as "Bit Pazar," "Tetovo Para-University case," "Radolista," "Gostivar case," "Aracinovo," and so forth.

9. "UNPREDEP—United Nations Preventive Deployment Force: Mission Backgrounder," (New York: Department of Public Information, June 1997).

10. See Jan Oberg, "The Kosovo War: No Failure, All Had an Interest In It," *TFF PressInfo*, No. 42, 17 August 1998.

11. Officially the Macedonian president and the government in their request to the UN claimed a possible military danger from the north (FRY) as well as potential spillover effects from other crisis points. De facto, it was clear that Macedonia was not on the military agenda of the Belgrade regime, because it had no priority at that time. Namely, Yugoslavia was busy with the clashes in Croatia and Bosnia while Macedonia was not perceived as a hostile neighbor and certainly not as a militarily relevant opponent. Milosevic always thought that Macedonia would not be a difficult territory to gain—one way or another. In the course of time, representatives of the UN mission in Macedonia also had become aware that the conflict potential within the country was more relevant than the external sources of instability.

12. For additional detail, see: Biljana Vankovska, "UNPREDEP in Macedonia: Diplomacy-Security Nexus in the Balkans," *Romanian Journal of International Affairs* 4, No. 2 (1998): 146–58.

13. Tomi Aleksovski, "NATO—Expensive 'entertainment' for poor Macedonia," *AIM Press-Skopje*, 13 June 1996. Available on the Internet at <http://www.aimpress.org> (accessed 30 March 2001).

14. Only a week before the session of the UN Security Council that should have extended the UNPREDEP mandate for one more term, the Macedonian foreign ministry issued its official state recognition of Taiwan. China's response was to cease diplomatic relations with Macedonia, so its veto was certainly no surprise.

15. Ole Weaver, "Securitisation and Desecuritisation," *COPRI Working Papers*, No. 5, 1993, p. 8.

16. On the day of the local elections (10 September 2000) in the western part of Macedonia, a unique clash occurred among Albanian party activists. Unprecedented terror was imposed on the mainly Albanian population in the villages near the towns of Debar, Struga, Tetovo, and Gostivar. The total account of the first round included the death of a twenty-year-old man and the wounding of ten other people. Only two weeks later during the second round of the elections, a second wave of violence involved thousands of citizens, this time mostly in the eastern part of the country. Even in the additional third round of the elections, one armed clash in Ohrid left one casualty.

17. Robert McMahon, "Balkan Instability Feeds Rise in Crime," *RFE/RL Report.* Available on the Internet at <http://www.centraleurope.com/yugoslaviatoday> (accessed 30 March 2001).

18. "The Balkan Medellin," *Jane's,* 1 March 1995.

19. Francesco Silvestri, "The Role of Drugs in the War of Kosovo," *Drugs and Development #16 (The Monthly Newspaper of ENCOD),* June 1999.

20. From the interview with Dr. Natalija Nikolovska to the Macedonian weekly *Start,* 29 December 2000, p. 20.

21. Peter H. Liotta, "The 'Future' Republic of Macedonia: The Last Best Hope," *European Security,* 9, no. 1 (Spring 2000): 68–97.

18 ✦ Romania: Security at the Periphery

Daniel N. Nelson

Romanians saw themselves as threatened from a variety of internal and external sources during the 1990s.[1] Post-Communist Romania's goal, by emotional consensus and pragmatic urgency, is Western integration—joining, participating, contributing. Romania wants "in,"[2] but thus far it sees itself consigned to the antechamber, gray zone, or periphery of Euro-Atlantic security.[3]

Obstacles in the path of Romania's Western movement deserve scrutiny. Larger questions are, however, implicit. Can capacity-poor states in threat-rich environments ever be "secure"? Or is a kind of perpetual state of lesser security "preordained" for some political systems and peoples? If true, is the pursuit of the security that others enjoy—via membership in institutions such as The North Atlantic Treaty Organization (NATO)—politically quixotic?[4]

During four and a half decades of Communist rule, under both Gheorghe Gheorghiu-Dej (who brought sovietization to a halt, obtained a Soviet troop withdrawal, and presided over the 1964 party declaration of Romania's separate path) and Nicolae Ceausescu, Romania sought to limit Moscow's presence in southeastern Europe, to ingratiate themselves with other powers and to disrupt any movement that could have provided autonomy to the Hungarian minority.

In its foreign policy, the Ceausescu regime portrayed itself as independent within the Warsaw Pact, as a "developing socialist state" tied to the nations of Africa and Asia, and as a bridge between East and West. This strategy of cultivating worldwide contacts and maintaining a high international profile from a position of uniqueness within the Warsaw Pact was successful for a decade and a half. At least through the 1970s, Ceausescu was seen as an important actor in East-West affairs, arranging diplomatic initiatives in the Middle East and helping to inaugurate some of the initial

U.S.-Chinese meetings in the Nixon administration. The United States recip-rocated by granting "most favored nation" (MFN) status to Bucharest, and Washington repeatedly extended it despite mounting reports of human rights abuses. American efforts to support differentiation within Eastern Europe, while indicating disfavor with Romanian actions against religious practice, artistic diversity, and political dissent, took the form of visits in the mid-1980s by top officials, including then Vice President George Bush, Secretary of State George Shultz, and many congressional delegations.

Romania's international role had become more limited by 1980–81, to such an extent that in a 1981 assessment of the country's prognosis for the rest of the decade, I concluded that "the 1980s will see more internal and external constraints. . . . The latitude available for military and foreign policy deviation, already limited, will decline as will Romania's ability to pursue economic plans independent from world markets and energy supplies. . . . Romania's ability to 'go it alone' will decline."[5]

Ceausescu's star began to fade in part because of high levels of debt and secrecy about Romania's economy, both of which heightened the risk of direct foreign investment. In December 1987, Ceausescu unilaterally ended payments to the World Bank.

And, of course, Mikhail Gorbachev had enabled the United States, Germany, and other countries to establish far more direct relations with Moscow, obviating the "need" for Ceausescu's intermediary role. At the same time, Gorbachev's leadership led to a geometric expansion of Roma-nia's political distance from Moscow. Ceausescu's regime was detrimental to Gorbachev's efforts to reinvigorate Communist Party states through eco-nomic and political reform, and the Romanian leader made it abundantly clear, only eight months after Gorbachev took office, that Bucharest would stay the course of state socialism. Ceausescu's human rights abuses and the regime's espionage activities abroad also heightened Western indiffer-ence to or suspicion of Romania from the late 1970s through 1989.

Ceausescu had, moreover, alienated the Romanian Army during the 1970s and 1980s by insisting on a national defense strategy euphemistically called the "struggle of the entire people" (*lupta intregului popor*). Further, the Army's manpower and equipment were increasingly used to build Ceausescu's gigantic construction projects, ranging from canals to the mas-sive "House of the People" in Bucharest.[6]

Ceausescu's bizarre and costly tyranny led Romania further from Europe and alienated the country as it had never been before from virtually all significant states, multilateral institutions, or other international actors. Romania, by 1989, was in the midst of a political, economic, and cultural catastrophe—all of which fed a sense of threat.[7] Highly insecure, Romanians were susceptible to appeals of politicians who promised to constrain change and limit domestic turmoil.

Threat Assessment

At the crux of Romanian foreign policy lies interwoven goals of avoiding isolation and any single power's domination over the region, protecting a unitary state while ensuring the country's cultural and political integration with Western Europe. In the post-Communist era, however, Romania has been only marginally successful in these goals.

Influential Romanian political figures, analysts, and commentators are well aware that Bucharest, notwithstanding two quite different governments in the 1990s (President Ion Iliescu, 1990–96, from the left, and President Emil Constantinescu, 1996–2000, from the center-right), has not been able to gain more than partial, limited acceptance by principal Western institutions. The first Iliescu presidency received no credit for avoiding conflict with neighbors or for maintaining a semblance of social peace; at the same time, Iliescu and his advisers were upbraided for being former Communists who allegedly "stole" the revolution.

A second Iliescu presidency, after victory in the 10 December 2000 run-off election, began with much of the same international credibility gap. Typical Western media coverage during the 26 November and 10 December 2000 votes referred to Iliescu and his Party of Romanian Social Democracy (PDSR) as "leftist," "ex-Communists," ousted from power in 1996 "amid corruption and economic stagnation" and with an "unsavory reputation in the West for cronyism and putting the brakes on needed reforms of the economy." The same reports alleged that Iliescu's victory, plus the large vote for right-wing nationalist presidential candidate Corneliu Vadim Tudor, would "deliver . . . a blow to the economy and Romania's EU prospects" and that the election "showed that Romania is ready to be carried out on a stretcher."[8]

That said, there was no chance for Romania quickly to climb the steep wall to respectability. Added to such a biased image were the policy predilections of Iliescu and his party to question privatization, especially when imposed by international financial institutions. It is not surprising that, as the European Bank for Reconstruction and Development reported in 1995, more than 50 percent of all income in Hungary was from privately owned enterprises or businesses, while less than a third of Romanian income was derived from the then-private sector.[9] Similarly, at the end of 1999, it was estimated that two-thirds of all employees in Romania continued to work in state-owned companies, most of which operate at a loss.[10]

The influential daily *Adevarul* editorialized in August 1998 that, despite the "long road that [Romania] has traveled in the past two years . . . one can notice that Romania has not managed to cross the finish line in any of its major foreign policy objectives such as NATO, the European Union or the free travel of Romanians in Europe."[11]

As a closely related phenomenon, Romania also has not been able to generate investor confidence sufficient to bring in substantial new foreign capital. In the first nine months of 1999, a mere $145 million of new foreign direct investment arrived in Romania.[12] U.S. capital has been slow to make its way to Romania; through 1997, "well under $200 million in direct U.S. investments have arrived in Romania since 1990, with only $18 million in new investments added in 1997."[13]

Economic data during 1998 and 1999 did not renew confidence; 1998 was the worst year for Romania's economy since 1989, with industrial output down by 17.3 percent, while the trade deficit reached $2 billion (33 percent more than in 1997). Results were no better for 1999. Under the tutelage of economist qua nonparty prime minister in 2000, Dr. Mugur Isarescu, modest recovery was achieved; inflation was reduced to 45 percent, for instance, and a bit of gross domestic product (GDP) growth was reported.

Yet reports of growing black market activity now estimate that 22 percent of Romania's 1998 GDP was unreported and untaxed, up from about 12 percent in 1997.[14] Standard & Poor's long-term credit rating for Romania was lowered in October 1998 from "single-B-plus to single-B-minus," while the country's short-term credit rating was lowered to "single-C." These constitute serious negative trends in the creditworthiness of Romania. Contributing substantially to such a poor rating was concern about potential default in 1999 on $2.2 billion in commercial debt. That the default did not occur is a testimony to the planning and creativity of Isarescu while he served as governor of the National Bank (a post he held from 1990 through 1999). The fear implanted in minds of investors, however, was palpable. While growth in 2000 into 2001 may lessen that fear, Romania's direct foreign investment will be diminished for some time.

The Constantinescu presidency and both Prime Minister Ciorbea and his immediate successor, Radu Vasile, were unable to restart structural reforms for which the principal international financial institutions are waiting.[15] Constantinescu's own popularity, once very high, plummeted after only two years in office; by October 1998, the president received only a 25 percent approval rating, down from 38 percent in June 1998 and almost 60 percent in mid-1997. In a poll published in September 1999, only 10 percent of Romanians surveyed identified Constantinescu as the political personality they trusted most, while Ion Iliescu led political figures with 22 percent.[16]

Constantinescu's support slipped further after the fifth *mineriada*—that is, the fifth time miners staged a large-scale revolt since the late 1970s, this time an abortive march by tens of thousands from the Petrosani mining area toward Bucharest in February 1999 led by Miron Cozma. Initially and for some time thereafter, Constantinescu and his prime minister, Radu Vasile, were perceived as having given in to most of the miners' financial demands, while Cozma himself was seen as a self-proclaimed regional strongman.[17]

That the interior ministry had performed abysmally—its forces being routed at one roadblock and hundreds taken prisoner by the miners— forced the Army to ominously suggest that it might have to use force. But, the Army itself saw this as a disastrous outcome of a political process for which the Constantinescu-Vasile government should take the blame, not the Army. In a scathing indictment of the interior ministry specifically and government policy by implication, the chief of the General Staff singled out "grave tactical and leadership errors" that had contributed to this perilous episode for Romania's nascent democracy.[18]

Eventually seeing that his presidency could not be salvaged, Constantinescu withdrew from the electoral contest in mid-2000. Unprepared for such a step, the various parties and personalities of the "center" slowly and painfully committed political suicide, waging rhetorical war against one another, proving to the electorate the absence of a cohesive, moderate alternative. Theodor Stolojan (a former prime minister and thereafter World Bank official), Theodor Melescanu (former foreign minister in the first Iliescu presidency and, later a Senator who founded his own break-away moderate left party), and Mugur Isarescu managed to garner a cumulative quarter of the presidential vote in the first round. Benefiting greatly from the shrinking center was Tudor's Romania Mare (Greater Romania) party, whose own presidential bid came closer than many thought to defeating even the former president, Ion Iliescu.

As a consequence, the sense of being relegated to a "gray zone"—neither in nor out, not part of the Euro-Atlantic Community and without any viable alternative—became palpable by the late 1990s.[19] And, in addition to public statements or diplomatic language, less guarded views saw it more bleakly:

> In the early 90s, we saw a dim light at the end of a tunnel. We did exactly as we were told, behaved well, and were told to keep going. We got closer and closer, and we could just about make out figures, faces, and things recognizable. We thought we had almost made it. Then, some invisible hand pulled us back—way back. Suddenly we no longer see any light and we're not even sure we're in the tunnel. But it is very dark, and there are strange, frightening noises all around.[20]

Promises made by President Bill Clinton and other U.S. emissaries in the aftermath of the NATO Madrid Summit regarding a "strategic partnership" between Washington and Bucharest were, likewise, met with doubt by astute Romanian observers—doubt that deepened in 1998–99.[21]

Even when Romanian policymakers deny that a gray zone exists, they acknowledge NATO's unwillingness "to involve itself in a new strategic set of challenges" concerning central and southeastern Europe. Former president Constantinescu's principal adviser on foreign policy, Zoe Petre, asserted the indivisibility of European security but, at the same time, acknowledged that "Romania's main and not very comfortable characteristic was to be the very border of different, even divergent, civilization areas." To simultaneously reject the divisibility of the continent's security while buying into thoughts that parallel if not replicate Samuel Huntington's "clash of civilizations" thesis is a tough fence to sit astride—yet Petre insisted on trying: "Situated on both sides of these rifts of civilizations, Romania was, too often, the victim of its status of a 'multiple border.' "[22]

Romania is thus dealt a blow by geopolitics—taking on the qualities of "fate" or "nature," condemned to a periphery. With a heavy dose of martyrdom, Romanians imply that a Latin nation, sandwiched between Slavs, Turks, and Germans, has been neither accepted nor appreciated. With Romanian policymakers seeing global forces in such deterministic ways, gray tones quickly become the backdrop to images that others form about the country.

Driving this sentiment are the vicissitudes of a nascent democracy and fledgling market economy. Still just over a decade after the end of tyranny, Romania lacks prolonged experience with democracy over the twentieth century and has yet to fully institutionalize the making and implementation of foreign and security policies.

The "control" of Romania's national security agenda and foreign policy is one important issue. In a country with a constitutionally strong presidency, Cotroceni (the presidential palace) is viewed as the locus of many key security decisions, particularly as prime ministers and coalitional arrangements come and go. Yet the sheer volume of decisions and issues cannot be handled by Cotroceni alone, and the centralization of foreign and security policy in the presidency is itself deleterious to Romania's larger goal of integration.

A Supreme Council of National Defense (CSAT in the Romanian acronym) exists, but its constituent parts are far more important than the council itself. Yet, neither the minister of defense nor the minister of foreign affairs, both of whom are in the CSAT, have the institutional clout to become the locus of security and foreign policy decision making. Occupants of either role can, moreover, greatly affect the office's potential simply, because the office itself is still underdeveloped. Victor Babiuc, defense minister during most of the Constantinescu presidency, was at least as much a political leader (he served as vice president of the Democratic Party led by Petre Roman) as he was minister of defense. His deputy minister from late 1996 through early 1999 (when he was moved over to head the interior ministry in the aftermath of that ministry's wretched performance in the miners' crisis of January 1999), Constantin D. Ionescu, is politically active in a conservative party, the Peasants (which performed terribly in 2000 elections, in a way punished by voters for four desultory years).

Among Romanian foreign ministers of the late 1990s, Adrian Severin talked himself out of the post by making indiscreet allegations while abroad about corruption or worse at the highest levels in Bucharest,[23] and he was succeeded by Andrei Plesu, an intellectual humanist without any experience in foreign and defense policy making. Plesu's inexperience and lack of political backing led, in turn, to Petre Roman's appointment as foreign minister in a late 1999 cabinet shake-up, because Constantinescu was desperately trying to resurrect his presidency. Roman (often presidential candidate himself, Democratic Party founder, and briefly prime minister in 1990–91) was, likewise, focused on the political landscape, not foreign policy. Leadership in Romanian foreign and defense policy, therefore, suffered between 1996 and 2000.

It therefore falls, in many instances, to Cotroceni—the president and a few advisers—plus a few people drawn in from the Romanian intelligence community and army officers to "make national security policy." Romania's paucity of active and organized nongovernmental organizations remains evident a dozen years since Ceausescu was ousted, and academe plays a very minimal role in foreign or security policy discourse. Major issues for Romania—for example, the strategy by which the Constantinescu government sought to attract NATO's interest for rapid inclusion of Bucharest as the Alliance enlarges—are decided by very few people. Often these are the same people who were active in Romanian foreign policy in the Communist era. The second Iliescu presidency has deployed many of the same faces—seasoned and "hardened," but not particularly pluralistic in their decision-making style.

In the intelligence realm, for example, a spring 1998 estimate suggested that the Romanian Intelligence Service (SRI) still employed thousands of Ceausescu-era personnel (almost 41 percent of SRI's payroll consisted of carryovers from the old regime).[24] Meanwhile, a companion organization meant to focus on foreign-directed intelligence gathering and analysis, the Foreign Information Service (SIE), spends much of its time today on fighting political and public relations battles rather than generating analyses. Catalin Harnagea, director of SIE from early 1997 through 2000, had less success than his predecessor, Ioan Talpes, lacking a background in either military or intelligence issues; further, Harnagea (like civilians in the defense ministry) was very tied to political activity and dependent on the president's popularity. In the second Iliescu presidency, from the end of 2000, Talpes is back—now as a top adviser in Cotroceni to President Iliescu.

The degree to which Romania is truly part of a common European socioeconomic, political, and cultural identity is also at issue. For intellectual Romanians, "European-ness" is unquestioned, and the country's rightful place in European and Euro-Atlantic institutions is natural.[25] The rejection of "Balkan" designation, not readily accepted by anyone it seems, was begun in the Iliescu government and carried over into the Constantinescu presidency—the preferred term describing Romania's location being "Central Europe."

Romanian intellectuals, wrestling with the dichotomy between what they think they are vis-a-vis how the world perceives Romania, often lament their country's weak government and "chaotic democracy." Their analysis, just as often, tends to emphasize Romania's "historic handicap"—the bad hand dealt to Romania's democrats and reformers that, from the start (December 1989), meant that the country's efforts and potential would be hindered and slowed.[26]

As a Croatian political scientist perceptively observed, however, the rebirth of national identity in post-Communist Europe underscores a fundamental difference between the eastern and western halves of the continent:

> The denial of national interest during the communist era was a form of deprivation for Eastern Europe [and] the recovery of the national interest in the post-Communist era has been a form of emancipation. . . . While liberty for the older nations, such as France and Britain, translated to the pluralism, tolerance and mediated conflict of democracy, East European liberty represents release from oppressive for-

eign rule, assertion of identity and the establishment of the nation-state.[27]

Such an emphasis on national identity in post-Communist Europe stands in
contrast to the broader European vision of submerging nation within larger
institutions that reduce sovereign prerogatives. Romania's willingness to peel
away layers of hard-won independence and sovereignty is uncertain at best.

That Romania, Bulgaria, and others have been kept at arms length is sometimes explained as a consequence of poverty and still heavily "statist" economies. Tardy efforts to privatize principal economic sectors, inadequate banking reform, and many other fundamental aspects of a market economy are
often cited as problems precluding the assimilation of Romania into the Western "club." Yet, Greece and Ireland were extremely poor when the EU accepted Athens's and Dublin's applications. Very low Portuguese, Greek, or
Turkish living standards, relative to European averages, and substantial government ownership did not preclude NATO membership.

Other factors must be more powerful explanations for Romania's difficulties with both institutions. Romanians suspect that those other explanations rest in the realm of an erroneous judgment about Romania, in inadequate information or, sometimes, a darker conspiracy against their country.
And Romanian journalists and analysts note with considerable irony any
occasion where Romania's needs are ignored or slighted.[28]

Romanians' earnest desire to avoid isolation is shared by all social strata
and corresponds with a strong positive sentiment about the United States,
France, Britain, and Germany—although opinion about the latter is clouded
by uncertainty about long-term intentions.[29] These mass feelings are not
manufactured by an elite campaign; rather, such views are steady, resilient,
and considered. Romanians want to "join," to be a member of "the club,"
to be appreciated and seen as a valued part of the Euro-Atlantic community.
That Romania has something to offer the West is, also, a view widely
shared—as a contributor to peacekeeping operations such as Angola and
Albania, or as an example of a stable multicultural Balkan state.

NATO's decision to enlarge without including Romania—announced at
Madrid in July 1997, and implemented at the Washington Summit in April
1999—hurt. Romania had pushed hard—very hard—in 1996–97 for inclu-

sion in the initial round of NATO expansion. The arguments used to develop Romania's case were numerous and presented themselves through diplomatic visits, the media, and publications.[30]

Even those Romanian officials who, in both the (first) Iliescu and Constantinescu presidencies, had been engaged deeply in pressing Romania's case in Washington, Brussels, and other European capitals, were unsettled by the implications for their country. For example, Defense Minister (in the second Iliescu presidency) Ioan Mircea Pascu, who had been deputy defense minister during 1993–96, wrote in 1997 that it had become painfully clear that Romania had been placed in the company of other states such that "its [Romania's] accession to NATO . . . [was put off] into the distant future."[31] Other well-known Romanian commentators on international politics likewise warned that Romania's inability to make its case with NATO may risk turning optimistic and patient Romanians into impatient pessimists.[32]

A sense of unfairness is felt acutely within upper echelons of the Romanian military. Although these sentiments will not be seen in print, people who work at the ministry of defense will, with a mixture of bitterness and resignation, point to accomplishments in restructuring, downsizing, and depoliticizing the army, often in the face of considerable political and intra-Army opposition. The West, however, appears to hold Romania to higher standards—largely political and economic—that the general staff and ministry cannot affect. They fear, not without foundation, permanent exclusion from the Western security "club" despite their best efforts.

Adding to that fear has been an increasingly vociferous opposition within the military to drastic force cuts that will, in 2002–2003, bring active duty troops down to one hundred and fifteen thousand. Romania's armed forces had numbered more than twice that number in the early 1990s and close to three hundred thousand during the Communist era. Some external consultants, for example, from the RAND Corporation, have even suggested much lower numbers based on what the country can afford to equip and train. The defense policies of the second Iliescu presidency are unlikely to endorse rapid downsizing given an absence of signs from NATO about future membership; still, budgetary constraints will leave no choice but to reduce (perhaps more slowly) the military's active duty ranks.

Discontent related to such reductions is nowhere near breaking out into insubordination, but it affects morale. Severe budgetary constraints imposed as the country tried to live within International Monetary Fund deficit ceilings meant that the military leadership had no money with which to implement even modest civil defense measures or deployments in response to the fighting next door between the Slobodan Milosevic regime in Belgrade and NATO in spring 1999.[33] Closely intertwined with officers' opposition to force reductions and budgetary cuts are severe personal consequences for many military families for whom inadequate housing exists while in the Army, and nothing awaits them once "retired" from active duty. Corrupt practices among officers and noncommissioned officers arising from these conditions have been reported as commanders and subordinates desperately seek alternative sources of cash and subsistence by pilfering supplies, selling equipment, or other schemes.[34]

Why the Romanian Army's woes are linked to NATO membership may be convoluted to outsiders, but it makes perfect sense to those on the inside. That Romanian requirements to meet NATO's recommendations "are much more severe than our neighbor's [that is, Hungary]," and that "our Army is forced to pay for politicians' and bankers' mistakes" are examples of more critical remarks that are now audible.[35]

Politicians have played a role in exacerbating military concerns. At a conference at the George C. Marshall Center in Garmisch, Germany—the principal U.S. government institution meant to enhance democratic control over armed forces and national security policy in post-Communist Europe—former Foreign Minister Teodor Melescanu (then senator, leader of his own Alliance for Romania, a center-left opposition party, and unsuccessful 2000 presidential candidate), spoke pointedly about "dangerous phenomena for [Romanian] society" evident in the Romanian Army. He further raised the potential that the Army, finding it "very difficult to comprehend and accept" some of the negative consequences of democracy, "might prefer to act according to their own views and ignore political decisions."[36]

Such words from a prominent politician, particularly public comments made at an U.S.-NATO event, were met with a sense of disbelief intermingled with harsh rebuttals and disavowals among Romania's senior military and defense leaders. Still, the psychic distance between NATO's criteria and Romania's achievements seemed to grow larger regardless of tangible national security and defense ministry reforms.

The NATO decision to exclude other applicants for the foreseeable future also brought to the surface fears of Hungarian membership while Romania is kept out, and of marginalization" in general.[37] When, in early February 1999, then-Prime Minister Radu Vasile visited Budapest, one important Bucharest daily—not known as particularly nationalist in tone—wrote that "Radu Vasile Enters the Den of the Young Wolf Viktor Orban" (Hungarian prime minister) while noting that the Hungarian press abstained from comments on the visit.[38]

Creeping Russian encroachments in southeastern Europe are also a concern, and the stuff for speculation in Bucharest. Potential Russian efforts to reassert control in Moldova from their foothold in Transnistria (a Russian populated sliver that broke off from Moldova in a violent miniwar during 1992) are thought to be simmering. Further, a dispute over the speck of land in the Black Sea between Ukraine and Russia, which is called Serpant's Island, and is important because of potential oil resources in the vicinity—and Moscow's behind-the-scenes role is suspect in Bucharest. Senior Russian officials are probed at almost every occasion about such matters, with a subtext of suspicion not far below the surface.[39]

During early and mid-1998, when the Russian firm, Lukoil, bought controlling interest in the Romanian oil company Petrotel, and amid sharp Russian statements against NATO enlargement, the Russian ambassador in Bucharest was often the focus of attention and some innuendo.[40] And, when the fifth attempt of miners to march on Bucharest occurred in January 1999, public speculation by a variety of politicians and journalists about Russian involvement—allegedly to create a crisis in Romania and thereby divert Western attention from Serbia—gained currency. Fortunately, cooler heads pointed to the foolishness of such phobia.[41]

Such concerns, although exaggerating Russian capabilities and interest in Romania today, nevertheless reflect Moscow's past record, including the Molotov Ribbentrop Pact that allowed the Soviets to absorb Bessarabia at the beginning of World War II. They also harken back to threats of Soviet invasion in 1968, when Ceausescu had opposed the Warsaw Pact's intervention in Czechoslovakia.

For public and political consumption, the Constantinescu government redoubled its efforts after Madrid, frequently and vigorously reiterating its intention to ensure Romania's entry via a "second tranche." Asserting that its 1998–99 arguments would be "strong and well presented, unlike we did in 1997," Foreign Minister Andrei Plesu and others tried to reinvigorate Romania's NATO campaign in spring 1998.[42] To visiting U.S. Deputy Secretary of State Strobe Talbott, Plesu said that "Romania's request to be admitted to NATO is not . . . local vanity or a rhetorical ornament, but rather a matter of objective necessity."[43] Yet, even Plesu admitted to doubts about his country's long-term success at entering NATO's "open door"; "in order to not remain isolated, on the outskirts of all empires, we need a 'beneficial' invasion."[44]

Many of the same arguments from 1996 and early 1997 continued to be recycled before the Washington summit of April 1999—that Romania has a "strategic position of interest for NATO" with an infrastructure vital for the Alliance's southern flank, a large military potential, and many other strengths.[45] External efforts that promoted Romania's interests, such as the Romanian-American Action Commission housed in and directed by the Center for Strategic and International Studies in Washington, D.C., likewise sought to promote the "strategic value."[46] Among Romania's putative assets were invariably mentioned its "strategic location," that is, at the intersection of several critical zones (Central Europe, southeast Europe, the Black Sea, and the so-called Caspian-Atlantic corridor), the Romanian government's "strategic commitment" (that is, to reform), and the country's "strategic contribution" (to peacekeeping and other likely NATO needs).[47] An undercurrent in discussions with France and Italy, too, was Romanians' culturally Latinate ancestry.

As with most other NATO aspirants, the sheer frequency of the word "strategic" was indicative of miscalculation. Unfortunately, those who make such "strategic" arguments forgot that domestic accomplishments that stabilize democratic transition will foster an appropriate image for NATO (or EU) membership far more quickly than the drumbeat of strategic value.

Capacities

Behind and beneath the continued focus on NATO were the formative stages of Romanian foreign and security policy options—propelled by the unmistakable sense that NATO's arrival will be delayed.

Post–Cold War Romania's unrequited NATOist foreign and defense policies began to fray in the aftermath of a Washington summit that provided no timetable or precise road map. The "Madrid plus" formula by which the April 1999 summit's script was written offered nothing more than further tutorials to Romanian and other NATO suitors. The Membership Action Plans (MAPs) that all aspirants were to produce evoked little enthusiasm in Bucharest, where responding to NATO's solicitations for documents, diagrams, and details consumed immense personnel time and scant resources.

Because of the war against Serbia, NATO's Washington summit offered some rhetorical security guarantees to "front-line" states such as Romania, Bulgaria, Macedonia, and Albania. Influential Romanian observers called this NATO offer "Article 4:45" ("*cinci fara un sfert*") in an ironic reference to the article of the 1949 Washington Treaty, applied fully to members only, that an attack on one is an attack against all.

Senior Romanian military and political leaders had made clear through every channel their hope that NATO would do more—a clear step-by-step road map with signposts, and a precise timetable. Western diplomats, hearing Bucharest's frequent and plaintive message, began to offer summaries in caricature—"please promise us something for the summit to make us feel better."

Denied what most Romanians viscerally want, even if the Washington Treaty's intricacies are unknown, any government in Bucharest will feel negative political consequences. Constantinescu, whose popularity as noted above fell substantially from 1996 to 1999, was in political trouble principally because of Romania's poor economy amid crime and corruption. Yet, messages from outside made his situation worse; that NATO and the EU kept their doors closed or barely ajar was a clear indication that Constantinescu and his various prime ministers and foreign ministers had achieved little European or global credibility. Given such a net assessment by Romanian voters in 2000, a recalibration and reassessment of Romania's "place" in Europe and the world are certain.

In microcosm, one early casualty of such national security reassessment was Romania's enthusiasm for an adapted Conventional Forces in Europe (CFE) treaty. Negotiations to adapt the 1990 CFE treaty, which had been placed into force when there were still two opposing Cold War military alliances, commenced in earnest in 1997. From the outset, Romania expressed its unease with the designation as a "flank" state, which grouped Bucharest alongside much of the former Soviet Union. Although such flank status meant little in practical terms for Romania, the exclusionary sound of the designation is disliked strongly in Bucharest. Moreover, the original 1990 treaty and subsequent amendments regarding military equipment allowed in "flank" areas meant that Romania was allocated considerably fewer tanks per capita (and other large conventional equipment) than, for example, Bulgaria—with a population much less than half as big as Romania. To Romanians, then, CFE smacked of "unfairness."[48]

Although CFE was approved by the Romanian parliament, these points of alleged unfairness, and the lack of more specific NATO guarantees to Romania, mean that conventional arms control remains an arena colored by the sense of poor treatment from Brussels and Washington. At the very least, CFE as signed at the Istanbul Organization for Security and Cooperation in Europe (OSCE) summit in November 1999 is regarded as NATO imposed, with far too much latitude for Russians and too little redress of Romania's concerns.

A broader questioning has also begun. No one yet talks, even guardedly, about giving up on NATO. But, ample discussion exists in Bucharest, or when Romanian analysts and policymakers are speaking abroad, concerning a "NATO-friendly, not NATO-dependent" strategy. At the same time, Romanian efforts to stay in NATO's sights and good graces, waiting for the day when a second tranche will be politically feasible, are increasingly seen as something other than as a public relations campaign talking about Romania's "strategic" value. Instead, emphasis is being placed on doing things—especially programs useful to Romanian security.[49]

One prominent editor, writing just after the NATO Washington summit on 27 April 1999 expressed this view rather succinctly: "The NATO summit is over, but Romania is left with its problems and anxieties. This moment should mark the end of illusions and a return to reality. It is good that we still have the attention of the NATO countries. . . . However, neither NATO nor the EU will fill in the black holes in the Romanian economy. . . . For now [the government] will have to demonstrate their commitment to western values by what it does to make Romania prepared for Euro-Atlantic integration."[50]

Already, Romania has been guarded on some matters of foreign and defense policy. During the 1991–95 wars in the former Yugoslavia, Bucharest enforced a UN embargo against Serbia and other combatants, losing perhaps $7 billion in revenues and sales. Yet, Romania exhibited reluctance during those years to distance itself from Belgrade or to create an irrevocable rupture in relations. During the Serb-Croat and Serb-Bosnian wars, Romania delivered oil to Belgrade, despite a UN embargo, through the Romanian firm Solventul in Timisoara,[51] and was reported to have negotiated deals to transship Russian and Ukrainian arms to Croatia.[52]

In the waning weeks of the 2000 electoral campaign, Romanian-Serbian contacts were trumpeted by outgoing President Emil Constantinescu in a transparent effort to discredit Ion Iliescu, at least in the eyes of international observers. Constantinescu alleged evidence of very high-level involvement in arms shipments to Belgrade, thereby breaking the UN embargo and commitments to Washington and other European powers as well. These were not new allegations, and no "smoking gun" was offered—although it is widely acknowledged that arms trafficking occurred regularly and at substantial levels from most countries surrounding the zone of conflict from 1991 through 1999.

In 1998, as Kosovo slid into full-scale war, caution about backing NATO threats of air strikes against Serbs was echoed from the opposition and government in Bucharest.[53] Several days before NATO air attacks commenced, President Emil Constantinescu did issue an endorsement of unspecified "NATO intervention," making no mention of force and emphasizing a much greater Romanian desire for success of the Rambouillet Agreement.[54] Romanian military and diplomatic channels did make U.S. authorities aware of the availability of Romanian airspace if the need arose, and the parliament eventually voted to endorse such an offer; but, Romania had not sought or encouraged the use of force and studiously avoided the most severe condemnations of Serbia or its government.

Both the second Iliescu presidency and attitudes within the Romanian military and security community are inclined to restore strong links with Belgrade. When Vojislav Kostunica was elected and then installed as president after street protests drove Milosevic from office on 5 October 2000, the Romanian armed forces wasted little time in reestablishing defense cooperation with "Yugoslavia." The two countries had cooperated in the

1980s to produce a jet fighter attack aircraft (which never went into widespread production), had shared intelligence since 1968, and had frequent defense meetings and consultations until the early 1990s.[55]

The consequences of this Balkan war (or the next conflict escalating as this was written in the late spring 2001) were not those from which Romania could take much comfort. With the Danube effectively closed to commercial traffic, both because of NATO's destruction of bridges and the Serb desire to "repay" Romania and Bulgaria for their cooperation with NATO, substantial economic losses were incurred; totals are imprecise, but net losses to the Romanian economy certainly added up to $2 billion or more.

But far more damaging to Romanians' sense of their own interests is the use of NATO power to ensure de facto independence for Kosovo, heretofore a province of Serbia. While most Western decisionmakers remain convinced that such force was necessary—to preserve standards of international behavior as well as to maintain NATO itself—Kosovo is seen as an unhealthy precedent by Romanian politicians. Regardless of party affiliation, Romanians prominent in their country's foreign policy making see NATO's apparent military success with uncertainty and even an ominous tinge. Sure that we have not seen the last of the wars of Yugoslav succession, Romanians are also afraid, justifiably or not, that other minorities can get the same idea—pushing violently for more than cultural autonomy, sensing that NATO will come to their side if a unitary state tries to reassert itself.

When Polish, Ukrainian, and Romanian foreign ministers met in late November 1997, there was also a hint of thinking in Bucharest about where NATO's enlargement was headed. Then foreign minister Adrian Severin noted at that meeting that NATO was "not only in the process of expanding, but . . . should increasingly become a system of collective security."[56] A consensus existed across parties and ideologies that OSCE would never suffice as a substitute for NATO; for example, Oliviu Gherman, the Senate leader while Ion Iliescu's party, the PDSR, governed before the November 1996 election, made clear the inadequacies of the OSCE for Romanian security.[57] Nevertheless, any notion that NATO itself will metamorphose into a collective security entity, although heard in Western capitals as well, departs from "mainstream" thinking within NATO states that intends the

Alliance to retain its core military function while developing new cooperative security roles.

In the same period, Romania's principal arms manufacturers, such as Aerofina and Romtechnica, garnered the attention of U.S. and NATO military analysts and intelligence circles for deals with governments and institutions that are not best friends of the democratic West. In some cases, these shipments were in violation of UN embargoes. Between 1994 and 1996, Aerofina (which manufactures missile components and guidance systems, among other products) negotiated with Iraqi emissaries, and actually signed an agreement with Iraq in 1995—forbidden by UN sanctions. Deliveries may have been prevented by coordinated intelligence agency sting operations, but the episode spoke poorly about control of Romania's military industry.[58] Moreover, it appears that Romania shipped large amounts of small arms to Rwanda in early 1997 via Yemen (to conceal the final destination), despite the UN embargo.[59] Other private discussions with Romanian officials have raised additional concerns about contacts regarding arms sales to questionable foreign governments.

Efforts to link Romania's considerable airframe and aircraft engine manufacturing capacity to NATO via licensed production agreements have been troubled. IAR (Intreprinderea Aeronautica Romana) and Turbomechanica are both large firms that carry over from the Communist era. In 1998 Bell-Textron thought, after discussions that some sources date from 1994, that a deal was finalized to build ninety-six advanced AH-1 Super Cobra attack helicopters, using the airframe and engines built by the two firms, with assembly in Romania.

But IMF objections and severe doubts with Romania that the country could afford to produce such a large fleet of very advanced helicopters, when the external market was questionable, led Finance Minister Daniel Daianu to resign in mid-1998. Although the project appears to have many lives, the budgetary consequences would affect Romania's ability to direct resources to other pressing needs. Requiring a Romanian investment of $1.5 billion or more, as compared with a defense budget of $950 (1998) million suggests a huge gap and large additional deficit even if the project is stretched over many years. For many Romanians who have led the drive to integrate with Western security institutions, such spending is a price the country must pay. Others see the Bell-Textron deal as yet another sacrifice made to enhance prospects for NATO admission.

Policy Innovations

In these and other respects, Romania's actions suggest recognition that, no matter how NATO-friendly Romania may be, complete dependence on the Atlantic alliance may be ill advised. NATO-related countries, such as Israel, have become close partners of Romania in modernizing MiG-21 and other aircraft, while vigorous exploration of markets for Romanian arms exports and technology will continue. At the very least, some aspects of Romanian security require a different calculus.

Part of that alternative strategy may be more of the commonsense policies that became accepted in the 1990s vis-a-vis Romania's neighbors. The potential flashpoint of Transylvania and relations with Hungary was defused through military-to-military contacts (for example, a simple but effective bilateral "open skies" arrangement for periodic overflights) and the inclusion of the principal ethnic Hungarian political party in Romania in the 1996–2000 Constantinescu coalition government. That Corneliu Vadim Tudor's party and presidential candidacy in 2000 resurrected antiminority sentiment in a proportion of the Romanian electorate is clear; still, cooler heads prevailed, and the second Iliescu presidency began by trying to incorporate the UDMR (Democratic Union of Hungarians in Romania) within a governing coalition.

Hungary's NATO membership and its advanced status in negotiations with the EU enable Budapest and the conservative coalition of Prime Minister Viktor Orban to hold substantial leverage regarding relations with Bucharest. Any effort to "veto" Romania's progress in either organization would be transparent and counterproductive, and thus far has not been attempted. Yet, Romanians of the left and right raise this danger in not-for-attribution conversations about Hungary. As long as Hungary's government restrains its own reactionary coalition partners, however, this danger (of Hungarian efforts to veto Romanian access to either NATO or the EU) remains speculative.

Similarly, what could have been a troublesome relationship with Moldova, or factions within Moldova, has mellowed into an issue of limited concern to almost everyone. Moldovan citizens of Romanian ethnicity (and language) have little interest in "unification" with Romania; as poor as they are, northeast Romania is poorer. And, culturally, their ties to Romania can be maintained without political unification. Romanians—elites and masses—also recognize that they have enough on their plate without complicating policy issues further. Beyond the Prut River, in Moldova, lie additional and volatile matters of Transnistria and other minorities (Russian, Ukrainian, Turkic, and so forth) with which Romania would not be able to deal. Moldova's constitutional and political uncertainties—suggested by the trouble selecting a new president in late 2000 and the election of a Communist government shortly thereafter—are added headaches that Bucharest has no discernible interest in absorbing. "Moldova is, for us, like a tiny version of Canada to Americans—interesting, similar, but neither well known nor anything we'd like to try to swallow."[60] And a Moldovan diplomat assigned to a West European post noted that "I enjoy knowing of my Romanian heritage—full stop."[61]

The search for additional (not other) anchors with which to maintain Romanian security in turbulent waters has also meant creating or strengthening ties with neighboring states. A concerted effort in this regard, which had the added benefit of underscoring the "strategic" importance of Bucharest's diplomacy, was the "Romania at the Crossroads" project launched by the Constantinescu presidency and the ministry of foreign affairs. Multiple bilateral and trilateral summits and ministerial meetings occurred in the 1997–2000 period, designed to cement bilateral or regional cooperative structures in Central and southeastern Europe, or linked to the German-generated, so-called "Balkan Stability Pact" (launched at a Sarajevo summit in July 1999).

Romanian engagement in the Southeastern European Cooperation Initiative (SECI), the brainchild of the Clinton administration National Security Council and State Department official Ambassador Richard Schifter, is likewise an outgrowth of Bucharest's hope that, one way or other, the gray zone can be avoided. The SECI, now with a link to the Balkan Stability Pact, and with a building and furnishings in Bucharest, has limited visibility.

France and Italy, Romania's "Latinate" NATO advocates, remain in favor of the Alliance's extension to include Bucharest and Slovenia. Romanian diplomacy cultivates these ties.[62] But such four-way (including Slovenia) cooperation also evokes memories of the entente between the wars, or of a "southern approach" to NATO's open door, neither of which seem to discerning Romanian policymakers to be a strong hand in the game of international security.

There is a danger that, under duress, people who have experienced the "comfort" of authoritarian rule—freedomless, but assured—will long for the assurance more than worry about an absence of freedom. The threshold at which such a tradeoff would be made is likely to be high— that is, ample research has demonstrated that socioeconomic pain and other threats would have to be extremely severe before a dramatic shift from democratic values would occur.[63] Yet, civil society can hemorrhage and ebb quickly once such a threshold is crossed.[64]

As the tenth anniversary of rebellion against Nicolae Ceausescu approached, most (51 percent) Romanians believed that life was better under Ceausescu, and 64 percent thought that Romania was "headed in the wrong direction."[65] At the same time, the extensive and prolonged NATO air war launched against Yugoslavia because of Milosevic's actions in Kosovo sent ripples of discomfort and fear through the Romanian population during spring and summer 1999.

Such unease bordering on panic—a sense that nothing was going right domestically or in their Balkan neighborhood—certainly fed Corneliu Vadim Tudor's large first-round presidential vote and made his Greater Romania (PRM) party the second largest in parliament. His support came disproportionately from Romanians in Transylvania, and from young, poorly educated voters. Among these people, microeconomic pocketbook issues and visceral fears of "others" prevailed. In style and message, Tudor and the RPM are demagogic, disbursing unfounded rumors and exaggerating threat to weaken public allegiance to tolerance and pluralism. Hungarians, Roma, and Jews are targets of slurs and allegations in almost every utterance.

There is no question that Tudor espouses and represents views incompatible with NATO and the EU. But, in circumstances of real or perceived threat to well-being or survival, the democratic niceties of such European and Transatlantic organizations fall by the wayside—whether in Romania, to almost 30 percent of Austrians in 1999, or almost a fourth of French voters earlier in the 1990s when Le Pen and the Front Nationale were surging.

A danger exists that the precarious sovereignty of small, poor states will confront increasingly strong challenges to territorial integrity, policy autonomy, and control over economic development.[66] While a post–Cold War environment has implied greater "freedom of action," the relative capacities of small states—particularly those without substantial wealth in a continent of great wealth and proximate powers—are mismatched with new latitude. Put another way, there is more "freedom" than they can use to their advantage. Such incapacity in the face of opportunity heightens national frustration and a perception of threat as perhaps nothing else could. Threat, in turn, is the bane of democratic norms and behavior.

For Romania, the "new world order" has been no picnic. Bucharest's policymakers have been peripatetic but ineffective, free to roam but without a place to land. Even a few years after 1989 it was abundantly clear that Romania confronted "numerous intractable problems that [made] the country less secure than most of the other formerly communist states of Eastern Europe" and that Romania had "neither the military nor the economic capacity to confront such threats."[67] If that was true in the early 1990s, it became far more poignant by the decade's close.

By mid-1998, Romanian views were much more blunt. Catalin Harnagea, then chief of Romania's Foreign Intelligence Service (SIE), spoke publicly about the palpable dangers of mafia-like groups taking over instruments of power in a given country using economic force and violence—and Romania, specifically, was endangered by large-scale organized crime.[68] As Romanians looked at NATO enlargement from which they were excluded, they wondered about Hungarian intentions—and listened, perhaps much too closely, to each conspiracy. And, reflecting on Romanians' hope to enter NATO with a European strategy (given U.S. disinterest), the venerable ex-Communist intellectual, Silviu Brucan, wryly noted that Romania would have improved its chances of getting into NATO with a Middle East strategy—by renewing old ties with the Middle East, and thereby both generating new trade and heightening Bucharest's added value for the alliance.[69] Still Europe focused, but reading the tea leaves very accurately, Bogdan Chirieac wrote in early February 1999 "Adio NATO—Europe, the

Only Hope." Led by German chancellor Schroeder, but endorsed by other Alliance leaders at a critical meeting in Munich, it was flatly stated that NATO would not be inviting anyone else soon. Accordingly, bilateral ties with principal European countries, not the United States, should be the country's security focus.[70]

Future Prospects

In this milieu, humble Romanian diplomacy is probably nearing an end; having been denied assurance about climbing aboard the NATO bandwagon, many Romanians may not want to climb back on. Already, this is an audible subtext to elite discussion. Even former Foreign Minister Plesu, while insisting that Romania has no alternative to NATO membership, points out that "one cannot rely on metaphorical pronouncements with an indefinite time scale."[71] Were that to become a popular consensus, however, the national and ideological components of Romania's international policy would become much more prominent. Several of the trends—moving away from NATO dependence and focusing on real or perceived internal dangers with foreign components—bode ill for domestic tolerance and civil society.

At the very least, the differentiation between internal political needs and external image offered to Brussels, Washington, and elsewhere is recognized more in the second Iliescu presidency. Although the victorious PDSR sought and ultimately achieved a coalition with, for example, the Liberals (PNL), the bases for such a coalition and the reasons for it were carefully delineated—not to "please" foreign audiences and observers but to respond to domestic needs. Inclusion of potential coalition partners, noted PDSR leaders, might satisfy those abroad but have negative domestic political consequences for PDSR constituencies.[72]

Yet these are close companions of rejection in the face of need. In the aftermath of Ceausescu's twenty-five-year tyranny, renewed sovereignty and a chance for democracy were cherished by Romanians. But their climb was long and steep—much more so than most other erstwhile Communist states. Expectations for assistance were unmet, many investors stayed away, and the Romanians' pursuit of Western institutions was spurned.

After more than a decade of post-communism, Romanians had only post-communism. That it was so is the "fault" neither of Romanians and their governing elites, nor of callous or prejudiced Western media and political institutions.[73] But the failures of both have now led to a 21st century potential for at least partial renationalization of Romanian foreign and defense policy. Were Romanian political figures or commentators increasingly to emphasize heightened threats and a need for their country to rely on its own capacities, rather than via integration with and security guarantees from the West, a troublesome corner will have been turned.

As the metamorphoses of states and European institutions continue, the message to small or poor states on the periphery may be unwelcome and keenly disappointing. Their needs are palpable and their preferences evident. Deferring such needs and preferences will sharpen and perhaps accelerate thought about a different calculus by which to ensure security. As that process unfolds, Romanian national identity will find new voice, particularly in the second Ion Iliescu presidency. Western institutions ought to listen closely and understand the inseparable link between security and the vital signs of democracy.

*This chapter is an edited, up-dated, and revised version of an essay that first appeared in Charles Carey, ed. *Romania in the 21st Century* (Boulder, Colo.: Westview, 2001).

Chronology

10 January 2000: Foreign Minister Petre Roman (Democratic Party, DP) makes clear that he will be a presidential candidate in late 2000 elections.

18 January 2000: Ion Ratiu, Peasant Party leader, dies in London at the age of eighty-two and is buried in Turda on 23 January.

22 January 2000: Balkan leaders meet in Hissar, Bulgaria, and call for more effective sanctions against Slobodan Milosevic and complain about slow implementation of the Stability Pact.

3 February 2000: U.S. Undersecretary Secretary of State Thomas Pickering meets with Petre Roman and signs a framework convention to enlarge the U.S.-Romanian "Strategic Partnership."

4 February 2000: U.S.-Romanian peacekeeping exercise starts at three airfields in Romania.

6–9 February 2000: President Emil Constantinescu travels to the United Kingdom.

February and March 2000: Ruling coalition in a governmental crisis, begun when Defense Minister Victor Babiuc resigns from his party, the Democratic Party.

1 March 2000: Romania introduces visas for Moldovans.

2 March 2000: General Wesley Clark, the Supreme Allied Commander Europe, meets Romanian governmental leadership, including Prime Minister Isarescu, and discusses military reform and NATO's readiness to assist.

14 March 2000: Romania and Bulgaria sign agreement to build a second bridge over the Danube between Vidin, Bulgaria, and Calafat, Romania— a project that will cost $155 million, with construction to begin in late 2001.

30 March 2000: EU-required child protection programs approved by Cabinet.

13 April 2000: Petre Roman promises flexibility in talks with Moscow on Basic Treaty, while criticizing Hungarian idea to open a consulate in Miercurea Ciuc.

14 April 2000: Hungarian Prime Minister Viktor Orban begins visit to Romania and raises issue of consulates; some Romanian protests in towns with Hungarian majorities and mayors in Harghita and Covasna.

mid-April 2000: Romania-Bulgaria Black Sea naval exercise Storm 2000 ends.

4 May 2000: Money-laundering charges surface against Adrian Costa, with ties to PDSR (Iliescu's party).

3 and 17 June 2000: Local elections reveal significant weakness in ruling coalition, and growing strength of PDSR.

14 June 2000: EU asserts Romanian officials stole aid sent to Bucharest for children.

5 July 2000: Ion Iliescu announces that Adrian Nastase will be his party's candidate for prime minister.

17 July 2000: President Emil Constantinescu withdraws from the presidential race.

28–30 July 2000: Hungarian Prime Minister Viktor Orban speaks out about Romania and the Hungarian minority, while Hungarian Foreign Minister Janos Martonyi meets with Petre Roman.

6 September 2000: Antidiscrimination legislation approved by the cabinet in line with EU standards.

20 September 2000: President Constantinescu rejects Belgrade's contention that NATO exercises in Romania have aggressive intentions toward Yugoslavia.

5 October 2000: Constantinescu, while on state visit to Italy, welcomes events in Belgrade (the ouster of Milosevic) and says that Romania is ready to resume dialogue and cooperation.

5 October 2000: Ion Iliescu announces his presidential candidacy.

20 October 2000: President Constantinescu invites Yugoslavia to join Black Sea Economic Cooperation Organization.

28 October 2000: German interior minister opposed lifting visa obligations for Romanians.

9 November 2000: Rumors of electoral "protocol" between PDSR and Liberals (PNL) surface for election and postelection cooperation.

21 November 2000: Corneliu Vadim Tudor (presidential candidate of the far-right Greater Romania Party) continues to pick up additional public support according to polls, and compares himself to recently elected George W. Bush in the United States.

21 November 2000: The EU reports that, among candidate countries, Romania lags behind all others, and completes (closes) only one of twenty-nine chapters in accession talks.

26 November 2000: National elections lead to substantial victory for the PDSR in parliament and a huge loss for the centrists, including an elimination of the Christian Peasant Party (PNTCD) from Parliament; Iliescu comes in first in the presidential vote, but is forced into a runoff by a strong second-place finish by Corneliu Vadim Tudor (Greater Romania Party). His extreme right-wing reputation evinces great concern elsewhere in Europe and the United States.

28 December 2000: New PDSR cabinet installed, with Adrian Nastase as prime minister, Mircea Dan Geoana as foreign minister, and Ioan Mircea Pascu as defense minister. The Liberals (PNL) and Democratic Union of Hungarians (UDMR) support the cabinet.

11 January 2001: Mircea Dan Geonea addresses OSCE as rotating chair, and spells out priorities.

30 January 2001: Statue of Marshal Antonescu to be erected in Bacau.

NOTES

1. See, for example, a study using public opinion data for the early and mid-1990s by Claire Wallace and Christian Haepfer, "Changes in Attitudes toward Internal and External Security in Post-Communist Europe," unpublished manuscript, 1998. The authors found Romanians to perceive more threat than Hungarians or Poles (ranking fourth among ten for which data were available).

2. United States Information Agency, "Romanians Prepared to Continue to Push for NATO Membership," *Opinion Research Memorandum* (6 October 1997).

3. These data were reported by the United States Information Agency *Opinion Research Memorandum* (28 April 1999), p. 6. Details about the sample were not reported.

4. Many of these general issues have been raised perceptively by Efraim Inbar and Gabriel Sheffer, eds., *The National Security of Small States in a Changing World* (London: Frank Cass, 1997), especially the "Introduction" (pp. 1–8), and Gabriel Scheffer, "The Security of Small Ethnic States," 9–40.

5. "Conclusion," in *Romania in the 1980s*, ed., Daniel N. Nelson (Boulder, Colo.: Westview Press, 1981).

6. More detail is provided in Daniel N. Nelson, "Ceausescu and the Romanian Army," *International Defense Review* 22, no. 6 (January 1989): 737–42.

7. For details about the Ceausescu catastrophe, see Daniel N. Nelson, "Romania: Economic, Social, and Political Disasters," in *The Legacies of Communism in Eastern Europe*, eds. Zoltan Barany and Ivan Volgyes (Baltimore, Md.: Johns Hopkins University Press, 1996), 198–226.

8. These examples were drawn from "First Count Confirms Leftist Win Romania Poll," *Reuters*, (27 November 2000); "Romanian Leftists Leading Elections," *AP International*, (27 November 2000), and "Left Surges in Romanian Poll," *BBC News Europe*, (27 November 2000).

9. European Bank for Reconstruction and Development (EBRD), "Transition Report, 1995" (London: EBRD, 1995), 28.

10. "Romania's Macroeconomy—A Thumbnail Sketch," *Country Market Assessment* (Alexandria, Va.: Global Concepts, Inc., 2000).

11. Bogdan Chirieac, "Petru NATO, Romania este unul de altele," *Adevarul*, (8 August 1998), p. 1.

12. *Romanian Digest* 4, no. 11 (November 1999): 7; earlier, similarly bleak 1998 foreign investment levels had been reported; see, *Romanian Business Journal*, 6, no. 4, 250 (29 January–4 February 1999): 1.

13. Center for Strategic and International Studies (CSIS), "U.S.-Romania: A Strategic Partnership," (Bucharest: CSIS, 1998), 3–4.

14. These data are from *Romanian.Digest@br.ro.* Accessed 10 April 2001 (November 9, 1998).

15. See this report in *Romanian.Digest@br.ro* (October 20, 1998).

16. Metro Media Transilvania, *Barometrul Politic* (September 1999), 17.

17. Constanta Corpade, "Miron Cozma se autonumeste conductator de zona si se urca deasupra oricarei legi," "Miron Cozma is an Autonomous Regional Leader and is Above Every Law," *Adevarul*, 4 February 1999, p. 1.

18. General Degeratu provided copies of his report on January 1999 miners' protests to me privately in the first days of February. The report was apparently leaked, however, and appeared in most Bucharest dailies on Saturday, 6 February 1999. See, for example, "Generalul Degeratu prezinta raportul MApN privind mineriada," "General Degeratu presents the Defense Ministry's Report Regarding the Miners' Protest," *Adevarul*, 6 February 1999, p. 1.

19. "Interviu Ioan Mircea Pascu: Anuntul facut de la Londra inseamna permanentizarea Romaniei intro-o zona vulnerabila, zona gri," "Interview with Ioan Mircea Pascu: The London Announcement means That Romania Will Permanently Be in a Grey Zone of Vulnerability," *Jurnalul National* (Martie 14, 1998), p. 17.

20. A senior diplomat at the Romanian ministry of foreign affairs in a conversation with me in early February 1999.

21. An early sign of such doubt about the Clinton administration's promises was Liviu Muresan, "Un parteneriat strategic prea indepartat?" "A Strategic Partnership too Distant?" *Lumea* (October 1997), 9. By late March 1998, the so-called partnership was being compared to "wishful thinking." See, Emil Hurezeanu, "Un Parteneriat Numit Dorinta," "A Partnership Named Hope," *Curentul* (23 March 1998).

22. Zoe Petre, untitled essay in response to CSIS draft document on Romania's strategic importance (October 1998), 1–2.

23. Severin had declared in September 1997 that he had "seen documents that showed 'without a doubt' that two or three publishers of large-circulation newspapers, as well as two or three well-known political party leaders, had been recruited by foreign intelligence agencies." See, for example, the report on Severin's resignation carried by AFP, "Romania's Foreign Minister Quits in Spy Row" (23 December 1997), http://www.atp.com (accessed January 12, 1998).

24. Rompres dispatch of 23 May 1998 as cited in FBIS-EEU-98-145 of 25 May 1998.

25. Teodor Melescanu, "The Accession to the European Union: The Fundamental Op-

tion of Romania's Foreign Policy," *Romanian Journal of International Affairs* 2, no. 4 (1996): 27.

26. See, for example, the rather ponderous study of Dorel Sandor, *Ambivalenta factorilor politici in sustinerea politicilor reformei in Romania*, [Ambivalent Political Factors in Sustaining Romanian Political Reform] manuscript (25 October 1999).

27. Branko Caratan, "The New States and Nationalism in Eastern Europe," *International Politics* 34, no. 3 (September 1997): 286.

28. For example, considerable bitterness was expressed on just one small bit of news—that World Bank agricultural investments had been $500 million for Poland and zero for Romania. See, for example, *Adevarul*, 4 February 1999, p. 1.

29. Many measurements of public opinion in Romania all point to the same pervasive support for NATO, the United States, and other Western countries and integration with the West in general. The U.S. Information Agency, for example, commissioned a number of national samples in Romania (and other countries of the former Warsaw Pact) about security perceptions, and found Romanians to be among the most positive regarding entering NATO and also vis-a-vis specific countries such as the United States. See, *The New European Security Architecture, II* (Washington, D.C.: USIA Office of Research and Media Reaction, September 1996).

30. A compendium of these arguments is presented in the Romanian ministry of foreign affairs' *White Book on Romania and NATO* (Bucharest, Romania: MFA, 1997).

31. Ion Mircea Pascu, "Security through NATO Enlargement and the Partnership for Peace: The Experience and Expectation of Romania," unpublished manuscript (August 1997), 12.

32. Liviu Muresan, "NATO si 'generalul Iarna' " [NATO and the General Winter], *Lumea Magazin* (September 1997): 30.

33. Conversation with General Constantin Degeratu, chief of the General Staff of the Romanian armed forces, Bucharest, 30 April 1999.

34. FBIS *Wirefile*, AU 0501154998 (5 January 1998); see also, FBIS, *Wirefile* AU2003185097 (May 20 1997) and AU160318397 (16 March 1997).

35. My conversations in Romania during visits in 1998.

36. Luminita Kohlami, "Afirmatii grave ale fostului ministru de Externe la Institutul George C. Marshall din Garmisch—Teodor Melescanu: In armata romana au loc fenomene periculoase pentru societate," "Grave Assertions of The Former Minister of Foreign Affairs at the George C. Marshall Center in Garmisch: In The Romanian Army Are Dangerous Phenomena for Society], *Cotidianul* (9 June 1998), 3.

37. For example, President Iliescu was quoted as having said, while on a trip to Bonn in late June 1996, that "Romania and Hungary should be admitted simultaneously in NATO if the Alliance wishes to avoid the production of tensions in Eastern Europe." See *Ziua* 26 June 1996, p. 2. Iliescu's last defense minister, Gheorghe Tinca, was quoted about the same time as having warned that "If we do not enter NATO . . . [with Poland, Hungary, the Czech Republic] Romania will be marginalized." See *Jurnalul National* 21 June 1996, p. 1.

38. "Radu Vasile intra in barlogul 'lupului tanar' Viktor Orban," "Radu Vasile Enters the Lair of the Young Wolf, Viktor Orban," *Cotidianul* 9, no. 229 (8 February 1999): 1.

39. See, for example, the interview with Vasily Lipitski, President Boris Yeltsin's senior adviser on constitutional matters, by Marcela Feraru in *Cotidianul* (6–7 February 1999): 5, "Vasili Lipitki: Relatiile dintre Romania si Rusia nu sunt dintre cele mai bune," "Vasile Lipitki: Relations Between Romania and Russia are Not Getting Better."

40. Interviu: Valeri Fiodorovici Keneaikin, Ambasadorul Federatiei Ruse: "Rusia este pregatita sa ofere orice garantii de securitate oricarui stat european," "Russia is prepared to offer all security guarantees to any European state." *Jurnalul National* (6 March 1998): 16–17. A wider interpretation of Russian strategic aims that threaten Romania was Bogdan Chirieac's editorial in *Adevarul* (9 March 1998). A long commentary on Lukoil's deal with the difficulties involving Bell Textron's helicopter production is by former foreign minister Adrian Severin in *Ziua* (28 August 1998).

41. Valerian Stan, "Rusofobia: un snobism pagubos," "Rusophobia: A Misplaced Snobbery" *Cotidianul* no. 229 (8 February 1999): 1.

42. "Bucharest Reiterates Commitment to NATO Entry," Rompres dispatch (5 March 1998), in *Daily Report*, FBIS-EEU-98-064 (6 March 1998).

43. "Plesu to Convince Talbott of 'Necessity' of NATO Entry," Radio Romania (17 March 1998), in *Daily Report*, FBIS-EEU-98-076 (17 March 1998).

44. Andrei Plesu, "The Indivisibility of Security," *Central European Issues* 4, no. 2 (1998): 26.

45. "Defense Minister Lists Arguments for Romania's NATO Entry," *Rompres Dispatch* (20 August 1998), in *Daily Report*, FBIS-EEU-98-232 (24 August 1998).

46. See, for example, "Policy Paper: Key Elements of Romania's Security Strategy," U.S.-Romania Action Commission, Security and Foreign Policy Working Group (Washington, D.C.: Center for Strategic & International Studies, October 1998).

47. Ibid.

48. My discussions with senior military and defense officials in Bucharest in February and August 1998. I was involved in CFE discussions during 1998 while serving in the U.S. Arms Control and Disarmament Agency, both in Washington, D.C., and Vienna, Austria, the location of negotiations.

49. Such an emphasis began to be apparent in 1998 with, for example, the submission of a twenty-one-page document to NATO proposing three regional NATO-AFP training centers in Romania—a center for defense resource management, a peacekeeping training center, and a simulation training center. That NATO was almost certain to avoid concentrating such centers in one country did not obviate the Romanian ministry of defense's attempt to draw resources for purposes critical to modernizing the Romanian military.

50. Dumitru Tinu, Editorial, *Adevarul* 27 April 1999, p. 1.

51. AFP Dispatch, "UN Gave Nod to Embargo Breach by Romania," 9 March 1998.

52. *Buletin de Stiri Telegrama*, no. 524 8 April 1996, part 2.

53. See, for example, Lucia Dumachita, "PDSR Vice Presidente Ioan Mircea Pascu: Despre Kosovo . . ." [PDSR Vice President Ioan Mircea Pascu: About Kosovo . . .], *Azi* (19 June 1998): 2.

54. Statement by Emil Constantinescu, President of Romania (19 March 1999), in English, as distributed by the Romanian embassy, Washington, D.C.

55. These renewed defense contacts were mentioned to me by senior Romanian military officers in November 2000. Exploratory at first, it is clear that the Romanian side took steps to initiate such conversations and that the range of potential collaboration covers training and education, intelligence, weapons modernization, and development, plus other arenas.

56. As quoted in an AFP Dispatch, "Polish, Romanian, Ukrainian Heads meet for Regional Stability," 26 November 1997, as cited at www.afp.com (26 November 1997), accessed 5 February 1998.

57. Ovidiu Gherman, as quoted in *Buletin de Stiri*, No. 549 (15 May 1996).

58. Cable News Network, www.cnn.com 3 December 1998, accessed 10 January 1999.

59. The Bucharest daily, *Evenimentul Zilei*, first reported this shipment (24 October 1997).

60. My conservation with senior ministry of foreign affairs individual, December 2000.

61. My conversation with Moldovan diplomat, Brussels, December 2000.

62. Dozens of ministerial and subministerial meetings took place in 1998, for example, involving diplomats or representatives of Italy or France or both and their Romanian counterparts. The second formal session of the "four-way cooperation" took place in Paris on 26 February 1998, at which Romania was represented by Deputy Foreign Minister Lazar Comanescu. See *Rompres* dispatch, 26 February 1998.

63. See, for example, Raymond M. Duch, "Economic Chaos and the Fragility of Democratic Transition in Former Communist Regimes," *Journal of Politics* 57, no. 1 (February 1995): 121–58. At the same time, punishing incumbents is likely, and other findings indicate substantial skepticism underlying most public attitudes about politics. See, for instance, William Mishler and Richard Rose, "Trust, Distrust and Skepticism: Popular Evaluations of Civil and Political Institutions in Post-Communist Societies," *Journal of Politics* 59, no. 2 (May 1997): 418–51.

64. See Daniel N. Nelson, "Civil Society Endangered," *Social Research* 63, no. 2 (Summer 1996): 345–68.

65. Radio Free Europe *News Report* (30 November 1998) cited an Open Society Foundation (a Soros-funded think tank in Bucharest) poll.

66. Inbar and Sheffer, *The National Security of Small States*, 4.

67. Daniel N. Nelson, "Post-Communist Romania's Search For Security," in *The Volatile Powerderkeg* ed. F. Stephen Larrabee (Washington, D.C.: The American University Press, 1994), 85.

68. Mugurel Ghita in *Adevarul* 10 July 1998, p. 16.

69. Silviu Brucan, interview on ProTV, 5 February 1999.

70. Bogdan Chirieac, "Adio NATO! Europa, singura speranta" [Good Bye NATO! Europe, The Only Hope], *Adevarul*, 8 February 1999, p. 1.

71. Andrei Plesu, "From the Madrid Summit to Washington and Beyond," text in English as distributed by the press office of ministry of foreign affairs, 15 February 1999.

72. My conversations with PDSR leaders, 28, 29, 30 November, 1 December 2000. See also the press conference of Ioan Mircea Pascu, 29 November 2000.

73. A good feel for American media's extreme bias toward southeastern and Eastern Europe (all of the regions excluded from EU or NATO enlargement) is presented by Katia McClain, "The Politics of Discourse in US Media Coverage of Eastern Europe," *International Politics* 36, no. 2 (May 1999).

19 • Serbia and Montenegro 2000: As Good as It Gets?

Stan Markotich

W as the 5 October 2000 Belgrade revolution really a popular civilian uprising, or was it closer to a police and military coup? It will take many years before we finally know. But what is already clear is that the muscle that stormed the parliament and state television station came from men who learned the trade of war in Croatia, Bosnia, and Kosovo—and had past or current links with Yugoslavia's police, army, and paramilitary groups. They wanted rid of Slobodan Milosevic, not because of his international crimes, but because he had become Serbia's albatross.[1]

In Serbia, the economy had collapsed during a decade of Milosevic's cronyism and misrule. The Federal Republic of Yugoslavia (FRY) was an international pariah because of the regime's all too transparent roles in fomenting a series of regional wars, beginning in the early 1990s. The first serious conflict came in 1991 with Croatia, followed soon in April 1992 in Bosnia by the bloodiest campaigns fought in Europe since World War II. That was the legacy of Bosnia and Herzegovina (BiH), and an uneasy peace came with the signing of the Dayton Peace Accord in December 1995. Next came the war beginning 24 March 1999, in which NATO confronted Milosevic over his horrific misrule in the province of Kosovo. Several efforts to achieve a negotiated peace culminated with Rambouillet, which ultimately Milosevic rejected, prompting the showdown. While the Western Alliance waged an air campaign for seventy-eight days, Milosevic unleashed his own ground war and ethnic cleansing against the Kosovo citizenry, turning some 80 percent of the province's population into displaced persons or refugees. Yugoslavia's slide into repression and conflict correlates exactly with Milosevic's rise.[2]

As 2000 began to unfold, there appeared little evidence that Milosevic would go by year's end, or that the prospects for his ouster or any kind of reform were bright. During the last few days of 1999, Milosevic did almost precisely what he had done roughly a year before. He adopted a combative attitude toward the outside world and focused on shaking down the military hierarchy. Those who had taken the hardest pro-Serb line were honored with promotions. Among the chief beneficiaries was General Vladimir Lazarevic, former commander of the Pristina Corps until Yugoslav forces withdrew from Kosovo.[3] Lazarevic, becoming head of the Third Army, had become known for vowing that Yugoslav fighters would return to the ethnic-Albanian populated province. Advanced alongside was General Milorad Obradovic, made leader of the Second Army, which was tasked with Montenegrin security. While at year's end Milosevic went on record as saying that Podgorica was free to leave the federation if it wished to do so,[4] Obradovic's appointment reopened speculation that the FRY dictator's real agenda included forcing a violent showdown with the Montenegrin authorities.

On 13 January 2000 relations were strained further, as supporters of Milosevic's Socialist Party of Serbia (SPS) were present and spoke publicly at a mass rally in Podgorica designed to stir emotions and support for the union with Belgrade. Police and security officers provided a presence that may have prevented tensions from being acted out. Only two days later, Montenegrin president Milo Djukanovic spoke to independent media in Serbia. He said that Milosevic would have to be held accountable for his crimes and the FRY president could face extradition if he ever showed up in Podgorica.[5]

The same day Djukanovic's remarks became public, an incident took place in Belgrade, which, with hindsight, amounted to a macabre foreshadowing of what was to happen with many familiar figures who had dominated public life in Serbia for roughly a decade. Notorious paramilitary leader Zeljko Raznatovic, alias Arkan, was slain gangland style at the Interkontinental Hotel.[6] Arkan's resume included being an indicted war criminal, political leader, and someone wanted by Interpol for a range of capital crimes. His assassination was the first in a wave of killings, abductions, and beatings that raised widespread fears throughout Serbia that the republic was on the verge of social breakdown, if not civil war. In another high-profile incident, Milosevic's former mentor and subsequent critic, Ivan Stambolic, was kidnapped on 25 August 2000 while jogging. Many rumors about motives for the kidnapping circulated, including that he was grabbed to prevent his candidacy for president. Presumed by most to be dead, no trace of him has been found.

As long as the dictator Milosevic remained at the helm, FRY, and specifically Serbia was seen as the only state in southeastern Europe for which violence was seen as a plausible policy choice. Arkan and Stambolic, the reasoning went, were but the victims of what had become standard practices. Simplified crudely, observers maintained that the dictatorship would rather turn to troops in a bid to protect and shield the regime from internal and external opposition. Not even a modicum of power would be given up. Milosevic, indicted by The Hague tribunal on charges of war crimes and crimes against humanity, would prefer to unleash another bloodletting and cling to power rather than give up even a shred of his authority. Many observers, with at best a superficial grasp of the internal dynamics of Serbian politics, also likened Milosevic and his wife, Mirjana Markovic, to the tyrannical Romanian ruling couple, the Ceausescus. The latter couple met their violent end with the collapse of Communism in Eastern Europe in 1989, and the Milosevics were thought to face, eventually, an identical fate.

For the Federal Republic of Yugoslavia to find favor with the international community, the totalitarian ruler, the Butcher of the Balkans, one Yugoslav president Slobodan Milosevic, needed to be ousted from power. As long as Milosevic remained in office, Serbia was subjected to sanctions. While the list of proscriptions is far too lengthy to be dealt with in detail here, measures included a ban on international flights and an oil embargo. A UN Security Council resolution of 31 March 1998 produced a full arms prohibition. The government of the United States, moreover, maintained an outer wall of sanctions against Belgrade and introduced a rigid visa regime not only against FRY officials but aimed broadly at those suspected of war crimes and genocide. Washington tightened the noose on 18 July 2000 by "re-authoriz[ing] the limitation on US assistance to areas in which local governments are known to be harboring indicted war criminals."[7]

While 2000 opened along a familiar pattern, it would close on a radically different note. In the short period that the new FRY president, Vojislav

Kostunica, has been in office, the country has resumed its membership in the Organization for Security and Cooperation in Europe (OSCE) and the United Nations. Then on 9 October 2000, immediately following Kostunica's formal accession to power on 7 October 2000, European Union foreign ministers agreed in principle to the lifting of sanctions against Yugoslavia.[8]

The process of Belgrade's reintegration into the international community was well under way.[9] That momentum continues. A day before leaving office, one of U.S. president Bill Clinton's eleventh hour acts was the lifting of sanctions against the FRY. President Vojislav Kostunica, on his first official visit to Sarajevo on 19 January 2001, stressed bilateral cooperation. One headline, positioned above a photo of Kostunica shaking hands simultaneously with all members of Bosnia and Herzegovina's tripartite presidency, heralded "The End of Balkanization and the Fragmentation of the Balkans."[10]

There are times when the removal of a dictator proves no easy endgame, with concomitant public upheaval yielding violence, bloodletting, and social dislocation. This was not the case in Serbia. The Milosevic autocracy died at the ballot box, with almost no bloodshed. In that respect, his demise has more in common with the 1989 Velvet Revolution in Czechoslovakia than the fate endured by Romania's Communist ruling clan. That Milosevic was arrested and jailed on domestic corruption charges and eventually extradicted to The Hague, marks a major achievement of Western pressure and Carla del Ponte's (chief prosecutor) perseverance. Despite some large protests by the former dictator's supporters, any threat of social violence appears to have receded, although isolated incidents cannot be ruled out.

The balloting that removed Milosevic took place on 24 September 2000, with opposition observers announcing the same evening that Kostunica had won an absolute majority, eliminating the need for a second round of voting.[11] Two days later, the electoral commission almost agreed, saying Kostunica was ahead, but had only roughly 48 percent of the votes, necessitating a crucial runoff.[12] Had Milosevic been able to force another vote, he likely would have resorted to ballot manipulation. The opposition held firm, insisting no revote was necessary. Milosevic's room to maneuver shrank. With the opposition supported by mass rallies and de facto by police and security forces unwilling to take action against peaceful protest, or at best making only token efforts to obstruct opposition demonstrators, Milosevic fell.[13]

It was just one week before Kostunica took power that one of the bluntest admissions of possible deal making with Milosevic was leaked. On 1 October 2000 the *Observer* reported that the Russians, who had been Milosevic's close allies, and especially also Germany's chancellor, Gerhard Schroeder, wanted to negotiate a deal, such that the Serbian dictator would step down, be granted safe passage to another country, and thus save himself from prosecution. The report alleged German officials felt that if there were any hope of Milosevic handing power peacefully to the opposition, there had to be bargaining that would allow him some sort of immunity from prosecution. A senior unnamed German diplomat was quoted saying "officially [we] are in favor of [The Hague Tribunal and its indictment on war crimes charges of FRY President Milosevic, however] we need an exit strategy and that means getting him off the hook."

What happened next was anticlimactic. The Democratic Opposition of Serbia (DOS) and the ruling Socialists worked out arrangements for an interim administration while preparations took place for Serbian parliamentary elections where few expected the opposition to lose. The date set was 23 December 2000 and results became official on 27 December 2000. DOS swept into office with 64 percent of the vote, winning 176 out of a possible 250 seats. Milosevic's SPS still emerged as the largest single party in the new legislature, securing thirty-seven seats after taking about 14 percent of the vote. Only two other parties won representation. The nationalist Serbian Radical Party (SRS) of Vojislav Seselj received 8.5 percent of the vote and twenty-three seats, while, in a surprising result, the party of slain warlord Arkan won slightly more than 5 percent of the votes, claiming fourteen seats.[14] Several stalwarts, notably Vuk Draskovic's Serbian Renewal Movement (SPO) and Milosevic's wife's party, the Yugoslav United Left (JUL), fell off the political map entirely.

Serbia's new, reformist leadership said immediately that it wanted improved relations with the outside world, yet at first it also hinted that violence and redrawing regional borders were aims that may not have evaporated with Milosevic's exit. New FRY foreign minister Goran Svilanovic went on record, as 2000 drew to a close, with the thinly veiled threat that any further deterioration of the existing Yugoslav federation would produce "serious regional consequences" and "especially within BiH." He clarified: "I'm not prepared to link directly the status of the Republika Srpska with that of Kosovo. However, if the [status] of Kosovo is violated, it would be most difficult to explain what was taking place and why the same thing or something similar couldn't be done in the case of the RS."[15]

Yet on relatively numerous other occasions, FRY officials have said that Belgrade, now under new management, is in fact a guarantor of regional stability. Svilanovic, in the days surrounding the establishment of diplomatic relations with Sarajevo, stressed firm support for the Dayton Accord and its borders. He went one step further, suggesting that perhaps the act of normalizing relations was predicated on an exchange—that Bosnia and Herzegovina offer support for the territorial integrity of its neighbor. BiH press quoted Svilanovic as declaring: "If it just isn't clear to someone, I shall repeat it: The Federal Republic of Yugoslavia is one of the guarantors of BiH's territorial integrity. We are waiting for BiH to receive precisely the same kind of guarantee from each of its neighbors. Furthermore, we are also hoping that with BiH we have a very strong guarantor of the territorial integrity of the FRY."[16]

As it turns to the international community for assistance and legitimacy, will Belgrade altogether abandon past policies that not only promised to antagonize great power relations, but also sought to elevate Serbia and Montenegro to the rank of major player in the world stage? As long as Milosevic held on to political power, the threat of involving Russian interests in regional brinkmanship was real. Perhaps no better manifestation of this damaging potential occurred than in the immediate aftermath of the NATO bombing campaign, ending in June 1999. After seventy-eight days of NATO action, Milosevic seemed to cave in quickly, negotiating a halt to war. While the Russian political establishment may have attempted to play a constructive negotiating role, Russia's armed forces were behind Milosevic. A dash by the Russian military to the Pristina airport appeared to be nothing less than an attempt to carve up the province, presenting the Western allies with a fait accompli. As one report observed:

Just as everything began to seem as though it were falling into a routine, with NATO countries focusing on an interpretation of events in such a way as to stress Belgrade's capitulation, the Russians entered the scene. On 11 June a Russian contingent of 200 Bosnia-based troops raced into Pristina, the Kosovar capital, and occupied the local airport, refusing to allow NATO access until political negotiations between Washington and Moscow had produced an outcome acceptable to the Russians regarding their role in the peace-keeping mission. Evidence that continues to dribble out suggests the Russian venture had been planned well in advance, possibly with roots as far back as late May.[17]

Some speculation and dark forces conspiracy theory making the rounds in Belgrade's cafes suggested, after 5 October 2000 that, if Milosevic were allowed to leave the FRY and escape to Russia as part of an exit strategy deal, he would have been an invaluable tool to the Russian intelligence services and military. He could be more dangerous outside Serbia than in, where his secrets about the FRY political and security establishments could allow Russian and Chinese security forces to meddle in FRY affairs more efficiently. That, it must be stressed, is only theory.

That the FRY plans and expects a return to the European fold is evidenced by a number of events that transpired in 2000. During the election campaign, EU representatives said that a change in the FRY government would be enough to ease sanctions and trigger the normalization process. That Kostunica sees his salvation more in Europe than in America was also demonstrated by varying reactions to any role in government for the Serbian Democratic Party (SDS). The Europeans either seemed not to care or to say that its presence in government was OK. The United States, by contrast, expressed vehement opposition to the presence of the party of indicted war criminal Radovan Karadzic. There is also the attitude of President Kostunica, who in 2000 refused meetings with Clinton administration officials, going so far at one point as to snub U.S. secretary of state Madeleine Albright. Kostunica thinly concealed his uneasy relations with the Democratic administration, suggesting that if the Republican Party had controlled the White House, the bombing would not have taken place. Once the Bush administration took office, residual hostile rhetoric faded and relations began to move toward a civil, if not cordial, footing, although the issue of war criminals remained contentious.

Threat Assessment

Has the international community, by acting so quickly to recognize the new FRY/Serbian leadership guided by Kostunica and Djindjic, in fact conveyed a message—that the root cause of the violence that dragged much of the West Balkans into wars in the 1990s can be overlooked as long as it is submerged, or reined in by the new political leadership?[18] What triggered the zeal of Serbian paramilitary and fighting forces was a propaganda-stirred nationalism, and one that found expression in ethnic cleansing campaigns.[19] To believe that the mere exchange of leaders at the top level alone can effect structural social and ideological changes over-looks the potency of Serbian nationalism.

Meanwhile, the leaders of the nationalist parties themselves are far from having gone quietly. Although Arkan is dead, his party made more of an impact in recent December 2000 elections than it ever did while its patriarch lived. Further, Seselj's Radicals continue to occupy space on the political spectrum, and his paramilitaries, or Chetniks, have merely resorted to the age-old Balkan strategy of hiding underground until political conditions become more accommodating for overt activity.

In early 2000, ultranationalist politicians, still in control of Federal political institutions and the government in Serbia, once again became vocal about their intent to gather together all Serb-populated lands, by force if necessary. In April, Seselj, in a not atypical statement, said the Federal Republic of Yugoslavia was nothing more than a political expedient. It could be tolerated, he stressed, but only until the move to create greater Serbia might be taken up strategically, in a relatively opposition-free environment. "The Republic of Serb Krajina [or RSK, the self-proclaimed state carved out in Croatia, but eliminated in 1995 following successful military campaigns by Zagreb] will live as long as there are Serbian people, and the Serbian people will never forget their holy debt, their holy obligation to liberate the RSK. The SRS will never ever give up its struggle to liberate the RSK," Seselj said on 27 April 2000.[20]

What most nationalists saw as the enemy continued to surface throughout the year in the guise of the Western world, and specifically in the form of the United States. Nationalist politicians continued to decry the NATO bombing campaign from the previous year and insisted that the greatest threat to FRY stability was Washington. Even nationalist politicians who looked to the West for aid and salvation at times concluded that the seemingly haphazard commitment to Serbian reforms was at best "controversial" and at worst counterproductive, potentially contributing to Serbia's internal political decay. Predrag Simic, foreign policy adviser to the Serbian Renewal Movement, said even when the United States wanted to act and acted in ways that were meant to be helpful, the result was invariably to the contrary. He noted early on in 2000 that: "the American moves directed at Belgrade are controversial and at present there's an obvious disarray in the American diplomatic approach to Yugoslavia. . . . While on the one hand the US offers financial aid to the opposition towns, it shows a readiness for a certain normalization of relations with Belgrade. Nevertheless, it does not fail to criticize others for making similar moves."[21]

Currently, the only real threat to FRY security is internal. The existing Yugoslavia is no longer home to a community with a singular view of what constitutes either the state or nation. This is not to suggest that socialist Yugoslavia ever was successful at creating a consensus without force, slogans such as "Brotherhood and Unity" notwithstanding. FRY now houses Serbian nationalism, along with Albanian and Montenegrin varieties.

Kosovar Albanians, who made up 90 percent of that province's 2 million inhabitants before the 1999 war, agree on the question of relations with Serbia—that rule by Belgrade is no longer an option. While Kosovo's Albanian population divides support among political parties, there are no apparent divisions over the consensus that independence from the Federal Republic of Yugoslavia is the endgame. Belgrade's influence in Kosovo is now restricted to the Serb regions or enclaves, with its unofficial capital in the city of Mitrovica. Claims at exerting jurisdiction over the entire province and the whole of its people are possible only because of the existence of UN Resolution 1244 and the United Nations' administration in the province.

In reality, Kosovar society has existed as a state within a state during the entire period of Milosevic's oppressive rule. Pacifist Kosovar leader Ibrahim Rugova presided over the "shadow state" institutions. Understanding how such a shadow state arose requires some very basic knowledge of Kosovar society. With its insular nature and ancient tradition of dealing with hostile intruders by turning inward, the Albanian community in Kosovo met the repression of the Milosevic years by engaging in this time-honored method. While the Belgrade-backed authorities, notably the police, conducted official business marked by armed repression, Kosovars established a fully functioning and parallel system of state administration that accounted for the needs of citizens. A range of services was provided, including education with health care, the cost of which were met, as far as was possible, by a taxation system. Nonviolence and strict observance of passive resistance made up Rugova's approach. At least until recently, the call for independence was not on the agenda for Rugova's party, the Democratic League of Kosova (LDK).

Rugova's chief political rival, Hashim Thaci, by contrast, advocated violent means to end the Milosevic dictatorship and led the Kosovo Liberation Army (KLA). His main affiliation now is with a political faction, the Democratic Party of Kosova. With municipal elections held on 28 October 2000, Rugova's party swept into office with a vengeance, gaining some 60 percent of the ballots cast.[22] While opinions differ over tactics, there is no difference between the Kosovar leadership over the independence question. As one Western journalist observed after the Kosovo elections, Kosovar Albanians would demand their own state even if Mother Theresa were in charge in Serbia.[23] Even though the KLA has been called upon to disarm, estimates suggest that the organization has opted instead to follow a familiar Balkan pattern and go underground, posing the risk that it may be a factor in future Balkan upheavals.

An organization taking up the radical tactics of the KLA calls itself the Liberation Army of Presovo, Medvedja, and Bujanovac (UCPMB). Its goal is to sever the Presevo valley, home to an estimated eighty thousand ethnic Albanians, from Belgrade, and to unite with Kosovo. That the organization is likely to win no sympathy from the international community has been made clear by constant reference in Western media to UCPMB as guerrilla forces. Kostunica has made repeated calls for the Kumanovo Agreements, defining Serbia's demilitarized zone with Kosovo, to be revised to allow the Yugoslav Army to confront the UCPMB. While resisting those demands for months, Western diplomats express an understanding of Belgrade's situation. While on a visit to Sarajevo on 21 December 2000, NATO secretary-general Lord Robertson recognized that "the Serb government is frustrated by what's happening in the safety zone . . . and so am I." Robertson urged restraint for Belgrade, leaving the door open to cooperation.[24] By mid-March 2001, Serbian forces were allowed to return to the demilitarized zone, albeit with some constraints on force levels; in effect, to control Kosovar Albanian violence, NATO turned to the Serbs.

The Montenegrin challenge to FRY stability can also be addressed quickly. While Milosevic threatened regional security, one way of stemming Serbian expansionism involved supporting democratic alternatives to the dictatorship. Montenegrin president Milo Djukanovic had been an opponent of Milosevic since 1995, and eventually Montenegrin independence became a supportable option. With Milosevic gone, international backing for Djukanovic's calls for independence have evaporated. That Djukanovic may be losing vital support, reducing the likely impact of this threat, is evidenced by two developments. On the one hand, his own governing coalition has shown signs of tearing apart. On 28 December 2000 Vice President of the People's Party Predrag Popovic said his party was withdrawing its support from the government. He stressed his organization would not stipulate that the international community "recognize the independence of Montenegro" as a condition for talks with Serbia, and "blamed Djukanovic" for pressing such "unacceptable" demands.[25] Such a point of view is grounded in the reality that perhaps up to 50 percent of Montenegrins either identify themselves as Serbs or feel a kinship with Serbia. In addition, some governments, specifically the Italian, appear to be tiring of Montenegrin black market activities, and thus are now publicly condemning the smuggling traffic and considering indictments of war criminals in lieu of entertaining discussions of Montenegrin independence. Increasingly and with less ambiguity, as was evidenced in a 22 January 2001 *Reuters* report, foreign governments are showing less tolerance for Montenegrin independence moves:

> The European Union openly sided with Serbia on Monday in its dispute with its sister republic Montenegro over whether its tiny neighbor should remain in the Yugoslav federation or become virtually independent. Foreign ministers of the fifteen-member EU, hold-

ing their first regular monthly meeting of the year in Brussels, said Serbia and Montenegro must decide on a new constitutional arrangement "within an overall federal framework."[26]

The question that remains open at this point is whether or not the current "democratic" authorities will be able to cling in practice to democratic methods. In mid-January 2001, Kostunica was caught partaking in the dubious—seemingly conspiring with the indicted former president, Slobodan Milosevic. Over the weekend of 13–14 January 2001, the two men met discreetly.[27] Djindjic claimed he knew nothing about the encounter and said he had to learn about it over the radio, the way everyone else did. The get-together triggered a wave of speculation about Kostunica's motives. Much centers on the suspicion that the current president was attempting to make a deal with his predecessor whereby the indicted Milosevic would not be extradited to The Hague to face war crimes charges, but would be tried in Serbia for corruption. Alternatively, another analysis had Kostunica working on a fallback strategy involving allowing Milosevic to disappear into exile. Proponents say the evidence lay in the fact that Milosevic's wife, just before the Milosevic-Kostunica meeting, flew to Moscow and then Baku, to be with their son Marko. Whatever the case, Kostunica has used the opportunity to articulate disdain for The Hague tribunal and the war crimes trial process, saying that he would refuse to meet with Chief Prosecutor Carla del Ponte when she arrived in Belgrade on 23 January 2000.[28] This prompted ultranationalists to cheer Kostunica.[29] The same ultranationalists, however, were unable to counter heavy international pressure, including economic leverage, that ultimately forced the new Belgrade government to produce the former dictator for the tribunal.

Capacities

Serbia's most important capacity or tool is, simply, its crop of new politicians. They are softening Serbia's image in the Western media.

Djindjic has completed the transformation to progressive activist. Whereas mass market dailies and weeklies until only recently thrived on the image of warmongering Butcher of the Balkans, now the focus is on the sharply dressed man. Djindjic, the "radical chic" is "tall and elegantly attired . . . [and] looks different from the gauche, lumpy apparatchiks who surrounded Slobo."[30] But, in case of doubt that style also translates into substance, the media add that much in Djindjic's past prepared him for a break with old ways. From the start, he was different, and caused the old order alarm: He "has a doctorate in philosophy. During Tito's iron rule, his student activism led to his arrest." He also boasts a proven track record since "Insiders credit him with fine-tuning the street strategy that dumped Milosevic." He is depicted as just what Serbia needs right now. As visionary, "Djindjic says he wants Serbia to have a transparent political system—a necessity for joining Europe's economy."[31]

For his part, Kostunica seems to be well aware of how much mileage he gets with the international community simply because he is not Milosevic. Those looking to Kostunica as the genuine reformer who will begin the process of healing and of bringing to justice those responsible for the war may have to content themselves with disappointment. While progress on many counts has been made in neighboring Croatia (see Jed Snyder's chapter on Croatia in this volume), Kostunica harkens back to Milosevic's approach. First, he continues to signal there will be no unilateral apologies for war crimes committed by ethnic Serbs, clinging to the line that each ethnic group must accept a share of the blame.[32] Moreover, he reminds international audiences of the alleged fact that regional political stability will depend in large measure on his good will. In an interview aired on the BBC on 18 January 2001, he stressed that the Dayton Peace Accord lacked legality, being signed by the president of Serbia (and not FRY) and never having been ratified by the federal Yugoslav parliament, thereby claiming its acceptance by his government was voluntary.[33] Kostunica has, however, gone on record saying that Dayton is "a constitution" under which "the FRY has to live."[34]

When asked about war criminals and war crimes, Kostunica makes several points. First, the arrest or detention of war criminals is not the responsibility of the FRY president. There are, he stresses, ministries and bureaucracies designed for that. Second, he continues to resist unequivocal cooperation with The Hague. While professing his desire to establish a working relationship with the International Criminal Tribunal, he betrays the belief that in his opinion the body is little more than a political weapon representing interests that undermine Yugoslavia. To be taken seriously in Kostunica's office, the tribunal would have to bring charges against the international community for crimes against the FRY. As one recent report notes: "I thought about just not receiving [Chief Prosecutor Carla del Ponte on 23 January 2001] because I am very busy. Yet there are a great many things that just made me change my mind," Kostunica said at a regular press conference. He said the information about the effects of depleted uranium ammunition (used by NATO air forces while bombing Serbia and targets in Kosovo) on the health of the public had influenced his change of mind. Further, according to the new Serbian president, his mind had been changed by new information on the murder of ethnic Albanians in the Kosovo village of Racak that "served as blackmail at Rambouillet [peace talks] and later as one of the reasons [justifications] for the bombing of Yugoslavia."[35]

Djindjic, meanwhile, also continues to demonstrate an unwillingness to break entirely with Milosevic's old ways, or at the very least with the dictator's erstwhile allies. To be sure, over the past few years Djindjic has been an outspoken Milosevic critic. Yet most recently he lobbied successfully behind Dusan Mihajlovic's bid to become Serbia's new minister in charge of the republic's police forces.

Mihajlovic, leader of a small political party called New Democracy (ND) that joined the Democratic Opposition of Serbia (DOS), had for years supported Milosevic's Socialist Party of Serbia in the Serbian parliament.[36] ND's unquestioning support for the Socialists enabled Milosevic to wield total control over a de facto majority government.[37] ND was among the parties that defended the regime most strenuously during the NATO air campaign. During bombing over Easter weekend 1999, ND bought a full-page ad in a major Belgrade daily condemning NATO and the West with the words, superimposed over a picture of an Easter egg: "They believe in BOMBS, we believe in God!"[38] Even after parting ways with the SPS, and spending time in the political wilderness, Mihajlovic for some time refused to say that cooperation with the Socialists and Milosevic was at the very least a tactical mistake. Instead, Mihajlovic became defensive about his years in government, as one of his public statements near the end of 1998 made clear: "I have no contact with any functionaries of the SPS, but

I have many, many friends among the party rank-and-file. And I can only say that in the past I never met or worked with any SPS functionary who supported the idea of co-operating with the Radicals. . . . I can say that the SPS is a victim itself, and the biggest political loser because its working with Seselj cost it [voters]."[39]

The seventy-eight-day war with NATO, which began on 24 March 1999, saw little damage done to the FRY's fighting capacity. Going into the conflict, Belgrade controlled Europe's sixth-largest army. One report noted that "In recent decades, Yugoslavia has built a hodgepodge of arms from the Soviet Union and the United States, and from arms factories." The same document, citing data and experts from *Jane's Defense Weekly*, concluded the overall letter grade the country's air defenses warranted was "a C-plus." It contained "1,850 anti-aircraft artillery pieces. . . . The deadliest weapons are the sixty radar-guided SA6 anti-aircraft missiles, which are networked with SA2 surface-to-air missiles, plus radars and command-and-control centers." The army also used Russian-produced T-72 tanks and was estimated to be 114,000-strong, with 20,000 men in Kosovo at the time the war broke out and another 20,000 near Serbia's border with Kosovo.[40]

After nearly five weeks of fighting, some observers noted that NATO had done very little to degrade Yugoslavia's arsenal. Paul Richter of the *Los Angeles Times* reported that the country "still has 80 percent to 90 percent of its tanks, 75 percent of its most sophisticated surface-to-air missiles and 60 percent of its MiG fighter planes, according to official estimates released over the past week. . . . Yugoslav troops in Kosovo still have nearly one-half of their resupply capacity, the Pentagon estimated last week, and have been able to maintain—or perhaps even expand— the force of 40,000 they had when the bombing began on March 24."[41]

Early figures may, in fact, have even overestimated the damage inflicted. A combination of NATO tactics, the ground strategy of attacking Kosovo villages when pilot visibility was reduced, and the effective use of dummy targets all contributed to the Serbian fighting forces emerging relatively unscathed. As one report noted:

In its first days, the bombing campaign struck military targets including air defense and communications installations. Though the bombing succeeded in completely grounding the Yugoslav air force it did not succeed in destroying its air defense, even though this was seriously damaged by the end of the war. NATO pilots were ordered to fly at altitudes above 15,000 feet to avoid the continuing threat of Yugoslav air defense systems. . . . The large number of decoy targets hit suggests that pilots were not able to make positive visual identification before attacking. . . . NATO attacks in Kosovo did relatively little damage to FRY ground forces. In spite of the bombing, the FRY military forces attacked the KLA rather successfully throughout Kosovo.[42]

But the real question is how trustworthy are Yugoslavia's forces. There is wide disagreement about how many troops would remain loyal to Belgrade, or how many would defect to the Montenegrin side in case of a showdown between federal authorities and Podgorica. With the new diplomatic climate and the chances of any clashes in 2001 seriously reduced if not eliminated, such issues are best consigned to the realm of speculation.

Policy Innovations

A recent historical perspective enables a view as to what may have been a critical policy innovation on Milosevic's part. These were, perhaps, not by him alone, but rather also by those around him who collectively supported the regime. While Montenegro and Kosovo posed the greatest threat to the territorial integrity of the FRY throughout 2000, Milosevic, hindsight now informs, not only left these issues unaddressed, but also swept them out of sight. Instead, what became the focal point of his attention was the threat posed by the domestic Serbian opposition. To be sure, the pro-Milosevic media kept alive the specter of a defenseless, innocent Serbia targeted by the international powers. No effort was spared to paint internal opposition, especially the student *Otpor* movement, as just the tip of a giant conspiracy aimed at destroying Serbia's statehood. Whether this focus on internal threats was conscious policy, or merely something that blind luck produced, is highly debatable. At minimum, Milosevic's preoccupation with domestic Serb opponents may have stopped him from starting any further wars before he left office.

On 4 May 2000, military officials made public warnings that mass demonstrations of a coercive nature would meet zero tolerance. Specifically,
"threats" against Milosevic, whether against "his person" or the "office of
the presidency," would prompt a reaction.[43] The clampdown against *Otpor*
and the renewed attack on independent media triggered the usual condem-
nation from opposition politicians, but in 2000 a growing number of public
figures increasingly attributed Milosevic's behavior to his loss of ability to
engineer political events. On 18 May 2000, for example, *Vesti* reported that
Ivan Stambolic, speaking in Nis, said that Milosevic grew even more knee-
jerk as Serbia slid further into a domestic political vacuum. Was the Army,
then, acting to keep tempers from flaring and to calm public disaffection
that could have erupted?

Evidence from just days before the presidential vote in 2000 suggests
the military was preparing to take a hard-line approach. Its representatives
doled out familiar harsh rhetoric. Speaking on TV Montenegro on 21 September 2000, Chief of Staff General Pavkovic said the Army was prepared
to defend national sovereignty. In a statement seen as a declaration that
an opposition win would represent a Western intervention into domestic
FRY politics, the general declared that "a nation cannot be free which is
colonized and enslaved." That the Army ultimately accepted Kostunica's
win proves that, as an institution, its defense of Milosevic was not regardless
of costs.

While the opposition prepared demonstrations against the regime,
quieter events unfolded that ultimately catapulted Kostunica from obscurity
to the forefront of public life. On 6 July 2000 the Yugoslav parliament
passed three sweeping amendments to the Yugoslav constitution, changing
how federal presidents were elected, how they served, and what powers
they could exercise. Until that point, the term of the federal executive was
limited to one four-year term. Election was indirect, through the parliament.
Henceforth, voters were to pick their presidents directly, and a tenure
of two four-year terms was now legal and possible. Thus, Montenegro's
influence in deciding the executive was greatly diminished. The small
republic's influence in national politics also decreased by changes that had
members of the upper house elected by popular vote rather than in equal
number by the Serbian and Montenegrin legislatures. That the president,

under the terms of the new constitution, could also dismiss ministers at will had the potential to restrict Montenegrin input at the highest office.[44] Podgorica's parliament not only denounced these changes, but on 8 July 2000, by a vote of thirty-six to eighteen, the republic's legislature also condemned the constitutional revisions as not only "illegal and illegitimate" but as "a gross violation of Montenegrin rights" and "a destruction of [the FRY] constitutional order."[45]

While constitutional changes did not signal that Milosevic had abandoned his policy of resorting to force if that served his interests, they did provide the means for his stepping off the political stage. As far back as late 1998, he was making statements in public that might have been intended as clues to his intentions. Speaking to the *Washington Post* in December of that year, he noted that, while he might not withdraw from public life, he would consider leaving public office.[46]

In 1999, and during the NATO air campaign, the pro-Milosevic media began profiling a relatively minor political figure—perhaps telegraphing that if not Milosevic personally, then his supporters surely would not mind seeing that person play a more substantial political role. The individual in question was Vojislav Kostunica, then known, if at all, for his sincere commitment to Serbian nationalism, and for leading the minor Democratic Party of Serbia (DSS). One report filed by the International Crisis Group (ICG) in late June 1999 detected an emerging phenomenon, observing: "[T]he electorate is now being urged to consider the alternative [to Seselj]— Vojislav Kostunica and his Democratic Party of Serbia. Western observers ought not to be surprised if upcoming elections give the DSS a marked boost."[47]

Was Milosevic, even back in 1999, calculating or perhaps even gambling that Kostunica would one day be a possible successor acceptable to himself, the Serbian electorate, and the international community? A profile of Kostunica offers potential clues. Again, turning to the ICG archives, one sees this:

Even less flamboyant politicians, such as Vojislav Kostunica, leader of the nationalist Democratic Party of Serbia (DSS), held steadfast to his ultra-nationalist, defiant posturing. For many years, Kostunica cultivated the image of a moderate standing in contrast to the extremist policies cluttering the political landscape. In truth, Kostunica's long-held views about the possibility of co-operating with ultra-nationalists and including them in governing coalitions betrayed his underlying extremism, although his dirth of charisma actually masks the excesses of his ideology, lulling some observers into the belief that he may be a genuine democratic alternative. While his phrases were far less antagonistic than Arkan's and even a shade more subdued than Seselj's, Kostunica made it clear on the eve of the peace breakthrough that his sympathies lay with the regime. According to the DSS, it was Washington that was aiming to destabilize the peace process, and it was "America that was against peace." He claimed that the indictment of members of the FRY and Serbia's top leadership was an effort to derail a negotiated settlement to the Kosovo crisis and that "The Hague tribunal is a political, and not legal instrument. . . ." With the newfound media attention gracing the DSS and Kostunica, it is tempting to speculate that Milosevic may have plans for the nationalist leader.[48]

Some firmer evidence surfaced well before the 24 September 2000 elections that Milosevic may have reconciled himself to life outside politics. On 4 September 2000, the daily *Oslobodjenje* in neighboring Bosnia and Herzegovina cited the *Sunday Times* when it reported that the FRY dictator, rather than plotting to keep power, was busy building a bunker. There he would hide if attempts were made to arrest him in the eventuality of an electoral defeat, the story explained. Moreover, on that same day, another Sarajevo daily, *Vecernje novine*, quoted an independent journalist working in the Republika Srpska, and now Kostunica's media affairs adviser in Belgrade, regarding the September 2000 elections. This journalist, Aleksandar Tijanic, said that Kostunica was all but assured victory: "The people simply want a normal state, normal government, and a normal leader." Before that, Tijanic was only optimistic about Kostunica's fortunes. Still more evidence, or a foreshadowing, of Milosevic's fall came through in remarks made by BiH foreign minister, Jadranko Prlic, days before polling. Prlic briefly hinted he could envision the normalization of relations with the FRY in the near future. He added the opposition in Serbia was prepared for improved ties, but declined to be specific about the factors fuelling his optimism.[49]

In reality, for someone who was an international pariah, Milosevic somehow never failed to engage the outside world. Back on 7 April 2000 reports circulated that Australian officials were taking much heat for stating openly that the intent was to resume relations with Belgrade. Reacting, Canberra's foreign affairs representatives said the decision to name an ambassador to Belgrade was prompted by several factors, including the reality that a significant number of Serbs lived in Australia and that Canberra worked on the principle of recognizing states, not governments.[50] Only days later, London's the *Sunday Times* reported that Washington, which had been among the most disparaging of Australia, was itself engaging in "bargaining" in order to open channels to the FRY. According to the report, the State Department felt in the dark about goings on in Serbia and needed to communicate. The same account added that the way to reestablishing dialogue had been opened by Russia and Greece, governments that never acceded to the notion of isolating the FRY.[51] Official State Department sources denied the account. It is tempting to speculate that deals aimed at an exit strategy for the dictator were discussed as early as April 2000.

Future Prospects

Most of this chapter has concentrated on diplomatic and political developments in FRY in the year 2000. This is necessary, because Serbia's security prospects in this past year have been defined by the diplomatic and political. While Balkan relations are fragile at best, 2002 is likely to be a year in which diplomacy will triumph over violence. This is far from saying that Balkan wars are a thing of the past for all time, or that peace has been achieved in our time. Clashes in Macedonia that escalated sharply as spring approached in 2001 (see Biljana Vankovska's chapter in this volume) suggest the ongoing potential for regional turmoil.

As has been hinted obliquely throughout this chapter, there are three, at times certainly not mutually exclusive, scenarios that give insight into how the FRY may evolve. Each has an impact on whether regional stability and an absence of war, if not peace, can be achieved. First, Kostunica can now count on international support while trying to stabilize FRY's existing borders. In turn, he will be expected to make good on such assurances as respecting the territorial integrity of neighboring states, particularly Bosnia, and vowing that Belgrade's intentions are not to test points of regional instability. Svilanovic has signaled that Belgrade can live with the idea of fellow Serbs living outside the FRY's borders, in the Republika Srpska (RS). However, the Kostunica government expects to have some influence in the RS, which they argue the "special relations" clause in the Dayton Peace Accord allows. That the international community conditioned good relations and assistance on additional commitments, including Belgrade's turning over Milosevic to The Hague tribunal, forced the new government to cooperate. Further cooperation, however, may be difficult to ensure.

Another scenario, in the short term an unlikely one, sees Kostunica becoming a president without a country and thus an office. Tensions between Serbia, Montenegro, and Kosovo can be buried for a while, but a profound, long-lasting resolution to various grievances will take effort and time. For his part, Kostunica may even harbor the desire that the Yugoslav state disappear, as it represents a tie to a socialist legacy that is no doubt abhorrent to the new president. The question for him may be whether or not a new state, a Serbia-Montenegro, for instance, may peacefully arise, phoenix-like, from the ruins.

If internal tensions rise and hit the boiling point within the next year, FRY may undergo rapid dissolution, reigniting regional instability. At present, international diplomatic capital continues to be invested in Kostunica and the well-being of his government, suggesting that pressure is being applied behind the scenes on leading figures in Pristina and Podgorica to at the very least keep political waves to a minimum. The outstanding question is whether or not the collapse, should there be one, can be contained. Can the effects from an imploding FRY be minimized or eliminated, so as not to trigger other regional demands for a redrawing of the broader Balkan map? At the very least, diplomatic concerns from Greece and Albania will likely sound should FRY cease to exist. And, even if the implosion is contained, can it be confined only to the political? Some observers, including President Djukanovic's American economics adviser, Professor Steve

Hanke, see the positive in a friendly or "democratic" parting of the ways, because that would allow each of the emerging states to concentrate on the critical problems of internal reform.[52] Yet, if a century of Balkan history can function as any indicator, any hope of an amicable divorce is naive. Montenegrin elections in spring 2001, which led to a narrow victory for Djukanovic's party and its independence allies (together about 53 percent of the vote), was too close to give the Montenegrin leader new strength for a drive toward an independence referendum. The FRY's future is far from resolved, and the absence of a clear electoral mandate for either side (independence or a renegotiated linkage to Belgrade), leaves an uncertain future in 2001–2002.

A third scenario, linked to the second, accounts for the paramilitaries and gangsters who not only survived but also thrived under Milosevic's political umbrellas. That they have opted for the moment to retreat and go underground does not mean they have abandoned politics for good. As the Arkan assassination cited above suggests, a government in their hands would not shy away from rough justice. At worst, a system run by their authority would not only see Montenegro and Kosovo breaking away, but would also see the wholesale internal decay or collapse of Serbia's internal social and political framework. Resulting anarchy could make street murders a daily occurrence. In search of a cohesive identity and ideology, the tendency would be to turn back to the nationalism of a greater Serbia, prompting wholesale regional instability, impacting first and foremost on Bosnia and Herzegovina. That the police and military essentially stood by while Kostunica took office following the 24 September 2000 election, however, suggests this civil war scenario is the least likely of all, for the foreseeable future. That acquiescence demonstrated by the armed forces discloses a great deal of discipline, further betraying that Serbia is not yet if at all on the threshold of any internal institutional collapse.

The international community's mad dash to alleviate sanctions and recognize Kostunica's win demonstrates a willingness, for the time being, to welcome Serbia back into the community of nations and to prop up the FRY. If the strategy of the international community hinges on gaining guarantees of fundamental social, economic, and political reforms only well after the political changes are consolidated within Yugoslavia, it must also consider that subsequent or delayed efforts may meet with resistance from Belgrade. That resistance could be emboldened by international public opinion, which is now told that "NATO is on the run. It's not difficult to see why. The moral crusader against Serb barbarism wielded a sword made of depleted uranium, called DU for short. And as more and more evidence proves a terrible connection between DU weapons and an explosion of cancers and leukemia among thousands of civilians who were close to DU detonations, the sword now appears far more disturbing than the object of the crusade."[53]

Chronology

28 December 1999: Milosevic promotes nationalist military leaders. The move prompts fears that Belgrade is preparing for war with Montenegro.

13 January 2000: Milosevic supporters back anti-Djukanovic rally in Podgorica, adding to fears of coming conflict.

15 January 2000: Paramilitary leader Arkan slain in Belgrade. Some observers worry this is the first volley in what may trigger civil war in Serbia.

28 February 2000: Yugoslav Army beefs up presence in Montenegro, along Albanian border, raising fears of a violent showdown.

2 March 2000: General Vladimir Lazarevic makes a public statement, accusing NATO of supporting UCPMB in its bid to destabilize southern Serbia.

7 April 2000: Australia makes public its intention to reestablish relations with Belgrade.

27 April 2000: Nationalist leader Vojislav Seselj makes a press conference vow to return to building a greater Serbia, when conditions permit and the time is ripe.

4 May 2000: Yugoslav Army issues provocative declaration. Delivered is the message that public protests of a threatening nature will not be tolerated and that no attacks on Milosevic's person or office will go unpunished.

18 May 2000: *Vesti* reports that Ivan Stambolic, Milosevic's mentor during the socialist period, delivers scathing remarks about his protege while speaking in Nis. Stambolic reportedly claims repression in Serbia is growing because the state plunges ever deeper into a political vacuum.

22 May 2000: Thaci reelected leader of his party in Kosovo.

6 July 2000: The Yugoslav constitution is amended, allowing Milosevic to seek a popular mandate to stay as FRY president for up to another two terms.

8 July 2000: Montenegrin legislature condemns changes to the FRY constitution, stressing that the unilateral move is an "illegitimate" and "illegal" usurpation of the small republic's authority.

15 August 2000: DOS goes public with its election platform, describing it as a "contract" with the electorate. Presidential elections are slated for 24 September 2000.

25 August 2000: Stambolic is kidnapped near his house while jogging.

24 September 2000: FRY presidential elections held. Kostunica scores first-round win, but for nearly two weeks tensions rise as Milosevic wavers on recognizing the returns.

25 September 2000: *Montena-fax* reports that just under 25 percent of eligible voters in Montenegro participated in the poll. The Montenegrin government, refusing to recognize the legality of the constitutional changes, had called for a boycott on election day.

29 September 2000: General strike and mass rallies aiming to pressure Milosevic into recognizing the inevitable get under way. Kolubara miners play a key role.

1 October 2000: The *Observer* reports that deals to have Milosevic evade prosecution in exchange for his stepping out of power had been entertained by international diplomats.

5 October 2000: Milosevic steps down. Kostunica becomes the first democratically elected president of the Federal Republic of Yugoslavia. He is sworn in two days later.

28 October 2000: Rugova's moderate party wins landslide victory in Kosovo local elections, securing roughly 60 percent of the total vote.

27 November 2000: On this date, Serbia is welcomed back into the OSCE. While in Vienna for the occasion, Kostunica snubs U.S. secretary of state Albright, prompting one Washington official to call the president "unnecessarily rude."

11 December 2000: Ibrahim Rugova tells Germany's *Der Spiegel* that Kosovo is de facto independent.

15 December 2000: FRY and BiH establish diplomatic relations.

19 December 2000: News reports say Kostunica seeks a revision to the agreements ending the 1999 war with NATO. The FRY president seeks to reduce the demilitarized zone with Kosovo and allow the Yugoslav Army to deal with the threat posed by the UCPMB. While the international community does not agree, two days later NATO secretary-general Lord Robertson, while on a visit to Sarajevo, expresses an understanding of the problems Belgrade faces in southern Serbia.

23 December 2000: Serbian parliamentary elections held. DOS wins a landslide margin, destroying Milosevic's power base in the republic's parliament.

3 January 2001: News breaks in Western media about growing concern in the West, especially in Italy, about possible ill health effects of depleted uranium, used in some ordnance dropped over several Balkan countries, now thought to be posing harm to peacekeepers. The DU is blamed for a spate of cancer deaths. Within days, the news is headlining throughout Serbia. Kostunica seizes the issue, insisting the information helps to substantiate claims of "NATO war crimes."

16 January 2001: Radio-Television Serbia (RTS) opens an office in Zvecan, Kosovo. The action is an assertion of Belgrade's sovereignty over the province, but may be seen as potentially provocative by the province's mainly ethnic Albanian population.

19 January 2001: Kostunica makes first official visit to neighboring BiH. In Sarajevo, he makes public statements about cooperative relations and his commitment to Dayton and support for Dayton boundaries.

22 January 2001: EU foreign ministers call for Serbia and Montenegro to solve their problems "within an overall federal framework."

NOTES

1. Gillian Sandford, "Almost the Same Old Serbia," *Guardian*, 18 January 2001.

2. For further background on the 1990s, see Stan Markotich, "Serbia and Montenegro" in *Eurasian and Eastern European Security Yearbook 2000*, eds. Ustina Markus and Daniel N. Nelson (Washington, D.C.: Brassey's, 2000).

3. *Radio-television Serbia* and *Tanjug*, 28 December 1999.

4. *Politika*, 30 December 1999.

5. Author's notes from *Radio B 92* broadcast, 15 January 2000.

6. See coverage in *Blic*, 16 January 2000. Also author's notes from *Radio B 92* broadcast, 15 January 2000.

7. "Sanctions against the Federal Republic of Yugoslavia" (as of 10 October 2000), *ICG Balkans Briefing*, 10 October 2000. Available on the Internet at <http://www. crisisweb.org/projects/showreport.cfm?reportid=42> (accessed 19 November 2000).

8. European officials and members of parliament had called for a lifting of sanctions even before Kostunica's actual victory. Author's notes, *Deutsche Welle* broadcast, 26 September 2000.

9. For a comprehensive listing of sanctions against the FRY, see: "Sanctions against the Federal Republic of Yugoslavia" (as of 10 October 2000).

10. *Jutarnje novine*, 20–21 January 2001.

11 Supporting Kostunica was the Democratic Opposition of Serbia, or DOS. This organization consists of eighteen opposition parties, dominated by Zoran Djindjic's Democratic Party (DS) and Kostunica's own Democratic Party of Serbia (DSS).

12. Radio Free Europe/Radio Liberty (RFE/RL) South Slavic Service, 26 September 2000.

13. This is not to say that the police were entirely passive. Some protesters were detained, and units resorted to removing some of the demonstrators' barricades by force. Singled out as a target by the state judiciary were the strikers at the Kolubara mine. Many workers at that facility, as well as student activists, were rumored to have been named in arrest warrants. A wave of detentions occurred on 3 October 2000 just days before Milosevic's ouster. See RFE/RL South Slavic Service, 3 October 2000. That the workers played a pivotal role in carrying public sentiment is undeniable. After their pivotal involvement in organizing a general strike in the last three days of September and first few days of October, the Kolubara miners came to the attention of FRY chief of the General Staff Nebojsa Pavkovic, who appealed to the workers to end their job action.

14. Radio-television Serbia, 27 December 2000.

15. *Beta*, 28 December 2000. See also Stan Markotich, "Special Relations," *Independent Media Commission (IMC) Briefing Paper*, no. 55, 30 December 2000, available on the Internet at <http://www.imcbih.org> (accessed 18 January 2001).

16. Exclusive interview with Svilanovic in *Dnevni avaz*, 15 December 2000. It was on this very same date that BiH and FRY established diplomatic relations.

17. Cited in "Back to the Future: Milosevic Prepares for Life after Kosovo," *ICG Report*, 28 June 1999. Available on the Internet at <http://212/212/165/2/ICGold/projects/kosovo/reports/kos25main.htm> (accessed 20 December 2000).

18. A critical comment on the West's initial euphoria about the 5 October 2000 events and Kostunica's installation as president was Daniel N. Nelson, "Don't Confuse the Belgrade Uprising with Democracy," Tirana *Albania*, 22 October 2000.

19. On this point, see Stan Markotich, "Serbia: Extremism from the Top and a Blurring of Right into Left," in *The Politics of the Extreme Right: From the Margins to the Mainstream*, ed. Paul Hainsworth (London: Pinter, 2000), 268–86. See also Markotich, "Extremism in Serbia," RFE/RL Research Report, no. 16, 22 April 1994.

20. *SRNA*, 27 April 2000.

21. *SRNA*, 10 April 2000.

22. RFE/RL South Slavic Service (in Albanian), 29 October 2000.

23. See column by Steven Erlanger in *International Herald Tribune*, 30 October 2000.

24. Cited in RFE/RL Newsline, 22 December 2000.

25. *Beta* and *Montena-fax*, 28 December 2000.

26. *Reuters*, 22 January 2001.

27. See *Radio B 92*, 14 and 15 January 2001. The Kostunica-Milosevic meeting became grist for the media in neighboring Bosnia and Herzegovina where much of the concern was focused on how BiH-FRY relations and Balkan stability might be impacted if Kostunica failed to honor The Hague indictment by working out a deal with Milosevic. See, for example, Sarajevo's *Oslobodjenje*, 16 January 2001. For his part, Kostunica described the meeting as brief, a matter of protocol, and an "uncomfortable" affair. He has flatly denied that any "deals" with Milosevic were discussed, stating that Western officials were much more interested in the question of deals and Milosevic than he was. See "Hardtalk" on *BBC World*, 18 January 2001.

28. *Beta* and *Tanjug*, 15 January 2001.

29. See, for example, *Truth in Media's GLOBAL WATCH Bulletin 2001*, 1–3, 16 January 2001.

30. See "Serbia's New Man: A TIME Field Guide," in *Time*, 8 January 2001.

31. Ibid.

32. (Croatia) *Republika*, 19 January 2001.

33. "Hardtalk" on *BBC World*, 18 January 2001.

34. *Dnevni avaz*, 18 January 2001.

35. *Beta*, 18 January 2001.

36. *Institute for War and Peace Reporting (IWPR) Balkan Crisis Report*, no. 210, 17 January 2001.

37. Serbian parliamentary elections took place in December 1993. The SPS emerged with 123 of a possible 250 seats. With the backing of six ND deputies, the government functioned for nearly four years.

38. *Vecernje novosti*, 10 April 1999.

39. *Danas*, 26–27 December 1998.

40. These citations and data are contained in Richard Parker, "Yugoslav Force's Capacity a Concern for Pentagon," *Detroit Free Press*, 23 March 1999.

41. "Yugoslavia's War Machine Largely Unhurt," available on the Internet at <http://seattletimes.nwsource.com/news/nation-world/html98/stri 19990429.html> (accessed 27 December 2000).

42. Cited in "International War Supervenes, March 1998 [sic]–June 1999," *Independent International Commission on Kosovo*, available on the Internet at <http://www.kosovocommission.org/reports/7-supervenes.html> (accessed 17 January 2001).

43. *Radio B92*, 4 May 2000.

44. See *Radio B92*, 6 July 2000. See also RFE/RL Newsline, 7 July 2000.

45. *Montena-fax*, 8 July 2000.

46. Cited in *Nedeljni telegraf*, 16 December 1998.

47. "Back to the Future."

48. Ibid.

49. See interview with Jadranko Prlic in Sarajevo's *Dnevni avaz*, 21 September 2000.

50. *Reuters*, 7 April 2000.

51. *Sunday Times*, 9 April 2000.

52. RFE/RL Newsline, 18 January 2001.

53. *Independent*, 17 January 2001. The piece was authored by British commentator Robert Fisk. The counterclaim, bolstered by the UNEP's findings, suggests that the risks of exposure to dangerous levels of uranium in Kosovo has been very low. See UNEP's fact sheet at <http://www.who.int/inf-fs/en/fact257.html> (accessed 1 February 2001).

20 ◆ Slovenia: West in the Direction of Brussels

Ivan Hostnik

Background

In June of 1991, in defiance of dire warnings from the international community, Slovenia, the small Alpine northern part of former Yugoslavia, declared independence.[1] In so doing, its people and leadership embarked on a path that has brought Slovenia prosperity, unchallenged sovereignty over its own territory, and a prospect of becoming a Central European centerpiece in the vanguard of regional economic and security developments.

Slovenia's successful emergence as an independent state out of the aftermath of a dissolved Yugoslav socialist federation was not a foregone conclusion at the time. Before Slovenia's sovereignty could be confirmed, Yugoslav Air Force jets would strafe its borders and threaten to blow up a nuclear power plant, armed skirmishes would be fought for at least ten fateful days, and the international community would turn its back on Slovenia's democratic resistance. At the beginning of the new millennium, in the year 2001, it is only too easy to lose sight of this fragility that characterized Central and East European independence movements, like Slovenia's. It is easy to forget the utter uncertainty in which they were compelled to exist.

The Republic of Slovenia would not have gained independence in 1991 without the dramatic democratic turnaround in the eastern half of Europe that started in the late 1980s. During the 1990s, the region underwent dramatic change, which greatly affected Slovenia's geopolitical position in four critical ways.

In the mid and late 1980s, and at the very beginning of 1990s while still a republic of the former Yugoslavia, two different, but interwoven and complementary processes were taking place in Slovenia. First, it underwent a process of achieving independence from the common Yugoslav state on the basis of the right of self-determination of nations. Equally important, Slovenians were changing fundamental social relations, that is, the transition from a socialist system to one of political pluralism and market economics.

In the end, Slovenia maintained democracy and sovereignty thanks to several factors. It was geographically distant from Belgrade, the dissemina-tor of destabilization in the former Yugoslavia. Its population was homoge-nous and had become accustomed to struggle in order to preserve its distinctive cultural, ethnic, and political identity. In fact, Slovenia existed long before the turmoil of 1991. For over seventy years, it was a part of Yugoslavia, but before then it belonged to the Austro-Hungarian Empire. Strong cultural and historical tides with Central Europe were never broken. And it was fortunate enough to be led by a brave, resourceful, and agile political elite that led a successful resistance and provided the intellectual underpinnings for the establishment of a new state.

The unraveling of the former Yugoslavia could be said to have begun in Slovenia. Yugoslav Army actions against Slovenians in 1991 were only a brief curtain raiser for the horrific warfare Belgrade would inflict just a few years later on Croatia and Bosnia and Herzegovina (further discussed in this volume's chapters on those countries). It was in Slovenia also that the international community first tested its shallow and feckless policies toward the Balkans, only to refine these stances in the later mismanagement of Serbian aggression in Croatia and Bosnia.

According to superficial analyses, Slovenia actually carries the stigma of having consciously started the dissolution of the former Yugoslavia. It was as if Slovenian leadership and Serbian dictator Slobodan Milosevic had entered into some unholy agreement to enclavize Slovenia, allowing it to bolt from the federation, while leaving the rest of the former federation to the mercy of the winds of war. Such an analysis defies the facts on the ground and, more important, represents a grave injustice to the effective political, intellectual, and paramilitary resistance Slovenia mounted—against formidable odds—to counter aggression and preserve its way of life.

Certainly, according to cultural stereotypes developed in certain parts of the former Yugoslavia, the Slovenes were not supposed to fight or to resist. They were perceived as "farmers, merchants, businessmen, and skiers." Historically, they had no national military tradition and no strong nationalist fervor. In the end, however, the resistance these "farmers, merchants, businessmen, and skiers" were to organize would defy a dictatorship that stood down the entire international community for years afterward; would defeat, or elude actually, one of the largest armies in Europe; and would set the stage for the successful democratization and "etatization" of peoples—the granting and recognition of sovereignty—throughout southeast Europe.

Rather than offering support and assistance to the Slovenian resistance, the United States and the other states of the West were united in a policy of isolating this movement (with an arms embargo declared in 1996), refusing to recognize its newly emerged state institutions, and encouraging it to appease Serbian demands. U.S. and other Western statesmen were frequent visitors to the region, as they actively discouraged Slovenia, Croatia, Bosnia, and other Yugoslav republics from declaring independence. Luxembourg Prime Minister Jacques Poos—then head of a three-person European Union (EU) triumvirate trying to encourage a negotiated solution—met with Slovenia's President Milan Kucan in an attempt to persuade Slovenia that it was too small to be a viable state. This message from the head of government of a state with a population of some *400,000* must have been met with some puzzlement, if not outright amusement, by President Kucan, leader of 2 million Slovenes. Later, then U.S. Secretary of State James Baker told Kucan that even Baker's children would not extend to Kucan's children recognition of an independent Slovenia.[2] (Baker himself announced U.S. official recognition, a complete turnabout, less than one year later.) During 1992, the European Union and later the United States recognized Slovenia and Croatia. The United States also extended recognition to Bosnia, an addendum that was to have historic consequences. By this time, all-out war had broken out in both Croatia and Bosnia, and Slovenia was largely allowed to develop and consolidate its state institutions relatively divorced from the conflict raging to its south.

Uncertainty about international intentions in the region, concern about the fragility of its own newly minted independence, and continuing anxiety about the long-term plans of Belgrade were all factors that made up the political consciousness of Slovenia throughout the early 1990s. As a result, Slovenia strove to highlight its Central European as opposed to southeast European traditions. When UN peacemakers were searching for a base for operations in Croatia, for example, they were forced to pass over Slovenia— eventually establishing in Bosnia—partly because the Slovenes were horrified that such a mission would, at worst, drag them into the warfare, or, at least, fortify the identification they were trying to escape of being part of the Yugoslav crisis.

While individual figures, notably Kucan, cultivated strong relationships with dissident personalities in other parts of former Yugoslavia, few of these contacts received attention or appreciation among the Slovenian public. In addition, there was a deep personal mistrust between Kucan and Milosevic that had certainly gained impetus when Kucan led his Slovenian delegation on a walkout of what would be the Yugoslav Communist Party's final federal meeting in Belgrade in January 1990.

Throughout the 1990s, the commerce-minded Slovenians frantically reshaped their economy to accommodate their country's new position. Slovenia had been a veritable "export engine" of the former Yugoslavia. In the days of the federation, fully 70 percent of all its products had been marketed in other parts of Yugoslavia. Now, with the disappearance almost overnight of these outlets, an abrupt and major reorientation had to be forged. Within a few years, the statistics had been successfully reversed, and some 70 percent of Slovenian products were being exported to Western Europe.[3]

Overall, Slovenia has been successful in maintaining since 1993 an economic growth rate at an average annual rate of nearly 4 percent. In the year 2000, in fact, the growth rate was nearly 5 percent. Inflation is currently well under 10 percent per annum, while unemployment is also under 10 percent. Parliament is making strong progress in adopting new legislation in harmonization with the EU. Since 1996, Slovenia has had an association agreement with the EU and in October 1999 the EU issued a positive report on Slovenia's prospects for early (first tranche) membership.

Under its sharp-minded governor, Franc Arhar, the National Bank of Slovenia resisted international pressure to liberalize regulations on international capital flows. The National Bank limited inward portfolio investment and kept close control over cross-border movement of capital. These policies stifled competitiveness, but they also kept a lid on domestic inflation and allowed Slovenia to avoid the fate of the Czech Republic, where a more liberal regime resulted eventually in uncontrolled capital outflows.

As far as security attitudes were concerned, in the first half of the 1990s, Slovenes appeared to be actively considering two options. One was that of "armed neutrality," espoused by its neighbor to the north, Austria. The other was actively seeking membership in the North Atlantic Treaty Organization (NATO) alliance. With the demise of bipolarity in the European security environment throughout the 1990s, the "armed neutrality" option waned in significance. By the latter half of the 1990s, the only viable option for Slovenia was eventual NATO membership.

In many ways, in fact, the option of NATO membership reflected a historical continuity in the Slovenian people's security strategy over many centuries. In modern times, Slovenia had not existed as a separate state, but rather had traditionally sought to preserve its national identity within the security aegis of a larger and more powerful entity. For several centuries, this larger entity was the Austro-Hungarian Empire. After the demise of Austro-Hungary during World War I, this role was assumed and continued throughout most of the twentieth century by the Yugoslav state. But, with the dissolution of Yugoslavia in the early 1990s, a security vacuum resulted that was effectively filled by NATO, though more in the form of the Alliance's sporadic reactions to individual incidents of violence in the Balkans, than by design.

Opinion polls taken among the Slovenian public in the mid-1990s reflected this shift in thinking toward favoring NATO membership. In January 1995, the published results of perhaps the first authoritative poll in the newly independent state revealed that some 75 percent of Slovenes ranked "good relations with neighboring states" as the best means of achieving security. "Defense agreements with other states" was highlighted by 50 percent of respondents. No more than 40 percent said NATO membership was important for national security. And, only 30 percent or so believed that building up Slovenia's own domestic armed forces was an essential ingredient for national security.[4]

In similar polls, public support for government actions aimed at joining

NATO increased from about 45 percent in 1994 to nearly 64 percent by 1997.[5] This stand in contrast to many other Central European states, including—remarkably—some already in the Alliance, where public opinion is often weak in its support for government actions connected with NATO.

At the same time, the number of those who disagreed with this policy also rose, but only slightly. (See table below.) The most interesting point in these polls came out in the October-November 1997 survey based on an extended sample. This survey found that the proportion of public opinion, despite the lack of an invitation to join NATO in between (July 1997), remained nearly the same as in March 1997, when pro-NATO public and political euphoria was at its peak. The percentage of supporters was around 9 percent lower than in March 1997, but people who no longer supported NATO membership for Slovenia became undecided, not opponents, of enlargement.

SUPPORT FOR SLOVENIA'S EFFORTS TO JOIN NATO

	Oct 1996	Jan 1997	Feb 1997	Mar 1997	Oct/Nov 1997	Jun 1999
Yes	66.4	61.3	58.3	64.1	55.4	56.5
No	15.7	20.5	21.1	18.3	18.4	16.1
Undecided	17.9	18.2	20.7	17.6	26.2	27.4
N=	958	996	942	965	2031	1001

Source: Malesic Marjan, ed. *International Security, Mass Media and Public Opinion* (Ljubljana, Slovenia: ERGOMAS, Faculty of Social Sciences, 2000).

Of course, all of this must be viewed in terms of both a growing awareness and education about NATO among the Slovenian public and the broader regional security environment at the time. For example, although the war in Bosnia appeared to end with the accords signed in late 1995, this armistice was still fresh and fragile going into 1996, Yugoslavia was still firmly ruled by the Milosevic regime, and the world had not yet even begun to witness the "blitz" ethnic cleansing campaign Belgrade would unleash just a few years later on Kosovo.

In such an uncertain regional security environment, it is hardly surprising that Slovenia looked to a larger alliance, in this case NATO, for protective purposes. NATO was to bomb the Serbs three times: over Gorazde in eastern Bosnia in April 1994, throughout eastern Bosnia in mid-1995, and, throughout Yugoslavia itself in 1999 during the Kosovo conflict. NATO's de facto security umbrella over southeast Europe at this time was a clear and present reality for Slovenians.

During many of these actions, the Slovenian government gave permission for overflights of Slovenian airspace by NATO planes, as well as for use of the Mediterranean port of Koper by NATO ships on patrol in the Adriatic on sanctions enforcement duty. Permission was also given for NATO and Implementation Force (IFOR) convoys to transit through Slovenian territory by rail and road. But, lack of full coordination between Brussels and Ljubljana sometimes resulted in momentary tremors in public and parliamentary support for NATO, until a more coordinated system was eventually elaborated.

In January 1994 NATO introduced the Partnership for Peace (PfP) program. Slovenia quickly became a charter member and initiated discussions with NATO Headquarters in Brussels on its Partnership program. Already in 1993, the Slovenian parliament had passed a resolution calling, somewhat tentatively, for "close association" with NATO. By April 1996, however, a Slovenian parliamentary resolution was more forward leaning, stating that "Slovenia wishes to ensure its fundamental security interest within the system of collective defense enabled by membership in NATO." Collateral legislation called for military hardware procurement within the context of interoperability with NATO.

Threat Assessment

Throughout the latter half of the 1990s, Slovenia adopted a modernization program that envisioned, among other things, enhanced cooperation with Western militaries, particularly NATO, and greater participation in regional peacekeeping missions. Unlike other Central European states, Slovenia's armed forces were derived not from the Warsaw Pact, of which Yugoslavia was never a member, but from the former Yugoslavia's system of territorial self-defense. Originally designed to counter a supposed attack from the West after Tito's break with Stalin, these defenses became more universal after the Soviet intervention in Czechoslovakia in 1968. Finally, during the dissolution of the socialist federation, territorial defense systems, their units, and their weaponry fell largely into the hands of local citizenry, which formed the backbone of republic-by-republic resistance against aggression by the original federation capital, Belgrade. The originators of this system could not have imagined in their wildest nightmares that this system would eventually be used against an internal enemy, rather than against an external invader.

Slovene concerns about developments in the southeast European region revolve around the belief that continuing instability there can have a negative impact on Slovenia's developmental progress. Especially given Slovenia's reliance for its welfare on maintaining vigorous international commercial trade, regional instability would have a disproportionate influence on this progress. Given Slovenia's relative small size, it must also be concerned about the societal and economic impact of potential inflows or cross-flows of refugees, should the wars of Yugoslav dissolution continue.

With the evolution of developments, however, the possibility of a direct military threat against Slovenia from another state in the region has receded. Especially after the political demise of Milosevic, Serbia is much less of an immediate danger and at least slightly less likely to be the source of continued instability in the region. But, there are still unsolved questions about the future status of Kosovo and Montenegro and disputes among Albanians and Macedonians in Macedonia—all of which are remaining sources of instability in the region. Such instability, of course, is considered by Slovenes as an indirect threat to their security.

The geopolitical change since 1989–90 as well as the results of recent wars in the Balkans have diminished or removed altogether several credible threats to Slovenia's security. However, some potential challenges to regional stability and welfare have remained and have even become more acute. Slovenia's concerns today include: 1. the possibility of a new flare-up of armed hostilities in the Balkans; 2. conceivable conflicts in the region over contested borders, dissatisfied national minorities, insufficient natural resources, and access to international communications (primarily seas and rivers); 3. transregional organized crime and terrorism; 4. large-scale economic dislocation, mass unemployment, and illicit labor migration; 5. illicit traffic in arms and drugs and mass smuggling; and 6. possible ecological disasters. Formidable challenges of these kinds require that a small state such as Slovenia develop new kinds of capacities and stronger ties to international institutions.

Correspondingly, economic, social, ethnic, religious-related, ecological, health, and other nonmilitary challenges gained substantially in importance in public opinion in Slovenia. A public opinion poll conducted in Slovenia in the summer of 1999 confirmed that the perception of foreign military threats has greatly declined (to 2.21 on a scale from 1 to 4). At the same time, the perceptions of acute nonmilitary threats rose and dominate the public mind today—crime (3.46), drugs (3.46), ecological disasters (3.35), and unemployment (3.35). When respondents were asked about military threats from abroad, some (15 to 16 percent) pointed to the Balkans as a possible source of such peril.

According to official assessments, however, Slovenia at present does not face any visible or realistic military threat to its sovereignty and independence.

Among immediate neighbors, Slovenia has made considerable forward progress in forging good bilateral relations. None of its neighbors constitutes a military threat, though unsettled issues with some could impact on economic and political stability. Of its neighbors, some unresolved issues remain with Croatia from the dissolution of Yugoslavia, of which both states were once parts. Relations with Austria and Italy are good, although such relations are sometimes buffeted by purely domestic politicking in both of those states.

Among relations with its neighbors, Slovenia probably enjoys the best bilateral relationship with Hungary. There are no outstanding unresolved bilateral issues. There is a relatively short common border with a small number of co-nationals living on each side. Hungarians in Slovenia are accorded a high level of minority rights. For example, they even have the right to a distinctive passport with a cover printed in both languages. The Hungarian minority, which numbers only a few thousand, also has a permanent position in the Slovenian parliament. Both of these privileges extend far beyond standards and principles practiced in other parts of Europe. The situation with the Italian minority on Slovenia's western border is similar. They enjoy special rights as defined by 1989 constitutional amendments, and both minorities are automatically represented by one parliamentary representative each.

Historically, Slovenia has had a close political and cultural association with Austria, since both were parts of the Austro-Hungarian Empire that dissolved during World War I. Afterward, the demarcation of a border between what had become two separate states left tens of thousands of Slovenes on the Austrian side of the frontier. This was to become a point of contention during World War II and intermittently thereafter in Austria's relations with the Tito government in Yugoslavia. Most recently, Austria has provided strong support to Slovenia's drive for independence, although from time to time various political parties have seized on Slovenia-related issues for domestic Austrian maneuvering. These issues have included the status of national minorities on both sides of the border, the AVNOJ (Anti-Fascist Council of Yugoslavia) declarations of 1943, which rightest parties in Austria apprised as being anti-German, and among Austrian environmentalists, the future of Slovenia's nuclear power plant at Krsko.

Slovenia and Croatia enjoy good bilateral relations, partly perhaps because they found themselves in a de factor spiritual alliance against Belgrade during their mutual resistance movements in the early 1990s. Both states declared independence, in fact, in June 1991 within one day of each other. Curiously, there was only sporadic military cooperation between them before and immediately after independence, a subject of some contention even today. Unresolved issues outstanding from the days of the former Yugoslavia include: demarcation of the border in three places, including the Bay of Piran; disposition of Croatian accounts in Ljubljanska Bank; and management of the Krsko nuclear power station. None of these questions threaten security, however, and will probably be resolved over the course of time because both sides have a strong desire to do so.

Slovenian relations with Italy have perhaps been the most problematic. Within Italy's complex internal politics, in the early 1990s northern Italian political parties began exploiting purely local issues for bargaining purposes. One of these was the status of members of the Italian minority that had left Slovenian territory following World War II. A new agreement on settlement for compensation was not signed between Slovenia and Italy until February 1996. Only then did Italy cease obstructing Slovenia's efforts to gain membership in the EU and became instead a sponsor of the newly emerged state. Overall, however, Slovenian-Italian relations are good and are becoming better. Italy is an EU and NATO state and, as such, certainly poses no direct security threat to Slovenia.

A further step toward better relations with Italy occurred in early 2001 when the Italian parliament finally passed the Law on the Global Protection of the Slovene Minority. Legal protection of the Slovene minority was a key duty of Italy according to the Osimo Agreement between Italy and the former Yugoslavia in 1975.

Capacities

Unlike many other Central and Eastern European states, Slovenia did not inherit its armed forces from the Warsaw Pact, since Yugoslavia was not a member of that bloc. Neither did it inherit much from the Yugoslav People's Army, since these units were transformed by Belgrade into an invading force after Yugoslavia's dissolution. Slovenia's armed forces then, as noted previously, were derived from a citizen-based territorial defense system that called for local fighting units to be formed for the purposes of local defense.

At the time of Yugoslavia's dissolution, Belgrade called for territorial defense weaponry to be "returned" to Belgrade. Slovenia is estimated to have relinquished perhaps half of its arsenal, retaining another half for its own use. (In contrast, Croatia gave up almost all its territorial defense weaponry.) Slovenia augmented this by importing some of its weaponry (illegally at first, because of the international arms embargo) and also by improvising the domestic production of small quantities of ammunition.

Currently, Slovenia's standing military forces number about ten thousand, including some forty-two hundred professional soldiers and five thousand to six thousand conscripts. Total peacetime forces, including reserves, number about fifty-six thousand. The Slovenian Army possesses approximately one hundred tanks, most upgraded T-72s and T-55s left over from Yugoslav days. Slovenian Armed Forces also have twelve light Swiss-made trainer aircraft, some of which have been refitted to carry arms. They also have eleven helicopters, mostly Bell 204 and 412, most of which have been deployed with Slovenia's contribution to IFOR in Bosnia.

It is important to mention that the Slovene Army enjoys, however, a high and stable degree of trust among the population. A survey in March 2001 showed that, in this respect, the Army (with 3.43 points on a scale from 1 to 5 points) trails only the president of the republic, prime minister, national bank, and the national currency.[6]

With Slovenia's adherence to PfP, an increased emphasis has been placed on professionalization of the armed forces and on enhancing peace-keeping capabilities. In this regard, Slovenian forces have participated in PfP exercises abroad as early as 1995 and as far away as Louisiana in the United States. In 1997 Slovenian forces participated in the Italian-led "Operation Alba" in Albania. With its neighbors Hungary and Italy, Slovenia has signed a trilateral agreement on military cooperation, infrastructure upgrading, and training coordination.

Slovenia's contributions to regional military cooperation, however, have been limited by domestic political considerations and other factors. Al-though it is a member of the Southeast European Defense Ministerial Group (SEDM), for example, it does not contribute troops to this organization's joint peacekeeping unit. Slovenia has also steadfastly refused to permit U.S. and NATO aircraft to use bombing ranges on Slovenian territory. In this regard, Slovenia successfully resisted U.S. pressure, which had been based on the Department of Defense's desire to cut costs associated with paying overnight lodging for crews based in northern Italy who conducted bombing practice runs at distant sites. But a strong Slovenian environmen-talist tradition, mirroring a similar concern throughout Europe, precluded this sort of cooperation.

Slovenia's severe disappointment at not receiving an invitation to join NATO—together with Poland, the Czech Republic, and Hungary at the 1997 Madrid Summit—was soon reflected in Ljubljana's intensified attention to the EU, even while NATO remains a key foreign policy objective. It is yet to be seen how Slovenia—and other states in the region, for that matter—will sort out NATO and European Security and Defense Policy (ESDP) considerations in the future.

Policy Innovations

Slovenia is striving to achieve security on two different levels: On the national level, Slovenia has made an effort to create smoothly operating national security structures. On the international level, as a member of the UN, the Council of Europe, the Organization of Security and Cooperation in Europe, and the Central European Free Trade Association (CEFTA), the country desires integration in the key economic, political, and security circles in Europe, that is, NATO and EU.

New initiatives in Slovenian security policy can be divided into several categories: the political shift to cooperation on regional matters, agreement on several public documents on security policy, and the decision to adapt to NATO standards regardless of membership in the Alliance, particularly in the areas of equipment interoperability and force downsizing.

In October 2000 elections, former Prime Minister Janez Drnovsek and his Liberal Democrats were returned to power and Drnovsek was once again asked to form a government. During his nomination hearings before the Slovenian parliament in November 2000, Slovenia's current defense minister, Anton Grizold, identified several directions for the future. In his testimony, Grizold highlighted the need to be aware of budgetary limitations, an ineffectual military procurement system, an emphasis on domestic defense coupled with fulfilling obligations in the region and beyond, and, the necessity of ratifying as soon as possible a whole series of security documents through the government and parliament.[7]

On budgetary matters, Slovenian security planners envision an increase in military expenditures from the current level of 1.5 percent of gross domestic product (GDP) to 2.3 percent of GDP by 2003. In terms of future procurement, Slovenia will have to continue to finance the purchase of Swiss-built trainer aircraft and Bell helicopters, while it also considers an advanced air control radar system. However, a short-lived domestic discussion about whether to obtain F-16s or other similar combat aircraft appears to have been decided in favor of declining this option in view of Slovenia's limited budgetary means and rather truncated geography.

This chapter has already traced the development of Slovenia's participation in some regional efforts. Slovenia is active in the Stability Pact for Southeastern Europe, and is cochairing Working Table I in the first half of 2001 concerning the establishment of the International Center for Interethnic Relations and the Protection of Minorities. Slovenia is active also in some other regional activities such as the trilateral cooperation, Adriatic-Ionian Initiative, and Alpe Adria. Another regional program, the

International Trust Fund for Demining (ITF), was launched jointly by Slovenia and the United States in 1995. Although technically available to the entire Balkans, it has actually focused on Bosnia. So far, the program has been relatively successful and has been well received in Bosnia itself, where the bulk of the demining efforts have been conducted. In three years of operation in Bosnia, Croatia, Kosovo, and Albania, the ITF cleared more than 12 million square meters of mine-infested territory and provided for the rehabilitation of four hundred mine victims. This places it among the most successful organizations for demining in southeastern Europe.

Future Prospects

To ensure a comprehensive basis for planned and coordinated development and the functioning of the various elements of the national security system, Slovenia is preparing two basic documents: a resolution on national security strategy and a defense strategy.

Both documents have been approved by the government and the "National Security Strategy" resolution has to be accepted by parliament, but final ratification is expected during the course of the year 2001. This entire exercise should contribute to the development of a cohesive approach to defense reform and modernization. It should also engage and develop the support of the general public, think tank, media, academe, and parliamentarians through a broad public discussion of Slovenia's security needs in the new millennium.

The resolution on the national security strategy will provide fundamental guidance for Slovenia in the area of national security. The document will deal on a strategic level with the phenomenon of the security of a modern state and society and focus on various elements of national security, such as the political, economic, social, demographic, ecological, and military aspects of their interactions and mutual effects. Basic national interests and national security goals, sources of threat to the state and citizens, and the mechanisms for ensuring the security of the state and its citizens will be set out in the document.

The defense strategy, which will be based on the national security strategy, will determine guidelines for developing the entire defense system, thereby ensuring coordinated military and civil defense systems and, in war, the civil protection and disaster relief system (Civil Emergency Planning—CEP).

As of spring 2001, the Slovenian government has adopted a military defense strategy, which set out the orientations for the organization and functioning of the Slovenian Armed Forces (SAF) and a national strategy for inclusion in NATO, which defines the country's basic orientation for activities aimed at joining NATO. Both documents will be reviewed and brought into line with the strategic and doctrine documents when they enter into force.

According to these documents, restructuring the SAF will create small but well-armed and equipped forces, able to participate in Euro-Atlantic security integration. Restructuring should be finished by 2010. By that time, Slovenia's armed forces will have been reduced to 33,000 active and reserve personnel from the current 56,000. The ratio between reserve and professional soldiers should thereby increase in favor of the latter.

In the midterm planning period (1999–2003), a new force and unit structure is anticipated, and the formation, personnel, and material activities connected to rapid reaction forces are to be completed. The main brigades will be upgraded, territorial forces reorganized into reserve forces, and changes in logistics implemented.

During the 2003–2010 period, the final structure and size of the Slovenian Armed Forces, particularly its career personnel, modernization and ratios between the active and reserve forces should be established. If all this is accomplished, Slovenia's armed forces will be available for collective defense deployments. The SAF will be organized into rapid reaction forces, main (or active duty) forces, and reserve (or support) forces. Rapid reaction forces will be organized into a multipurpose brigade equipped and trained to operate over the entire territory of the Republic of Slovenia, as well as to participate in humanitarian activities and peace support operations.

Active-duty (main) defense units are to compose the biggest part of the Slovenian Armed Forces and will consist of professional and active reserve units, as well as of recruitment structures. Support defense forces should consist of inactive reserves, which could be mobilized with or without the help of active-duty cadres. The tasks of the support defense forces would, if mobilized, involve combat, protection and security, logistical, support, or other activities. To carry out these changes, the current Defence Law must be amended, and appropriate funding must be found.

Slovenia understands that NATO's decision on new invitations will be based on individual progress and the fulfillment of Membership Action Plan (MAP) goals. At the same time, Ljubljana is aware of the political nature of new invitations. The MAP process is, by its nature, individual. However, this does not exclude joint activities with the other eight candidates on an ad hoc basis. Slovenia expects that earnest discussions about enlargement will commence in mid-2001 in preparation for NATO's 2002 Prague Summit.[8]

In June 2001 Slovenia celebrated its 10th anniversary of independence. Slovenia's success, during these ten years, is evinced by memberships in numerous Western multilateral structures and by its bilateral cooperation with many countries. Taken together, these achievements suggest that a small state can, indeed, build up its domestic and international political prestige to guarantee security in the framework of contemporary European security settings.

Chronology

7 June 2000: New government with Dr. Andrej Bajuk as prime minister.

31 August 2000: Government of the Republic of Slovenia adopts the defense strategy.

15 October 2000: Elections for national assembly take place.

23 November 2000: Slovenia offers 180 men from the units that have already taken part in international peacekeeping operations to participate in the EU Rapid Reaction Forces.

30 November 2000: New government with Dr. Janez Drnovsek as prime minister. Dr. Anton Grizold appointed as new minister for defense.

5 April 2001: North Atlantic Council reviews Slovenia's progress in the preparations for NATO membership.

19 April 2001: Government of the Republic of Slovenia adopts the national security strategy and sends it to parliament for discussion and endorsement.

22 April 2001: Representatives of nine NATO candidate countries meet in Slovenia.

NOTES

Note: This article benefited from extensive consultation with Ambassador Victor Jackovich, Associate Director, George C. Marshall European Center for Security Studies.

1. The area of Slovenia is 20,273 square kilometers and the total population is around 2 million. It is a Central European country regardless of the fact that some authors place it in southeast Europe or even in the Balkans. It is much smaller than Scandinavian countries, Switzerland, and Austria but many times larger than the smallest NATO member, Luxembourg. Slovenia has the higher gross national product per capita among the Central and central eastern European states in transition and is comparable, in this respect, with the least affluent members of the European Union.

2. According to senior U.S. administration official present at this meeting.

3. The real determinant of the long-term future of the Slovene economy is foreign trade of goods and services. Some Slovenian economic analysts estimate that the recent trends in the structure of trade will continue: the share of processed products will grow and trade patterns will be more dispersed. In addition, the current most important Slovenian foreign trade partners (Germany, Italy, France, Austria, United Kingdom, the Netherlands) will remain the same in the near future.

4. *National Security of Slovenia* (Ljubljana, Slovenia: Faculty of Social Sciences, Defense Research Center, 1994).

5. *Politbarometer* (Ljubljana, Slovenia: Center for Public Opinion Research, Faculty of Social Sciences, March 1997).

6. *Politbarometer* (Ljubljana, Slovenia: Center for Public Opinion Research, Faculty of Social Sciences, University of Ljubljana, March 2001), table 2.3.

7. *Delo* (largest Slovenian daily newspaper), 29 November 2000.

8. Slovenia's bid to become a NATO member was given a high rating in a recent RAND Corporation volume. According to RAND, "Slovenia is the most qualified and attractive candidate for membership from NATO's strategic perspective." See Thomas Szayna, *NATO Enlargement 2000–2015* (Santa Monica, Calif.: RAND Corporation, 2001).

Conclusion: Central and Eastern Europe's Incomplete Security Metamorphoses

Daniel N. Nelson

Welcome to a New Millennium

What did we really expect? A better century, perhaps?

In the latter part of the twentieth century, the frequency of major conflicts (where one thousand or more people die) and serious violence within or between states remained stable or rising.[1] A *pax democratica,* announced with scholarly eurekas during the 1980s and 1990s,[2] failed to explain why careful and repeated analyses have found democratizing states to be no less war prone (and perhaps even more so) than authoritarian or fully democratic states. Further, the nature of crises can be more powerful than the kind of regime in predicting the likelihood that a country will engage in serious conflict or war; democratic states, if they sense no reciprocal peril or threat in a crisis of their initiation, are actually more likely to go to war than nondemocratic systems.[3]

Among chapters in this survey of 2000–2001 in Europe from the Baltic to the Balkans, few tales of untarnished success are found. Indeed, a dozen years after events that many thought were a harbinger of a "Europe whole and free," little of the kind is evident.

Were we to look at the Middle East's never-ending violence, South Asia's nuclear race, Central Africa's wars and genocides motivated by diamonds and tribes, and countries like Colombia, Angola, or Sri Lanka—all being ripped apart by a quest to control wealth, people, or territory—Central and southeastern Europe may not seem too bad.

Yet, there was immense hope and great promise in 1989–1991; Europe's existing institutions such as the North Atlantic Treaty Organization (NATO) and the European Union, supported by many others, had the tools and capacities to meet challenges and overcome obstacles. As one of the world's

431

wealthiest regions (only the United States and Japan having greater per capita gross domestic products[4]), with ample infrastructure for political and socioeconomic strength, Europe's potential to end the Cold War and begin anew was widely seen as a good bet.

It didn't work out. In this *Brassey's Central and East European Security Yearbook,* we see unequivocal evidence that, even in the best cases, a "new Europe" has not emerged. The continent is neither whole, everywhere secure, nor wholly free.[5]

What went wrong?

Shattered Illusions

Perhaps too much was expected.[6]

In Russia, Chechnya, the 1998 currency collapse, and the return of a quasi-nationalist, mafioso-ridden, KGB-led government of Vladimir Putin changed quite a few minds. Russia's transformation, however, was always unlikely to meet Western democratic standards.[7]

Southeastern Europe's trauma since the early 1990s cost an immense number of lives and led to U.S. and NATO interventions. Not until Macedonia's explosion in spring 2001, however, were Western "spin" and some participants' self-inflation about conflict containment and crisis management shown to be vacuous.[8] NATO, the icon of cooperative security, even with tens of thousands of troops deployed in next-door Kosovo and Bosnia, confined itself to rhetorical cheerleading and ineffectual arm twisting while deaths began to mount and the rule of law unraveled.

Elsewhere in post-Communist Europe, peace and democracy were not so obviously challenged. But they were endangered nonetheless. Illiberal practices or intolerant attitudes raised the potential of social strife, while corruption and rampant crime wiped away public trust in nascent democratic institutions. Central Europe and the Baltics have no wars, but neither do they have assured tolerance and pluralism, or complete and effective reform of key institutions (for example, armies and defense ministries). And, further to the east—in Belarus, Ukraine, Russia, the Caucasus, and Central Asia—"transition" seems to be in reverse gear (see Ustina Markus and Daniel N. Nelson, eds., *Brassey's Eurasian Security Yearbook, 2001*).

At the core of the region's incomplete metamorphosis and troubled transitions are fundamental conceptual errors. Some of these baseline confusions simultaneously raise false expectations throughout the region *and* generate mistargeted Western assistance and investment.

Making "free and fair elections" the litmus test of democracy, for example, and inundating countries with international election monitors ignores normative bases for democracy (tolerance, pluralism, and transparency) and enables people with dubious credentials to claim the mantle of popular legitimacy. Yet, Western governments and nongovernmental organizations (NGOs) for years have made such a criterion the first and biggest test of compatibility with the European Union (EU), NATO, and other institutions. Consequently, the moment Vojislav Kostunica was elected (and installed after Slobodan Milosevic's 5 October 2000 ouster), most governments, NGOs, and investors rushed to Belgrade—ignoring that Kostunica's nationalism, while less violent, is no less virulent than his predecessors.

Likewise, some smart but naive economists who became gurus of post-Communist economic transitions decided that cold turkey capitalism, with rapid shifts of ownership to private hands and sudden withdrawal of the state from economic matters, was the surest route to a market system. Maybe. But what kind of market is then created? The answer seems to be one in which monopolies are recreated, held by indigenous criminal organizations or foreign investors who have resources to buy up entire industries (telecommunications, energy extraction or distribution, and so forth). The notion of free competition remains a long way off in most of the region, although advances in private ownership are reported proudly by governments, the World Bank, and other institutions.[9]

For political and economic transitions, the elections-equal-democracy and privatization-equals-market equations lead to disappointments, antagonisms, fraud, and waste. They do not, however, lead to war—or, at least, not directly.

In the security realm, however, evidence of dangerous misperceptions exists. These, left uncorrected, enlarge the probability that insecurities will become the genesis of violent conflict or war.

Origins of Incomplete Security Metamorphoses

Strong biases in the West tend to blame insecurity on those who suffer it, and to expect democracy (and market) to produce better and more pacific behavior. These same biases, the adoption of which are implicit to joining the clubhouses of NATO and the EU, then permeate a region such as central to southeastern Europe. Security is understood by both institutions as a commodity provided to those who deserve it, who are "ready" to receive it, and who will not endanger the security of those who already possess the clubhouse key. Security is not a public good available to everyone, including those who need it.[10]

Those who are insecure, and who thus confront an imbalance between threats and their own capacities, must find themselves in such conditions because of their own failings or inadequacies. Were a state (or community or individual) truly able, it would create or procure bases for security; the able and adaptable survive, a la Darwin applied to the realm of politics. Alternatively, those "worth" being secured by others will be identified as such as the "free market" of security will provide such a good to deserving countries and peoples.

Such approaches may not embody much idealism, but they do incorporate views expressed by both a Hungarian diplomat and a Polish scholar (on different occasions):

I'm not sure why we, who fought the Soviets in 1956 and then managed to scratch out a better life by developing a non-socialist second economy, should now think the same benefits of NATO admission or early EU entry ought to go to countries that resisted no one and enjoyed the fruits of state socialism for five decades.[11]

If NATO had thought that Balkan states or elsewhere were better candidates than we, the Czechs and Hungarians, they would have admitted them and not us. We were simply the most ready, could contribute the most, and were best able to become compatible with Alliance standards.[12]

Closely related to these viewpoints is the expectation that "freemarketde-mocracy" (which is so often said as one word that we might as well write it as such) generates or is associated with pacific traits.

The liberal peace and democratic literature, a few cases of which were cited above, was adapted and absorbed by policymakers from Washington to Brussels and beyond in the early 1990s. If the "democracies don't fight democracies" logo were anywhere embedded, it was in the February 1995 American national security strategy evocatively entitled "Engagement and Enlargement"—a product of the early Clinton years' enthusiasm for nation-building and other global endeavors.[13] "[D]emocratic states," said President Bill Clinton, "are less likely to threaten our interests and more likely to cooperate with the U.S. to meet security threats and promote free trade and sustainable development."[14] Bruce Russett and other scholars engaged in the empirical research upon which the democratic peace literature was built are no doubt troubled by the way their work was crudely used as a political and policy tool.

Yet, it was not a new theme in U.S. and West European policy. Indeed, U.S. President Ronald Reagan and his first Secretary of State, George Schultz, inaugurated the democratization theme in the mid-1980s as part of an anti-Communist crusade. By the 1990s, however, the message had changed: if one's credentials as a "freemarketdemocracy" grow, we (the West) will pay more attention to your security and prosperity. The bargain was clear—you (substitute any country's name) help us by opening your economy and behaving democratically, and the safety and prosperity of integration with us will be possible and even likely.

One problem with such a quid pro quo was and remains, in a region such as Central and southeastern Europe, that many political leaders and opinion makers rejected the deal. An HDZ loyalist during the Franjo Tudj-man era in Croatia said, succinctly, "We are told constantly to democratize. . . . But, let me tell you, we'll do all of that when we feel secure. Not before." He was right.

Indeed, the relationship between security and democracy is not really addressed in the academic literature, because it focuses on the relationship between war proneness and regime type (democratic versus nondemocratic). A prior and even more fundamental question is not raised—who become democrats? As discussed elsewhere, there is ample reason to suspect that democratic values and behaviors are security dependent—at the level of individuals, groups, nations, and states.[15] If ambient threat (perceived or real) is high and capacities are low, insecurity exists. In such conditions, tolerance, pluralism, and other normative dimensions of democracy will suffer. Demagogues, armed with the blunt instrument of such a threatening milieu, can and do attack democracy as a luxury the state and "people" cannot afford. Behavioral manifestations, including attacks on scapegoat minorities, xenophobia, the media, and other institutions embodying democracy follow.

Unfortunately, this causal path has not guided Western policy or the policies of political leaders in the still-young democracies of the region.

Further, an irresistible penchant for stability and an end to overt violence lead to premature or incomplete "solutions" that respond to today's crises. Cynically, this behavior among Western policymakers or Central and East European elites can be seen as little more than an effort to rid television and Internet images of such untidiness, because this frightens taxpayers and investors alike. Yet among NGOs, diplomats, and regional leaders, the sincere belief that mitigating tension or halting combat is a first step toward reconciliation fosters efforts to negotiate.

That stability is not security and an end to conflict is not peace, however, are truths too often mislaid in the midst of crisis. Communist states had ample stability during those decades, and such stasis holds little promise— although the appeal of guaranteed employment still galvanizes many voters throughout the region. The need for instability as a precursor to new bases of security, however, is often missed. Hungary may have managed a "negotiated revolution" over several decades until 1990 because the country's transition had begun long before.[16] Romania's Communist cult was so entrenched, however, that nothing but a cathartic rebellion in December 1989 could have started that country on the road to transition; even then, it took some time. Getting rid of the old structures, ousting bureaucrats, disbanding parties and ideologies, pursuing justice against those who harmed others—these steps and more constitute instability, but are necessary if not sufficient components of a genuine stability based on security.

A process of separating feuding factions or combatants, insulating them, and then observing them for violations of a social or military cease-fire has become ersatz peace. In the Caucasus and Moldova, and in Bosnia-Herzegovina and Kosovo, these are formalized by treaties and militarized via NATO. In other countries, efforts continue to ensure such a quasi-peace between majority populations and Roma, between ethnic Hungarians and either Slovaks or Romanians, or between Latvians and Russians. And, in many states, the battle that is not being fought because of concern to maintain peace and stability is one against the corruption of kleptocrats, or the criminal networks engaged in drugs and human trafficking, counterfeiting and racketeering. For a struggle against these threats to security, substantial instability would be required, and nonwar would not seem very peaceful.

Summary

In an annual volume such as this, our endeavor is to chronicle and to analyze events that have happened and processes under way, while offering informed thoughts about future scenarios. None of the contributors has a crystal ball. But take note that few are sanguine, and some might be read as seeing events in melancholy terms. In 2001–2002, the expectations of many countries about entry into NATO will be disappointing (a few may be pleased), and the ramifications for domestic constituencies will not be welcome. Continued economic difficulties, domestic and foreign criminal and corrupt elements, and social unrest from those and related problems will plague the region. Ukraine and Belarus, and their instabilities, raise dark vision of a reconstituted Russian-dominated union at the borders of Central and southeastern Europe and are menacing to the Baltic states. In Macedonia, specifically, the prognosis is uncertain at best, and bleak at worst.

If one is in Warsaw, Prague, and Budapest, these concerns may be transient—sometimes apparent, but usually in the socioeconomic and political background. They are omnipresent in Skopje, poignant in Latvia, and deeply worrisome in Sofia. The security metamorphoses of Europe from the Baltic to Balkans is far from complete.

NOTES

1. For summaries of such data, see *SIPRI Yearbook 2000* (Oxford, U.K.: Oxford University Press, 2000), and the Center for Defense Information (CDI) web site <http://www.cdi.org>, "World at War" (accessed 12 February 2001).

2. The liberal peace and democratic literature of contemporary international relations—

not to mention its Kantian intellectual roots—is now vast and incorporates many assumptions about the pacific effects of democratic processes, institutions, or norms. Perhaps the most indicative of this literature is by Bruce Russett, *Grasping the Democratic Peace* (Princeton, N.J.: Princeton University Press, 1993), especially chapters 2 and 6. Further, see John M. Owen, "How Liberalism Produces Democratic Peace," *International Security* 19, no. 2 (Fall 1994), 87–125.

3. A very useful synopsis of literature in democratic peace theory, and its critics, is provided by Hemda Ben-Yahuda and Iris Margulies, "Regime Type and State Behavior in Threat and Opportunity Crises: A Monadic Study of the Democratic Peace Theory, 1918–1994," *International Politics* 38, no. 2 (June 2001). Their research on the role of crisis types vis-a-vis regime types pokes more holes, albeit of a different kind, in the democratic peace literature.

4. See the data for 1999 in the *CIA World Factbook*, available on the Internet at <http://www.cia.gov/cia/publications/factbook/fields/gdp_per_capital.html> (accessed 15 March 2001).

5. Two organizations that offer judgmental measurements of freedom and corrupt practices, Freedom House (FH) and Transparency International (TI), gauge and rank states by their chosen indicators of such concepts. While not scientific, such judgments might be indicative. As such, Europe offers a highly variegated portrait—and, to be sure, few of the countries in Central and southeastern Europe do very well on both. For ratings of political liberties and other concepts, see <http://www.freedomhouse.org/ratings/index.htm>; regarding the "international corruption perceptions index" that compares such perceptions by country, see <http://www.transparency.org/documents/cpi/index.html>. In both of these cases, data suggest impressions among foreign elites that states such as Serbia (Yugoslavia), Albania, Croatia, Romania, Macedonia, Bulgaria, Latvia, and Slovakia are among the world's most corrupt systems. Only Slovenia, Estonia, Hungary, the Czech Republic, and Poland from Central and southeastern Europe rank among the best fifty countries (in that order) on TI's "corruption perception index."

6. "Early warning" against expectations of a smooth transition were in Daniel N. Nelson, "Europe's Unstable East," *Foreign Policy* 82 (Spring 1991), 137–58, and in the same author's "Democracy, Market, Security," *Survival* 35, no. 2 (Summer 1993), 156–71.

7. See Daniel N. Nelson, "Russia's Perilous Course," *Christian Science Monitor,* 2 April 1993.

8. For Richard Holbrooke, his was the key role, and "the war" he "ended" via Dayton, had others understood as he did, would have successfully maintained Balkan peace. Holbrooke's memoirs and reflections are in his *To End a War* (New York: Random House, 1998).

9. The World Bank's annual *World Development Report* (Oxford, U.K.: Oxford University Press, annually) includes data on "from plan to market" and privatization. Individual countries have, during the 1990s and in 2000–2001, continued to issue periodic reports on privatization. For example, Slovakia (as just one example) regularly produces a report *privatizacia na Slovensku, actualne probleme a otazy* (privatization in Slovakia: current problems and questions).

10. Greater detail on this notion of a clubhouse versus public good was offered in Daniel N. Nelson, "Conclusion," in *Brassey's Eurasia/East European Security Yearbook 2000,* ed. Ustina Markus and Daniel N. Nelson (Washington, D.C.: Brassey's, 2000).

11. A Hungarian diplomat in conversation with me, May 2000.

12. My conversation with a Polish scholar, January 2001.

13. The White House, *A National Security Strategy of Engagement and Enlargement* (Washington, D.C.: February 1995).

14. Ibid., 1.

15. Daniel N. Nelson, "Threats and Capacities: Great Powers and Global Insecurity," *Contemporary Politics* 3, no. 4 (December 1997), 341–63.

16. This is Rudolf L. Tokes's term from his book of the same title, *Hungary's Negotiated Revolution* (Cambridge, U.K.: Cambridge University Press, 1996).

INDEX

About the Editors

Daniel N. Nelson

Daniel N. Nelson (Ph.D., Johns Hopkins) is professor of democratization and civil-military relations at the George C. Marshall Center for European Security Studies in Garmisch, Germany; editor of *International Politics,* a peer-reviewed quarterly journal published by Kluwer (New York, N.Y., and The Hague, The Netherlands); and senior consultant for an international consulting firm, Global Concepts, Inc. in Alexandria, Virginia. He was CEO of Global Concepts, Inc. from its founding in 1992 through 1998. From 1992 to 1999, he was founding director (1992–95) and professor in the graduate programs in international studies at Old Dominion University, Norfolk, Virginia. He was a NATO research fellow in 1995–96, William Foster Fellow (scholar in residence) at the U.S. Arms Control and Disarmament Agency of the State Department in 1998, and visiting scholar at the National Security Education Program of the Department of Defense in 1999. Previously, he served as a foreign policy consultant in Senator Tom Harkin's (D-Iowa) presidential campaign (1992), as the senior foreign policy adviser for Richard Gephardt (D-Mo.) when he was the majority leader of the House of Representatives (1990–91), a senior associate at the Carnegie Endowment (1989–90), and a professor of political science at the University of Kentucky (1977–89). He has also taught at Georgetown University, The Johns Hopkins University's School for Advanced International Studies, and George Washington University. His forthcoming books include *Global Society in Transition* (Kluwer, 2001) and *At War with Words* (Mouton de Gruyter), edited with Mirjana Dedaic. Among nineteen other books by Daniel Nelson are *Post-Communist Politics* (Ashgate Books, 2001), edited with Stephen White; *After Authoritarianism* (Praeger, 1995); *East European Security Reconsidered,* edited with John Lampe (Johns Hopkins, 1993); *Romania after Tyranny* (Westview, 1992); and *Balkan Imbroglio* (Westview, 1991). He is a member of the Council on Foreign Relations.

Ustina Markus

Ustina Markus (Ph.D., London School of Economics) is a senior field analyst for the International Crisis Group (ICG). She is based in Osh in the Ferghana Valley following security developments in Central Asia. Before joining the ICG she worked at the Defense Threat Reduction Agency in the U.S. Department of Defense, writing on disarmament in the former Soviet Union. From 1993 to 1997, Dr. Markus was an analyst and then a senior analyst at the Radio Free Europe/Radio Liberty Research Institute in Munich, Germany, and its successor institute, the Open Media Research Institute, in Prague, Czech Republic. In 1991 she completed a Ph.D. on Soviet counterinsurgency doctrine at the London School of Economics. Dr. Markus has authored nearly a hundred articles and book chapters on the former Soviet Union (FSU) and has coauthored a book on nuclear disarmament in the FSU.

About the Contributors

Margarita Assenova

Margarita Assenova is a professional journalist (M.A. in linguistics, University of Plovdiv, Bulgaria). After working as a senior journalist in Bulgaria from 1987 to 1997, she came to Stanford University in the United States on a Knight Fellowship, and is now affiliated with the Center for Strategic and International Studies in Washington, D.C. She is also the Washington, D.C., correspondent for *Kapital,* the principal political and economic weekly in Sofia, and also writes regularly for *Radio Free Europe/Radio Liberty,* Newsline and Balkan Report publications. She was the founder of the "Journalists for Tolerance Foundation" in Bulgaria and has promoted ethnic and religious tolerance in Bulgarian society through mass media since 1995.

Sophia Clement

Sophia Clement graduated in political science and international relations from the University of Paris II and the Institute of Political Science. She has specialized on European security and defense issues, transatlantic relations, and crisis management in the Balkans. From 1991 to 1996, she was attached to the Centre d'Etudes et de Recherches Internationales (CERI) in Paris of the Western European Union (WEU). Since then, she has been part of the delegation of strategic affairs of the French ministry of defense in charge of NATO-EU relations and transatlantic issues. She is the author of monographs entitled "Crisis Management in the Balkans" and "Bosnia and the Transatlantic Debate" (both Chaillot Papers of the WEU Institute) and, most recently a monograph from the Diplomatic Academy of Vienna (summer 2001) on "European Defense and Transatlantic Relations."

Pal Dunay

Pal Dunay (Ph.D., Budapest University of Economics, and J.D., Eotvos Lorand University) has been director of the international training course

465

in security policy at the Geneva Centre for Security Policy since 1996. Previously, he was deputy director of the Hugarian Institute of International Affairs (1994–96), head of the Arms Control and Security Policy Department of the Hungarian ministry of foreign affairs in 1991, and legal adviser to the Hungarian delegation to the Conventional Forces in Europe negotiations in 1989–90. He was also a faculty member during the 1980s and 1990s at Eotvos Lorand University. Dunay has published scores of scholarly articles and authored or edited numerous books, including (most recently) *Ungarns Aussenpolitik 1990–1997* (with Wolfgang Zellner) (Baden-Baden, Germany: Nomos Verlagsgesellschaft, 1998).

Heinz Gartner

Heinz Gartner is a senior researcher at the Austrian Institute for International Affairs specializing in European security and international politics. In 2002, he will be a Fulbright visiting professor at Stanford University and, from 1997 to 2001 was guest professor at the Institute for Political Science at the University of Vienna. Previously, Gartner served as a visiting professor at the University of Erlangen, a visiting fellow at the Institute for International Relations in Vancouver, Canada, a visiting fellow at St. Hugh's College, Oxford, and a resident fellow at the Institute for East-West Security Studies in New York, N.Y. His work on European security, crisis management, small states, and international relations theory has appeared in many European and American journals.

Peter van Ham

Peter van Ham (Ph.D., University of Leiden, 1991) is a senior research fellow at the Netherlands Institute of International Relations "Clingendael." He has held teaching and research positions at the George C. Marshall European Center for Security Studies (Garmisch-Partenkirchen, Germany), the WEU Institute for Security Studies (Paris), Columbia University (New York City), and the Royal Institute of International Affairs (London). His books include *Mapping European Security after Kosovo* (edited), *European Integration and the Postmodern Condition,* and *A Critical Approach to European Security.*

Graeme P. Herd

Graeme Herd is a lecturer in international relations and deputy director of the Scottish Center for International Security at the University of Aberdeen. Dr. Herd has published articles on political and economic issues relating to Russia, the Baltics, and Black Sea security politics. He has also managed EU PHARE-TACIS projects analyzing democratic security building in the Baltic and Black Sea areas.

Ivan Hostnik

Ivan Hostnik is now counselor to the government of Slovenia and head of the Division for International Security at the ministry of defense's Centre for Strategic Studies. He holds a postgraduate degree from the University of Ljubljana in political science and public administration. In 1991 he became an adviser to the ministry of defense for organization and recruitment and has worked at the Centre for Strategic Studies in the ministry since 1992, of which he was head from 1996 to 1998. Mr. Hostnik is author of several professional articles in the field of defense systems operations, management of defense in democracy, and international security organizations.

Mel Huang

Mel Huang has worked as the Baltic editor of the award-winning electronic magazine *Central Europe Review* since its inception in 1999. Before that he has worked as an analyst with Radio Free Europe on its flagship Newsline publication and has published frequently in various media in English and Estonian.

Robert E. Hunter

Robert E. Hunter (Ph.D., London School of Economics) is senior adviser at RAND (Washington, D.C.), vice chairman of the Atlantic Treaty Association, and chairman of the Council for a Community of Democracies. His most recent government service was as U.S. ambassador to NATO (1993–98). He is coauthor of *Taking Charge: A Bipartisan Report to the President-elect on Foreign Policy and National Security,* <http://www.RAND.org>, "Maximizing NATO" in *Foreign Affairs,* and *The New Era: Globalizing*

Economics and Unsteady Regional Geopolitics (Washington, D.C.: National Defense University, 2001). He is a member of the Council on Foreign Relations.

Victor Jackovich

Ambassador Victor Jackovich is Associate Director of the George C. Marshall European Center for Security Studies in Garmisch-Partkenkirchen, Germany. Prior to this, his most recent postings abroad were as U.S. Ambassador to Slovenia (1995–1998), the first United States Ambassador to Bosnia-Herzegovina (1992–1995), and Chief of the U.S. Mission to Moldova (1992). He holds an M.A. from Indiana University, Bloomington in Slavic Languages. Among his awards for exceptional service are the Distinguished Presidential Award (1994) for work in the Balkans and the American Bar Association's Max Kampelman Award (1998) for advancing the rule of law in Central and Eastern Europe and the former Soviet Union. In 2000, he was accorded an honorary degree from the University of Sarajevo and declared an "Honorary Citizen of Sarajevo."

Stan Markotich

Stan Markotich (Ph.D., Indiana University, Bloomington) is senior policy adviser for the Communications Regulatory Agency (CRA) in Sarajevo, Bosnia-Herzegovina. Previously, he worked as research analyst with the Radio Free Europe/Radio Liberty (RFE/RL) Research institute in Munich, the Open Media Research Institute (OMRI) in Prague, and the International Crisis Group (ICG). He has extensive fieldwork and teaching experience and has published numerous academic and analytical essays, for example, in outlets such as *Jane's* and in books such as *The Politics of the Extreme Right* (London: Pinter, 2000).

Andrew A. Michta

Andrew A. Michta is the Mertie Willigar Buckman professor of international studies at Rhodes College, in Memphis, Tennessee. He holds a Ph.D. from the Johns Hopkins University School of Advanced International Studies and is the author of *The Soldier-Citizen: The Politics of the Polish Army after Communism* (St. Martin's Press, 1997), *The Government and Politics of Postcommunist Europe* (Praeger, 1994), and *Red Eagle: The Army in Polish politics, 1944–1988* (Hoover Institution Press, 1990). Dr. Michta is also associate editor of *Problems of Post-Communism,* and an associate of the Institute of European, Russian, and Eurasian Studies at George Washington University.

Alpo Rusi

Alpo Rusi (Ph.D., University of Helsinki) is professor of international relations at Lapland University, on leave from the Finnish ministry of foreign affairs. Previously, he served as Finnish ambassador for European affairs and (from 1994 to 1999) as foreign policy adviser to the president of Finland. He was also EU coordinator for the Sarajevo Summit in 1999 and deputy special coordinator for the Stability Pact of Southeastern Europe (Brussels, 1999–2000). His books are *After the Cold War: Europe's New Political Architecture* (London: Macmillan, 1991) and *Dangerous Peace; New Rivalry in World Politics* (New York: St. Martins, 1997).

Ivo Samson

Ivo Samson received his B.A. in history from the University of Brno (formerly Czechoslovakia) in 1981. Thereafter, he worked in the Slovak Academic of Sciences in 1990–92, and in the Slovak Institute for International Studies in the ministry of foreign affairs from 1993 to 1994. After completing his Ph.D. in Germany, he returned as an analyst at the Slovak Foreign Policy Association in Bratislava and as a visiting professor at the Central European University in Budapest, Hungary. His many studies about Central European security include recent books such as *Integration of Slovakia into the Security System of the West* (Bratislava, Slovakia: Slovak Foreign Policy Association, 1997) and *The Security and Foreign Policy of Slovakia in the First Years of Independence* (Baden-Baden, Germany: Nomos Verlag, 2000).

Fabian Schmidt

Fabian Schmidt is Deutsche Welle Radio's director for Bosnia-Herzegovina. Previously, he served as a senior analyst at the Open Media Research Institute (OMRI) in Prague and at the Sudost Europa Institute in Munich,

Germany. He has also worked as the director of the Albanian Media Monitoring Project in Tirana from 1997 to 1998 and as a journalist for Radio Free Europe/Radio Liberty.

Jed C. Snyder

Jed C. Snyder is senior national security adviser with DynCorp, a private U.S. firm providing national security support and services, as well as strategic planning assistance for the international defense community. Before joining DynCorp, Mr. Snyder was the senior adviser for strategic planning and defense policy with another private U.S. firm, MPRI. During this period, he was posted in Zagreb from 1997 to 2000, working with a succession of Croatian ministers of defense and armed forces chiefs of staff on a multiyear program to modernize the Croatian ministry of defense.

Marybeth Peterson Ulrich

Marybeth Peterson Ulrich (Ph.D., University of Illinois) is a graduate of the U.S. Air Force Academy, was an officer in the U.S. Air Force, and taught at the Air Force Academy and the Naval Postgraduate School. She is now professor of government in the Department of National Security and Strategy at the U.S. Army War College in Carlisle, Pennsylvania. Her writing in strategic studies and emphasis on national security democratization in post-Communist Europe, has included the book *Democratizing Communist Militaries: The Cases of the Czech and Russian Armed Forces* (Ann Arbor: University of Michigan Press, 1999). She is a member of the Council on Foreign Relations.

Biljana Vankovska

Biljana Vankovska (Ph.D., University of Skopje, Macedonia) is scientific adviser for the Geneva Centre for Democratic Control of Armed Forces (DCAF) and professor of political science at the University of Skopje. She also serves as international adviser at the Transnational Foundation for Peace Research (TFF) in Lund, Sweden. She was a guest senior research fellow at the Copenhagen Peace Research Institute (COPRI) from 1997 to 2001. Among her recent publications is *Between the Past and Future: Civil-*

Military Relations in the Post-Communist Balkan States (London and New York: I. B. Tauris, forthcoming).

John R. Wise

Jay Wise currently works on Balkan affairs and peacekeeping issues at the Washington, D.C., office of the RAND Corporation. Previously, he was head of research at the D.C. office of the Open Society Institute and served on the State Department's Kosovo History Project. A graduate of the University of Chicago, he was a Fulbright Scholar in Hungary from 1996 to 1997.